Wilhelminism and Its Legacies

Standing, left to right: Benedikta von Scherr-Thoss, Robbie Arnold, Holger Nehring, Robert Gerwarth, Yaron Pasher. *Sitting, left to right:* Christian Haase, Julia von Dannenberg, Hartmut Pogge von Strandmann, Jocasta Gardner, Anna Menge.

Wilhelminism and Its Legacies

German Modernities, Imperialism, and the Meanings of Reform, 1890-1930

Essays for Hartmut Pogge von Strandmann

Edited by
Geoff Eley and James Retallack

Berghahn Books
New York • Oxford

First published in 2003 by

Berghahn Books

www.berghahnbooks.com

©2003 Geoff Eley and James Retallack

Library of Congress Cataloging-in-Publication Data

Wilhelminism and its legacies : German modernities, Imperialism, and the meanings of
  reform, 1890-1930 : essays for Hartmut Pogge von Strandmann / edited by Geoff Eley and
  James Retallack.
     p. cm.
  Includes bibliographical references and index.
  ISBN 1-57181-223-7 (alk. paper)
   1. Germany--Politics and government--1888-1918. 2.
  Nationalism--Germany--History--19th century.   3. Germany--Social
  conditions--1871-1918. 4. Germany--Economic policy--1888-1918. 5.
  Imperialism--History--19th century. I. Pogge von Strandmann, H. (Hartmut) II. Eley,
  Geoff, 1949-   III. Retallack, James N.

DD228.W58 2003
943.08'4--dc21   2002043662

British Library Cataloguing in Publication Data

A catalogue record for this book is available from the British Library

Printed in United Kingdom by Biddles/IBT Global.

Contents

Foreword
    by *Volker R. Berghahn*   vii

Acknowledgments   x

Introduction
    by *Geoff Eley* and *James Retallack*   1

1. Making a Place in the Nation: Meanings of "Citizenship"
   in Wilhelmine Germany
   Geoff Eley   16

2. Membership, Organization, and Wilhelmine Modernism:
   Constructing Economic Democracy through Cooperation
   Brett Fairbairn   34

3. "Few better farmers in Europe"? Productivity, Change, and
   Modernization in East-Elbian Agriculture, 1870-1913
   Oliver Grant   51

4. The Wilhelmine Regime and the Problem of Reform:
   German Debates about Modern Nation-States
   Mark Hewitson   73

5. *Lebensreform*: A Middle-Class Antidote to Wilhelminism?
   Matthew Jefferies   91

6. Imperialist Socialism of the Chair: Gustav Schmoller and
   German *Weltpolitik*, 1897-1905
   Erik Grimmer-Solem   107

7. "Our natural ally": Anglo-German Relations and the Contradictory
   Agendas of Wilhelmine Socialism, 1897-1900
   Paul Probert   123

8. The "Malet Incident," October 1895: A Prelude to the
    Kaiser's "Krüger Telegram" in the Context of the
    Anglo-German Imperialist Rivalry
    Willem-Alexander van't Padje   138

9. Colonial Agitation and the Bismarckian State: The Case
    of Carl Peters
    Arne Perras   154

10. The Law and the Colonial State: Legal Codification
    versus Practice in a German Colony
    Nils Ole Oermann   171

11. Max Warburg and German Politics: The Limits of
    Financial Power in Wilhelmine Germany
    Niall Ferguson   185

12. Continuity and Change in Post-Wilhelmine Germany:
    From the 1918 Revolution to the Ruhr Crisis
    Conan Fischer   202

13. A Wilhelmine Legacy? Coudenhove-Kalergi's Pan-Europe
    and the Crisis of European Modernity, 1922-1932
    Katiana Orluc   219

14. Ideas into Politics: Meanings of "Stasis" in
    Wilhelmine Germany
    James Retallack   235

Notes on Contributors   253

List of Publications by Hartmut Pogge von Strandmann   257

Index   261

Foreword

When Hartmut Pogge von Strandmann took up his studies at Hamburg University in 1958 and became a student of Fritz Fischer, he could perhaps conceive of himself as a professional historian; but it is unlikely that he could have imagined himself as topping his academic career with a professorship at Oxford University and becoming one of the best-known experts on Wilhelmine Germany in England. He reached this influential position in recognition of his achievements as a scholar and teacher.

That he would be an excellent teacher, who for the past thirty-five years has shaped the analytical skills and devotion to history of hundreds of undergraduates and dozens of graduate students, was already evident when in 1962 he was awarded a scholarship to continue his studies at St. Antony's College, Oxford. Meeting him in those years was always an intellectually stimulating experience. It was not just that he had immersed himself deeply in the history of the Bismarckian Empire and debated the new ideas that had come out of the Fischer school with clarity and commitment; his friends and colleagues were even more impressed with his encyclopedic knowledge of virtually every social or political issue under the sun. Helped by a truly remarkable memory for facts and figures, he would often leave his interlocutors grasping for a counter-argument.

His knowledge of history and contemporary affairs made him an ideal tutor in the Oxford system—one who would challenge his students, question the lines of argument in their essays, and encourage them to be skeptical of orthodoxies. This was also the secret of his success at Sussex University, where small-group seminars were the principal teaching device. Having completed a course with him meant that you came away feeling not only that you had learned something, but also that you had begun to explore some really intriguing ideas.

This was also what, I think, attracted a large number of students to write their dissertations with him. For when it came to questions of historiography, he was a *Querdenker* who encouraged others to go against the grain as they developed their thesis topics. As his own work became more focused on the Bismarckian Empire, he was in fact among the first to point to the importance of pressure group politics and the impact of extraparliamentary associations on both official foreign and domestic policymaking and on the mobilization of people at the grassroots level of society. He was also to be found in the first line of those who began to challenge Hans-Ulrich Wehler's interpretation of the German Empire. He queried the latter's notion of the primacy of domestic politics, voiced doubts about the feudalization hypothesis, and drew attention to the many modern features of pre-1914 Germany. He began to think about the ambiguities of modernity and the role of the bourgeoisie, particularly as embodied by the personality of Walther Rathenau.

All of these ideas, it is true, are to be found in his essays; he did not bring them together in a larger study of the basic character of the Wilhelmine Empire and of "Wilhelminism" as some of his friends urged him to do. But his students listened to him, as they were themselves looking for ways of escaping the "new orthodoxies" of the "Bielefelders." It was not easy to do this, as Geoff Eley has recorded in the introduction of his *From Unification to Nazism*. But Hartmut Pogge never stopped telling his students to develop the ideas they had been discussing, urging them not to be intimidated by those magisterial German professors. So they went ahead producing important work of their own, and even if they ran into hostile criticism, their long-term impact on the direction of research on modern German history has been profound.

That impact is also reflected in this volume, which is not a traditional Festschrift containing disparate essays by a large number of friends and colleagues. Rather, this anthology is a clearly focused volume with a coherent theme, presented in essays written exclusively by Hartmut Pogge's students, all of whom are now well launched on their own careers and have made major contributions to the field of "Wilhelminism and Its Legacies."

No less important, the reader who compares the themes of the essays in this volume with those of the honoree will find that quite a few of them appear in Hartmut Pogge's own writings. The editors and contributors hope that their tributes to their teacher will stimulate further research and raise critical questions of the kind that he encouraged them to ask when they embarked upon their work.

However impressed I am with the weighty scholarship in this volume, let me end on a lighter note. There were two of Hartmut Pogge's friends who remained rather more stubborn when he regaled them with his revisionist ideas. He first met them in somewhat unusual circumstances in Potsdam in 1963 after they had all been given permission to work in the East German archives. In fact, the flood of three applications, all from England, so overwhelmed the authorities that, in the absence of hotels in that place, they booked two of them into a tiny room with only one bed at a local bed and breakfast. Piling into this one bed was not what Hartmut Pogge and John Röhl, the other budding historian, had expected, but it quickly sealed a lifelong friendship between them. The third person in this trio, Volker Berghahn, arrived in Potsdam a day or two later. He was luckier in that he was given a room to himself and the luxury of running water, with a bucket under the washbasin that had to be emptied after every wash.

These experiences of GDR hospitality bonded the three of them together. Yet, however persuasively Hartmut Pogge debated problems of modern German history with the other two, he failed to convince them to follow the route that he and his students took. John Röhl pursued "*personalisierende Geschichtsschreibung*" by devoting his entire professional life to writing about Wilhelm II. Volker Berghahn remained an old-fashioned "structuralist." But regardless of such minor differences, both friends are truly happy to join his students in this fitting celebration.

Volker R. Berghahn

Acknowledgments

A s with any Festschrift, our principal expression of gratitude is directed toward the honoree. We thank our friend and mentor, Hartmut Pogge, for giving us this opportunity to undertake and complete a labor of love.

We are also indebted to the contributors, who allowed us to realize our goal of producing a coherent and cohesive volume of essays—one that takes up themes of direct interest to Hartmut Pogge and of wider appeal to students of modern German history.

For their assistance in bringing this volume to fruition we owe a special debt to Marion and Vivian Berghahn of Berghahn Books, and, for his Foreword, to Volker Berghahn. At various stages of editing, proofing, and indexing, we were assisted in Toronto by Erwin Fink and Lisa Todd, and in Ann Arbor by Roberta Pergher.

James Retallack is grateful for the opportunity—initially during a time of heavy administrative duties and then while holding a visiting appointment in Göttingen—to undertake new research for his own essay and to oversee the final stages of the volume's production. These tasks would have impossible without the support of the Dean of Arts and Science and the Chair of History at the University of Toronto, Carl G. Amrhein and Ronald W. Pruessen, respectively. He is also grateful to his host at the University of Göttingen, Bernd Weisbrod and, for financial assistance, to the DAAD / University of Toronto Joint Initiative in German and European Studies; the York / U of T Institute for European Studies; the Social Sciences and Humanities Research Council of Canada; the TransCoop Program; and especially the Alexander von Humboldt Foundation.

Geoff Eley would like to thank the Department of History and the College of Literature, Science, and Arts at the University of Michigan for providing the sabbatical leave, research support, and incomparable intellectual environment that made the production of this volume possible. He is further grateful to his fellow German historians at the University of Michigan, above all Kathleen Canning, Belinda Davis, Andrew Donson, Young-sun Hong, Jennifer Jenkins, Kristin McGuire, Warren Rosenblum, Roland Spickermann, Dennis Sweeney, and Lora Wildenthal, who over the years have continued deepening his education in the complexities of the Wilhelmine era.

Ann Arbor and Toronto,
October 2002

Introduction

⟨⇒·◇·⇐⟩

GEOFF ELEY AND JAMES RETALLACK

I

M ore than three decades have now elapsed since the "Fischer Controversy" dramatically opened the *Kaiserreich* for serious historical research.[1] The interpretations that quickly established their ascendancy during the initial rush of publication will be familiar enough. They amounted to a powerful claim about German exceptionalism—Germany's differentness from "the West." That claim was rooted in arguments about political backwardness and Germany's persisting authoritarianism, which allegedly stacked the decks (or set the points) in favor of the eventual triumph of the Nazis. From the upsurge of scholarship produced between the mid-1960s and mid-1970s came a series of lasting and almost axiomatic perspectives: the importance of direct continuities linking Bismarck with Hitler; the effects of a structural contradiction between economic modernity and political backwardness that destabilized the *Kaiserreich*'s political institutions; the view that Germany never experienced the crucial emancipatory transformation of a bourgeois revolution in the nineteenth century, remaining subject instead to the authoritarianism of old-style "preindustrial elites" in the political system; the notion that those elites ruled by repression, social imperialism, and other manipulative techniques of rule; and the belief that German history was stamped by a calamitous "misdevelopment" in contrast to the healthier trajectories of societies farther to the west.

What came to be termed the "new orthodoxy" of the mid-1970s converged in important ways with an existing Anglo-American body of interpretation produced largely by emigrés and often drawing upon older, pre-1933 critical traditions of German political life. But the revisionist West German historians of the 1960s and 1970s sharpened these earlier claims and carried the argument much further. They insisted that backward political interests—the traditional power elites and their preindustrial mentalities—preempted any democratic modernizing of the political system and allowed what Karl Dietrich Bracher termed "authoritarian and anti-democratic struc-

Notes for this section begin on page 13.

tures in state and society" to persist. The resulting paradigm of "backwardness"—
and especially the *continuity* of backwardness—was then taken to be crucial for the
conditions eventually enabling the rise and success of the Nazis. In those terms, the
approach implied a conspicuously deterministic framework of explanation, in which
Nazism's primary origins became located somewhere in the middle of the nineteenth
century (or even earlier, in the epoch of Napoleon and the French Revolution), when
Germany failed to take the "Western" path of successful liberal-democratic evolution.

Constructive critiques of these perspectives developed in the late 1970s, partly
from dissentient voices inside the West German historical profession (most notably,
Thomas Nipperdey),[2] but also from across the North Sea in Britain, drawing upon
a different set of national historiographical traditions. The first sign of the latter was
a volume of essays edited by Richard Evans in 1978,[3] followed by further publications on the part of several of its contributors in both essay and book form. David
Blackbourn and Geoff Eley published a book-length assault on the fundamental
framework of the post-Fischer perspectives, initially in West Germany (1980) and
then in expanded and revised form in English (1984).[4]

By the mid-1980s, the breadth of this critique was readily apparent. Taking
direct aim at the so-called *Sonderweg* thesis—the established teleology of German
exceptionalism, which treated the spectacular and undeniable difference of Nazism as
evidence of a deeper-rooted historical pathology marking German history *in general*
as different from the history of the West—the new critiques argued the heuristic value
of trying to see German history between the 1860s and 1914 in its own terms. This
was *not* an argument against comparison as such. Rather, it was a plea for rethinking
the appropriate contexts in which comparisons could best be made. As a consequence of such rethinking, it was argued, German history under the *Kaiserreich*
might start to look less damaged and dangerous beside the histories of Britain and
France (to take the two most consistently implied, but rarely explicated, referents
invoked by adherents of the *Sonderweg* thesis). Of those differences that remained,
the critics argued, many might look less straightforwardly aligned with the events of
1930-1945, so that the deterministic grip of 1933 on discussions of the preceding
periods might be pried loose. And, of particular importance for the present volume,
they suggested that the sources of Germany's domestic and international crises in the
half-decade preceding World War I might have to be disengaged from the longer history of the *Kaiserreich*—not absolutely, of course, but certainly as the encompassing
argument of first recourse to explain German "deviance" from "norms" of democratic, parliamentary, and international behavior. In consequence, the whole idea of
the *Sonderweg* needed to be rethought.

There followed a decade of invigorating debate. Though with differing emphases
and drawing different conclusions, German and Anglo-American scholars focused
particularly on the need to revisit the history of the German bourgeoisie. The goal
was to reassess the bases of the bourgeoisie's sociocultural cohesion and forms of organization, to reappraise its values and collective sense of itself, and to rethink the
nature of its impact on the new German society, the new national state, and the new

political culture created from the 1860s onward. One result was to send West German historians back to the drawing board in major research projects on the social and cultural history of bourgeois class formation, most significantly in Bielefeld under Jürgen Kocka (on the forms of bourgeois culture and civility)[5] and in Frankfurt under Lothar Gall (in a series of city-by-city investigations).[6] By the early 1990s, presaged by a variety of densely packed conference volumes, the book-length monographs from these projects were starting to appear.

During this time, three additional developments had been independently maturing and now also began to converge. First was a new sophistication in the writing of women's history, which transmuted during the 1980s into an increasingly accepted emphasis on gender. Second, the initially quite marginalized and contentious movement of *Alltagsgeschichte* (history of everyday life) was being co-opted by the 1990s into the German versions of the new cultural history. Third, driven in part by the events of 1989–90, historians both intensified their effort to investigate hitherto neglected regions and localities in the *Kaiserreich* and developed more sophisticated means to consider the interpenetration of local, regional, and national identities. After the groundbreaking study by Celia Applegate,[7] which demonstrated that Germans after 1871 did not need to abandon their attachment to the locality even as they embraced the German nation, the interpenetration of social, political, and cultural approaches to German nationalism allowed historians to demonstrate that beliefs, idioms, and symbolic representations generated on the local and regional level really did matter.

II

From the vantage point of 2003, various substantial changes can be seen. Most importantly, the powerful post-Fischer consensus regarding the historic weakness of the German bourgeoisie—which has itself exercised almost canonical standing in the larger discourse of comparative social science—has dissolved. Certain nostrums of the historiography of the 1960s and 1970s, such as the "refeudalization of the bourgeoisie" or the subordinate status of bourgeois cultural values, the so-called *Defizit an Bürgerlichkeit*, have been abandoned. Indeed, as one commentator noted recently, except for certain rear-guard actions the *Sonderweg* concept no longer serves very well as a compelling thesis against which to build an alternative explanation.[8]

Why is this so? On the one hand, the *Kaiserreich*'s dominant culture is now widely acknowledged to have been explicitly and self-confidently "bourgeois." More generally, however, and also more importantly, current research has acquired such richness and diversity—on particular cities; on the sociology and culture of the professions; on entrepreneurship in various branches of the economy; on different sectors of policymaking; on the universities, science, and the academic disciplines; on bourgeois taste and moral codes—that it is difficult to overlook (or sidestep) the implications inherent in the fractured nature of today's historiographical "state of the art." Studies of religion, to take just one example, have recently reemphasized the heterogeneous vitality of bourgeois culture and its forms of sociability between the 1860s and World War I. But there is a growing sense of urgency among historians that we must work harder to reconnect the disparate worlds inhabited by Protestants, Catholics, and Jews in the Empire. Similarly, region and locality have been properly and successfully claimed as legitimate sites for writing the history of the *Kaiserreich*, thereby loosening the remarkable tenacity of Prussocentric assumptions in German historiography. Our knowledge about particular regions has quickly surpassed any definition of "critical mass," and we have become aware that the grand syntheses of the 1980s and early 1990s privileged national aggregates and Prussian peculiarities at the expense of local conditions "that were messy, spasmodic, and unpredictable— just like life itself."[9] Nonetheless, we are less certain that we have adequately grasped the real significance of processes whereby the locality, the region, and the nation were simultaneously constructed by contemporaries—spatially, culturally, and symboli- cally. We feel intuitively that the federated Empire and its histories (in the plural) were profoundly conditioned by "the 'placeness' of place."[10] Yet the symbolic repre- sentations of territoriality, together with their constant renegotiation, have remained largely disconnected from the specific political consequences to which they gave rise.

Despite the many areas in which *Kaiserreich* historiography has been questioned, revised, and enriched by research of the past twenty-five years, the post-Fischer con- sensus remains broadly intact in perhaps the most important dimension of all— namely, the treatment of the *Kaiserreich*'s political system and the characterization of its reformist potential. Whereas the complexities of German society and its dominant culture are now generally acknowledged, with few historians any longer doubting that Germany's dynamic modern economy brought with it far-reaching transformations of the social structure and the prevailing cultural value system, little seems to have changed in the analysis of the *Kaiserreich*'s political history more narrowly conceived. Despite the striking concessions made in the areas of social and cultural history, most advocates of the *Sonderweg* thesis would find little with which to argue in general accounts of the *Kaiserreich*. Most of those accounts—overviews, textbooks, syntheses, to be sure, but also specialized monographs that try to provide a larger context for their empirical findings—still insist on the backwardness of the Imperial state, the pet- rification of its central political institutions, and the unreformability of its practices. In the realm of the state, it is argued, preindustrial interests and elites remained ascen- dant, armored inside the institutional core of Prussianism. Secured by the 1871 Constitution, those interests were preserved against the changes occurring elsewhere. In particular, general studies of the *Kaiserreich* and analyses accompanying primary sources for student readers continue to list the same familiar elements in the long- established narrative of backwardness: "[M]ilitarism, a political system where the leg- islature had no control over the executive, and the right of the King of Prussia to appoint his own ministers, which as German Kaiser he was also given at the Imper- ial level," as one new general account summarizes them.[11]

Given the rather surprising persistence of this paradigm, the purpose of this vol- ume is to push forward and accelerate the process of opening up the political history of the *Kaiserreich* for alternative readings. The volume's contributors propose a more complex and differentiated understanding first and foremost of Wilhelmine Germany's extraordinarily dynamic and rapidly transforming society in its own right, but also of its possible lines of development when viewed from a longer historical perspective. This double proposition will certainly involve disengaging the analysis of the Imperial era from the violent and divisive histories that came afterward—histories into which the main interpretations of the *Kaiserreich* have been so persistently and powerfully subsumed. Once again, though, our purpose is not to refuse the necessity of the longer-term perspectives; after all, we propose looking at crises *and* continuities. Instead, we aim to fashion a more careful basis for allowing the questions of continuity and change to be judged. Likewise, if our volume treats the framework of German exceptionalism skeptically, proposing ways in which the "peculiar" elements of German history might be redescribed and given more specificity, this is not to dissolve the purposes of comparison altogether, still less to make German history simply the same as any other. On the contrary, if less familiar bases of comparison can be found and less well-known elements of particularity be mined from the historical record, allowing German history's "differentness" as well as its "sameness" to be explored, then national specificities can properly begin to emerge.

III

The following considerations are important in setting the scene for this project:

Within the late-twentieth-century framework of comparative thinking about political development and the progress of democracy, "Germany" has usually acted as a sign for setbacks and difficulties, as the place where the necessary modernizing reforms failed to break through. Accordingly, for the first half of the twentieth century, German history is taken to be the site of modernity's *defeat*. This was especially true of democracy and citizenship, of women's emancipation and pacifism, and, more ambiguously, of rationalism and the rise of science. In other areas—notably the rise of the welfare state and industrialization—Germany was considered to have demonstrated resistance to modernity or, at best, to have been the site of ambiguous modernization. Yet even here historians tended all too quickly to abandon even these elements of complexity and ambivalence, reverting to a view that stressed the familiar (but no less violent) central contradiction of German history: between the dynamism of economic modernization on the one hand, and the handicaps of political backwardness on the other.

The earlier optimism behind narratives of progress in social science and historiography has been badly compromised by the events of the last quarter of the twentieth century: from the crisis of the welfare state and the demise of Keynesianism to the environmental catastrophe and widespread popular disillusionment with science. Contemporary logics of "globalization" have also damaged earlier confidence in the expansion of democracy within national states. In the specifically German context, moreover, the burgeoning historical scholarship on science, medicine, public health, social policy, social planning, rationalization, and the technologies of expertise under the Third Reich profoundly questions the progressive valency of reform discourses based on those ideas earlier in the twentieth century, whether in the Weimar Republic or the *Kaiserreich*.

As understandings of "progress" and "reform" start to shift and realign in the present, their meanings in the past also pull apart. The political valencies of "reform" in Imperial Germany start to seem very contradictory and confused. For example, in existing historiography the supposed relative weakness of "reform movements" is thought to be a key aspect of Imperial Germany's persisting authoritarianism and political backwardness. Our reconsideration of this view extends in two directions. First, we would argue that those reform potentials were stronger, richer, and ran more deeply through social and political movements than previously assumed. Second, the very multiplicity of "meanings of reform" meant that reformist impulses were also often lacking in the conventional progressivism that historians' teleologies of reform have usually ascribed. Thus, even though such innovations as the advent of labor exchanges in big cities may have served employers' interests specifically and the cause of social control generally, the possibility that they could have—or perhaps actually did—contribute tangibly to the prospects for social peace in Germany cannot be denied out of hand. Conversely, ideas and movements traditionally identified with German "anti-modernism"—with "anti-reform" in that sense—may actually have carried forward-looking and modernizing aspirations. Examples here would be *Heimatschutz* and other "romantic" forms of preservationism, *Lebensreform* and related ideas of ethical reform, various kinds of radical nationalist agitation, and so forth.

The main reform narratives identified with political modernity—those of democracy and citizenship, the welfare state, women's emancipation, industrialization, science, and cultural modernism—are typically assumed to be consistently interrelated and positively articulated together. Yet there is no inherent reason why "modernizing" initiatives in one area should reinforce the interests of "modernization" in another. One of the pressing needs of Wilhelmine historiography, in fact, is to deconstruct the long-established dichotomous framework of "modernizing economy" and "backward political culture" in order to open up the interesting and underexplored spaces in between. Once that difficult rethinking is underway and the heterogeneous meanings of "the modern" become unpacked, unexpected connections and coalitions can come into view.

For the *Kaiserreich* as a whole, the 1890s have long been seen as the crucial watershed. Bismarck's departure from office has been the oldest basis for this, reinforced since the 1960s by the socioeconomic periodization proposed by Hans-Ulrich Wehler, Jürgen Kocka, and others for the transition to "organized capitalism" and the end of the so-called great depression in 1895-96.[12] The era that opened in 1890 was also defined by the impact of Wilhelm II: if John Röhl and his former students are atypical in seeing the Kaiser's role in government as decisive, that role is taken almost universally to reflect the Imperial state's structural backwardness.[13] In the foreign and colonial spheres, the proclaiming of *Weltpolitik* and the advent of massive naval construction after 1896 further defined this Wilhelmine era, in ways emphasized both by the Fischer school and by Wehler's framework of "social imperialism." Finally, as debates over the *Sonderweg* emerged from the late 1970s and early 1980s, a growing body of literature focused on the growth of popular politics in the period 1890-1914. That literature emphasized not only the general significance of "politics in a new key" under the Reichstag suffrage, but also the specific effects of intensified electoral competition and demagoguery, of expanding popular participation and the growth of mass-based political parties, of the restructuring of a national electorate through changes in local and national public spheres, and of the impact of regional electoral cultures conditioned simultaneously by newer as well as more traditional political elements. In all of these ways, a specifically "Wilhelmine era" has long figured in the vocabulary of German historians without being accorded firmer conceptual form. By using the term "Wilhelminism," we seek to give it that form. Moreover, in also addressing its legacies, we find that attention can be focused both on the notoriously under-researched years 1900-1918 and on the transitions undergone by German society, politics, the economy, and intellectual thought in the revolutionary era of 1917-23.

There presently exists a partial, fragile consensus among historians that one distinctive configuration of politics (the "Bismarckian") was replaced by another (the "Wilhelmine") during the 1890s. Notwithstanding the likelihood that this transition will continue to attract scholarly interest, the Wilhelmine era was characterized by two dimensions that are difficult to reconcile and therefore need further explication. One dimension is illuminated by considering the limited stabilization of politics within the given constitutional forms and parliamentary rules, in a pattern lasting until the eve of World War I. The other dimension became more readily apparent after 1900, when both popular and elite grievances against the remaining blockages to reform drove Wilhelminians to consider new solutions to old problems, and when new scientific, industrial, and international developments also combined to impress contemporaries with the growing possibilities for meaningful, comprehensive, rational reform. Despite the upsurge of scholarly work on the *Kaiserreich* since the late 1960s, we remain surprisingly underinformed about the party-political and legislative histories that would allow us to flesh out this argument. Klaus Tenfelde noted recently that as historians we are unlikely to make further progress either by using such concepts as partial or restricted (*gebremster*) modernization to describe the *Kaiserreich*'s trajectory or by simply agreeing among ourselves that contemporaries in Wilhelmine Germany were ambivalent about the arrival of "the modern."[14] Instead, as Tenfelde also observed, when we consider Germany's political culture more broadly and look for signs of change outside the formal organization of the state, we discover that it was precisely the most conservative, traditional elements of Wilhelmine Germany's political constellation "that could create or accelerate a wholly distinctive modernity [*eine ganz eigentümliche Modernität*] in certain social and political realms [*Teilbereichen*]."

If we take a broader view of "political modernization," carefully uncoupled from the usual assumptions about stronger forms of liberal democracy and parliamentary control, and more keyed theoretically to aspects of efficiency, state intervention, and governmentality, then the two decades before World War I begin to coalesce rather differently within the twentieth century's larger normative frame. In a variety of key areas—the growth of corporative logics in the management of national economic policy; the state's regulative interest in the family as the vital site for the health of the national body; the interest in education, philanthropy, and other fields of social policy under the banner of national efficiency; the turning to science as the primary means to address social problems—new departures occurred whose reach extended well into the 1920s and beyond. For making sense of *these* changes, we would argue, the hoary dichotomy of "modernizing economy" versus "backward political culture" does not provide much guidance, particularly because the crosscutting effects of social, intellectual, and cultural change complicate this dichotomy so fundamentally. In fact, if we consider contemporary Germans and take *their* logics and purposes as our defining criteria, the Wilhelmine polity does not look very "backward" at all. Perhaps, then, we need to reevaluate the viability of the *Kaiserreich*'s political institutions on this basis, rather than continuing to regard Imperial Germany's political culture as self-evidently less "modern" than those of Britain or France. Arguably, we need to rethink the category of "the modern" altogether.

One of the most influential of existing efforts at doing this, that of Detlev Peukert, certainly reevaluated the strength of reformist forces in the *Kaiserreich*'s final two decades. But Peukert did so by giving reformism a sinister, rather than a progressive, valency.[15] He turned the previous meanings of reform almost entirely on their head, stressing control, regulation, and disciplinary power in contradistinction to the qualities of improvement and emancipation usually associated with reform, and endowing "modernity" with a kind of totalizing logic thought to have been generative of the future potential for Nazism. Moreover, in Peukert's neo-Weberian and Foucauldian-like perspective, the particular political struggles previously central to the thinking of Wilhelmine historians became almost entirely bracketed from the account. Thus it becomes increasingly important to find ways of connecting those impersonal logics of social discipline, biopolitics, and disciplinary power to the political agency of individual and collective actors as earlier social and political historians have understood it. We need to ask: How were these new forms of intervention concretely encountered in the active contexts of organized political life and the public sphere?

What was the specifically "Wilhelmine" aspect of this distinctive configuration that encompassed forward-looking socio-economic developments, expanding state capacities, "normalizing" parliamentary politics, and popular mobilizations? We would locate this somewhere inside the nexus that formed around the turn of the century between capitalist dynamism, national state formation, and social improvement in the doubled context of domestic societal conflict and intensified international rivalry. Here we use the concept of "Wilhelminism," originally proposed by Hartmut Pogge von Strandmann and epitomized by Walther Rathenau:[16] embracing both the national state and the new industrial-capitalist economy; enthused by the technologies of industrial power; acutely aware of the "social problem"; determined to reform the Wilhelmine state through criticism, though on condition that reform serve the cause of national efficiency; and opposed to the Conservatives and Social Democracy alike. Wilhelminians of Rathenau's ilk took their stand positively on the ground of a status quo that was rooted in the undeniable achievements of the nineteenth century yet was dynamic, unfolding, and unequivocally oriented toward the twentieth. For these Wilhelminians, the Imperial polity itself was the best guarantee of modernity, particularly when confronted with two as-yet-untested alternatives: a coup d'état from above (*Staatsstreich*) and a liberal-democratic parliamentary state.

That Rathenau assumed many public roles—"the intellectual, the visionary, the social-political philosopher,... the politician [and the] ... industrial organizer"[17]—reminds us that it is patently insufficient, and even misleading, to describe Imperial Germany or its citizens as simply Janus-faced. To be sure, like Rathenau they were caught between past and present, between stasis and reform; like him, many of them anticipated their role in Weimar of "outsider as insider." But Rathenau's critical conception of Wilhelmine Germany's reformist potential was more complex, more impermanent, and more fraught with internal inconsistencies and tensions than the Janus image would suggest. Indeed, the range of issues accumulated and anticipated in the present volume was already prefigured in a series of articles Rathenau published in the Viennese *Neue Freie Presse* on the eve of World War I. Hartmut Pogge's discussion of Rathenau as representative of the Wilhelmine age highlights the remarkable range of issues he addressed, including: "the bureaucratization of politics, the lack of qualities of leadership in Germany, the unequal distribution of burdens in the State, the concentration of power in the hands of a small but powerful class, the political indolence of the middle classes, the economic materialism, the impotence of the Reichstag, Germany's loss of its position of hegemony in European politics, and the lack of political goals."[18] Together with these criticisms of political and social conditions in Wilhelmine Germany, adds Pogge, Rathenau "developed ideas which dealt *inter alia* with Anglo-German relations, with France's policy of alliances, with the general usefulness of colonies, with a central European customs union, and with the Monroe Doctrine." Many of these topics, too, are taken up by contributors to this volume, though the Monroe Doctrine is, of course, *ein weites Feld*.

IV

In this volume, then, we have planned a series of carefully focused essays exploring aspects of this general argument and bringing those aspects into new, perhaps untested proximity with an existing literature and with each other. At root, we wish to examine what was distinctive—and distinctively "modern" (or not)—about the Wilhelmine era. We want to explore a variety of ways in which certain elements of "the modern" emerged in the social, cultural, political, and international realms during this period. In so doing, we hope to revisit existing approaches to Wilhelmine political history in order to question the frameworks of modernity and backwardness in which it has normally been constrained. In order to address these complexities, we seek to demonstrate that the language of "anti-modernism," "failed modernization," "misdevelopment," and "backwardness" is unsuited to the purpose. Even as we suggest ways to dismantle that older framework, we hope to clarify the comparative significance of Wilhelmine political developments in relation to political histories elsewhere and to the later possibilities of German history after 1918. In doing so, we also hope to honor an outstanding scholar, teacher, and friend.

V

Born in May 1938, Hartmut Pogge took his *Abitur* at the Johann-Heinrich-Voss Gymnasium in Eutin (Holstein, Germany). He then studied history, philosophy, geography, politics, and economics at the universities of Bonn, Berlin, and Hamburg. During his time as a student in Germany, he also worked for six months in the Economic Department of the Mannesmann industrial group. He passed the first part of his university examinations with a first-class mark and in 1962 was awarded a Senior Scholarship to St. Antony's College, Oxford. After that point, he pursued his academic career in Britain. He was a Research Fellow of Balliol College in 1966-70, also serving there as College Lecturer and Junior Dean. From 1970 to 1977 he was a Lecturer in Modern European History at the University of Sussex, after which he returned to Oxford, first as a Fellow of University College and University Lecturer and, since 1996, as a Professor of Modern History.

Teaching and examining undergraduate and graduate students at Oxford is intensive and requires a high level of commitment. Yet Pogge has in addition held a number of prestigious visiting appointments and research positions. In 1985 he was Oxford Visiting Professor at the University of South Carolina, Columbia; in 1991 he was DAAD Visiting Professor at Rostock University; and in 1993 and 1995 he was DAAD Visiting Professor at Namibia University, Windhoek. Since 1999 he has also served as Director of the Modern European History Research Centre in Oxford. In this capacity, Pogge was instrumental in establishing a Master of Philosophy graduate course in Modern European History—an initiative designed to increase the profile of European history at Oxford.

Having studied with Fritz Fischer in Hamburg, and benefiting from Fischer's close relationship with Oxford University at that time, Pogge was very much at the center of the controversies raging around Fischer's work, both in the West German historical guild and in the broader public sphere. Although he was not one of Fischer's *Assistenten* in Hamburg, Pogge, too, grappled with the Wilhelmine background to German expansionism before and during World War I. Indeed, in his contributions to the three Festschriften[19] for Fischer and in a volume of lectures on the origins of the war that he co-edited in 1988,[20] Pogge has continued throughout his career to reconsider the implications of the "Fischer Controversy." He has refined (in some respects also refuted) the findings that made the scholarly impact of Fischer's early work so dramatic. One enduring scholarly product of those early years was a slim volume Pogge published with Imanuel Geiss in 1965, which laid bare the radicalism of Pan-German ideology for the first time.[21]

At the end of 1969, Pogge submitted his Oxford doctoral dissertation on Imperial Germany's Colonial Council (*Kolonialrat*); he passed his oral examination a few weeks later.[22] Pogge's pioneering work moved away from the narrowly based studies of government policy-making that took Bismarckian colonial policy in the 1880s as their focus or that followed a colony-by-colony approach to the subject. By contrast, Pogge identified and explored the vital consultative nexus among government, economic interests, and the nationalist associations espousing a particular colonialist ideology. In so doing, he managed to establish a more complex interplay of relationships between colonialism and German society than the straightforwardly instrumentalized logic implied by Wehler's manipulative model of social imperialism. In the premier British journal *Past & Present*, Pogge developed larger arguments about German imperialism—not limited to Africa—that both built upon and further fueled these more subtle interpretations.[23]

Pogge's work on the *Kolonialrat* then spawned further interests, or rather entwined them. The two most prominent were, on the one hand, the figure of Walther Rathenau, whose colonial journeys preceded his rise to become what Pogge termed the "grandmaster of capitalism" in Wilhelmine Germany, and, on the other, the politics of German industry. His interest in Rathenau developed quickly, with the publication of Rathenau's diaries, first in German in 1967 and then in much expanded and revised form in English in 1985 with Oxford University Press.[24] Well before the English edition was prepared, however, Pogge had conceived a book-length biography, building upon his wide-ranging introductions and drawing on the accumulating monographs produced by colleagues and students in the early 1970s. Here Pogge's relationship to James Joll in London (also Hugh Trevor-Roper) was very important, dovetailing with his role as a key mediator between the West German and British historical scenes and suggesting a left-tending, cosmopolitan type of "pro-European" British liberalism.[25] The common interest in British-German relations before World War I and in Rathenau as a figure who was decidedly "German" and yet intellectually attuned to international cultural and intellectual movements was another natural bond. Given his Hamburg background and the historic mercantile relationship linking Hamburg to Britain, Pogge was excellently positioned to guide the Hanseatic Scholarships and other scholarship programs aimed at internationalizing Oxford's institutional culture while bringing the British and German academic scenes in particular more closely together. These activities contributed to the establishment of the Anglo-German Committee of Historians, which counted Pogge among its strongest supporters, in turn feeding into the launching of the German Historical Institute in London.

The confluence of industry and politics pulled Pogge forward from the Wilhelmine into the Weimar years. Generously supported by the Volkswagen Foundation, Pogge's research was able to deepen and complicate the relationship between heavy industry and politics postulated by Dirk Stegmann and others. A monograph on the Mannesmann firm was the product of this work,[26] as were various essays that provided only a tantalizing glimpse of the pioneering and wide-ranging archival work Pogge conducted in Germany during these years. Meanwhile, the Rathenau connection converged with a developing interest in Rapallo and in German-Soviet relations between the wars. This interest in industrial politics over an extended time frame underscores the broad-gauged quality of Pogge's writing, which studiously avoided any narrow concentration on *Interessenpolitik* in the formal sense, exploring instead the wider political field in which industry's pursuit of politics occurs.

Thus, whereas many of Pogge's interests have found their best expression in compact, often circumspect scholarly essays, these have ranged temporally, geographically, and thematically over considerable ground. One thinks of his work on urban liberalism in the *Kaiserreich*,[27] on Mecklenburg (and the Pogge family) in the mid-nineteenth century,[28] on radical nationalist interest groups,[29] on colonial policy, and on German relations with Britain and Russia. More of the same can be expected from Pogge's current research on the German armaments industry—from a European perspective—on the eve of World War I.

Nevertheless, by helping bring the world to Oxford and by supervising doctoral dissertations as diverse as the essays collected in this volume, Pogge vitally shaped historians' growing enchantment (and perplexity) with the Wilhelmine epoch. Eschewing the common practice of imposing dissertation topics on newly arrived supervisees, he nonetheless ensured that existing Wilhelmine historiography would be supplemented with new work that he believed was badly overdue, for example, on the nationalist *Verbände*, on the German Civil Code of 1900, on Reichstag elections and the 1902 tariff controversy, on the colonialist Carl Peters, on German conservatism, and much more besides. In these ways, Pogge nurtured the seeds that grew into monographic studies authored by a new generation of scholars, patiently allowing the idea of a specifically "Wilhelmine" moment to coalesce in his own thinking and, as the present volume demonstrates, in that of his students. Embracing distinctive notions of industrial dynamism, reform, and colonialism, the concept of "Wilhelminism" gradually became embedded within the contexts of crisis and continuity on the one hand and international relations on the other that continued to figure prominently in Pogge's own thinking. He never allowed his lifelong interest in Rathenau "the man" to constrain his curiosity about "the times"—that is, the larger questions of modern German history that found their confluence in the Wilhelmine age.

Accordingly, the red thread tying this volume together has more than one strand. As students of Pogge, each of us has tried to consider one or more dimension of Wilhelminism. Some of us follow Pogge in taking Rathenau as representative of his age, and particularly of its industrial-capitalist face. Others focus more squarely on the continuities and crises in German colonial administration or German-British relations, while others consider the meanings of reform (or its opposite) as indicative of recent realignments in German historiography. As the diversity demonstrated here reveals, Pogge's influence extends in many directions: geographically, institutionally, and thematically. Indeed, few friends or colleagues realize how diverse a group of people and dissertation topics Pogge has supervised.

Nevertheless, this volume celebrates three prominent aspects of Pogge's long-term achievement that have a patently self-reinforcing (and thus unifying) effect: he has trained a surprisingly large proportion of scholars currently working in the Wilhelmine period; he has consistently challenged his students to consider all that changed, rather than all that remained the same, during the reign of Wilhelm II; and he was more sensitive than many scholars trained in the 1960s to the ways in which elements of "the modern" emerged simultaneously in the social, cultural, political, and international realms during the Wilhelmine time. Hence, the themes of this volume closely reflect something of the same vision of German history and historiography that Pogge expressed and explored through the concept of Wilhelminism.

In bringing this volume to fruition, but also over the longer duration of our careers, we have discovered just how richly Pogge influenced our thinking—questioning orthodox assumptions, seeding ideas, and releasing bees that have continued to buzz in our bonnets ever since. Of course, he was an excellent taskmaster as well, keeping us to deadlines and insisting that we bring our work quickly into print. Timed to coincide with an important birthday celebration in May 2003, this volume has given us an opportunity to bring our friend's ideas into wider circulation and accord them the honor they deserve. We hope readers will feel the same way.

Notes

1. Due to limits of space, no attempt can be made here to cite even the most important historical literature. See the endnotes to the individual contributions for specific references. While hardly representing the current state of the art because of their date of publication, in earlier historiographical résumés we have each tried to take stock of various aspects of the debate: Geoff Eley, "Introduction 1: Is There a History of the *Kaiserreich*?" and idem, "German History and the Contradictions of Modernity: The Bourgeoisie, the State, and the Mastery of Reform," in *Society, Culture, and the State in Germany, 1870-1930*, ed. Geoff Eley (Ann Arbor, 1997), 1-42, 67-103; James Retallack, *Germany in the Age of Kaiser Wilhelm II* (Basingstoke and New York, 1996); idem, "Introduction: Locating Saxony in the Landscape of German Regional History," in *Saxony in German History: Culture, Society, and Politics, 1830-1933*, ed. James Retallack (Ann Arbor, 2000), 1-30.

2. Thomas Nipperdey, "Wehlers 'Kaiserreich'. Eine kritische Auseinandersetzung," (orig. 1975), in idem, *Gesellschaft, Kultur, Theorie. Gesammelte Aufsätze zur neueren Geschichte* (Göttingen, 1976), 360-89.

3. Richard J. Evans, ed., *Society and Politics in Wilhelmine Germany* (London, 1978).

4. Geoff Eley and David Blackbourn, *Mythen deutscher Geschichtsschreibung. Die gescheiterte bürgerliche Revolution von 1848* (Frankfurt a.M., 1980); David Blackbourn and Geoff Eley, *The Peculiarities of German History: Bourgeois Society and Politics in Nineteenth-Century Germany* (Oxford and New York, 1984).

5. Jürgen Kocka, ed., *Bürgertum im 19. Jahrhundert: Deutschland im europäischen Vergleich*, 2 vols. (Munich, 1988).

6. Lothar Gall, ed., *Stadt und Bürgertum im 19. Jahrhundert* (Munich, 1990).

7. Celia Applegate, *A Nation of Provincials: The German Idea of Heimat* (Berkeley, 1990).

8. Thomas Kühne, "Das Deutsche Kaiserreich 1871-1918 und seine politische Kultur: Demokratisierung, Segmentierung, Militarisierung," *Neue Politische Literatur* 43, no. 2 (1998): 206-63, here 248.

9. Alon Confino, "On Localness and Nationhood," *Bulletin* of the German Historical Institute London 23, no. 2 (2001), 7-27, here 13.

10. Celia Applegate, cited in Retallack, "Introduction: Locating Saxony," 18.

11. Matthew S. Seligmann and Roderick R. McLean, *Germany from Reich to Republic, 1871-1918: Politics, Hierarchy and Elites* (New York, 2000), 173.

12. Hans-Ulrich Wehler, *Deutsche Gesellschaftsgeschichte*, vol. 3, *Von der "Deutschen Doppelrevolution" bis zum Beginn des Ersten Weltkrieges 1849-1914* (Munich, 1995); Jürgen Kocka, *Unternehmensverwaltung und Angestelltenschaft am Beispiel Siemens 1847-1914. Zum Verhältnis von Kapitalismus und Bürokratie in der deutschen Industrialisierung* (Stuttgart, 1969).

13. See John C. G. Röhl and Nicolas Sombart, eds., *Kaiser Wilhelm II: New Interpretations* (Cambridge and New York, 1982).

14. Klaus Tenfelde, "1890-1914: Durchbruch der Moderne? Über Gesellschaft im späten Kaiserreich," in *Otto von Bismarck und Wilhelm II. Repräsentanten eines Epochenwechsels?*, ed. Lothar Gall (Paderborn, 2000), 119-41, here 140.

15. Detlev J. K. Peukert, "The Genesis of the 'Final Solution' from the Spirit of Science," in *Reevaluating the Third Reich*, ed. Thomas Childers and Jane Caplan (New York, 1993), 234-52.

16. Hartmut Pogge von Strandmann, ed., *Walther Rathenau: Industrialist, Banker, Intellectual, and Politician. Notes and Diaries 1907-1922* (Oxford, 1985), Introduction and passim.

17. Ibid., 11.

18. Ibid., 183, and for the following.

19. *Deutschland in der Weltpolitik des 19. und 20. Jahrhunderts. Fritz Fischer zum 65. Geburtstag*, ed. Imanuel Geiss and Bernd-Jürgen Wendt with Peter-Christian Witt (Düsseldorf, 1973); *Industrielle Gesellschaft und politisches System. Beiträge zur politischen Sozialgeschichte. Festschrift für Fritz Fischer zum 70. Geburtstag*, ed. Dirk Stegmann, Bernd-Jürgen Wendt, and Peter-Christian Witt (Bonn, 1978); *Deutscher Konservatismus im 19. und 20. Jahrhundert: Festschrift für Fritz Fischer zum 75. Geburtstag und zum 50. Doktorjubiläum*, ed. Dirk Stegmann, Bernd-Jürgen Wendt, and Peter-Christian Witt (Bonn, 1983).

20. Robert J. W. Evans and Hartmut Pogge von Strandmann, ed., *The Coming of the First World War* (Oxford and New York, 1988).

21. Hartmut Pogge von Strandmann and Imanuel Geiss, *Die Erforderlichkeit des Unmöglichen. Deutschland am Vorabend des Ersten Weltkrieges* (Frankfurt a.M., 1965).

22. Hartmut Pogge von Strandmann, "The Kolonialrat. Its Significance and Influence on German Politics 1890 to 1906" (D.Phil. diss., University of Oxford, 1970). Cf. idem, "Consequences of the Foundation of the German Empire: Colonial Expansion and the Process of Political-Economic Rationalization," in *Bismarck, Europe and Africa: The Berlin Africa Conference 1884-1885 and the Onset of Partition*, ed. Stig Förster, Wolfgang J. Mommsen, and Ronald Robinson (Oxford, 1988), 105-20.

23. Hartmut Pogge von Strandmann, "Domestic Origins of Germany's Colonial Expansion under Bismarck," *Past & Present* 42 (1969).

24. Walther Rathenau, *Tagebuch 1907-1922*, ed. Hartmut Pogge von Strandmann (Düsseldorf, 1967); *Walther Rathenau, Industrialist, Banker, Intellectual, and Politician: Notes and Diaries, 1907-1922*, ed. Hartmut Pogge von Strandmann (Oxford, 1985, rpt. 1988). The latter translation was significantly aided by the linguistic expertise of Hilary Pogge von Strandmann.

25. The Joll Festschrift was published as *Ideas into Politics: Aspects of European History, 1880-1950*, ed. R. J. Bullen, H. Pogge von Strandmann, and A. B. Polonsky (London, 1984).

26. Hartmut Pogge von Strandmann, *Unternehmenspolitik und Unternehmensführung. Der Dialog zwischen Aufsichtsrat und Vorstand bei Mannesmann 1900 bis 1919* (Düsseldorf, 1978).

27. For example, Hartmut Pogge von Strandmann, "The Liberal Power Monopoly in the Cities of Imperial Germany," in *Elections, Mass Politics, and Social Change in Modern Germany: New Perspectives*, ed. Larry Eugene Jones and James Retallack (Cambridge and New York, 1992), 93-117.

28. For example, Hartmut Pogge von Strandmann, "Revolution in Mecklenburg. Die liberale Verfassungsbewegung vom Vormärz bis zum 'Sieg der Reaktion' im Jahr 1850," in *Modernisierung und Freiheit. Beiträge zur Demokratiegeschichte in Mecklenburg-Vorpommern*, ed. Michael Heinrichs and Klaus Lüders (Schwerin, 1995), 165-185. Cf. Hartmut Pogge von Strandmann and Robert J. W. Evans, eds., *The Revolutions in Europe 1848-1849: From Reform to Reaction* (Oxford, 2000).

29. See Pogge's contribution on "Nationale Verbände zwischen Weltpolitik und Kontinentalpolitik," in *Marine und Marinepolitik im kaiserlichen Deutschland 1871-1914*, ed. Herbert Schottelius and Wilhelm Deist (Düsseldorf, 1972), 296-317.

– 1 –

Making a Place in the Nation
Meanings of "Citizenship" in Wilhelmine Germany

GEOFF ELEY

Nation and Citizen in Imperial Germany

The inchoateness of national affiliations in the nineteenth century made the boundaries of national categories in Europe anything but stable and mature.[1] Indeed, for current writing on nationalism, that nonfixity has become almost axiomatic, emphasizing the indeterminacy, constructedness, and contingency with which national identity came to be formed. Within that general "constructionist" idiom, however, national affiliations can easily appear far too malleable and free-floating, reflecting an unresolved tension between the insights of the new theorizing and the analysis needed for national identity in particular places and times. After 1918, for example, national identifications certainly became hardened along juridical, institutional, and ideological continuities among others, whereas before 1914 the full-blown ideal of the nation-people-citizenry as the basis for state-political organization was still only in the process of being proposed. If we are to grasp those dynamics of emergence, therefore, we need to temper the idea of nationalism's changeability and unfinishedness by keeping in mind the instituted and material finiteness of the resources available for nationalist action, however creative and bold, at any one time.

Thus, the passage to statehood marks a key watershed for any nationalist movement. Owning the nation-state, with its juridical machinery of constitutions, legal codes, courts, and police; its centralized administrative systems; its society-wide institutions in governmental, party, and associational terms; and its organized cultural life, enormously alters both the strength of national identifications and the modalities for building them. The ideal of "the nation," as against other principles of state-political organization, became a source of extraordinary legitimizing power in the centralizing drives of the nineteenth century, enabling demands on people's loyalties far beyond the expectations of earlier forms of government. As Benedict Anderson famously put it, the willingness to die for the nation, to sacrifice one's own body, in an emotionally gripping call on the citizen's deepest loyalties, memorialized in poetry and monuments, became the extreme heroic form for this suturing together of the individual and the nation.[2]

It made an enormous difference to this discourse of sacrificial inscription—inescapably gendered in its allegories and public symbolics—whether the nationalism concerned was that of a campaigning or insurgent movement demanding its rights, or that of a state already wielding its independence. Different temporalities of state formation pertained. For one, infrastructures of national identification in the old states of Western Europe (coming from cumulative histories of legal and institutional sedimentation) allowed practical consciousness of national belonging to coalesce. For the other, purposeful movements of political creation generated demands for national independence. Thus, the coordinates of nationalism in England and France differed profoundly from those in Germany and Italy, and still more from the moving nationalist frontier of Eastern Europe. Outside the "core" states of Western Europe, nationality lacked the faculty of an established statehood. For early German nationalists of the anti-Napoleonic wars, the *Vormärz*, and the 1860s, the arduous work of instituting the national category—of inventing the nation as a political program—was conducted without benefit of existing state power. The architecture of national identification and the process of imagining the nation as an organized, proselytizing act, in a politics of continuous nationalist pedagogy, depended on private more than official bodies, on individuals and voluntary associations more than governments. Further, this process of proposing the German national category was coterminous with the emergence of a public sphere in Habermas's sense, so that "the nation" became conceived simultaneously as a political community of citizens.[3] Indeed, the very virtue of "publicness" in its civic sense and the associated coalescence of civil society were entailments of demands that the nation be formed.

The complex interpenetration of these two ideas—"nation" and "citizenry"—in the political languages of the nineteenth century was extraordinarily important. A key tension ran through processes of national unification between the slow coalescing of national consciousness in institutional ways (as an effect of longer-term histories) and the campaigning of the nationalist movement per se. A political identity of Germanness might have cohered institutionally over a longer period in response to state policies, constitutional frameworks, juridical definitions, and political opportunity structures, but German nationalism as such required new languages of political subjectivity that called on the inhabitants of this Central European region to restyle themselves in national, as opposed to other, ways.[4]

This tension required both the inventedness of national identity and the constraints under which inventiveness had to work. On the one side, the element of political innovation vitally structures how we think of nations and nationalism nowadays: nationality was *not* a natural consequence or outgrowth of common culture of great antiquity, and nations were not so much discovered or awakened as they were invented by the labors of intellectuals. That is, nationalisms rested on specific political histories and ideals of citizenship far more than arising spontaneously out of preestablished cultural communities. Moreover, achieving continuity in national culture required hard, repeated, creative ideological and political efforts by intellectuals and nationalist leaderships. It did not occur naturally by itself. Yet on the other side, nationalists could only work with the cultural materials at hand—that is, not with cultures of their own choosing, but with cultures directly encountered, given, and transmitted from the past. Despite all the power of our contemporary "constructionist" insight (the inventedness and contingency of nations), it was this complicated dialectic of political innovation and actually existing cultures that provided the key to the particular histories that nation building involved.

This fissiparous and fractured quality of nineteenth-century political cultures was critical to nineteenth-century nationalisms. Eventually, nations attained a presence independently of the political practices that originally proposed them. They acquired an instituted and renewable everydayness, which built them into the underlying framework of collective identification in a society, part of the assumed architecture of political order and its commonsense intelligibility. With the attainment of sovereignty or political self-determination at the latest, the nation became a discursive formation—ideologically, institutionally, culturally, practically, in myriad small ways—of immense power, which already prescribed the possible forms of political action and belief—what was thinkable and what was not. In Tom Nairn's words, nationalism turned into "a name for the general condition of the modern body politic, more like the [overall] climate of political and social thought than just another [freestanding] doctrine."[5] But in the nineteenth century, this hard-wiring could not yet be presupposed. Accordingly, the histories of nationalist belief and practice before 1914 concern the processes permitting this to happen.

For us today, nationality or "nation-ness"—the complex, conscious, unspoken, and inescapable modalities of "being national" in the territorialized constitutional polities of the period since the 1860s—delivers the generic languages of political identity formation in the public and everyday conditions of life of the twentieth century. We are "national" when we vote, watch the six o'clock news, follow the national sport, observe (while barely noticing) the endemic iconographies of landscape and history in television commercials, imbibe the visual archive of suggestion and citation in the movies, and perform the nation day by day through our unreflected repetitions of political recognition. We are interpellated in mundane ways as national subjects in that sense. As Lauren Berlant suggests, this is what talk of "a common national character" implies, whereby "National Subjects are taught to value certain abstract signs and stories as part of their intrinsic relation to themselves, to all 'citizens,' and to the national terrain." She calls this the "National Symbolic": "… the order of discursive practices whose reign within a national space produces, and also refers to, the 'law' in which the accident of birth within a geographic/political boundary transforms individuals into subjects of a collectively held history. Its traditional icons, its metaphors, its heroes, its rituals, and its narratives provide an alphabet for a collective consciousness or national subjectivity; through the National Symbolic the historical nation aspires to achieve the inevitability of the status of natural law, a birthright."[6]

In defining "the *political* space of the nation," this "National Symbolic" exceeds the legal discourse of citizenship, seeking "to link regulation to desire, harnessing affect to political life through the production of 'national fantasy.'" This is how the idea of "the nation" works, figuring history and geography into a landscape of familiarity and promise, inciting memories and hopes of citizenship, and bringing its claims and demands into the intimate and ordinary places of daily life. "National fantasy" captures the process by which "national culture becomes local—through the images, narratives, monuments, and sites that circulate through personal/collective consciousness."[7]

Nation and Modernity

As national belonging became the common currency of public personhood during the nineteenth century, the national idea supplied the languages through which disputes about citizenship became encoded. For many German historians after 1945, such conflicts became conceptualized around a "modernity" versus "anti-modernism" divide, from which the potentials for authoritarian, illiberal, and eventually fascist political mentalities and cultures of rule were thought to have formed. Yet for nineteenth-century commentators, in contrast, German unification had captured the progressive momentum of history, replacing a mess of petty particularisms with a national state fitted for the dynamism of change. Later, that progressivist view became mainly effaced, and the "modernist" valency of the creation of "Germany"—its forward-looking meanings in the larger process of European constitution making in the 1860s –expunged. Instead, to take one salient version, the extreme modernity of the pre-1914 German economy was thought *not* to have been matched by comparable modernizing of the political culture, in which on the contrary recalcitrance, the authoritarianism of core political institutions, and the primacy of preindustrial traditions still prevailed.

According to this view, this contradiction fostered an anti-modernism or illiberalism that overwhelmed unification's progressive potential. Historians saw popular anti-modern and illiberal ideologies carrying nationalism away from that ground of citizenship, where democratic claims might have been pressed, toward a romantic and irrationalist terrain increasingly overrun by ideas of race. In this distinctive environment, "Germanness" then became a pseudo-scientific inscription of cultural superiority and difference rather than a narrative of constitutionally secured capacities and rights. Such arguments were typically pursued under the rubric of the German *Sonderweg*. But the following will show how political phenomena may be redescribed positively *inside* the languages of citizenship rather than in opposition to them, enabling the Imperial era's conflicts to reappear as contests *within* the framework of modernity rather than as resistances *against* it. This allows the character of German politics before 1914 to become suggestively depathologized, making the period less an incubator for dominant "proto-Nazi" or "pre-fascist" continuities than a source of complex and functioning normality, in which competing possibilities could form.

The Local and the National

Embeddedness in local affiliations, from city elites down to petty hometown notables, supplies one key dimension of the illiberal "apoliticism" and absence of civil courage that historians have repeatedly invoked in explaining Germany's susceptibility to Nazism. Fritz Stern gave bourgeois mentalities under the *Kaiserreich* this classic description: "At every juncture in his career, a German would learn illiberal attitudes or see illiberal models in positions of authority," which were imposed by the political system, sharpened by class antagonisms, embodied by the revered army, and taught by schools and universities. A culture of passivity and deference to authority ensued, working against the chances for a vigorous liberalism. Thus, the Germans of the Empire were stunted and disabled in their exercise of citizenship, refusing "the kind of voluntary, civic activity that attracted their English or American counterparts." This crucially adumbrated the German *Sonderweg*: "Civic initiative takes practice, and German society never fostered it. Most Germans looked to the state for guidance and initiative."[8]

Stern called this syndrome "civic nonage," a failure of civic virtues to flourish.[9] It opened a gap between the German *Bürger*'s social standing in his local domain and the lodgment of political authority in the state. In contrast to the growth of self-government in "the West," an active culture of citizenship was lost. The *Bürger*'s relationship to the state went unmediated by the liberalism of representative institutions or the public performance of civic duties. Consequently, "the new faith in nationalism" became a kind of compensation, a flight forward and upward to the "supreme value of the nation-state," which dismissed civic action and lacked intermediary mechanisms or habits of participatory citizenship in between. Stern's *Politics of Cultural Despair* presented this as a rebellion against the "modern world" per se.[10] The political values of liberalism ("tolerance, dissent, debate, openness") were rejected for an aggressively "Germanic" philosophy. German differences from Britain and France became elaborated into a nationalism based on "racial thought, Germanic Christianity, and Volkish [*völkisch*] nature mysticism," doubling as an "anti-modern" cultural critique.[11] It was rooted in romantic celebrations of local identity—focused on landscape, folkways, and "blood and soil," yet joined upwards to exaggerated love of nation.

Recent works have revisited these old tropes of German parochialism and the lost cultures of civic participation. The German idea of *Heimat* associated with Wilhelm Heinrich Riehl has been integral to that older interpretation, suggesting traditionalist recalcitrance fortified against threats of modernity.[12] But against that presumption of tradition-bound conservatism, Celia Applegate has foregrounded

Heimat's novelty as a complex of meanings specifically generated from unification's modernity. Using the Rhenish Pfalz, a distinct southwestern border region between the Rhine and France that was annexed to Bavaria after the Napoleonic wars, she relates the idea to a complex dialectic of regional and national identifications working together. In her view, the artfully cultivated discourse of *Heimat*—as home, homeland, community, belonging, the cultural locatedness of identity—became fashioned into an idiom for negotiating the complexities of civil affiliation during a time of dramatic transitions. It was not the place from which modernity was resisted, but the ground where workable accommodations could be embraced. *Heimat* was an adaptable and hybrid construction, securing identity through the firm bearings of a familiar locality, but reinscribing them with new national associations. It mediated not just the tensions between the Pfalz and the physically distant Bavarian state, but also the social disruptions wrought by industrialization and especially the emerging meta-identity of Germanness, now institutionalized in the new national state of 1871.[13]

Paradoxically, a term focused on localness and tradition turned into a medium for forward-looking integration and management of supralocal change. *Heimat* represented "the modern imagining and, consequently, remaking of the hometown, not the hometown's own deeply rooted historical reality." In shaping this idiom, its architects called on the "old"—folk customs and speech, the community of village life, the power of the landscape—to engage the need for the new—loyalty to the larger German entity: "Those who created and promoted *Heimat*, consciously or not, were suggesting a basic affinity between the new, abstract political units and one's home, thus endowing an entity like Germany with the emotional accessibility of a world known to one's five senses." This was the quotidian and sensual suturing of nation-ness to the lived world of individuals that was essential if the emotional life of citizens was to be harnessed for the needs of a national culture, while the national culture in turn could insert itself into the local. The "national" could make itself "local" in that sense, delivering some of the materials for "a collective consciousness or national subjectivity."[14] After 1871, "the invented traditions of the *Heimat* bridged the gap between national aspiration and provincial reality," offering "the Germans a way to reconcile a heritage of local political traditions with the ideal of a single, transcendent nationality." And: "*Heimat*'s depiction of the small town as a 'cradle' of the greater political unity both eased the transition and defined an entirely new, more malleable kind of localness."[15]

This approach builds the on ideas of "imagined community" and "invented traditions."[16] It sees the transformations and adaptability of the new German society rather than its resistance to modernity. Instead of being counterposed against forces of change, *Heimat* becomes a creative and integral part of them, a specifically local modality of the nationally emerging public sphere. The early institutional expression of *Heimat*, the Pfalz Historical Association, was formed at the height of German unification in 1869, dually focused on preserving "the region's cultural integrity ... as the surest constituent of German nationhood."[17] Its patrons came from the ascendant political force of the time—regionally dominant National Liberal notables, unification's main bearers and beneficiaries in the Pfalz. National Liberals ruled local government and regional Reichstag representation until the 1890s, stamping the early *Heimat* activity. But when National Liberalism fell into crisis during the 1890s, challenged by new popular mobilizations from radical agrarians, Catholics, and the labor movement, the Pfalz Historical Association was also left behind. In Applegate's argument, this marked the transition from "*Heimat* patronage" to a diverse and contested "*Heimat* movement."[18]

In this new phase, local *Heimat* activity flourished in three main areas. One was the celebration of nature and the countryside through preservation and beautification societies, followed by hiking and other outdoor associations, which both discovered and memorialized the natural world. The second embraced the "revival" of folk custom, song, dance, and dress through multiform cultural invention. The last saw the reshaping of memory through a new genre of *Heimat* histories, in which "staging festivals, building monuments, and touring castles" complemented writing per se. This intensified activity climaxed in the new Historical Museum in Speyer in 1910 and a protracted controversy over the invention of a territorial Pfälzer flag. This last project galvanized difficulties with the Bavarian government, widening the spaces for political disagreements.

In this way, Applegate shows the complex imbrication of local and regional rootedness with the new project of building consciousness of nation, which required a wide repertoire of activities emanating from civil society. Alon Confino's study of *Heimat* in Württemberg also approaches the nation as a "local metaphor," focusing on museums, other *Heimat* organizations, and visual representations of locality and landscape via postcards, posters, paintings, and magazine art.[19] Again, the *Heimat* idea's specificity was its spatial hybridity, joining a grand story of national origins to the forms of lived identity in local and everyday environments. This provincialized grounding of the nation "enlarged local existence to its ultimate imaginary boundaries by transforming local history into national history." It connected "the abstract nation" with local and personal circumstances, thereby "making national history as tangible as local history." In fact, by bringing the national down to the local, the local became nationalized in return.[20]

In Württemberg the same liberal hegemony coalesced, in this case around the German Liberals, those regional notables who embraced Bismarck's solution to the German problem in the late 1860s. These National Liberals then dominated Württemberg politics up until the later political watershed of 1895, when the region's Catholics and left liberals began supplanting them much as in the Pfalz, paralleled by Social Democratic advances in the industrial towns. In emphasizing liberalism's dominance in the political culture of the 1860s and 1870s, Confino's treatment converges with earlier work on Württemberg by Langewiesche, Blackbourn, and others that focuses on liberalism's constructive achievement in the Empire's foundation rather than its capitulation before Bismarck.[21]

In Charlotte Tacke's comparison of national monuments in Germany and France—the Hermannsdenkmal and Vercingetorix monument—the region also functions as the setting wherein "the local" and "the national" worked creatively together. Tacke locates these parallel cultural narratives in a comparative social history of class formation in the respective regions of Lippe and the Auvergne, showing in each case how rootedness in locality dovetailed with the desire to affiliate with the nation. Crucially, that process required extensive civic activism, sometimes state generated but emanating more frequently from civil society. Indeed, the building of these two emblematic monuments presupposed the emergence of the civil societies necessary to sustain them, borne by the organized efforts of voluntary associations, fund-raising activities, and public cultures of commemoration.[22] Interestingly, Tacke also shows the political cohesiveness of regional elite formation in the German case, whose notables enjoyed greater success than their French counterparts in keeping popular participation at bay.[23]

Of course, when cultural contexts of innovation form in this way, disputed territory is usually being created, in which competing interventions can occur. Recent studies of the place of religious conflict in the dynamics of the Empire's emerging national polity take exactly this as their starting point, defining the *Kulturkampf* as a vital site of contention around the terms of national affiliation.[24] During the unification years of the 1860s and 1870s, liberalism's grand narrative of German nationhood was ineluctably Protestant in character, so that the *Kulturkampf* unfolded simultaneously as a demand for progress and as the projection of a national culture that was confessionally enframed. Viewed through the lens of religious conflict, the discourse of belonging to the nation was plural and mobile, appropriated by both sides of the *Kulturkampf*, rather than supplying some unitary language of society-wide political integration.

This undecidedness concerning the possible languages of national identification also emerges from Jennifer Jenkins's study of cultural politics in Hamburg, where bourgeois reformers projected ideals of national unity onto their campaigns of public education and cultural uplift, while seeking to domesticate an unruly mass public and the associated technologies of mass communication. The commercialization of culture and the social disorder of the modern city, combined with the deculturing of respectable taste into kitsch, produced anxieties not only among the bourgeois notability, but also the intellectual advocates of the modernity of the new national state. The resulting projects of national/ist pedagogy provide another setting in which the cultural, social, and political coordinates of the new German citizenship were open to definition.[25]

The "National Symbolic" and the Public Sphere

These examples illustrate the origins of national unification at the grassroots level. National identification under the *Kaiserreich* was fashioned by the efforts of voluntary associations, in regionally and locally bounded everyday experiences, and in energetic forms of civic action. Identification with the new Germany couldn't be produced mainly from above by the actions of the Imperial government and the states. State-

centered or manipulative accounts alone can't explain the emotional power of nationalist appeals. Elaborate and subtle forms of consciousness of nation, strong patterns
of patriotic solidarity, emotional attachment to national symbols and stories, and the
inscription of personhood in the languages of national citizenship all required grassroots activity, sutured to everyday life. Public authorities certainly contributed enormously to this, via schooling, the churches, conscription, and sundry encounters with
officialdom. Workplace experience mattered vitally, too.[26] But national identification
presumed a more general circulation of ideas, which entailed the contest of values in
a public sphere. Civil society supplied the concrete settings for this to occur.

The growth of a locally rooted nationalist public—and the main rhythm of organized nationalist campaigning—accelerated with the 1890s. The transition to heightened and diversified *Heimat* activity was one trend, launched in 1904 by the national
Bund Heimatschutz and related campaigns for protecting historic buildings.[27] By
then, the nation's images were being diffused on a mass scale, densely textured into
the visual symbolic landscape of turn-of-the-century Germany. The public machinery
of patriotism encompassed state ritual and iconography, conscription as the "school
of the nation," schooling and other pedagogies, the press and mass literary forms, the
commemorative calendar of public institutions, and so forth. Identification with the
German nation was being performed in the practices of public life, inside institutions,
in official settings, and on the wider social stage.

Popular culture supplied rich materials for collective identification. The new
urban environments became saturated with cultural references and commercial stimuli,
in visual languages whose "Germanness" became increasingly automatic. Commodi-
fied images now circulated through an expanding economy of consumption—through
travel guides; posters; postcards; collectors' picture cards in packets of cocoa, choco-
late, and other consumer goods; commercialized bric-a-brac; advertisements; and the
spread of tourism. The opposite of a neutral process, this trend inspired extensive
debate over the socio-political implications. While awakening anxieties about cultural
degeneration (via pulp fiction, penny dreadfuls, early films, and all kinds of kitsch), this
new mass market and allied commercial entertainments invited campaigns of uplift and
edification, for which nationalist pedagogy became a natural idiom.[28]

This visualizing of the nation was simultaneously unregulated yet profoundly organized. It was on the one hand decentered, involving mass circulation of images in a lib-
eralized public sphere teeming with rival and competing discourses, embracing the full
spectrum of party politics. Yet on the other hand, the nation was increasingly defined
by common representational frames. Inside these frames, some agencies wielded dis-
proportionate social, organizational, and ideological power—most obviously the state
in its various guises, but also some special interests and political parties over others.

Rudy Koshar calls this process "the formation of a national optics," or "a mul-
tifaceted way of seeing the historical nation in the physical environment." It involved
situating the nation's evolving presence in a visualized landscape of ascribed antiquity.
But it also required a visible and convincing claim on the future. Accordingly, this
"myth of a national community originating in the mists of time" simultaneously

"depended on the saturation of local communities with visual markers of the nation's perdurability." In a time of expanding literacy and accelerating communications, the project of making the nation "real" necessarily worked off the available iconography of landscape and built environment: "Urban communications and transportation networks created a need to 'read' more public symbols, commercial markets created compact advertising messages designed for visual seduction rather than contemplation, and the realistic images of photography and film created new possibilities for visual memory. Most important for our purposes was the national state's need to create objectified symbols of national identity that offered a point of contact and easily recognized visual referent for many disparate groups."[29]

The overbearing and bombastic monuments to unification constructed around the map of Germany—physical analogues to the pomp of Sedan Day—perfectly charted this two-way street: unmistakably glorifying the new state, either via heroic embodiments of Imperial rule or by the sheer scale of their grandiosity, yet growing from the subscriptions of private citizens. The Hermann (1841-75) and Niederwald Monuments (1871-83) were finished earlier. But the 1890s were again the key decade—when projects were either brought to completion, such as the massive Kyffhäuser Memorial or Deutsches Eck, both finished in 1897, or else first conceived, such as the Siegesallee in Berlin (1898-1901) or the centenary Monument to the Battle of the Nations in Leipzig (launched in 1894, inaugurated in 1913). Such monuments came thickly laden with historical citations, calculated to ground the new state's legitimacy in a landscape of officially consecrated memory. This also harmonized with a growing trend toward ceremonialism in institutions like the army and schools. In the Schöneberg Prince Heinrich Gymnasium, ten substantial ceremonies were held between August 1895 and March 1896, "including ample commemorations of battles in the [Franco-Prussian] war, celebrations of the Emperor's birthday, the official handing-over of a portrait of an Imperial Prince, illuminations and public addresses on the war of 1870-71, on the development of the Imperial idea during the war, the character of the Hohenzollern dynasty, etc."[30]

These were certainly "the ritual practices, badges and symbols through which identification with the new Germany (as distinct from any other kind of Germany or any other German state) was internalized."[31] But this activity shouldn't be attributed mainly, let alone exclusively, to the state. It came from civil society. Each major monument was sustained by private initiative and voluntary subscription, often with minimal official subsidy. On a smaller and local scale, some five hundred of Wilhelm Kreis's Bismarck Towers were built during 1900-1910, usually with civic support, requiring little of the state's backing. Such commemorations drew momentum mostly from nonofficial sources. The National Festival Society (formed in 1897) emerged from the earlier Central Commission for People's and Youth Sports (1889), which in its turn had descended from the earlier choral and gymnastic movements, with their civic modeling of the future German nation. By 1900, the occasions of patriotic celebration were laden with dignitaries and officialdom. But the drive and imagination came from private individuals and associations.[32]

Radical Nationalism: Citizenship and its Ambiguities

The constitutional and territorialized conditions of political life under the *Kaiserreich*, which shaped the national polity after the 1870s via precepts of parliamentarism, the rule of law, and a liberal public sphere, instated a thoroughly "modern" construct—politically, juridically, culturally—of the active male citizenry as the embodiment of the nation. By Bismarck's fall, this understanding had even become thoroughly hegemonic, providing increasingly the shared terrain of political exchange and contestation, the generally presumed political commonsense. If during the 1890s a new popular politics cast the founding structure of liberal notability politics into disarray, this led to a broadening of the public sphere rather than any anti-modern process of cutting it back.[33]

This normalizing had many aspects. The end of Bismarck's rule and the Anti-Socialist Law confirmed the cumulative channeling of political life into established constitutional paths, further propelled by the post-1895 economic upswing and an increasingly massified public sphere. The impetus came partly via intensified electioneering and popular agitation. Right-wing efforts at reducing political freedoms and severing parliamentary politics from the broader political nation—if necessary by overturning the Constitution—became decisively blocked. By the 1898 elections, the Social Democrats (SPD) and Centrum could capture the initiative from the government by forcing it to respond to their own campaign issue of the "Constitution in Danger." This successful indictment of the right's hankering for *Staatsstreich* helped institutionalize parliamentary sovereignty and the democratic franchise into an attested national good.

If by misrecognizing the Imperial polity's "modernity" historians have obscured the potentials for pluralism and even democracy in the new languages of nation and citizenship, however, those languages clearly allowed space for the radical right, too. But although the right's politics have usually been associated with resistance to modernity, they just as commonly treated modernity as a vital good. Here the emergent forms of right-wing politics can be used to unsettle our familiar assumptions about modernity and anti-modernism under the *Kaiserreich*.

A key case was radical nationalism, or the politics of "national opposition," which was associated with the *nationale Verbände* (nationalist pressure groups) between the 1890s and 1914. Radical nationalists were clearly on the right. An ebullient populism notwithstanding, they were largely anti-democratic and obdurately anti-socialist to the core, apparently subscribing to the aggressive and anti-modernizing authoritarianism that so many historians read as preserving the *Kaiserreich*'s backwardness. Yet radical nationalists didn't fit this framework. Sociologically, they were not the casualties or opponents of modernization, but the self-assured beneficiaries of Wilhelmine Germany's new industrial civilization. Politically, they celebrated the new national state's powerful modernity, using a novel *deutsch-national* (German-national) rhetoric. Most obviously, this was focused on *Weltpolitik* and the naval arms drive, but it embraced a range of further concerns, including an anti-cler-

icalism that originated in the *Kulturkampf* and a relentless hostility to all particularisms, especially that of Catholic Bavaria, but ultimately including the Prussian par-
ticularism of aristocratic privilege east of the Elbe.

The common thread was the positive desire for a unitary state. The political
drive for strengthening the Empire's centralized fabric produced a range of specific
reform commitments, including the demand for an Imperial system of national taxation to harness the nation's resources and the pressure to "nationalize" the school curriculum, which in its turn was linked to the call for "civic education" or "a crusade of
national education."[34] During a bitter confrontation with the government in 1907-8,
radical nationalists angrily disrupted the given patterns of right-wing politics identified with the Imperial government. Tendentially, these were even anti-royalist.

In all of these ways, radical nationalism professed a modernizing ideology of
"national efficiency" that was extremely threatening to traditional conservatives.
While the militants of the *nationale Verbände* remained vociferously anti-socialist and
bitterly hostile to aspects of the parliamentary system, they were entirely unfazed by
the entry of the masses into politics. Indeed, they berated conservatives for ignoring
the new dictates of popular politics and the fact (as one of them said) that "the
masses have come of age (through elementary schooling, mass conscription, universal suffrage, and the cheap oil lamp)."[35] "Parts of our fatherland," another complained, "are unfortunately still dominated by traditional bureaucratic residues of the
'narrow subject mentality'." Such diehards were obstructing "the *elevation* of all
parts of the nation to consultation and *participation* in national affairs."[36]

Many leading radical nationalists came from strongly liberal backgrounds,
formed as children or young adults in the cultural crucible of German unification. But
radical nationalism's rhetorics of "freedom," "independence," "the will of the people," and the importance of a "free political life" were more than the fossilized traces
of an older discourse dating from that time. Rather, such language articulated real
desires of the Wilhelmine present, issuing angry commentaries on the inability of an
earlier generation's liberalism to organize sufficient popular support for contemporary
needs. Radical nationalist critiques crucially fractured the established terms of right-
wing political legitimacy. Repeatedly assailing the government for its inactivity, they
contrasted the "courtly sneaks, empty-headed jingoes, and undignified sycophants,"
who currently monopolized influence, with the "independent citizens, intrepid patri-
ots, and responsible tribunes of the people," who alone provided "what the German
people needed."[37] Radical nationalism in that sense was a complex and ambiguous
hybrid, sui generis to the Wilhelmine era. How this new political formation might be
fitted into the conventional "tradition versus modernity" schema of German historiography is unclear.

Radical nationalists proclaimed the healing properties of the "national idea"—
its ability to consummate Germany's internal unity by transcending divisions of class,
religion, region, and party—with a missionary zeal, thereby revealing the ambiguities
of the search for an effective nationalist pedagogy. Superficially, educational reform
seems to support functionalist accounts of the Imperial government's needs for inte-

gration, legitimating the Empire's institutions against SPD attacks and establishing new forms of national cohesion over older particularist, confessional, and parochial solidarities. The two Prussian School Conferences of 1890 and 1900, which debated the societal purposes of a state system of education, offer strong support for this view.[38] But those debates over classical versus "German" learning themselves contained a "modernizing thrust," because the language of Germanizing the curriculum was also practical and technocratic, aimed at rendering German society dynamic and efficient for an age of industrial culture and intensifying international competition.

There are two points here. First, the basic project of devising and promulgating a national pedagogy was the common currency of popular politics before 1914, attracting liberals and even socialists no less than governmental conservatives and their radical nationalist critics. But then second, all manner of ideas could coexist with the desire to promote the learning, knowledge, and skills needed for Germany's entry into the twentieth century. Being an extreme modernist for these purposes was no hindrance to a variety of racialist, anti-democratic, and otherwise right-wing beliefs. In these terms, we need to deconstruct the system of distinctions around which Imperial Germany's alleged deficit of modernization has usually been defined. This can be illustrated by two examples.

Hermann Rassow was a senior *Gymnasium* teacher in Elberfeld before moving after 1900 successively to headmasterships near Magdeburg and in Potsdam. He was the most tireless and creative of nationalist agitators, inspired by a mobile political eclecticism, unattached to parties, equally comfortable with populisms of "left" and "right." In the naval expansion of the 1890s, he found an issue ideally suited for raising "the German national consciousness," for easing the workers' "return to patriotism," and for "winning back the embittered masses" to the monarchy. For these goals, he used all manner of platforms—the local Pan-German League (he was also a member of its National Council), Young Men's Associations, networks of former pupils, the Elberfeld Christian-Social Association, the Elberfeld Evangelical Workers' Association, the Royalist Association of Railway Craftsmen, the Provincial Conference of Conservatives in the Rhineland, the Elberfeld "Tuesday Society," and all sorts of workers' clubs and "patriotic associations." A supremely well-connected *Bildungsbürger*, Rassow was the prototype of the disinterested nationalist intellectual. Driven by an ideal of social conciliation beneath the banner of national community and formed in the experience of unification, he made loyalty to the nation-state per se his guiding light.[39]

Rassow was centrally positioned inside Wilhelmine Germany's evolving modernity. He straddled the line perfectly between supporting the Imperial polity in its given constitutional framework and enthusiastically welcoming the new political methods. Likewise, he both defended capitalism's unequal social relations and pressed for an active response to the social consequences of industrialization. Accepting that Social Democrats had to be reasoned with rather than banned and evincing a lively interest in the "social problem," he made the expanding capitalist economy his answer to working-class discontent rather than remedial reforms from the state. In this double respect, the primacy of nationalist loyalty to the state, and an acceptance of capitalist Germany's evolving social reality, Rassow was truly a child of the Empire, in that sense a *Wilhelminian*, attracted neither by the anti-capitalist counter-utopia of conservatives nor by the prospect of a more democratic political system. He loved the new technologies of industrial power, both in the battleships that focused his nationalist desire and in the varied media of his popular agitation. He collaborated with the Navy Office, threw himself into backing the Reich Finance Reform in 1908-9, and was drawn electorally to the imperialist strands of left liberalism. In the 1890s, he was simultaneously an admirer of Adolf Stöcker, Friedrich Naumann, and Friedrich Lange.

An anti-Semitic advocate of a Germanic "aristocracy of race," the author of the well-known racialist tract *Reines Deutschtum* (1893) and the founder of the Deutschbund (German-Union) in 1894, Friedrich Lange was superficially a prime candidate for a simplistic anti-modernist proto-Nazi pedigree.[40] Yet he emerges as a far more complex figure. He specifically repudiated that "ecstasy of habitual German patriotism" and "beloved self-deception," which harked backward to the tradition of "Arndt, Jahn, Körner," insisting instead on the radical newness of the Wilhelmine era's nationalist agenda. He denied that the Deutschbund was "a refuge for *Deutschtümelei*." On the contrary, "it knows how to think *modern*."[41]

One of Lange's favorite issues was school reform. In the 1880s, culminating in 1889, he initiated the movement to launch the Society for School Reform. Its central demands for a modern curriculum and the unitary grammar school reflected not only a desire to "Germanize" the classical education, but also a response to technocratic calls for national efficiency. Similarly, Lange's critique of Christianity and search for a new secular religion of nationality, with its stress on the "native idealism of our popular stock," had affinities with the cultural criticism of the non-SPD left: in 1893 his anti-capitalist and anti-clerical play *Der Nächste* was performed by the New Free People's Theater in Berlin. Lange's advocacy of a "national socialism," which he described as "economic nationalism with a better balance between work and leisure," certainly had prophetic intimations. But when we find him speaking of "natural science and socialism" as "the main levers of recent time," we should pause before assimilating him too easily into an irrationalist and anti-modern prehistory of Nazi ideology.[42] His ideas cannot be located midway on a simple continuum between romanticism and Nazism. They were a complex hybrid of "progressive" and "reactionary" motifs, sui generis to the period between the 1880s and 1914.

Conclusion

Germany was a new state in which allegiances had to be newly made. From a governing perspective, loyalties needed to be reordered and refashioned. Consciousness of belonging to a nation had to be refocused from its earlier objects onto a new encompassing ideal, one commensurate with the complexities of the fledgling national state.

This shaping of a national culture occurred at a time of unprecedented societal change: demographic upheaval, industrialization, rural flight, urbanization, capitalist transformation. The physical landscape was transmuting into a new type of built environment—not everywhere at the same time or speed, but with momentous consequences for social vision. The larger entity of "Germany," where people now imagined their futures, needed to be revisualized. This realignment of affiliations and reimagining of the societal form were also accompanied by revolutionizing changes in the technologies and media of communication, by new methods for circulating ideas in the public sphere, and by new modalities of publicness and public exchange. The infrastructure for identity formation on a society-wide scale was being rebuilt.

These three axes of change in state, society, and public sphere supplied the shifting coordinates of political agency and political subjectivity—of citizenship—for Germans of the Wilhelmine era. But the broadening faculties of citizenship were more than simply an effect of large-scale processes and weighty determinations. Nor can they be grasped exclusively within juridical frames of state-bounded duties and rights, because full citizenship in those terms came only to adult men enfranchised under the 1871 Constitution. Citizenship was shaped by far more dynamic contexts of thought and practice, defined by the organized social action of parties, clubs, committees, and associations; by the shifting boundaries of public and private; and by the exchange of ideas and images in an increasingly mass-mediated public sphere. It also grew from the individual and collective efforts of citizens themselves. Seen dynamically as a mobile aggregate of expanding or contracting political capacities, the process of becoming a citizen might be only unevenly ratified in national politics or institutionalized into law. Further, the claims of citizenship might either stabilize an already constituted state or unsettle it via pressure from below. The juridical nation could be constantly challenged by the uncompleted citizenship of those still on the outside.

Approaching citizenship as a "set of practices—juridical, political, economic, and cultural—which define a person or through which persons define themselves as competent members of society" opens the political history of the *Kaiserreich* for a more complex analysis than the older intepretative frameworks allowed.[43] Civil activism and civic agency were crucial for the reconfiguring of Germanness in the mid nineteenth century, both sustaining the wider mobilizations that accompanied unification in the 1860s and proliferating during the new state's continuing construction. During Germany's accelerating transformation at the turn of the century, the mushrooming of organized activity then greatly expanded the scope for political self-fashioning, as ever more Germans made themselves into citizens by actively claiming a place in the nation. German historians have traditionally seen this process from above, as a state-driven stabilizing of authority that concentrated popular identities around an unreformed political system. Yet that view misunderstands both the evolving dynamism of the *Kaiserreich*'s governing system and its consequences for society, because those new forms of governmentality simultaneously produced new fronts of citizenship. As the example of radical nationalism suggests, the issue was not the *existence* of civic agency, but the unsettling directions and valencies it displayed—not the presence of citizenship as such, but the *kind* of citizenship being developed.

It makes no sense to consider Wilhelmine politics through the lens of "backwardness" or the language of "authoritarian continuities" and "preindustrial traditions," for those years were the site of far more complex and open-ended innovations. The ensuing conflicts are distorted by those older narratives of stagnation and rigidity, in which the forces of change became blocked by the forces of tradition and preindustrial elites perpetuated their power. Stasis of that kind was the opposite of what Wilhelmine society promised and contained. In trying to capture the complexities of that Wilhelmine modernity, the best starting point is the present tense of the period itself, its specificities of social and cultural history and the new forms of politics they spawned. German society was in the midst of full-throttle capitalist transformation between the 1890s and 1914, and in those terms it was change that supplied the Wilhelmine era's strongest continuity. In any case, traditions are only as old as the practices and relations that ground or upset their meanings. To put it another way, the only constancy in the new societal circumstances of Wilhelmine Germany came from the drama of the unceasing pressures of change.

Notes

1.   In regard to the matter of citizenship, I'm especially indebted to the following: Margaret R. Somers, "Citizenship and the Place of the Public Sphere: Law, Community, and Political Culture in the Transition to Democracy," *American Sociological Review* 58, no. 5 (1993): 587-620; Lauren Berlant, *The Queen of America Goes to Washington City: Essays on Sex and Citizenship* (Durham, 1997); Kathleen Canning and Sonya O. Rose, "Gender, Citizenship, and Subjectivity: Some Theoretical and Historical Considerations," *Gender and History* 13, no. 3 (2001): 427-43; Kathleen Canning, "Embodied Citizenships: Gender and the Crisis of Nation in Weimar Germany," unpublished manuscript.
2.   Benedict Anderson, *Imagined Communities: Reflections on the Origin and Spread of Nationalism*, rev. ed. (London, 1991), 7, 9ff.
3.   See Jürgen Habermas, *The Structural Transformation of the Public Sphere: An Inquiry into a Category of Bourgeois Society* (Cambridge Mass., 1993); and Geoff Eley, "Nations, Publics, and Political Cultures: Placing Habermas in the Nineteenth Century", in *Habermas and the Public Sphere*, ed. Craig Calhoun (Cambridge Mass., 1992), 289-339.
4.   For an institutional approach to nationhood, see Abigail Green, *Fatherlands: State-Building and Nationhood in Nineteenth-Century Germany* (Cambridge, 2001).
5.   Tom Nairn, "Scotland and Europe," in *Becoming National: A Reader*, ed. Geoff Eley and Ronald Grigor Suny (New York, 1996), 80.
6.   Lauren Berlant, *The Anatomy of National Fantasy: Hawthorne, Utopia, and Everyday Life* (Chicago, 1991), 20.
7.   Ibid., 5.
8.   Fritz Stern, "Introduction," in idem, *The Failure of Illiberalism: Essays on the Political Culture of Modern Germany* (London, 1972), xviii, xx. Stern's statements speak from the core of the early postwar belief in Germany's exceptional and historic authoritarianism. See also "The Political Consequences of the Unpolitical German," ibid., 3-25.
9.   Stern, "Introduction," xix.

10. Fritz Stern, *The Politics of Cultural Despair: A Study in the Rise of the Germanic Ideology* (Berkeley, 1961).

11. Stern, "Introduction," x; George L. Mosse, *The Crisis of German Ideology: Intellectual Origins of the Third Reich* (London, 1964), 1.

12. Riehl (1823-97) was a social theorist, folklorist, ethnographer, and general cultural critic, best known for his writings on the "rich multiplicity" of German rural life, especially *Die Naturgeschichte des deutschen Volkes*, 3 vols. (Stuttgart, 1851-55), and *Die bürgerliche Gesellschaft* (orig. 1851), ed. Peter Steinbach (Frankfurt a.M., 1976).

13. Celia Applegate, *A Nation of Provincials: The German Idea of Heimat* (Berkeley, 1990).

14. Berlant, *Anatomy*, 20, 5.

15. Applegate, *Nation of Provincials*, 8, 9f., 13, 11.

16. Anderson, *Imagined Communities*; Eric Hobsbawm and Terence Ranger, eds., *The Invention of Tradition* (Cambridge, 1983). See also Arjun Appadurai, "The Production of Locality," in *Modernity at Large: Cultural Dimensions of Globalization* (Minneapolis, 1996), 178-99.

17. Applegate, *Nation of Provincials*, 44.

18. Ibid., 17.

19. Alon Confino, *The Nation as Local Metaphor: Württemberg, Imperial Germany, and National Memory, 1871-1918* (Chapel Hill, 1997).

20. Ibid., 149. See also Georg Kunz, *Verortete Geschichte: Regionales Geschichtsbewusstsein in den deutschen Historischen Vereinen des neunzehnten Jahrhunderts* (Göttingen, 2000); Rolf Petri, "Deutsche Heimat 1850-1950," *Comparativ* 11, no. 1 (2001): 77-127.

21. See Dieter Langewiesche, *Liberalismus und Demokratie in Württemberg zwischen Revolution und Reichsgründung* (Düsseldorf, 1974); David Blackbourn, *Class, Religion and Local Politics in Wilhelmine Germany: The Centre Party in Württemberg before 1914* (London and New Haven, 1980); Klaus Simon, *Die württembergischen Demokraten. Ihre Stellung und Arbeit im Pareteien- und Verfassungssystem in Württemberg und im Deutschen Reich 1890-1920* (Stuttgart, 1969); James C. Hunt, *The People's Party in Württemberg and Southern Germany 1890-1914* (Stuttgart, 1975).

22. Charlotte Tacke, *Denkmal im sozialen Raum. Eine vergleichende Regionalstudie nationaler Denkmalsbewegungen in Deutschland und Frankreich in 19. Jahrhundert* (Göttingen, 1995). See also Patricia Mazón, "Germania Triumphant: The Niederwald National Monument and the Liberal Moment in Imperial Germany," *German History* 18, no. 2 (2000): 162-92; Rudy Koshar, *From Monuments to Traces: Artifacts of German Memory, 1870-1990* (Berkeley, 2000).

23. For background to Tacke's argument, see Thomas Nipperdey, "Nationalidee und Nationaldenkmal in Deutschland im 19. Jahrhundert," *Historische Zeitschrift* 206 (1968): 529-85; and "Verein als soziale Struktur in Deutschland im späten 18. und frühen 19. Jahrhundert," in idem, *Gesellschaft, Kultur, Theorie. Gesammelte Aufsätze zur neueren Geschichte* (Göttingen, 1976), 174-205.

24. Helmut Walser Smith, *German Nationalism and Religious Conflict: Culture, Ideology, Politics, 1870-1914* (Princeton, 1995). See also David Blackbourn, *Marpingen: Apparitions of the Virgin Mary in Bismarckian Germany* (Oxford, 1993); and Edward Mathieu, "Protestant Home Towns: Religion and the Middle Class in Thuringia, 1871-1914" (Ph.D. diss., University of Michigan, 2002); also Margaret Lavinia Anderson, *Practicing Democracy: Elections and Political Culture in Imperial Germany* (Princeton, 2000).

25. Jennifer Jenkins, *Provincial Modernity: Local Culture and Liberal Politics in Fin-de-Siècle Hamburg* (Ithaca, 2002); and idem, "The Kitsch Collections and *The Spirit in the Furniture*: Cultural Reform and National Culture in Germany," *Social History* 21, no. 2 (May 1996): 123-41.

26. See Dennis Sweeney, "Work, Race, and the Transformation of Industrial Culture in Wilhelmine Germany," *Social History* 23, no. 1 (1998): 31-62; and idem, "Corporatist Discourse and Heavy Industry in Wilhelmine Germany: Factory Culture and Employer Politics in the Saar," *Comparative Studies in Society and History* 43, no. 4 (2001): 701-34.

27. See William H. Rollins, *A Greener Vision of Home: Cultural Politics and Environmental Reform in the German Heimatschutz Movement, 1904-1918* (Ann Arbor, 1997); Kevin Repp, *Reformers, Critics, and the Paths of German Modernity: Anti-Politics and the Search for Alternatives, 1890-*

1914 (Cambridge Mass., 2000); Matthew Jefferies, *Politics and Culture in Wilhelmine Germany: The Case of Industrial Architecture* (Oxford, 1995), 53-100; Rudy Koshar, *Germany's Transient Pasts: Preservation and National Memory in the Twentieth Century* (Chapel Hill, 1998), 17-73.

28. See Rudy Koshar, *German Travel Cultures* (Oxford, 2000).

29. Koshar, *Germany's Transient Pasts*, 23.

30. Eric Hobsbawm, "Inventing Traditions in Nineteenth-Century Europe," in *Invention of Tradition*, ed. Hobsbawm and Ranger, 5-6.

31. Ibid.

32. See especially Nipperdey, "Nationalidee und Nationaldenkmal," 529-85.

33. For a fuller statement of this argument, see Geoff Eley, *Reshaping the German Right: Radical Nationalism and Political Change after Bismarck* (London and New Haven, 1980), especially 19-40, 206-36; also David Blackbourn, "The Politics of Demagogy in Imperial Germany," *Past and Present* 113 (1986): 152-84.

34. See the manifesto published by sixty-four mainly Pan-German intellectuals in the *Kölnische Zeitung*, 1 June 1909.

35. Hermann Rassow to Alfred von Tirpitz, 12 April 1898, Bundesarchiv-Militärarchiv Freiburg i. Br., 2223, 93943.

36. Heinrich Oberwinder, *Nationale Politik und Parteipolitik. Ein Beitrag zur Geschichte des Deutschen Flottenverein* (Dresden, 1907), 17, 21.

37. "The Victory in Danzig", *Rheinisch-Westfälische Zeitung*, 16 June 1908.

38. See Heinz-Joachim Heydorn and Gernot Koneffke, *Studien zur Sozialgeschichte und Philosophie der Bildung*, vol. 2: *Aspekte des 19. Jahrhunderts in Deutschland* (Munich, 1973), 179-238.

39. This account of Rassow's activities is distilled from Eley, *Reshaping*, 172-74, 57-58, 94-95, 131-32, 225-26.

40. The Deutschbund was a small Pan-German-like sect combining *völkisch* philosophy with clear-headed anti-socialist coalition building for elections. The best source for Friedrich Lange is still *Reines Deutschtum. Grundzüge einer nationalen Weltanschauung*, 3rd ed. (Berlin, 1904). See also Eley, *Reshaping*, 68, 186-87, 228-30, 246-48, 282-83; Uwe Puschner, *Die völkische Bewegung im wilhelminischen Reich. Sprache—Rasse—Religion* (Darmstadt, 2001), 62-63, 68, 78, 120-1, 152, 174, 223, 266, 270-72.

41. Lange, *Reines Deutschtum*, 375.

42. Ibid., 147, 72, x, viii.

43. Kathleen Canning, "Of Gender Stories and Master Narratives in the History of the Weimar Republic," unpublished paper, 9, citing Bryan Turner, "Contemporary Problems in the Theory of Citizenship," in *Citizenship and Social Theory*, ed. Bryan Turner (London, 1993).

[handwritten annotation:] Very little new, is energetic but unclear prose — but does like the 'Heimat' work to other 'grass-roots' perspectives. Never gets beyond to 'point' + the formal aspect of citizenship completely ignored

– 2 –

Membership, Organization, and Wilhelmine Modernism

Constructing Economic Democracy through Cooperation

⟫⬦⟪

Brett Fairbairn

Introduction

W hen, in the 1890s, British colonial officials began to consider how best to promote economic and social development in India, it was not to the British homeland that they turned for inspiration. Rather, their model for rural economic and social progress was Germany. Sir Frederick Nicholson, sent from India to Europe to study ways of relieving the peasantry of debt, returned with the advice: "Find Raiffeisen." The rural cooperative system initiated by Friedrich Wilhelm Raiffeisen, which in the 1890s was spreading rapidly throughout Germany, became the initial model for British-Indian development.[1] It was therefore logical, more than a generation later, when the British-Indian cooperative movement was languishing under excessive administrative control and lack of peasant commitment, that another British colonial official traveled to Germany, perhaps in an attempt to find even more Raiffeisen. M. L. Darling published a book about his travels in Europe in 1920-21 and the lessons that Germany, especially, had to teach about development in the modern era.[2]

The world-leading cooperative system that Darling found in Germany had been built up throughout the Wilhelmine era and was in many ways at its peak. He encountered a country that had tens of thousands of cooperatives; where approximately 80 percent of peasant proprietors were members of agricultural co-ops; and where total household membership in cooperatives of all types, rural and urban, amounted by his estimation to "about half of the present population of Germany."[3] The Wilhelmine economy—modern, industrial, and capitalist—rested at its social roots significantly on cooperative economic activity, and so has almost every succeeding German economic régime. The cooperative system, as it spread and developed and became institutionalized before 1918, is part of Wilhelmine Germany's legacy to posterity.

These observations cannot help but raise a host of questions for historians. The historiography of twentieth-century Germany has stressed, in varying measures, its complicated relationship to modernity and democracy, its conflicts and violence, its tortuous road toward stability. How is such a history to be reconciled with the massive development of cooperatives, which are inherently democratic and mutualistic institutions?[4]

The first step toward untangling the issues is to historicize the concept of democracy. In recent decades historians have managed to historicize many concepts earlier taken for granted, including modernity, gender, morality, the nation, and much more. Generally speaking, however, the historiography of Germany illustrates a reluctance, until recently, to historicize democracy. This may be the result of an understandable hesitation to sully a concept that many educated intellectuals still consider to be an unqualified good, possibly the last such. This tendency is manifested in a preoccupation with specific democratic failures or anti-democratic machinations, as if there is a natural path toward pure democracy, or some mythical other country that is truly democratic, from which deviations have to be explained. To historicize democracy, however, means to see it as embedded in process, always imperfect, always partial, contingent, and contextual.[5] It is important to note, for example, that by today's standards *no* country was democratic a century ago.[6] It is more profitable to pursue grounded comparisons of actual practice within the same time period, and to stress democracy as a process rather than a final state—something that can be "practiced"—as Margaret Lavinia Anderson has recently done with great effectiveness for Imperial Germany.[7]

The second step is to unpack the historical processes of democracy. Contemporary political theory stresses that democracy is not a mere mechanism of voting, but rather an institution that must be embedded in widespread culture, values, and practice. Robert Dahl sees democracy proceeding from an underlying "logic of equality," through foundational ideas including local assemblies, the principle of the consent of the governed, the concept of representation, and the idea of election.[8] It is clear that these notions, upon which formal democratic governance structures are based, are fostered in society at large through a number of means, among which associational life is particularly important. Democratic organizations develop concepts such as meetings, consent, representation, and election, prior to the institutionalization of these ideas in constitutions and electoral laws. We can, therefore, examine the development of democracy in society, parallel or prior to democratic franchises and governments, by looking at associations.

Examinations of the role of associations in Wilhelmine Germany typically came at the subject, up to the 1970s, from assumptions of anti-modernity, that is, that the development of associations compromised or impeded normal democratic development. Thus, interest groups were seen as competitors with parties, "a secondary system of social powers" that led to "a new, semi-political organization of the people, which stood at cross-purposes to their division into parties."[9] Another writer referred to a "tendency toward extra- and antiparliamentary democratization" by social groups opposed to democracy.[10] Hartmut Pogge turned this explanation partially around in saying that it was not pressure groups that were responsible for the state of the political parties; rather, the nature of the parties was what gave rise to the *Ersatzfunktion* of the pressure groups.[11] Pogge elsewhere took this line of thinking a step further, proposing that perhaps the political institutions should not, in the first place, be the measures of political modernization, and that the economic and social institutions— which in Wilhelmine Germany were largely controlled by the bourgeoisie—should instead be where we look to study German modernity.[12] Later studies, for example, by Geoff Eley and James Retallack, discovered unsuspected reformist dynamism within nationalist and anti-Semitic pressure groups.[13] It was particularly in connection with the new studies of the German bourgeoisie that the important role of associations became evident, now as local institutions of middle-class hegemony and "bourgeois success."[14] This literature leaves open, however, questions about the roles of associations that were not necessarily "bourgeois" (or "liberal," "right-wing," or "Social Democratic") in character.

In political theory, the development of voluntary and participatory associations is increasingly understood as an aspect of building and maintaining democracy. Different authors have used terms such as "civil society," "the public sphere," "civic virtue," and "social capital" to describe potentially democratic products of associational activity. Few such theorists have explicitly considered cooperatives, but some who have done so see them as a type of organization that is particularly conducive to the democratization of society. Cooperatives are important because they attempt to link democratic control to economic ownership, so to speak anchoring a developing social-political system within an economic one whose dynamics might otherwise be inconsistent with democratization. Also, the fact that cooperatives are designed to pursue economic gain builds into them an incentive toward bridging differences and divisions within society.[15] Are such effects apparent in the history of Wilhelmine Germany? To pose such a question demands an interrogation of unconventional sources using the available techniques of both social history and postmodernism; and it demands that the questioner grapple with a vast scale and range of organizations and people.[16]

Association and Community

As people of a distant time and perspective, we are rather like M. L. Darling, traveling to a Germany that is foreign to us in an effort to understand, from the outside, the inner meaning of its institutions. Darling's study mission offers a convenient way into the world of German cooperatives. One of the lessons that Darling tried to impress on his readers had to do with the connection between German cooperatives and community, expressed in what he called their "moral influence" and developmental effects:

After 60 years [of] experience Germany believes as firmly as ever in the village bank, and still regards it as the foundation of her agricultural cooperative system. Morally and materially there could be no better foundation; materially, because credit is the basis of all business, and morally, because in the village bank credit is based as much upon character as upon property. Moreover, the village bank is a school of business where the humblest peasant may take his diploma.... [T]he village bank is becoming more and more the business centre of the village, and through its moral influence it continues to uphold the best village traditions.[17]

Darling's language makes clear that the purpose of the cooperatives in his mind was to teach the peasants modern business, and to shape their individuality and identity—their morality—into modern, autonomous personhood. Presumably, only a cooperative could do this, because it was at the same time consistent with "the best village traditions."

Darling described another cooperative in "Duisdorf" helping its members both with loans for agricultural improvements and with cooperatively owned machinery, such as mills and scales for their deliveries. [18] The co-op was helping its members improve their productivity and conduct transactions in markets that they found untrustworthy. But one thing that particularly impressed Darling was the co-op's president:

As is so often the case in India, the success of this society is largely due to the character of its president, who was perhaps the most striking of the many presidents I had the good fortune to meet in Germany. He recalled the best type of our peasant proprietors. Past his prime, he was still energetic, intelligent and capable, with a vein of humour, and, if his face was any guide, absolutely straight. He has been president for 24 years and has spent his whole life cultivating his 100 acres of land. Four out of his five sons, he said, have been brought up to do the same.

Like "the best type" of "our" peasants, this local patriarch was someone with whom an official could deal—a larger and likely more commercial farmer than his neighbors, a man accustomed to leading.

Another association was the village bank at "Buller": "In 51 years it has only had two presidents, father and son, and two Secretaries. The present Secretary, who has been so for 40 years, is a good type of peasant proprietor."[19] This "good type" informed Darling that "the society was started to counteract the influence of the Jews who used to sell cattle to the villagers at extortionate prices," and who trapped peasants in debt and dependency: "These methods were common enough in the old days, but Co-operation has killed them." Darling noted that the bank lent "at the moderate rate of 4.5 percent. ... a member of a village bank can easily borrow 1.5 to 2 per cent. cheaper than Government and nearly 3 per cent. cheaper than if he dealt with a commercial bank." As the bank paid 3.25 to 3.75 percent on deposits, this meant it was operating on a margin of only about 1 percent between deposits and loans. "In 40 years no one in Buller Society has been expelled, nor has any defaulter had to be sued.... In Germany default on a serious scale is rare.... This partly explains why German village banks can work upon so [narrow] a margin."

Concerning member involvement, Darling described how the general assembly of members at Buller met only once per year, and the supervisory council, twice— "below the average." Like many societies, this one had a policy that members absent from a meeting should pay a fine, but this was not enforced. Instead, the co-ops tried to entice members to their meetings:

> Some societies attract members to their general meetings by providing refreshment or holding lotteries in which the prizes are agricultural implements, a rake, a hoe, and the like. The latter were very popular in the Rhineland before the war....
>
> Women are now allowed to vote at general meetings but this is a comparatively recent innovation. The old German ideal which taught woman to care only for children, kitchen, church and Kaiser has had to be modified. During the war, when almost the whole manhood of the country was mobilized, many societies were only kept going by women, and the work was often so well done that many have been retained as secretaries. It is therefore impossible any longer to exclude them from general meetings.

Rural cooperatives were authentic village institutions, which is not to say that they were strictly egalitarian. They were dominated by local leaders from within the peasant community, and their members were predominantly peasants. Energetic member participation, tumultuous meetings, or high turnover among leaders was apparently rare. Cooperatives provided useful economic services—strikingly, they lent money at less than the government discount rate, less than any commercial bank. Few peasants would want to dispense with such a service. We can infer that the cooperatives were economically important to small farmers, highly efficient, and well accepted; as Darling noted, their shoestring margins would never have survived any significant member dissension or disloyalty. Finally, we can identify a number of interesting topics observed by Darling, that merit further discussion below: inequality among members, anti-Semitism, the role of the state, regional and national identifications, the roles of women.

Association and Equality

Raiffeisen's great accomplishments, according to one official who praised him in 1896, sprang from the simple facts that "he was a Christian and a true German man." [20] Within these limits, Raiffeisen issued a "wake-up call to the old collective mentality [*Gemeinsinn*] of our rural communities." As we have seen, the inclusiveness of German rural cooperatives was conceptualized in a way strongly conditioned by the social realities of the time: "man," "Christian," and "German"—we could add, "landowner"— are not unimportant terms. There were important exceptions, especially in certain kinds of cooperatives, but for the moment, let us work with this characterization. A key issue for cooperatives was that this definition of membership, however narrow it seems, was rather broad in some important respects: it required co-operation between people of unequal social status and rank, and sometimes of different confessions or political parties. This was no accident. From the time of Raiffeisen onward, it was intended that rural cooperatives serve as a framework within which small peasants and large landowners, and others, could share in an economic community.

Raiffeisen had conceptualized participation in cooperatives as an issue of Christian charity and neighborly love. The wealthy in the community, and priests and officials, should join cooperatives precisely because they did not need them; through participation, they would bring benefits to their neighbors and the whole community. In this connection, it is significant that Raiffeisen cooperatives held fast (in many cases into the mid twentieth century) to the principle of unlimited legal liability. Members risked everything they owned when they joined such a cooperative; this was what guaranteed the success of the cooperative, and enabled it to borrow the capital it needed to supplement member savings. The decision by a large landowner to join such a co-op might be the key to the co-op's viability. Similarly, the participation of priests and local officials—strongly encouraged by Raiffeisen and his successors— added credibility and solidity to the undertaking.

It is very difficult to know what occurred in the members' meetings or board meetings of individual cooperatives; but some tensions around the issue of unlimited liability hint at questions of inequality among members. The new Reich cooperative law of 1889, passed after the death of Raiffeisen, allowed for limited liability incorporation. The general understanding was that unlimited liability was best, especially for credit cooperatives, while other kinds of cooperatives might function better with limited liability. These generally included larger, more urban, and more specialized cooperatives, in which the risk and scale of business were greater, and the mutual relations among the members weaker. The assumption remained that the small rural credit cooperative was the ideal of solidarity: "One for all and all for one," according to the Raiffeisen slogan.

Yet in certain regions of Germany, notably Saxony and Pomerania, limited-liability credit cooperatives were established. In these areas, there were a great number of very large and very small landowners. As Darling observed: "On the one side the landlord is unwilling to pledge all his property because he has so much, and on the other the peasant proprietor is equally reluctant, fearing that the default of one or two landlords may involve him in the loss of everything. If both are to join together in one society, limited liability may be necessary."[21] Limited liability allowed for diversity among members, as Darling found when he visited some Saxon cooperatives. He noted that one of them had a membership of thirty-nine landowners "and in addition a pleasant medley of market-gardeners, priests, shopkeepers, butchers, blacksmiths, cartwrights, shoemakers, and barbers; also a doctor, teacher, factory owner, merchant, shop assistant, builder, railwayman, locksmith and policeman, in all 75 members. So great a variety is exceptional, but it is more likely to be found with limited than with unlimited liability." In this sense, we can see the experimentation with limited liability as a reflection of implicit negotiation among the interests of materially unequal members. We can imagine cagey peasant proprietors weighing the risks and benefits of forming a cooperative business alliance with large landlords, and those landlords themselves weighing their alliances with each other. This is by no means a straightforward case of patronage or clientelism.

Above all, such examples indicate the ambiguities of democratic participation. When the peasants and the large landowners sat in the same room, their common membership in the co-op did not make them social equals. But at the same time, they were meeting and deliberating, voting and electing, within a formal procedural structure of equal membership and voting. This was democratic practice, the gradual familiarization with the procedural basis of democracy, within an actual social context. The existence of cooperatives did not fundamentally change the societal structure, but it was a change nonetheless.

The sometimes fragile and formally egalitarian solidarity of the village cooperative was held together by a shared commitment to an idea of village life, but also sometimes by shared representations of the enemy: markets, business, traders—and occasionally people came out and added, as they did to Darling, the Jew. It is difficult to assess the degree of anti-Semitism in the Wilhelmine cooperative movement, but there is no doubt it was present. A small number of formally anti-Semitic cooperatives were formed by anti-Semitic organizers and political parties, especially in Hessen. David Peal has drawn attention to the fact that the political anti-Semitic movement in Hessen endorsed cooperatives beginning in 1887-88, as part of a campaign against allegedly Jewish usurers.[22] An inquiry by government officials in 1892 showed that in the rural area around Marburg (one of the strongest centers of political anti-Semitism), as many as eleven of the forty-one existing consumer and credit cooperatives could be connected in some way to anti-Semitic agitation.[23] But these were considered negligible precisely because they were few and easily identified; officials and respectable co-operators deemed them beyond the pale.

Much more important, and much harder to evaluate, was the presence of implicitly anti-Semitic rhetoric within the broader cooperative movement. Here we find the figure of the "usurer" (*Wucherer*) in cooperative propaganda. Many accounts of the origins of credit cooperatives, including Raiffeisen's, began with usury and usurers; such accounts differed mostly in tone and degree.[24] A clergyman named Wuttig, in explaining Raiffeisen banks and stressing their Christian character in an 1895 publication, referred to "usurious middlemen" who undermined the morals and religion of their victims, who "had to give the disgraceful bloodsucker [*dem schändlichen Blutsauger*] their arms to satisfy their unjust claims."[25] Where the villainous activities of "usurers" are denounced in lurid, detailed, and sensationalist terms, the language converges with the language of anti-Semitism, and we may assume that such accounts were often tapping the same springs of prejudice. It is an open question whether it was possible, at the turn of the century, emotively to denounce bloodsucking usurers without evoking anti-Semitic imagery.

But while some, primarily local and regional, activists within the cooperative movement resorted to anti-Semitic allusions, their official leaders and organizations discouraged and criticized such activity. Not only Raiffeisen, but also his colleagues, allies, and successors used their platforms in the organized cooperative movement to criticize anti-Semitic tendencies. Raiffeisen himself toned down his rhetoric after the earlier editions of his book, and preferred to emphasize positive Christian values of neighborly love rather than denunciations of usurers. Pastor Adam Meyenschein, a prominent Raiffeisen organizer in Hessen at the turn of the century, made a point of telling how he got a friendly ride from a Jewish trader to his first cooperative meeting in 1892; there was no tension in this, he recalled, "although some people then already believed Raiffeisen to be 'against the Jews.'"[26] Of course, the fact that Meyenschein felt it necessary to criticize views in this way indicates that such views were in fact present. Cooperatives were organizations of real communities, mirroring their hierarchies, suspicions, prejudices, and ambiguities.

Association, Region, and Nation

One of the ambiguities of cooperatives was that members were joining highly local, community-based organizations, which, however, were fundamentally tied into extralocal networks. None of the middle-class cooperative founders and leaders of the 1850s to 1880s envisaged regionalism as a factor in cooperatives. Both the left liberal Hermann Schulze-Delitzsch (1808-1883) and the social conservative Raiffeisen (1818-1888) had imagined self-governing, autonomous local associations, federated together into unitary national movements. Indeed, for years Schulze-Delitzsch did not even limit his scope to Germany, and continued to include Austrian cooperatives in his statistical summaries and reports. The two founding men became national figures; their respective co-ops were to be associated with the national figureheads directly, without mediating bodies or levels. But regionalism crept in, and in the 1890s became a reorganizing principle for the cooperative movement. At issue were both identities and power. It evidently seemed appropriate to many Germans that one was a member of a cooperative as a Hessian, a Westphalian, a Bavarian, or a Pomeranian, and not just as a German. Somehow, because cooperatives were accepted as authentic and community based, it was presumed that they should also be regional: popular authenticity and regionalism were connected in people's minds. Berlin (or, for Raiffeisen, Neuwied) was too distant and nebulous a connection. But at the same time, such mentalities were shaped by power. State governments and their representatives were instrumental in remaking the German cooperative movement in the 1890s so that it conformed to the federal political structure of the Empire. At the moment in history when cooperatives were growing rapidly in numbers, states discovered the importance of engaging territorially with them. Cooperatives adapted, and agricultural cooperatives, in particular, formed partnerships with state governments.

Regionalism and provincialism in German cooperatives began with the third great founder of German cooperatives, a man less well-known than Schulze-Delitzsch and Raiffeisen who went on to found what became, in the Wilhelmine era, the world's largest cooperative federation. Wilhelm Haas (1839-1913) was a politician and official in the Grand Duchy of Hessen, a National Liberal who built his career around the promotion of agriculture and cooperatives. Crowds of people assembled to celebrate Haas's seventieth birthday in 1909, hailing him as the "Vice-Grand

Duke of Hessen."[27] While always paying tribute to Raiffeisen, Haas began in the 1870s to construct a separate cooperative movement based on distinctly different principles. His co-ops were more specialized in functions and more businesslike and secular in style than the Raiffeisen originals, and he developed and organized them within Hessian state-level organizations. A handful of other states and provinces formed their own cooperative federations in the 1880s, partly inspired by Haas, but the true breakthrough came in 1890. In that year, Haas formally united all his Hessian federations of different kinds of cooperatives into a unified Hessian cooperative federation, and he launched a new national federation rivaling Raiffeisen's. This eventually became the Imperial Federation of agricultural cooperatives, based for many years in Darmstadt and Offenbach.

The issue of regional decentralization divided and weakened the Raiffeisen movement. One of Raiffeisen's closest colleagues, cooperative organizer and academic Martin Faßbender, broke with him in the 1880s to help organize an independent Westphalian federation. Looking back years later, Faßbender identified a variety of reasons why rural cooperatives exploded in numbers after Raiffeisen's death in 1888. These included the impact of the new agrarian movements and peasant leagues, the new cooperative law of 1889, and new religious impulses towards social reform. But, concluded Faßbender: "[T]he most significant influence on the spread of cooperatives among German peasants was undoubtedly the implementation of the principle of decentralization, and the founding of state federations independent from the Raiffeisen central organization."[28] Regional decentralization was a key organizational innovation that permitted cooperatives to catch the energies of the new agrarian and reform movements.

Bavaria provides a clear instance of these developments. We know, in Bavaria's case, that the idea of setting up a separate Bavarian federation of cooperatives originated with the semiofficial Upper Bavarian Agricultural Association (Landwirtschaftlicher Verein). The Agricultural Association took up the issue with the government, and the minister of the interior, Freiherr von Feilitzsch, issued a call for a Bavarian organization. In 1892, officials and priests took advantage of a Raiffeisen conference in Munich to lead a delegation of co-operators to see Prince-Regent Luitpold and Minister von Feilitzsch; they went on to organize the founding meeting of the new federation in 1893. Like other such federations, it received a generous annual grant from the state government to subsidize the mandatory accounting services it offered to member cooperatives. A few years later, the Bavarian federation joined Haas's Imperial federation.[29] However, it was not an all-encompassing organization: in addition to the state-initiated Bavarian federation, a Raiffeisen organization continued to exist with Bavarian members; separate federations formed for Franconian and Swabian farmers; and the Bavarian Peasant Association (Bauernverein) under Georg Heim formed its own cooperatives and central cooperative organizations around the turn of the century.

A study by the Ministry of the Interior in 1899 concluded with satisfaction that with 1,704 co-ops in the Landesverband, "the whole of agriculture is ruled by the cooperative idea." The state's intervention was justified retrospectively by the "fragmentation" of the cooperative sector, which had hindered the movement's development and "made it difficult for the government … [to carry out] a truly supportive, targeted intervention."[30] It was customary in Wilhelmine Germany for "fragmentation" to be invoked as a justification for some kind of intervention, but in this case the claim is unconvincing. Cooperatives had been "fragmented" between the Schulze-Delitzsch and Raiffeisen federations, with few agricultural cooperatives in the former; now agricultural cooperatives were split between the state-sponsored Landesverband and the others. The real issue was Bavarian regional identity, and the need for the state to have a partner organization congruent to its territory. Peasants and their representatives presumably did not object—except for those in Heim's federation and the others. The Bavarian Landesverband continued to grow, and by 1914 had 3,114 member cooperatives.[31]

Peasants participated in local associations, but through those associations, they also acquired and reinforced broader identities. In the Wilhelmine era, peasants, through massive new cooperative systems, became regional. At the same time, even as they organized sectionally and regionally with an implicit fragmentation of the movement, this fragmentation was simultaneously the basis for a logic of inclusion. Wilhelm Biernatzki, an agricultural journalist turned cooperative leader in Schleswig-Holstein, expressed the cooperative logic of inclusion: "We are strong enough to be a power with which other economic groups must reckon…. The more members join our … association, the more influential our position."[32] Economies of scale and considerations of market power gave cooperatives a material incentive to bridge divisions. By some accounts, they did:

> Everyone is happily accepted into the federation, and the leadership repeats daily that politics must not be brought in…. Perhaps in the beginning a clergyman or a conservative might have been a rare face in the associations, but today, in the cooperative conference, the conservative sits harmoniously beside the socialist, [the socialist] beside the liberal, even if the different party leaderships are not in agreement with [their doing so].[33]

This passage was written in 1895, but the Wilhelmine era was characterized by an increasing tension between co-operation and politics. One of the forces creating this tension was the growing involvement of the Prussian state with the cooperative movement: in 1892, instructing its officials to support the formation of cooperatives; and in 1895, creating the Prussian Central Cooperative Bank (Preußische Central-Genossenschafts-Kasse, PCGK). In both cases the effect was to force cooperatives to sort themselves out into those that were willing to work with the state in support of agriculture and the *Mittelstand*, and those that were not. Strikingly, the centralizing policies of the PCGK were resisted not only by the left-liberal Schulze-Delitzsch federation, which was ideologically opposed to state intervention, but also in the end by the Raiffeisen and Haas federations. Even though they did not in principle disapprove of state involvement, they felt compelled to defend and articulate cooperative autonomy in order to keep their federations strong, inclusive, and economically viable.[34]

The cooperative movement and the state bank came into conflict as well over a key area of government policy: the Prussian government's Germanization campaigns in the Polish provinces of the east. The Poles had begun using cooperatives as an economic tool for their population in the 1870s; as the government stepped up its Germanization campaigns in the 1880s and 1890s, it sought to marginalize the Polish cooperatives and to support German ones that would help settle and retain German peasants and artisans. The PCGK was critical of both the Raiffeisen and Schulze-Delitzsch movements for admitting too many Poles as members, and for refusing to form a nationalist cooperative front in the east.[35] Haas went further and entered into discussions with the Polish cooperative federation, which applied for membership in Haas's Imperial Federation in August 1907. Haas himself seems to have been supportive of this move, likely being driven by the economic and political logic of cooperation, which required the broadest possible base on which to build a strong movement. Haas's own board included cooperative leaders who wanted to emphasize exclusively the economic functions of the federation and remain aloof from all politics, which implied admitting the Polish cooperatives, while others agreed with and supported the government's nationalist crusade.[36] Regional leaders in the eastern cooperatives—the non-Polish ones, that is—were typically German nationalists. Alfred Hugenberg, for example, took over the management of the Posen cooperative bank, federation, and wholesale cooperative in 1900.[37] Prussian officials were likely involved in organizing nationalist voices within the Reichsverband, but in spite of the internal pressure on Haas, they were worried that he would go ahead and conclude a deal with the Poles. To cut off any such possibility, officials in the Reich chancellery wrote to the minister of agriculture to suggest Haas be informed "of the inevitable economic and political consequences that an acceptance of the Polish cooperatives into the Reichsverband would have"—namely, "that after the acceptance of the co-ops, any support or promotion of the Reichsverband by the Prussian government would of course be out of the question."[38] Haas's organization was not strong enough to ignore this direct threat, and he had to let the matter lie.

The logic of co-operation was strong, and it led all of the major cooperative systems to pursue integration across ethnic and regional divisions, backing down only from direct confrontations with the state. It is clear that the state's policies and pressures deformed and divided the cooperative movement, and also that the cooperative organizations resisted these pressures for their own reasons.

Association and the Person

The logic of cooperatives was in one respect to create modern individuals, rational and autonomous agents functioning within the fields of modern markets and the state. As the Brandenburg rural cooperatives put it, cooperatives had fundamental state-citizenship (*staatsbürgerliche*) qualities of "thrift, precision [*Akkuratesse*], and order."[39] But co-ops were also expected to cultivate such qualities in a different or more effective way than would occur without co-operation—a way that would be a hybrid between conventional modernity and popular values. As one Raiffeisen publicist put it: "We seek to increase, in the economic sphere, property ownership; in the intellectual, education [*Bildung*]; in the moral, love. But that is not our final goal. Beyond all this, we want to make our rural population [*Landvolk*] strong, and when it is strong, it shall be free. Freedom is our final goal"—freedom from usurers, superstition, and internal conflicts and divisions.[40] We should not be misled, however, by the notion of reawakening the communalism of German peasants. The past being harkened back to was a mythical one; the idea of the peasant community was a construction. The tremendous effort put into organizing the cooperative movement made this clear. As one leader remarked, "the basic mistake of the German peasant is his lack of a sense of solidarity. He is a born singleton [*Einspänner*].... When his neighbor is doing well, the peasant is annoyed; when [his neighbor] is doing badly, he's happy...."[41] In short, German peasants were not naturally cooperative; they had to make themselves that way.

The cooperative movement was not, or not only, the result of spontaneous peasant activity; it was more directly the product of a tremendous organizational and educational effort. Especially in the beginning, this effort occurred through existing networks such as those of the clergy, officialdom, agricultural associations (in rural areas), and workers' associations (in urban settings). As time went on, however, the movement created a developmental infrastructure. A key role was played by the field agent (*Wanderlehrer*) who traveled from place to place explaining the idea of cooperatives, helping people set up a society, ensuring that the proper regulations were followed, organizing elections of officers, and training the officers in tasks related to their duties. [42] Karl Sparr, a *Wanderlehrer* in Pomerania, was said to have handed out co-op savings books to everyone he met on his walks to and from villages. He returned from his walks through the countryside with pockets full of money that people had given him for deposits.[43] Proper bookkeeping was another major emphasis; after the passage of the 1889 cooperative law, it was mandatory for cooperatives to join auditing unions that would supervise and review their bookkeeping. The efforts of instructors, officials, and federations were backed by a rapidly expanding cooperative press, libraries, and educational events.[44]

A 1908 essay contest asked contributors to address the question of how agricultural supply co-operation could be increased. The five prize-winning entries by co-op functionaries proposed the slogans "Enlightenment and Success," "Only the Great Powers Make an Impact!" "Help Yourself, and God Will Help You," "He Who Understands the Signs of the Times Will Interpret Them Correctly," and "By One's Own Strength!"[45]

Middle-class sponsors, functionaries, and educators saw cooperatives as a means for peasants to improve themselves, to educate themselves, to learn business and citizenship skills necessary to function in the modern world. The speeches and writings of such leaders make their perspective clear. We cannot, however, know what the peasants thought. It seems at least conceivable that peasants saw cooperatives as a coping

mechanism, as a way to get by, to reproduce a household and its community connections with the minimum necessary adaptation to the new economy and the outside
world. Peasants may not have been seeking to transform themselves into modern
individuals, but rather, to preserve what they most cherished by accommodating the
modern as little as needed. At root, the attitude of German officials toward German
peasants was not much different from the attitude of British colonial leaders toward
Indian peasants. Just as Indian peasants responded with changing mixtures of adaptation, resistance, apparent pliability or passivity, and forms of "hybridization," we
might expect German peasants—colonized, so to speak, by their own state—to have
been similar. Cooperatives were one forum in which the degree of adaptation to the
modern could be negotiated.

One of the most challenging aspects of the development of modern personhood
within cooperatives was in relation to gender. We have seen that, in general terms,
cooperatives were constructed as vehicles to develop men as economic and political
actors. And yet co-ops both explicitly involved women in a variety of ways—as members, customers, employees, or supporters and facilitators of men's involvement—and,
because they opened up egalitarian economic categories, implicitly allowed for female
economic and political agency. It seems as if some cooperatives went out of their way
to contain such possibilities.

It was difficult for women to participate in cooperative governance. The more
conservative Raiffeisen cooperatives discouraged or forbade female membership; the
liberal Schulze-Delitzsch ones permitted it, but often did not allow mixed-gender
meetings—women members had to be represented by proxy. Only the urban consumer cooperatives, on the English model, promoted active female membership.
Even within these restrictive terms, women were present, though one often has to dig
into local records to find traces of them. For instance, the solid, successful Speyer
Volksbank had 393 women members out of 1,790 total in 1899. These included
252 "without occupation"—many of these likely widows—but also 141 employed in
a wide range of livelihoods including independent artisans, retailers, and agriculturalists, as well as professionals, teachers, artists, and servants.[46] Some women could
rise to prominent positions within the movement, could achieve a status that likely
could not have obtained in any other economic institution. Emmeline Stegmann of
Pomerania is reported to have become the first female bank manager in Germany in
1907 when she was elected to the management committee of the co-op bank in
Schönlanke, where her father had been manager before her; she went on to be a
prominent figure at the national level for decades.[47] The logic of co-operation
inclined itself toward full involvement of all economic agents, but this logic was also
hindered by tremendous constraints.

Karl Korthaus, an important national organizer and leader of *Mittelstand* cooperatives, wrote and published in the 1920s a series of short stories in which he tried
to combine literature with contemporary social themes. The first of these is a story
about a widow, Johanna Westerhold, who discovers on the death of her businessman
husband that he was heavily indebted to numerous creditors. The widow bravely car-

ries on with the business, working her way out of debt while supporting her five-year-old son. Korthaus portrays her as an excellent business manager and successful entrepreneur; the manager of the Gewerbebank to which she is indebted, Direktor Beck, admires and supports her. However, her brother-in-law, who has mismanaged his own business, begins to pressure her, wanting to marry her and sell her business. Full of courage, business sense, and tact, she resists him as long as she can; but his machinations lead the board of the Gewerbebank to call in Johanna's loans, which would ruin her. At the end of Korthaus's story, she is saved when Direktor Beck realizes he is in love with her, uses his savings to pay her debts, and marries her. Much of Korthaus's story is written like a novel of manners, though with no great art: carefully chosen words, deliberate ambiguities, and broken-off conversations hint at the realities beneath a surface of urbane and polite behavior.[48]

Apart from the novelties of a romantic banker and love and intrigue in a co-op, Korthaus's story makes an interesting statement about the cooperative movement's acceptance of women. Korthaus challenged his readers with an image of a single-parent female entrepreneur, inviting their sympathy for her, and clearly indicating how dependence on men made her life impossible. There was implied social criticism in this. Korthaus aimed to inspire his readers with Johanna's plight, but at the same time he cast doubt on whether a woman really could make her own way. His story was only in a limited way an affirmation of female strength and independence. Korthaus reassured his readers by having her end up married again and not needing to support herself. One could take this to mean that cooperatives could help as many women as their bank managers could marry, but this would be unfair to Korthaus. He clearly felt a need to present the idea that women were, or could be, members, entrepreneurs, economic *persons*, and that the job of the cooperative was to respond to their needs in this role. His partial, tentative, and ambiguous authorial treatment says a great deal about the unfulfilled potential of the new structures of society.

Conclusion

German cooperative organizations provided an emergent democratic framework within which millions of Germans grappled with compelling issues: class divisions, regional and national identities, integration of minorities, anti-Semitism, acceptable forms of partnership with the state, market economics and its meaning for communities, gender. All of these issues were part of a larger complex, namely, modernity and its manifestations. The fact that we can see these constitutive issues being addressed within cooperative systems, and that we can see differences of opinion about them, is an indication that cooperatives were performing the role assigned to them by democratic theory. The presence of anti-Semites, Pan-German nationalists, anti-democrats, and sexists among the cooperative membership shows that the cooperatives were indeed broad and representative. Importantly, the cooperatives were also inculcating modern and democratic concepts and procedures. Through their educational structures, their leadership, and their interregional infrastructure of federations, they were making attempts to resist influences that lessened their autonomy and compromised their movement's inherent interests and values.

Cooperatives could not remain unaltered by the direct application of state power, however, and in the Wilhelmine era this shaped them in two important respects. First, the movement's division between rural and urban, between co-ops considered by the state to be patriotic and those of the working classes, was not entirely a natural development, and was pushed by the interventions of Prussia and other states, especially as these intensified in the 1890s. Second, this state intervention, combined with the thinking and ideas of Schulze-Delitzsch, Raiffeisen, and Haas, produced a distinctive constellation of ideas in which cooperatives were seen as being first and foremost vehicles for agriculture and the *Mittelstand*. Despite the contrary example of urban working-class cooperatives, and despite many contrary examples from other countries, this association of the cooperative movement with the interests of the *Mittelstand* became deeply entrenched in German cooperative thought. However we assess these factors, it seems clear that Wilhelmine Germany's cooperative movement was not considered backward, but rather struck contemporaries as innovative, progressive, and modern. In these respects, its complexities mirrored those of the society in which it was based.

Notes

1   Johnston Birchall, *The International Cooperative Movement* (Manchester, 1997), 166.
2   M. L. Darling, *Some Aspects of Co-operation in Germany, Italy and Ireland (A Report)* (Lahore, 1922).
3   Darling, Aspects, 5.
4   The most concise, official statement of cooperative values and principles is Ian MacPherson, *Cooperative Principles for the 21st Century* (Geneva, 1996).
5   Hence the important argument, developed by David Blackbourn and Geoff Eley in *The Peculiarities of German History: Bourgeois Society and Politics in Nineteenth-Century Germany* (Oxford, 1984), that explanations of German history have to proceed from a consideration of how developments were rooted in modern and democratic processes and institutions, and their instabilities, not in anti-modern or anti-democratic deviations.
6   Women's equal suffrage is now accepted as essential to democracy. Even if we reduce our standard to universal male suffrage, by one count only four countries were democratic in 1890—Robert A. Dahl, *On Democracy* (New Haven, 1998), 8. See also the introduction to Brett Fairbairn, *Democracy in the Undemocratic State: The German Reichstag Elections of 1898 and 1903* (Toronto, 1997).
7   Margaret Lavinia Anderson, *Practicing Democracy: Elections and Political Culture in Imperial Germany* (Princeton, 2000).
8   Dahl, *On Democracy*, 10 and 22.

9   Thomas Nipperdey, *Gesellschaft, Kultur, Theorie. Gesammelte Aufsätze zur neueren Geschichte* (Göttingen, 1976), 324.

10   Hans-Jürgen Puhle, "Parlament, Parteien und Interessenverbände 1890-1914," in *Das kaiserliche Deutschland. Politik und Gesellschaft, 1870-1918*, ed. Michael Stürmer (Düsseldorf, 1970), 340-77; here, 342-43.

11   Hartmut Pogge von Strandmann, "Nationale Verbände zwischen Weltpolitik und Kontinentalpolitik," in *Marine und Marinepolitik im kaiserlichen Deutschland*, ed. Herbert Schottelius and Wilhelm Deist (Düsseldorf, 1972), 296-317; here, 299.

12   Hartmut Pogge von Strandmann, "Widersprüche im Modernisierungsprozeß Deutschlands. Der Kampf der verarbeitenden Industrie gegen die Schwerindustrie," in *Industrielle Gesellschaft und politisches System: Beiträge zur politischen Sozialgeschichte*, ed. Dirk Stegmann, Bernd-Jürgen Wendt, and Peter-Christian Witt (Bonn, 1978), 225-40; here, 225-26.

13   Geoff Eley, *Reshaping the German Right: Radical Nationalism and Political Change after Bismarck* (New Haven, 1980); James Retallack, *Notables of the Right: The Conservative Party and Political Mobilization in Germany, 1876-1918* (Boston, 1988).

14   Many of the leading researchers are collected in *In Search of a Liberal Germany: Studies in the History of German Liberalism from 1789 to the Present*, ed. Konrad H. Jarausch and Larry Eugene Jones (New York, 1990).

15   Mark E. Warren, *Democracy and Association* (Princeton, 2001), 199.

16   This chapter will concentrate on the Raiffeisen-inspired rural credit cooperatives. Germany also had a large and, in the Wilhelmine era, rapidly expanding urban, working-class consumer cooperative movement. For an overview, especially on relations between the consumer co-ops and social democracy, see Brett Fairbairn, "The Rise and Fall of Consumer Cooperation in Germany," in *Consumers Against Capitalism? Consumer Cooperation in Europe, North America, and Japan, 1840-1990*, ed. Ellen Furlough and Carl Strikwerda (Lanham, 1999), 267-302.

17   Darling, *Aspects*, 5.

18   Ibid., 22 (and ff for the following).

19   Ibid., 26 (and ff for the following).

20   Landgerichtsrath Dr Brandt, *Raiffeisen als Wiedererwecker deutschen Gemeinsinnes: Vortrag gehalten auf dem VIII. Verbandstag der Thüringer ländlichen Genossenschaften (Raiffeisenscher Organisation) zu Coburg am 15. Mai 1895* (Neuwied, 1896), 3, and 15 for the following quotation.

21   Darling, *Aspects*, 29; and 31 for the following.

22   David Peal, "Antisemitism by Other Means? The Rural Cooperative Movement in Late Nineteenth-Century Germany," in *Leo Baeck Institute Yearbook XXXII* (1987), 135-153; here, 142.

23   Landrat Marburg to Regierungspräsident Kassel, 12 November 1892, in Staatsarchiv Marburg, Bestand 165 (Königliche Regierung zu Cassel, Präsidial-Abtheilung), Nr. 765.

24   F. W. Raiffeisen, *Die Darlehnskassen-Vereine als Mittel zur Abhilfe der Noth der ländlichen Befvölkerung, sowie auch der städtischen Handwerker und Arbeite* (Neuwied, 1866), 2. Raiffeisen probably did not intend to be anti-Semitic with such comments; they were less prominent in later editions of his book.

25   Adolf Wuttig, *Friedrich Wilhelm Raiffeisen und die nach ihm genannten ländlichen Darlehnskassen-Vereine. Ein Weck- und Mahnruf an alle, die unser Volk lieb haben*, 3rd ed. (Neuwied am Rhein, 1895), 13.

26   [Adam Meyenschein, ed.,] *Den Alten zur Her, Den Jungen zur Lehr, Dem Lande zur Wehr: Selbstbildnisse kurhessischer Raiffeisen-Männer* [2nd ed.] (Cassel, 1922), 55-56.

27   Adalbert Feineisen, *Wilhelm Haas: Gestalter einer großen Idee* (Neuwied, n.d. [c.1956]), 13. See also Rudolf Maxeiner, *Vertrauen in die Eigene Kraft: Wilhelm Haas. Sein Leben und Wirken* (Wiesbaden, 1976).

28   Martin Faßbender, *F.W. Raiffeisen in seinem Leben, Denken und Wirken im Zusammenhange mit der Gesamtentwicklung des neuzeitlichen Genossenschaftswesens in Deutschland* (Berlin, 1902), 227.

29   *Raiffeisen in Bayern, 1893-1968* (Munich, 1968), 23-29.

30   *Der Stand des landwirthschaftlichen Genossenschaftswesens in Bayern 1899* (Munich, 1900), 1, 3.

31   Ernst Hohenegg, *Die Landesorganisation des landwirtschaftlichen Genossenschaftswesens in Bay-
      ern* (Munich, 1927), 22.

32   From an annual report in the 1890s, quoted by Albert Lüthje, *Raiffeisen seit mehr als 100 Jahren
      in Bordesholm und Flintbek* (Bordesholm, 1984), 31.

33   Albert Knittel, *Beiträge zur Geschichte des deutschen Genossenschaftswesens* (Freiburg, 1895),
      119.

34   On the origins of the bank, see Arnd Holger Kluge, *Geschichte der deutschen Bankgenossen-
      schaften. Zur Entwicklung mitgliederorientierter Unternehmen* (Frankfurt a.M, 1991), 278ff. A dif-
      fering view can be found in David Peal, "Self-Help and the State: Rural Cooperatives in Imperial
      Germany," *Central European History* 21, no. 3 (1988), 244-66.

35   See the documents in Geheimes Staatsarchiv Preußischer Kulturbesitz (hereafter, GStAPK),
      Rep 151 I C, Nr. 10284, on criticisms of the Schulze-Delitzsch federation; and no. 10356 on how
      the Raiffeisen organization in the east was raided in 1911 and its cooperatives reorganized into the
      nationalist camp.

36   Oberpräsident Westfalen to Chancellor (Bülow), 15 August 1907, and (on the threat to withdraw)
      Abschrift, Präsident der Preußischen Zentral-Genossenschaftskasse, report on admission of Polish
      cooperative federations to the Reichsverband, dated 11 August 1907, both in Bundesarchiv Berlin
      [hereafter: BAB], Reichskanzlei Nr. 1125 (Film 12349/12350).

37   Friedrich Swart, *Diesseits und jenseits der Grenze. Das deutsche Genossenschaftswesen im Posener
      Land und das deutsch-polnische Verhältnis bis zum Ende des zweiten Weltkrieges* (Leer (Ostfriesl.),
      1954), 35.

38   Reichskanzlei, Diktat des K. Geh. Reg. Rat Wahnstorff [name not fully legible] an den Herrn
      Minister für Landwirtschaft, Domänen und Forsten, 17 August 1907, in BAB op cit.

39   *Genossenschaftliche Erfahrungen: Zugleich Geschäftsbericht der landwirtschaftlichen Provinzial-
      Genossenschaftskasse für die Mark Brandenburg und die Niederlausitz für das Jahr 1902* (Berlin,
      1903), 11.

40   Adam Meyenschein, "Die Bedeutung der Persönlichkeit für das Genossenschaftswesen," speech
      in Kassel, 14.7.1904, in Meyenschein, *Raiffeisen und das deutsche Dorf. Gesammelte Aufsätze und
      Vorträge fon Adam Meyenschein* (Berlin, 1917), 139.

41   W. Bode, *Die ländlichen Spar- und Darlehnskassen in gemeinschaftlicher Darstellung* (Offenbach,
      1897), 3.

42   See Konrad Mose, *100 Jahre genossenschaftliche Prüfung in Kurhessen. Eine Chronik des Prü-
      fungsdienstes des Raiffeisenverbandes Kurhessen e.V.* (Kassel, n.d. [c. 1982]), esp. 16.

43   Ernst Seer, *Karl Sparr und der Grundgedanke seiner genossenschaftliche Arbeit. Ein Lebensbild aus
      den Jugendjahren des pommerschen Genossenschaftswesens* (Stettin, 1930), 19.

44   Günter Link, *Das Bildungswesen des ländlichen Genossenschaftssektors in Deutschland. Funktio-
      nen, Formen und Probleme in historischer und aktueller Sicht* (Ph.D. Diss., Erlangen, 1969).

45   *Preisarbeiten über die Frage: "Durch welche Mittel läßt sich der genossenschaftliche Bezug von land-
      wirthschaftlichen Bedarfsartikeln seitens der Einzelgenossenschaften, insbesondere durch Vermittelung
      der Zentral- Ein- und Verkaufsgenossenschaften steigern?"* (Darmstadt, 1908).

46   "Mitglieder-Verzeichniß der Speyerer Volksbank e.G.m.b.H. in Speyer 1. Januar 1899"; found in
      Bayerisches Hauptstaatsarchiv ML Nr. 203.

47   Otto Ibscher, *Im Deutschen Genossenschaftsverband von 1893 bis 1938. Persönliche Erinnerungen
      und Erlebnisse aus 45jährige Tätigkeit* (Berlin, 1938), 119.

48   Karl Korthaus, "Gewertet und Gefunden," in Korthaus, *Den Weg entlang. Erzählungen aus dem
      Wirkungskreis der Deutschen Genossenschaftskasse* (Berlin, n.d. [1928]), 5-27.

"Few better farmers in Europe"?

Productivity, Change, and Modernization in East-Elbian Agriculture 1870-1913

OLIVER GRANT

Modernity and Economic Rationality

The test of economic rationality, the test of whether a system of production maximizes output or minimizes costs for a given set of input prices and a particular set of technological possibilities, is not the only test by which to assess the modernity of a system of economic and social relationships, but it is one that can help to elucidate certain aspects of these relationships. Economic rationality is generally included in lists of the characteristics of modernization. Its absence, particularly in the context of a society that rejects other aspects of the modernization agenda, provides prima facie evidence that this is a society prepared to pay a cost to maintain certain traditional values or institutions. There is, to use an economist's term, a revealed preference.

Where economic rationality *is* achieved but some other features of modernity are nevertheless rejected, then the situation is a rather different one. Such a society does not pay an economic price for these choices. For this reason, change will be harder to achieve. There will not be the opportunity to compensate the losers from modernization out of the economic gains from a more productive system. A society which is set on a path which combines economic rationality with the maintenance of certain traditional attitudes, forms of authority, and social and cultural relationships, will not be easily pushed from this path. Indeed, economic success, by apparently legitimizing this particular combination of the old and the new, may tend to entrench surviving traditions and institutions.

The *Kaiserreich* has long been considered an example of a society that combined undoubted economic success with other "un-modernized" features. East-Elbian rural society has often been given prominence in analyses of traditional or preindustrial characteristics which survived despite the industrial progress of Germany as a whole.[1] This chapter considers whether this view is justified. The main focus is on the economic performance of the rural sector east of the Elbe. Did incomplete modernization hold back the economic transformation of East-Elbian agriculture? How well did the sector perform in comparison with other parts of Germany, and with other European countries?

The chapter goes on to consider other aspects of East-Elbian agrarian society, in particular the system of labor relations. This included many features which have been described as patriarchal or precapitalist: payments in kind, harvest shares, labor service obligations, and so on. But, if these did not hold back economic progress, then other criteria must be used to assess their "modernity."

A Comparison with Other European Countries

Considered over the nineteenth century, the performance of German agriculture compares well with that of other European countries. There are different ways of measuring relative performance: figure 1 uses statistics provided by Bairoch for calories produced per male worker. This is an imperfect measure, but it has the advantage that estimates can be produced as early as 1800.[2]

Figure 1. Bairoch's estimates of agricultural productivity 1800-1910 (calories produced per male occupied in agriculture).

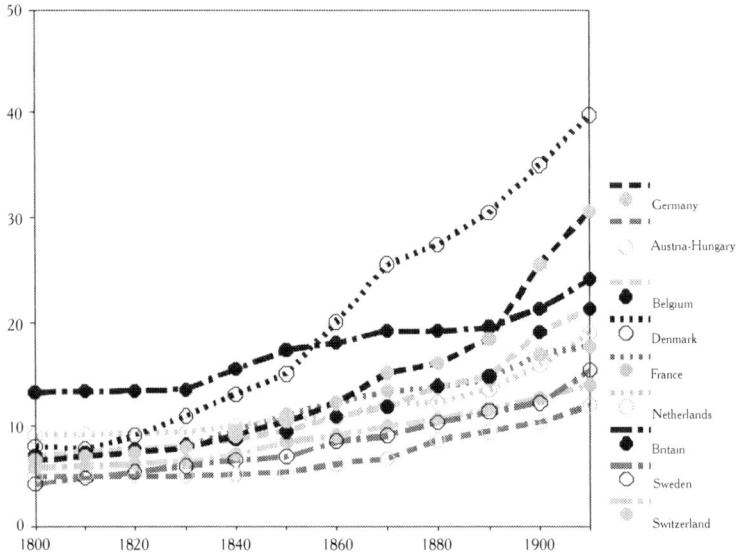

Source: Data from Paul Bairoch, "Les trois révolutions agricoles," *Annales*, 44, no. 2 (1989): 317-354.

The figure shows that Germany was placed in the middle of a group of lagging countries in 1800, some way behind Britain. However, by 1910 Germany was second only to Denmark. The imperfections of the measure mean that the relative strength of German agriculture in 1910 is almost certainly exaggerated, but the dynamism of the agricultural sector over the whole period is better founded. Germany was definitely moving up in the European rankings.

Looking at some indicators of agricultural progress, figure 2 shows wheat yields for a selected group of countries. In the mid century German wheat yields were on a par with France, little more than half the British level. By 1910, Germany had caught up with Britain and was closing the gap with Denmark (the European leader). France had been left some way behind.

Figure 2. Wheat yields, 1848-1913 (1,000kg per hectare, rolling five-year averages, log scale)

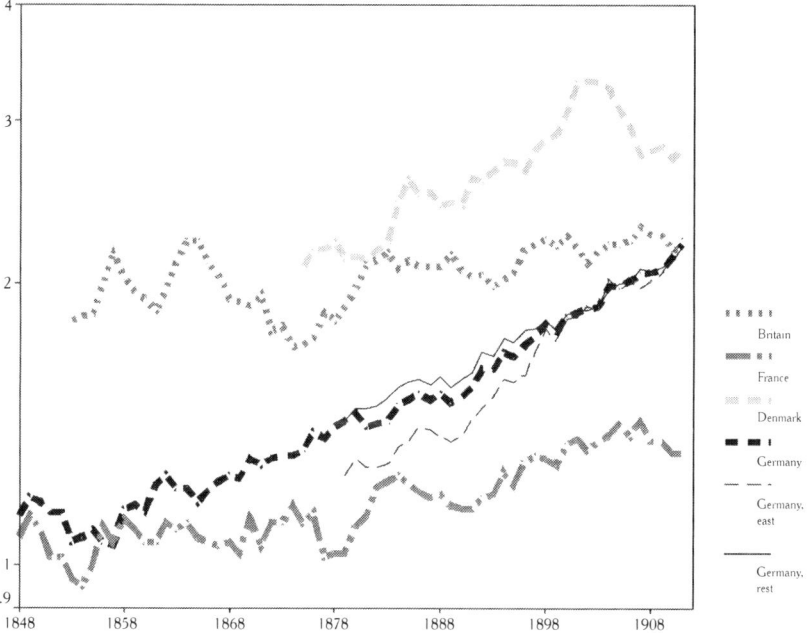

Sources: Calculated from data in Brian R. Mitchell, *European Historical Statistics 1750-1975* (1981), from national sources, but then adjusted using the 1905-9 Institut International d'Agricole comparison of cereal yields; Institut International d'Agricole, *Annuaire International de Statistique Agricole 1913/14* (1915), 28. The British figures were converted to metric tons using estimates of bushel weights from the 1879 *Encyclopaedia Britannica.*

The figure also shows average yields for Germany east of the Elbe and the rest of Germany. This shows that eastern yields were tending to converge with the rest of Germany, and that this was a factor in the rise in the average for the country as a whole.

Wheat was a less important crop for German agriculture than rye, and figure 3 repeats the analysis for rye (Britain is not included as rye production was insignificant). Here the German performance is even more impressive: Denmark was overtaken after 1900. The convergence of eastern yields is also very striking, and was a major contribution to the success of German agriculture in this sector.

Figure 3. Rye yields, 1848-1913 (1,000kg per hectare, rolling five-year averages, log scale).

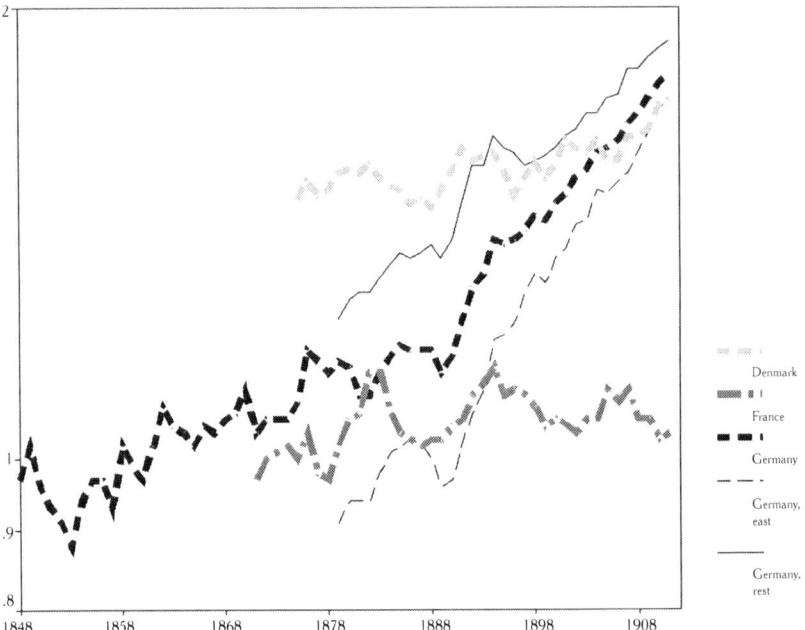

Sources: as for figure 2.

Finally, table 1 gives livestock intensity, a measure that is significant both for livestock production and arable production, as animal manure was the most important source of nutrients for crop production. Livestock intensity was calculated by weighting the different livestock categories and dividing the total by the agricultural area. The table shows that livestock intensity in German agriculture rose by more than the increase in France and Britain, but by less than the Danish increase (Denmark was shifting from cereal production to concentrate on the export of livestock produce). By 1912-13, German livestock intensity was around the same level as Britain, having been well below in the 1870s.

The composition of the livestock sector shows some significant differences. Sheep numbers remained high in Britain, reflecting the continuation of a relatively extensive sheep plus corn system. Arable areas were falling—the cereal acreage fell by 26 percent between 1871 and 1913—so that the available supply of nutrients could be concentrated on a smaller area. By contrast, in Germany, cereal areas were still rising, and the increases in yields shown in figures 2 and 3 were partly due to the increase in nutrient supply made possible by an intensification of the livestock sector, that is, the replacement of sheep by cattle and pigs. As the table shows, there was a sharp fall in the numbers of sheep, and a roughly equivalent rise in pig numbers.

Table 1. Livestock numbers (in thousands) and livestock intensity.

Germany	Horses	Cattle	Pigs	Sheep	LU/100ha
1873	3,352	15,777	7,124	24,999	45.0
1913	4,558	20,994	25,659	5,521	62.5
% change	+36.0	+33.1	+260.2	-77.9	+38.9
France					
1882	2,838	12,997	7,147	23,809	37.3
1913	3,222	14,788	7,036	16,131	39.9
% change	+13.5	+13.8	-1.6	-32.2	+6.9
Denmark					
1871	325	1,239	442	1,842	54.6
1914	487	2,463	2,467	515	105.1
% change	+49.8	+98.8	+458.1	-72.0	+92.4
Britain					
1872	1,258	5,625	2,772	27,922	57.8
1912	1,441	7,026	2,656	25,058	64.9
% change	+14.5	+24.9	-4.2	-10.3	+12.3

Sources: Data from Mitchell, conversion to Livestock Units (LU) uses weights from Peter Wagner, "Die Steigerung der Roherträge der Landwirtschaft im Laufe des 19. Jahrhunderts" (Ph.D. diss., University of Jena, 1896).

In comparison with Britain, the table shows that German agriculture responded well to the increased demand for livestock produce that was one of the main consequences of industrialization. The intensive livestock sectors, such as dairying and pig meat production, also benefited from the arrival of cheap grain imports from the United States. The poor performance of British agriculture in these areas is much less easy to explain than the problems of the cereal sector. By contrast, German agriculture took full advantage of these opportunities.

Regional productivity performance

Figures on the performance of German agriculture as a whole do not distinguish between the different regions. To do this, it is necessary to prepare estimates of regional productivity. This in turn requires the construction of regional agricultural accounts, giving production of the different crops and livestock output, deducting

Oliver Grant

from these allowances for the use of items of intermediate consumption (fertilizers, livestock fodder, etc.), and dividing the resulting figures for value added by an esti-mate of the labor input (adjusted to allow for differences in the extent of part-time farming). Estimates of this type are given in table 2.

The basic materials were taken from the various German agricultural censuses and from the annual production figures (where available). Estimates were prepared for three five-year periods, 1880-84, 1893-97 and 1905-9, and for twenty-one regions or regional units (amalgamating the smaller states). Given the uncertainties involved in the process, a range of estimates were prepared, which (on the basis of variance calculations) were considered to represent a 95 percent confidence range (the range over which the true figure is thought to lie with 95 percent confidence). The figures are given in constant 1913 prices, and thus represent estimates of real dif-ferences in productivity between the various regions and the different years.

Table 2. Productivity in German Agriculture.

| | Net Value Added per FLU (Full-time Labor Unit) | | | Annual % Rates of |
| | 1880-84 | 1893-97 | 1905-09 | Growth |
	Marks	Marks	Marks	1880/84-1905/09
East Prussia	480 (454-506)	745 (703-786)	934 (877-992)	2.71 (2.87-2.54)
West Prussia	648 (615-680)	923 (879-967)	1,078 (1022-1134)	2.07 (2.18-1.95)
Berlin/Brandenburg	731 (697-764)	1,001 (957-1045)	1,222 (1,163-1,280)	2.08 (2.19-1.97)
Pomerania	852 (811-893)	1,175 (1,121-1,229)	1,433 (1,363-1,503)	2.11 (2.22-1.99)
Posen	636 (607-664)	891 (850-932)	1,179 (1,124-1,234)	2.51 (2.63-2.38)
Silesia	550 (521-579)	765 (728-802)	960 (911-1,009)	2.26 (2.38-2.13)
Pr. Saxony/Anhalt	1089 (1,046-1,131)	1,356 (1,304-1,407)	1,388 (1,330-1,445)	0.98 (1.03-0.93)
Schleswig-Hol.	1,145 (1,072-1,218)	1,323 (1,243-1,403)	1,709 (1,600-1,819)	1.62 (1.74-1.50)
Hannover/Old/Brun.	779 (737-821)	1,075 (1,023-1,126)	1,136 (1,075-1,197)	1.53 (1.62-1.43)
Westfalia	579 (544-614)	865 (822-908)	834 (787-881)	1.48 (1.58-1.37)
Hesse-Nassau	524 (497-552)	798 (760-837)	769 (727-811)	1.55 (1.65-1.45)
Rhineland	535 (504-565)	761 (723-799)	757 (713-800)	1.41 (1.50-1.31)
Bavaria, excl. Pfalz	510 (484-536)	691 (654-729)	667 (623-712)	1.08 (1.16-1.00)
Pfalz	480 (458-501)	791 (756-826)	699 (664-735)	1.53 (1.61-1.44)
Saxony	789 (744-834)	1,052 (999-1,105)	1,395 (1,316-1,474)	2.32 (2.46-2.17)
Württemberg/Hoh.	594 (565-622)	641 (608-674)	661 (619-704)	0.44 (0.47-0.41)
Baden	517 (492-543)	631 (601-661)	635 (599-671)	0.83 (0.88-0.77)
Hesse	685 (654-716)	949 (908-990)	1,016 (965-1,067)	1.60 (1.68-1.5)
Mecklenburg	1,267 (1,211-1,323)	1,442 (1,380-1,505)	1,716 (1,632-1,801)	1.23 (1.3-1.16)
Thuringia	750 (717-783)	1,029 (984-1075)	1,088 (1,034-1,142)	1.50 (1.59-1.42)
Alsace-Lorraine	596 (571-622)	609 (580-638)	676 (639-713)	0.51 (0.54-0.47)
Germany	672	855	982	1.53

Estimates from regional agricultural accounts in 1913 prices, 95 percent confidence intervals in brackets (for definitions of regional units see Appendix A).

Sources: Figures from chapter 5 of Oliver W. Grant, "Internal Migration in Germany, 1870-1913" (Ph.D. diss., University of Oxford, 2000); there is a fuller discussion of the methods used in Oliver W. Grant, "Productivity in German Agriculture: Estimates of Agricultural Productivity from Regional Accounts for 21 German Regions: 1880/4, 1893/7 and 1905/9," Oxford University Discussion Paper in Economic and Social History (2002), available at http://www.nuff.ox.ac.uk/Economics/History/.

The regional pattern changed over the whole period largely as a result of the improvements east of the Elbe. Of the seven East-Elbian regions, four had productivity levels below the national average in 1880-84. Two (Pomerania and Brandenburg) were somewhat above, and one, Mecklenburg, had the highest level of all the German regions. Productivity growth in all of the eastern regions, except Mecklenburg (which nevertheless retained its leading position), was above average for the 1880-84 to 1905-9 period. The result was that all of the eastern regions had above-average productivity in 1905-9, with the exception of East Prussia. A map of the increase in productivity by region shows the extent to which productivity growth was fastest in the east (figure 4). There was a process of "catch-up" or convergence as advanced agricultural techniques spread out from central Germany, which explains why some central regions, which had already adopted these techniques, had relatively slow productivity growth. But convergence was not automatic. Some lagging regions, notably those in the south and southwest, did not converge; indeed, they fell further behind. "Catch-up" was much stronger in the east.

Figure 4. Percentage increase in agricultural productivity for the period 1880-84 to 1905-9.

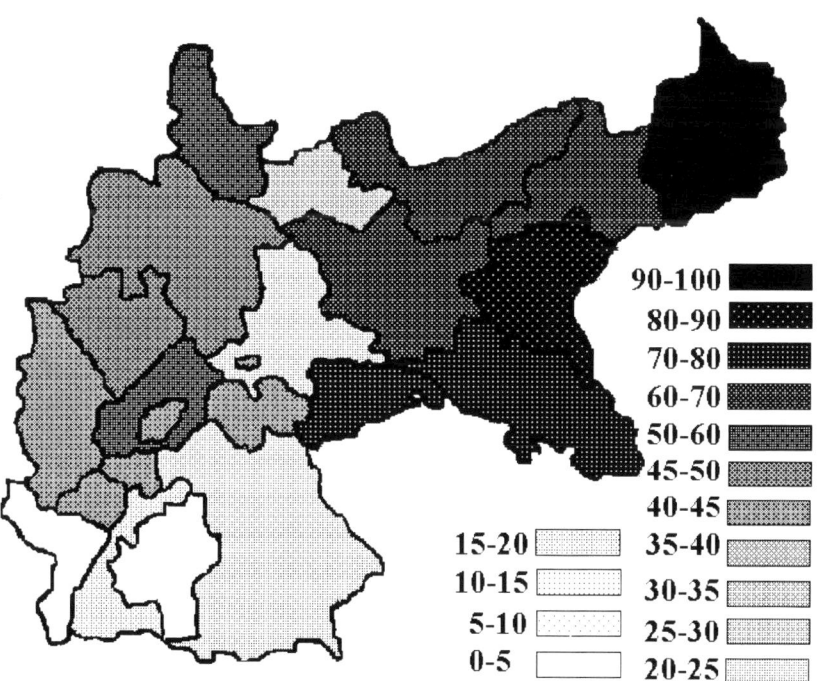

Increase in productivity 1880-4 to 1905-7 in %.

What drove this process of convergence? Analysis of the results shows that the main factor for the east was a rise in the yields of arable crops to somewhere near the national average from a point well below. In 1880-84, the East-Elbian regions (excluding Mecklenburg) had an average level of arable production per hectare that was 75 percent of the national average (crops valued at 1913 prices); by 1905-7 this had risen to 96 percent. As a result, whereas these regions had accounted for 31 percent of German arable production in 1880-84, this had risen to 41 percent in 1905-9. There is an important negative point here: productivity convergence was not driven by labor shedding as a result of mechanization on larger farms (the east's share of the total agricultural labor force remained roughly constant) yield convergence was a far more important factor.

An explanation of the rise in yields can be provided by making use of contemporary evidence, and combining this with statistical analysis (using yield figures for the Prussian *Kreise*). There were three main reasons for the increase in yields in the remoter areas of the east: improvements in communications, improvements in technology, and the diffusion of more intensive methods, which was partly, although not exclusively, connected with the spread of sugar beet cultivation.[3]

Statistical analysis shows that remoteness (as measured by the distance from major towns and cities) was an important factor in explaining low yields.[4] The costs of getting produce to market were high, reducing the incentive to invest in more intensive methods, and it was also expensive to bring in bulky inputs such as fertilizer or animal feed. But, as railways were constructed, and roads and waterways were improved, these problems were ameliorated. The construction of a fertilizer factory or a sugar beet refinery was made possible by these improvements.

The new agricultural technology of the second half of the nineteenth century was particularly valuable for the "hungry" sandy soils of eastern and northern Germany. The technology produced improved crops, as a result of scientific breeding, and mineral fertilisers, mainly potash and phosphate. Combined with a system of "green manuring" (plowing in nitrogenous crops to provide nitrogen) and the application of lime to reduce soil acidity, these new techniques could achieve dramatic increases in yields: average rye yields in *Kreis* Uelzen in the Lüneburg Heath rose 205 percent between 1882-84 and 1910-14, from a position 29 percent below the national average to one of 15 percent above.[5]

The diffusion of improved techniques was accelerated by the spread of sugar beet cultivation. Both estate records and the statistical analysis of yields in different *Kreise* suggest that there was a strong effect on the yield of other crops from the introduction of sugar beet cultivation. The reasons for this were, first, that sugar beet was a demanding crop both in terms of nutrient requirements and cultivation techniques; the improved husbandry could then be applied to other crops. Second, sugar beet needed good roads to move the beet to the refineries (both on and off the estate), and this made it possible to bring in fertilizers for other crops. Third, refining the beet produced a byproduct, sugar beet pulp, which could be fed to livestock, thus intensifying livestock production and raising the availability of nutrients from this source.[6]

However, the analysis shows that productivity also rose in areas where there was little sugar beet cultivation. East Prussia is one example: a region that was not suited to sugar beet but which had the largest productivity increase. There was a more widespread diffusion of improved agricultural knowledge. British observers were impressed by German agricultural education, and by the system of research institutes and experimental farms which demonstrated the new techniques to local farmers. This was also a factor in the improved performance of the east.[7] Moreover, the east managed to maintain its share in total livestock production while simultaneously devoting a larger area to cereal production. The east accounted for 33 to 34 percent of total livestock production, and fully shared in the general increase in livestock intensity previously shown in table 1.

Missing from this list is one characteristic of eastern agriculture that might be thought to have favored the use of new technology: the relatively high number of large farms and estates. In the documentary accounts, the leadership role of certain own-ers of larger estates is often stressed, and, in some sources, peasant farmers were crit-icized on the grounds that they were slow to use artificial fertilizers.[8] If this had been a general problem, it would be expected that *Kreise* in which larger estates predomi-nated would either show above-average yields or produce higher increases in yield as the new technologies were applied.

However, the statistical analysis provides a more nuanced view. There is, in gen-eral, no clear connection between the presence of large estates and the intensification of arable production between 1880-84 and 1905-7. Analysis of rye yields at the *Kreise* level shows that larger farms and estates did have an advantage in the early 1880s, but this had been substantially eroded by the 1890s, as the smaller holdings caught up. The larger holdings had a continuing advantage in wheat production, but this was a less important crop, and one that was not much grown on smaller farms.[9]

The pattern shown by figure 4 confirms this point. On the one hand, the south and southwest were the lagging regions, and these were areas where smaller holdings predominated. But although a cursory glance might suggest that the largest produc-tivity gains were in the eastern areas dominated by larger estates, the position was more mixed. The largest gains were in four regions: East Prussia, Silesia, Posen and the Kingdom of Saxony. Of these, larger estates were dominant only in Posen (52 percent of agricultural area was in holdings of over 100 hectares in 1895). East Prus-sia had 61 percent of the agricultural area in holdings of less than 100 hectares, and was a region where the typical farm was in the "larger peasant" (20-100 hectare) cat-egory. Silesia and the Kingdom of Saxony had even less land in the over-100 hectares category (34 percent and 16 percent respectively) and were areas with large small-holding sectors: 45 percent of the Silesian agricultural area and 55 percent of the Saxon area was in holdings of less than 20 hectares.

In short, while, initially, the economic "modernisation" of eastern agriculture may have been put in motion by the larger farms and estates, whose owners probably led the way in the introduction of sugar beet, for example, the smaller and medium-sized farms kept pace, and their contribution was an important factor in the extremely impressive overall gains made by East-Elbian agriculture in the period before 1914. Given the paucity of the documentary evidence on the performance of the small and medium-sized farm sector, the value of the statistical analysis presented in Appendix B is that it is able to rescue this aspect of the eastern performance from undeserved oblivion. The small and medium-sized farms were the unsung heroes of the modernization of East-Elbian agriculture.[10]

Social Relations and Modernization

Even if East-Elbian agriculture was modern in its use of advanced technology, there are other aspects that present a less progressive picture. The continued domination of local administration by the aristocracy, despite the *Kreisordnung* of 1872, is one example. Another is the distinctive system of labor contracts and tenurial relations, which was the subject of Max Weber's 1893 contribution to the survey of agricultural labor conditions organized by the Verein für Sozialpolitik.[11] This section will consider this aspect of conditions east of the Elbe.

It is useful to take a rather wider view of this issue. There has been a more general debate over the relationship between tenure systems and agrarian progress, conducted mainly by agricultural economists and rural sociologists working in the field of development studies. In the 1950s and 1960s, a simple formula held sway: cash payments were "modern." This meant, in particular, monetary rents—fixed in advance by formal agreements and not related to output—as the predominant form of landlord-tenant relationship, and wages paid in cash, on an hourly basis, as the normal way of rewarding agricultural laborers. These were the characteristics of a modern, "capitalist" agriculture—a view, incidentally, that was shared by Weber in 1893.

But this simple view has been replaced by one that exhibits more understanding of the role of different systems of tenure and labor contracts in conditions where credit is not easily available, where insurance can hard to obtain, where yields and prices are variable, and where the cost of getting produce to market can be prohibitively high. Systems such as share-farming and other forms of payment in kind can economize on monitoring costs and provide an element of risk-sharing. The cost of cash transactions can be high in regions where banking facilities are not widely available.[12]

These considerations provide the basis for a reassessment of the "modernity" of the system of contractual relations east of the Elbe. The first question to ask is *Cui bono?* Who benefited from the system? Table 3 provides some evidence on this point, derived from a survey conducted in the early 1870s. This survey compared the total income of agricultural laborers and their families from all sources: money wages, payments in kind, harvest shares as well as produce from their own small-holdings, and other activities within the household. It showed that the incomes of *Inste* and *Deputanten* households were, on average, rather greater than those of "free" day laborers. The difference was larger for the comparison with free day laborers who had no property of their own. In the regions west of the Elbe, there was little difference between the incomes of the contractually employed workers and those free laborers who had some property. East of the Elbe, there was a 13 percent advantage to those who were bound by the contractual systems of eastern agriculture.

Table 3. Annual incomes (in Marks) of farm households, 1872-73.

	No. of Replies	Incomes of Free Day Laborers with Property	without Property	Incomes of *Deputanten, Instleute,* etc.	% Difference Compared to Free Day Laborers with Property	without Property
East of the Elbe	221	191.6	179.6	216.8	+13.1	+20.7
Other Prussian Regions	216	232.5	199.3	234.3	+0.7	+17.6
All replies	437	211.9	189.3	225.4	+6.4	+19.1

Source: Calculated from figures given in Ernst Engel, "Die Ergebnisse der Classensteuer und der classificierten Einkommensteuer im preußischen Staate," *Zeitschrift des Königlich Preußischen Statistischen Bureaus* (1875).

For the *Inste* and *Deputanten* households east of the Elbe, the advantage of the contractual system was fairly clear: it produced more income. It also offered greater security, given that the amount of paid labor was fixed by contract and not subject to fluctuations.

What then were the advantages to the landowners? On the face of it, the contractual arrangements of eastern agriculture involved costs that were 20 percent higher than the wages paid to free day laborers (since landlords would not include the value of the laborers' own small-holding as a cost). But the system had important benefits for the landowners as well, and it may be surmised that these outweighed the drawbacks.

In the first place, it was flexible. Under the *Scharwerker* system, the eastern laborer was obliged to provide additional workers during the harvest and other periods of peak demand. These could be other family members or young, single workers (*Knechte* or *Mägde*), who lodged in the laborer's house. During slower periods, the landowner did not have to pay wages to underemployed workers, and the laborer and his family would occupy themselves on their small-holding or find some other form of household production.

Secondly, it economized on monitoring costs. As Weber noted, the *Deputanten* (who were predominantly occupied in the livestock sector) were, in effect, small contractors, who organized the tasks associated with livestock husbandry themselves. The landlords saved the cost of employing foremen and other supervisors to monitor the performance of their workers. The payment system ensured that the laborers had an incentive to perform their tasks diligently without direct supervision. Similar considerations apply to the payment of harvest shares to workers instead of fixed money wages.

Thirdly, it reduced cash outflow. This could be an important consideration for an estate in remote areas, or one exposed to large fluctuations in yields or prices. In years when prices were low, the costs of getting produce to market could be prohibitive. In these circumstances the normal response was to feed the surplus grain to live-stock, but this would not produce any cash until the livestock were sold. If the estate was unwilling or unable to borrow to cover this deficit, then a system of payment in kind would be one way to mitigate the problem. Effectively, some of the risk associated with producing for the market would be transferred from the landlord to the worker, since the monetary value of payments in kind would fall when prices were low (which might not have mattered much to the laborers, who probably consumed most of the produce received as payments in kind themselves).

Why, then, did the system erode as it did? Weber's survey revealed that in many areas cash payments were being substituted for the traditional system. By 1914, monetary payments were the norm in most eastern regions. Weber's argument was that this came about as a result of a change in landlord attitudes: traditional, patriarchal values were replaced by capitalist, entrepreneurial ones. Landowners changed to cash payments as they moved to profit-maximizing methods of intensive arable farming. This implies that in the earlier period landowners were foregoing some potential income in order to maintain traditional social relationships.

There are two main points to be made in answer to this. The first is that, as noted above, the contractual system offered landowners considerable benefits. The second is that there is documentary evidence that, as day laborer rates rose from the 1860s onwards, agricultural workers voluntarily gave up their contractual status and took employment as day laborers.[13] With rising industrial demand for labor, workers faced a widening range of employment opportunities. Moreover, with falling agricultural prices in the 1870s, the value of payments in kind was falling. To have matched rising day laborer rates, landlords would have had to offer increased harvest shares or give more land to their laborers for household production. There was an understandable reluctance to do this.

Moreover, conditions that had previously favored the contractual system of eastern agriculture were changing. Improved communications cut marketing costs. Access to finance was made easier by the spread of a modern banking system and the introduction of credit cooperatives, agricultural mortgage banks, and other institutions. Yield variability fell with improved husbandry and better crop varieties. Price variability was also reduced. Under these circumstances, the switch to cash payments favored the interests of both landowners and laborers.

What then remains of the concepts of "modern" and "traditional" as applied to the tenurial and labor systems of eastern agriculture? Once it is recognised that a variety of tenure systems can be efficient and appropriate in different circumstances, then simple distinctions between "modern" and "traditional" become much harder to apply. The "share-milking" system currently practiced in New Zealand dairying, widely recognized as the most modern and cost-effective dairy industry in the world today, is not dissimilar to the arrangements under which the *Deputanten* of East-Elbian agriculture looked after the landowners' cows in the nineteenth century.[14] If the dichotomy between traditional and modern is to have meaning and content, it is necessary to show that the maintenance of traditional systems involved giving up a potential benefit. There were, almost certainly, individual farms and estates for which this was indeed the case. But when we consider East-Elbian agriculture as a whole, the argument can be made that this was a system that was well adapted to the circumstances of the rural east in the mid nineteenth century. Subsequently, as circumstances changed, so did the system.

Challenge, Crisis, and Response in Wilhelmine Agriculture

The argument put forward so far—that East-Elbian agriculture was modern and responsive in its use of technology, in its institutions, and in its ability to evolve with changing circumstances—might meet with an obvious retort: If so, why were they making such a fuss? Why was membership rising in the agrarian pressure groups? Why was there such a heated debate over tariff treaties and other agrarian issues? Why was there a shift to agrarian radicalism, which became an important influence on German conservatism as a whole?

There are social, political, and cultural answers to these questions that cannot be treated here; instead, this section will consider the economic background to these issues. On the economic side, there were two main components to the agrarian crisis of the late nineteenth century: imports and debt.

The story of the "European grain invasions"—the effect on European markets of falling transatlantic transport costs and rising production in the U.S. and other exporting countries—is sufficiently well known.[15] What is perhaps less well understood is the extent of the impact on counties such as Germany that engaged in some degree of protectionism. The net import position for Germany with respect to trade in cereals is given in figure 5.

The broad picture is that between the mid 1860s and the late 1890s, Germany moved from a position in which net exports amounted to 2 to 5 percent of cereal production to one in which 12 to 15 percent of total domestic consumption was supplied by net imports. This position was maintained up to the outbreak of World War I.

Two points emerge from this analysis. First, the impact of tariff protection was, at best, to slow down the rise in imports. Second, this was a rapid swing from a net export position to one of net importation, with inevitable consequences for the cereal sector in particular. Tariffs may have prevented an absolute decline in the arable sector, as happened in Britain, but they did not avoid the loss of a substantial part of the domestic market.

Some more indicators of market conditions are given in figure 6. This figure shows the course of German arable producer prices, together with the price of imported cereals. The two series move together, with a "U" shape, indicating the extent to which German prices were influenced by foreign market conditions. Comparing five-year averages, imported prices fell by 34 percent between 1872-76 and 1893-97, while German producer prices fell by 23 percent, so that German farmers experienced about two-thirds of the fall on world markets. Between 1893-97 and

Figure 5. Net imports of cereals as a percentage of total domestic consumption (including use as animal feed), Germany (post-1871 boundaries), 1850 -1913.

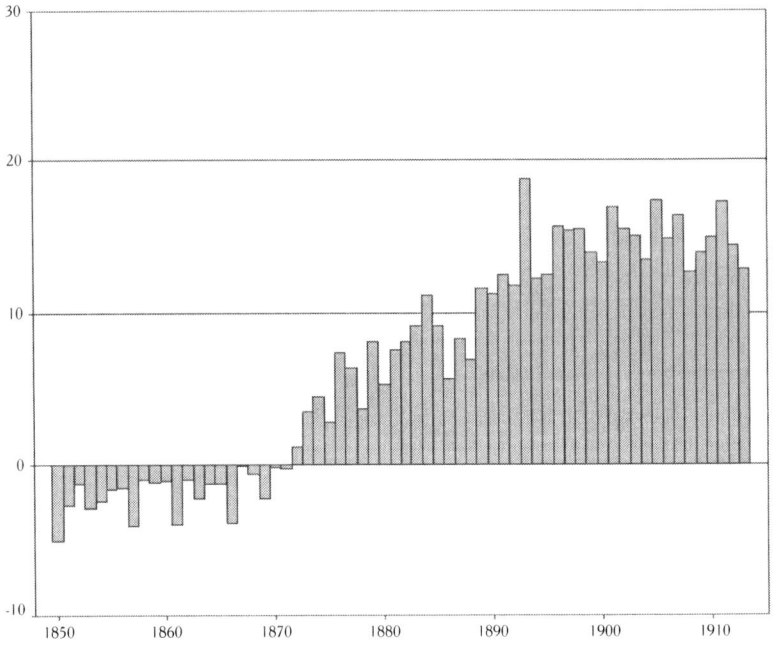

Source: Calculated from Walter G. Hoffmann, *Das Wachstum der Deutschen Wirtschaft seit der Mittel des 19. Jahrhunderts* (Berlin, 1966), 292-93, 530-35, and 537-43.

1909-13, imported prices rose by 40 percent and German prices rose by 30 percent, so rises on world markets were responsible for about three-quarters of the improvement after the mid 1890s.

The consequences can be seen from two other series included in the figure. Land prices fell by about 10 percent between the mid 1870s and the 1890s and then rose by 89 percent between 1895 and 1913. The numbers of forced sales recorded by the Prussian Statistical Office also fell sharply, although these had been falling before the low point in producer prices in the 1890s, indicating that Prussian agriculture was already adjusting to adverse market conditions.

Even in the 1890s, surveys found that the larger farms were still making profits. A survey of twenty estates in the early 1890s found an average return on all capital of 3.4 percent and a return on land and fixed assets of 2.6 percent, after deducting 7 percent interest on working capital (livestock, machinery, etc.). The problem was that such returns were not high enough to meet interest charges on the heavily indebted estates. Two out of the twenty estates made no return on land and fixed assets. These farms faced the need for a painful adjustment.[16]

There were regular surveys of farm debt whose results were published by the Prussian Statistical Office. These showed high debt-to-capital ratios, particularly in

Figure 6. Market conditions in German agriculture 1870-1913.

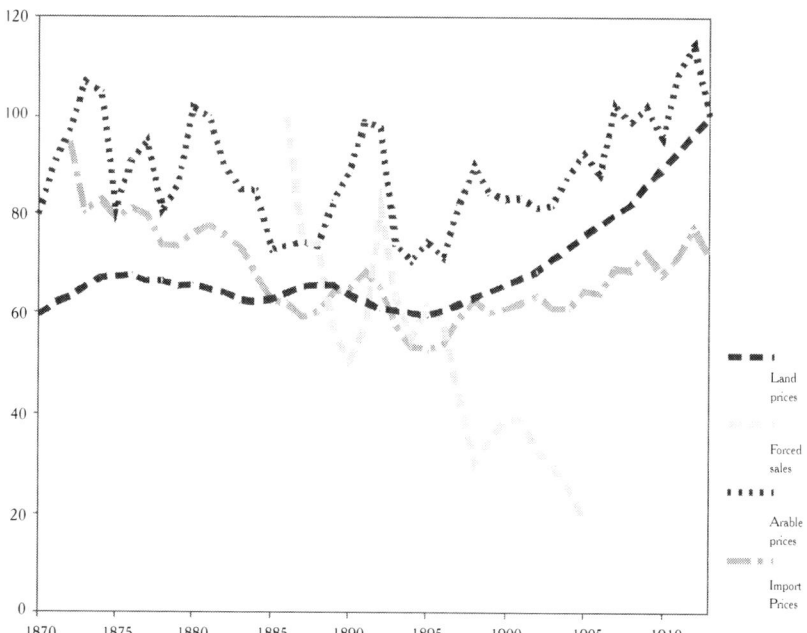

Note: Price indices for arable producer prices and imported cereal prices (100 = German prices for 1913); land prices (1913 = 100); forced sales (*Zwangsversteigerungen*) in Prussia, in hectares (1886 = 100)

Sources: Price data from Hoffmann; imported food prices were converted using price comparisons for 1905 from Board of Trade "Report of an Enquiry by the Board of Trade into Working Class Rents, Housing and Retail Prices Together with Rates of Wages in Certain Occupations in the Principal Industrial Towns of the German Empire," *Parliamentary Papers, Accounts and Papers (47),* cd 4032 (1908); *Zwangsversteigerungen* taken from various issues of the *Zeitschrift des Königlich Preußischen Statistischen Bureaus,* 1888-1907.

the larger East-Elbian estates. The surveys may well have omitted informal debts owed by smaller farmers, since they tended to concentrate on mortgages and other debts (*Grundbuchschulden*) that were recorded by the land registers. But the transition to a more intensive agriculture—in particular, the introduction of sugar beet—was a capital-intensive process, and it is not surprising that the rise in productivity in eastern agriculture had a cost in the form of rising debt: estate roads had to be improved, new buildings were required, and more expensive equipment was needed.[17]

The problem for East-Elbian farmers, large and small, was that the appearance of these new capital requirements coincided with the period of falling prices in the 1880s and 1890s, which meant that the process of transition was a painful one. The better managed farms and estates, or the less indebted ones, managed to survive; others went under. But, in contrast to Britain, land did not go out of production. Even in the worst period for forced sales—the late 1880s and early 1890s—the arable area continued to rise: the area under arable crops rose 4.3 percent east of the Elbe in 1884-94, compared to a rise of 2.6 percent for the rest of Germany. Bankrupt estates were taken over by new owners, who were better equipped financially or possessed more modern management skills, and the land remained in cultivation. This was a crisis of transition, not a structural crisis for the sector as a whole.

A "Preindustrial" Elite? Modernization and Junker Agriculture

The title of this chapter is taken from a remark by the British economic historian J. H. Clapham, which expresses opinions widely held by British observers of pre-1914 German agriculture:

> [T]here were few better farmers in Europe than the best of the Junkers in the later nineteenth century …; after the decade 1840-50 Germany had little to learn from any country in agriculture and forestry. In agricultural chemistry she was undoubtedly the leader.[18]

Some qualifications need to be made here. Clapham was, by implication, undervaluing the contribution made by smaller and medium-sized farmers east of the Elbe. Although the better managed aristocratic estates survived the transition to a modern and more intensive agriculture, others did not, and these were the main victims of the agricultural depression of the 1880s and 1890s. If the best were as good as any other farmers, there was still a less successful "tail" to the distribution. Nevertheless, in general, Clapham's judgment was a sound one, and the analysis presented in this chapter supports it.

In what sense, then, can East-Elbian agriculture be regarded as an example of incomplete modernization? Do the Junkers deserve the appellation, still frequently encountered, of being a "preindustrial" elite?

The term "preindustrial" is one that carries unspoken implications. As a simple statement that the Junkers were engaged in the production of nonindustrial goods it is factually correct. But this implies that modern agricultural technology—such as genetically modified crops, pesticide applications controlled by GPS satellite systems, and so on—are also "preindustrial," which is obviously absurd. It is also true that the ownership of many aristocratic estates was in the hands of families whose roots lay in the period before the onset of German industrialization. But by this token, the Rothschilds, whose banking activities in Continental Europe (if not in Britain) began in the period before industrialization, would also deserve the term. In any case, modern research has revealed a high turnover of estate ownership, so the number of landowners who could trace family ownership back to preindustrial times was falling.

The use of the term implies a resistance to industrialization or its consequences. This resistance is not limited to a dislike of democracy, for which the terms "antidemocratic" or "illiberal" are appropriate (though needful of more precise definition). The resistance is broader, including a reluctance to face the economic, social, and cultural consequences of the creation of a modern, industrialized society: urbanization, mass literacy, the popularization of art and entertainment, the erosion of traditional systems of rank and deference. This chapter does not attempt to deal with these broader issues; rather, it attempts to answer a quite simple question: If there was a sense in which East-Elbian society was "preindustrial," was there an economic price to this? The answer is that there was not. In the economic sphere, East-Elbian agriculture was "modern": flexible, technologically advanced, capable of responding to the demands and opportunities of industrialization.

Incomplete modernization, then, is a concept that needs to express more than just a taste for the ways of the past. In the political sphere, the Bismarckian legacy was a state that had undeniable difficulty in resolving issues that involved confrontation with well-entrenched interest groups. But it does not necessarily follow that this "political backwardness" was a consequence of broader deficiencies rather than a result of decision-making procedures that had their origins within the political system itself.

When Wilhelmine society is investigated with care, particularly when realistic comparisons are made with other European societies, the salience of its many modern and progressive features is revealed, as the example of East-Elbian agriculture has demonstrated.

Appendix A

Amalgamations to Produce Regional Units used in the Agricultural Accounts (all other regions correspond to the normal regional boundaries)

Regional unit used in table 2	Includes the following regional units used in German statistical publications
Pr. Saxony/Anhalt	Provinz Saxony and Anhalt
Schleswig-Hol.	Schleswig-Holstein, Hamburg, and Lübeck
Hannover/Old./Brun.	Hannover, Oldenburg, and Brunswick
Westfalia	Westfalia, Waldeck, and both Lippes
Württemberg/Hoh.	Württemberg and Hohenzollern
Mecklenburg	Mecklenburg-Schwerin and – Strelitz
Thuringia	Saxony-Weimar, -Altenburg, -Meiningen, and – Coburg-Gotha; both Reuß; and both Schwarzburgs

Appendix B

Statistical Analysis of Cereal Yields

The question whether large farms or small benefit most from new agricultural technology is one that cannot easily be answered using estate records and other documentary evidence. There are too few records of yields on smaller holdings to produce a reliable sample. But there are testable implications. If yields rise 50 percent on large holdings (with over 100 hectares) but are static on smaller ones, then it is a fairly simple calculation that average yields will rise by 15 percent in a *Kreis* with 30 percent of the land in holdings of under 100 hectares, and 35 percent in one with 70 percent.

To test the hypothesis that farm size has an effect on yield using this approach requires three elements: a sufficiently large sample, in this case data for yields in the Prussian *Kreise*; information for more than one year, so that the results are not unduly affected by weather conditions and other exceptional factors; and information on other factors that might affect yields, such as soil type.

The data set that was prepared included yields for 325 *Kreise* in the post-1815 Prussian provinces, together with information on soil type (the percentage classified as "sandy" and "sandy loam") and the average level of *Grundsteuerreinertrag* (the assessment of land value for taxation purposes). These were taken from August Meitzen's 1868 survey of Prussian agriculture.[19] The remoteness of the different *Kreise* was found to have an effect on yields, so variables for the distance to major towns and cities were included, as well as the percentage of nonagricultural employment within the *Kreis* (as an indicator of the strength of the market within the *Kreis*).

Yields for four years were analyzed, and the resulting estimates are given in table B1. The effect of three classes of holdings was examined. Of these, yields on holdings of between 20 and 100 hectares were not found to differ significantly from the *Kreis* average, and the results were erratic. In the larger holdings, however, yields were apparently rather higher, particularly in the earlier years. Yields on holdings of less than 20 hectares were rather lower than the *Kreis* average.

In the case of rye, the difference in 1878 and 1883 was a considerable one: yields on holdings of over 100 hectares were nearly 50 percent above those of holdings of less than 20 hectares in 1883, and 30 percent greater in 1878. But the gap had narrowed to 17 percent by 1897, and was down to 9 percent in 1900 (when the results are no longer statistically significant). These figures indicate that the smaller and medium-sized farms were catching up with the larger holdings, and would support the view that they, too, had access to improved technology by this later date.

Table B1. Results of statistical analysis of yields in 325 Prussian *Kreise*.

Estimated yields of farms of different sizes relative to the average for the *Kreis* (allowing for the effect of soil type and the location of the *Kreis*).

	1878	1883	1897	1900
a. Analysis of rye yields	(% difference from the average)			
Holdings of 100 hectares and over	+18.6**	+23.4**	+9.7**	+5.2
Holdings of between 20 and 100 hectares	-6.8	+14.0	+1.9	+2.0
Holdings of less than 20 hectares	-8.9**	-17.6**	-6.3**	-3.6
b. Analysis of wheat yields				
Holdings of 100 hectares and over	+18.4**	+33.9**	+33.4**	+23.5**
Holdings of between 20 and 100 hectares	-7.6	+7.9	+9.1	+9.5
Holdings of less than 20 hectares	-8.7**	-22.5**	-22.6**	-16.8**

** indicates a result significant at the 99% level
* indicates a result significant at the 95% level
coefficients without asterisks are not significant at the 95% level

One note of caution about these estimates should be sounded. The estimates assume that there is no learning effect running from large holdings to small. This means that the effect of larger holdings on average yields is entirely direct, due to increases in yields on such holdings. But if larger holdings had a leadership role, so that they had an indirect effect on yields on neighbors even if these were smaller farms, then the estimates given in this table will be too high. The significance of the result remains: the presence of larger holdings has a positive effect on *Kreis* yields, and this effect tended to decline in the case of rye. However, it would not then be possible to make a direct estimate of the gap between yields on different classes of holdings.

The position is rather different with regard to wheat. Here the gap between large and small holdings was a persistent one, which did not change much over time. Wheat was a more demanding crop and required better husbandry skills. It was also a crop grown for urban markets; not much was consumed by farm households. Thus, it was more attractive to the larger, market-oriented estates, and less useful to smallholder families intending to consume a large portion of their production themselves.

Notes

1. See, for example, the articles by Hans-Jürgen Puhle and Hanna Schissler in *Peasants and Lords in Modern Germany: Recent Studies in Agricultural History*, ed. Robert G. Moeller (London, 1986); see also the introduction to Heinz Reif, *Ostelbische Agrargesellschaft im Kaiserreich und in der Weimarer Republik* (Berlin, 1994).

2. The main imperfections are, firstly, that the use of a calorie measure overvalues the output of high-calorie crops such as potatoes or sugar beet, and undervalues "Mediterranean" crops such as fruit or wine; and, second, the exclusion of female labor (due to a lack of comparable figures) leads to an overestimate of productivity in countries where female participation was highest.

3. On the new scientific approach to arable production, see, inter alia, Sigmond von Frauendorfer, "Naturwissenschaften und Technik als dynamisches Moment," *Zeitschrift für Agrargeschichte und Agrarsoziologie* 4 (1956): 113-27, and Volker Klemm, "Die Agrarwissenschaften und die Modernisierung der Gutsbetriebe in Ost- und Mitteldeutschland," in *Ostelbische Agrargesellschaft im Kaiserreich und in der Weimarer Republik*, ed. Heinz Reif (Berlin, 1994). For a general discussion of developments in German agriculture, see John A. Perkins, "The Agricultural Revolution in Germany," *Journal of European Economic History* 10 (1981): 71-118.

4. The econometric analysis is presented in Grant, "Productivity in German Agriculture"; see also the discussion in Appendix B.

5. Figures from Franz Schneppe, "Die Ertragssteigerung auf den leichten Böden der Lüneburger Heide," *Zeitschrift für Agrargeschichte und Agrarsoziologie* 8 (1960): 14-22, who also gives details of government-sponsored research on the light soils of the Lüneburg Heath. It was a general complaint of German agriculturalists that the quality of German soil was poor. See, for example, the remark by Dr. H. Gerlich at a meeting of the Royal Statistical Society in 1899, *Journal of the Royal Statistical Society* 62, no.4 (1899). Sandy soils have advantages and disadvantages, high-fertilizer requirements being undeniably one of the latter. The author of this study farms on soils of this type in central Sussex. See also Hugo Thiel, "Der Verbrauch von Kunstdünger im Preußischen Staate," *Landwirtschaftliche Jahrbucher* 16 (1887): 447-79, for details of fertilizer use in the Prussian regions.

6. See, for example, the estate history in volume 1 of *Die deutsche Landwirtschaft unter Kaiser Wilhelm II*, ed. H. Dade (Halle, 1913), 19.

7. See the remarks on Germany in the survey of agricultural education in the *Journal of the Royal Agricultural Society of England and Wales* (1885): 126-64 and 518-46.

8. "In this area, as in the whole region, it is only the large farms and estates that make use of artificial fertilizers and concentrated livestock feed"; from a report on conditions in *Kreis* Stolp in 1890-91 in the *Landwirtschaftliche Jahrbücher* 19, suppl. 4 (1891). See, however, Robert G. Moeller, "Peasants and Tariffs in the *Kaiserreich*," *Agricultural History* 55 (1981): 370-84, and John H. Perkins, "Dualism in German Agrarian Historiography," *Comparative Studies in Society and History* 28 (1986): 287-306, for a more balanced view of peasant agriculture.

9. There is a summary of the statistical analysis in Appendix B.

10. And would, in many areas, be the main losers from the post-1945 expulsions. It is not possible, using accounts drawn up as for table 2, to differentiate between productivity levels in Polish-speaking and German-speaking areas, although the maps suggest that the Polish areas shared in the general "catch-up" east of the Elbe. Analysis of yields in the Prussian *Kreise* confirms that there was no difference between yields levels, or yield increases, in German-speaking and Polish-speaking areas (controlling for the effect of remoteness, farm size, and soil type). Polish areas also shared in the modernisation process.

11. Max Weber, "Die Lage der Landarbeiter im ostelbischen Deutschland," *Schriften des Verein für Sozialpolitik* 55 (1893).

12. See, for example, the discussion in chapter 9 of Yujiro Hayami, *Development Economics: From the Poverty to the Wealth of Nations* (Oxford, 1997), also Partha Dasgupta, *An Inquiry into Well-Being and Destitution* (Oxford, 1993), 229-34.

13. For example, a report in the *Jahrbuch für die Amtliche Statistik des Preußischen Staats II* (1867): 284.

14. Under the New Zealand share-milking system, a retiring farmer hands over the herd to a new entrant, who milks the cows in return for a gradually increasing share of the value of the herd. The *Deputanten* milked the landlord's cows in return for a share in the produce and the opportunity to keep some livestock of their own.

15. Kevin H. O'Rourke, "The European Grain Invasions, 1870-1913," *Journal of Economic History* 57 (1997): 775-801; see also Steven B. Webb, "Agricultural Protection in Wilhelmian Germany: Forging an Empire with Pork and Rye," *Journal of Economic History* 42 (1982): 309-26, for a discussion of the German response.

16. The survey results are given in Carl von Könitz, "Über die Verhältnisse zwischen Rohertrag und Reinertrag in landwirtschaftlichen Betrieben verschiedener Wirtschaftssysteme," *Landwirtschaftliche Jahrbücher* 24 (1895): 309-444. *Landschaften* loans generally paid 4 percent, and these were the best terms any landowner was likely to get.

17. There were regular surveys of agricultural debt published in the *Zeitschrift des Königlich Preußischen Statistischen Bureaus*. See also International Institute of Agriculture, Bureau of Economic and Social Intelligence, *The Landschaften and Their Mortgage Credit Operations in Germany 1770-1920*, by M. Tcherkinsky (Rome, 1926) for an overview; August Meitzen, "Ermittelungen über die durchschnittliche Höhe der Grundbuchschulden der bäuerlichen Besitzungen in 52 Amtsgerichtsbezirken der Preußischen Staat nach dem Stand des Jahres 1883," *Landwirtschaftliche Jahrbücher* 14, suppl. 2 (1885), 1-32, is a survey of debt on peasant holdings, but limited to *Grundbuchschulden*.

18. John H. Clapham, *The Economic Development of France and Germany* (Cambridge, 1921), 206.

19. August Meitzen, *Der Boden und der landwirtschaftlichen Verhältnisse des Preußischen Staates* (Berlin, 1868), vol. 4, part a; yield data came from various issues of *Preußische Statistik*; information on the land distribution was taken from the 1895 agricultural census, *Statistik des Deutschen Reichs* n.f. 112 (1896): 489-500.

The Wilhelmine Regime and the Problem of Reform

German Debates about Modern Nation-States

MARK HEWITSON

Introduction: Wilhelminism and Modernity

The Wilhelmine "system" was commonly believed to differ from its predecessors. Friedrich Naumann, one of the main critics of the system by 1907/08 and an important intermediary between politics, the press, and the universities, was an acute, representative interpreter of such "Wilhelminism." In his treatise *Demokratie und Kaisertum*, which first appeared in 1900 and went on to become a best-selling work of its kind, Naumann explained how the industrialization and democratization of Germany had created the conditions for a new type of political regime. Gradually, as a consequence of these changes, the "modern" idea of an emperor and empire were expected to replace "the traditions of conservative Prussian kingly rule". This, wrote the left-liberal politician and publicist, "seems to be the difference between the view of Wilhelm I and Wilhelm II, that the latter is more of an emperor [*Kaiser*] and the former more of a king [*König*], a difference, which is not based on personal inclinations alone, but whose basis lies in the fact that kingship [*Königtum*] is the constitutional form of an agrarian state [*Agrarstaat*] whereas empire [*Reich*] is the constitutional form of an industrial state [*Industriestaat*], and that the industrial state, through constant population growth, is becoming more powerful than the agrarian state."

In interpreting the advent of the new regime in such a way, Naumann relied on long-standing assessments of demographic trends and on a recent debate between the liberal economist Lujo Brentano and his conservative, "state socialist" opponent, Adolph Wagner, about the relative merits of *Industrie-* and *Agrarstaaten*. Acceptance of the implications of demographic growth and of the necessity of industrialization, in however limited a form, had subsequently become a shared assumption of Wilhelmine politics. The German regime, in which "the Hohenzollern state's pursuit of power is united with the national idea's pursuit of power," needed to harness resultant democratic and economic forces in a "realistic" fashion, continued Naumann. This understanding of the regime's expanding and novel role in terms of power rather than of tradition had introduced "a completely new era [*Zeitabschnitt*]."[1] Naumann, like many of his contemporaries, was convinced that the Wilhelmine state was functionally and legitimately "modern."[2]

There were, of course, many criticisms of the Wilhelmine state and of Wilhelminism, not least from the liberal circles around Naumann. Thus, the sociologist Max Weber was scathing about the role of the monarch, exposing the flaws of what he termed "*this* regime of *this* man," and of the system as a whole, including the damaging predominance of Junkers, the underrepresentation of the economic interests and liberal values of the *Bürgertum*, the "pseudo-constitutional" thwarting of parliamentarization and of political elites, and the isolation of the *Kaiserreich* abroad. "We are becoming 'isolated' because this man rules us in this way *and because we tolerate it and make excuses for it*," he warned Naumann in December 1906. As the *Daily Telegraph* affair had furnished further examples of misplaced royal interventions in 1908, the sociologist had concluded: "This is a fault of the system, not of the person." Yet Weber's point, echoing that of Naumann, was not that the existing Wilhelmine regime was a feudal remnant, although he certainly believed that it contained archaic elements, but that the transformation of the state, which had already begun in response to bureaucratization, the concentration of industry, and late unification, would have to be accelerated.[3] Even though they rejected his pessimistic conclusions, Weber's conservative academic opponents within the Verein für Sozialpolitik broadly concurred with his general analysis of the state. The bureaucratic regime, which had been a feature of the Wilhelmine era, had coped reasonably well with the stresses and strains of modernity, wrote the founder of the Verein, Gustav Schmoller, in 1906:

> [W]e still have a bureaucratic government [*Beamtenregierung*] today because this is the only possible form of government for us, and I believe that we have not on the whole, since 1888, done at all badly by it. Certainly, much has gone wrong, and often. But the great part of this lies in the temperament of the Kaiser, in his romantic rushes of blood. In any event, we have managed to avoid the creation of a feudal-clerical ministry, despite all the forceful striving, and despite the fact that we are obliged to govern with ultramontanes and conservatives. Caprivi, Hohenlohe, and Bülow have brought this about.... One can object: we must have a parliamentary regime. But we lack the aristocracy, the leaders, the great political parties. Bülow would be ready for a [parliamentary] ministry today, if he could see any prospect of achieving better results in this way than with the current bureaucratic ministry.[4]

Such turn-of-the-century claims and counterclaims concerning the modern state were nearly always set against a series of international comparisons. This was partly the result of changes in the means of communication—most notably, newsreels and photographic journalism in illustrated weeklies—and partly the corollary of a wider transformation of production, transportation, distribution, and consumption, which seemed to have brought industrial societies into closer proximity to each other. Thus, when commentators like Weber and Schmoller spoke of the Wilhelmine "system," they generally referred to a complex division of labor, modes of exchange, networks of communication, and relationships of power, some of which crossed the line between public and private spheres, and even the borders between national territories. Nevertheless, the state remained the core of the system, and the prominence of international comparison is explicable largely in terms of the centrality of a German nation-state in contemporary understandings of politics.

There were two reasons in particular, it seemed, why the Wilhelmine state could be understood fully only in an international context. First, the *Kaiserreich* had become the subject of a debate after the turn of the century in which critics such as Naumann began to cast around for possible foreign alternatives. Such thoughts had not crossed the mind of anyone who entered politics in the 1880s and 1890s, "since the size of economic-political and social tasks preoccupied him in such a way that everything else faded into the background," wrote the editor of *Die Hilfe* in 1908. "But it has emerged in the dealings over economic questions and social policy that the major decisions in all these affairs depend on who actually has power within the state."[5] Now it seemed necessary for both opponents and supporters to reconsider, by means of international comparison, the merits of a state that had previously seemed firmly entrenched. Second, journalists and politicians could—for the first time since unification—criticize the German nation-state, which appeared to many Wilhelmine commentators to have become "normal," without being condemned for "treason." Consequently, to compare the German state with its neighbors no longer seemed to threaten the integrity of the German nation. This was perhaps the most important reason why much of the right was prepared to participate in a discussion about the *Kaiserreich* as one type of regime among others.

Such prewar discussion has a direct bearing on the historiographical controversy, begun by the Hamburg and Bielefeld schools, about the legitimacy of the Wilhelmine polity and the political integration of Wilhelmine society. It also impinges on a related debate about the nature of modern German nationalism.[6] Here, I assume that the new German nation-state, even though it had a long-established national culture, lacked significant integrating political traditions typical of other western European states. Such traditions included a common political history, a clearly defined constitution, convergence between citizenship and nationality, and political parties closely associated with myths of unification or national struggle. As a result, the legitimacy of the Wilhelmine regime—and Wilhelminism in general—came to rest either on the rapid invention of political traditions or on a cult of modernity, confusingly mixed with archaism, that was designed to compensate for any political shortcomings. This chapter examines how Wilhelmine commentators invented such political traditions and assessed the modernity of the regime by means of international comparison. The next section investigates the way in which the *Kaiserreich* was distinguished from other countries on the periphery of Europe or beyond, while the third section demon-strates how it was compared favorably with the most modern Continental Great Power, France.

The *Kaiserreich* and the *Kulturländer*

Germans' assessments of other states around the turn of the century were influenced by a confusing number of preconceptions. In part, judgments of neighboring regimes rested on domestic confessional, class, and political affiliations. They were also affected by national rivalries, as different powers came to challenge the perceived eco-nomic interests and foreign policy goals of the German Empire. Arguably more sig-nificant than such domestic and national preconceptions of foreign powers, however, was a series of assumptions about races, cultures, and states, which was—with some exceptions—reinforced by popular distinctions between "young" and "decadent" powers, civilizations (*Zivilisation*) and cultures (*Kultur*), and the Old and New World. On the whole, such dichotomies served to reinforce the idea that the Wil-helmine state should be measured against the yardstick of other mainland European regimes, since these alone shared a common racial, cultural, and geopolitical heritage. It was as if many Wilhelmine commentators conceived of Germany and Europe as a single cultural entity, separated progressively from other countries by a series of con-centric circles, which corresponded to differences of race, culture, and politics. These differences, though not preventing the imitation of individual institutions, tended to make broad comparisons between the German Empire and extra-European states seem less useful than those between the regimes of Western and Central Europe.

Most Germans, like other Europeans, were swayed in their assessment of other states outside of Western Europe and North America by a belief in the superiority of their own culture and race. The basis of such judgment was not altered by sud-den shifts in the balance of forces and alliances nor by increased coverage in the press—including lustrous photographs—that showed the world beyond the "cul-tured countries" (*Kulturländer*) in a new light. Thus, even though Japan had become a Great Power, defeating Russia in Manchuria in 1905, it was usually dismissed as racially inferior, with the left-liberal satirical journal *Simplicissimus*, for instance, continuing to represent it as a small, ineffectual figure in the shape of a monkey or an insect.[7] In a similar way, Russia and other "Slav" states were disregarded either because they were believed to be racially inferior or, more commonly, because they were perceived to be culturally backward.[8] The main result of such distinctions was to underline that Germany stood at the center of a European-dominated sphere of *Kulturländer*, which extended to British dominions and former colonies in North America and the Antipodes.

Such "cultured countries" were believed to have been shaped by Greco-Roman philosophy, Christian morality, the science of the Enlightenment, industrial capital-ism, imperialism, and national sentiment. However, despite sharing a common culture and serving as a common foil for the construction of a supposedly unique German identity, the principal *Kulturländer*, it seemed, could also be distinguished from each other geographically, militarily, socially, and politically. These distinguishing features ensured that the United States rarely functioned as a model for German state building. It is true that constitutional experts such as Max Weber and the Heidelberg lawyer Georg Jellinek continued to point to parallels between federalism, separation of competencies, legitimacy, and powers of appointment and dismissal in both polities, resurrecting some of the arguments put forward in 1848-49.[9] At the same time, there was in Germany a growing familiarity with, and respect for, the economic achievement of the United States.[10] Yet even this image, which was perpetuated in well-known books such as Ludwig Max Goldberger's *Das Land der unbegrenzten Möglichkeiten*, published in 1903, arguably formed part of a long-standing European tableau of the New World, with its economic opportunities, its untapped resources, and its vast expanses of wilderness.[11] Such a composition, though becoming less romantic in an age of imperialism and industrial rivalry, continued to overshadow other, more realistic depictions of the United States, akin to that put forward by the German-American academic Hugo Münsterberg in *Die Amerikaner* in 1904. Unlike Münsterberg, the majority of Wilhelmine commentators appear to have begun from the premise that American society and culture, even if no longer seen as a tabula rasa, were fundamentally different from those of Continental Europe. Thus, the historian Karl Lamprecht's verdict in his popular diary of *Americana* in 1906 that "vis-à-vis the old culture of the European population, both the Germanic and the Romanic, the Americans are still behind" was widely echoed, as was the economist Werner Sombart's conclusion—in his 1906 treatise *Warum gibt es in den Vereinigten Staaten keinen Sozialismus?*—that economic and social conditions in the United States bore little resemblance to those in Germany.[12]

Wilhelmine depictions of the American polity were, in the majority of cases, clearly influenced by such premises. The right-wing historian Heinrich von Treitschke was typical of many observers, including those more sympathetic to the United States such as Max Weber and Wilhelm Roscher, who referred to the corruption of American bureaucracy and the machine-like nature of American politics.[13] The North Americans were "not in a position to create a reliable, good bureaucracy for themselves," nor to prevent "the basic democratic law of free economic competition" from altering their system of government and leading "to a domination of the stock exchange," declared Treitschke in his famous lectures on politics, which were published posthumously in 1898. The dangers of such developments had been contained only "because the young country is still making enormous progress in its living standards," and because its federal political system was unique, precluding the type of centralization and Caesarism experienced by France. In fact, he went on, the United States was not a single democratic polity, but rather "a bundle of democracies," which had been able to take root because of the untouched political and social soil of the New World. Different conditions in Europe meant that these American forms of government could not serve as a model for Germany:

Europe, by contrast, has an old history with monarchical traditions, which cannot be
swept aside without further ado; for this reason alone, it offers less promising soil than
America for a democratic form of government [*Staatsform*]. Furthermore, Europe needs
a very outward-looking policy that is temporarily not needed by North America, which
is without powerful neighbors and which thus, as Washington was able to boast, does not
know of national hatreds. In addition, social conflicts in Europe are much more glaring
than in the New World; thus, there is a lack here of an important foundation of democracy, equality. Finally, our old continent needs to be much governed, which is likewise difficult to reconcile with democracy.[14]

Although observers on the German left disagreed with Treitschke's analysis of democracy, they were unable—in the absence of guidance from Marx and Engels—to offer
a consistent alternative explanation of American politics.[15] For them, too, the pattern
of economic, social, and political development in the United States did not fit into a
Eurocentric understanding of state building and state intervention.

For most Wilhelmine commentators, Britain was a more obvious point of comparison than the United States. Certainly, it featured much more prominently in
press reportage of foreign affairs, with about 30 percent of newspaper and journal
articles on the main external objects of German interest—France, the U.K., Russia,
and the U.S.—concentrating on Britain, compared to 10 to 13 percent on the
United States, according to one calculation.[16] Some of the attention that Britain
received in Germany was a direct consequence of the two countries' economic, colonial, and—especially—maritime competition, which reached its zenith after the turn
of the century, with the British "world state" allegedly constituting the principal
obstacle to German ambitions overseas. More significant than such shifting international antagonisms, however, were the close historical, political, religious, and dynastic ties that had traditionally existed between the United Kingdom and the German
states. For much of the nineteenth century, Britain had been admired by German liberals for its balanced, constitutional system of government; its robust parliamentary
style of politics; its defense of basic freedoms of association, assembly, and expression;
and its pursuit of free trade and industrial growth. It had also been praised by many
conservatives—and a significant number of liberals—for its aristocratic parties; its
incremental, historical approach to policymaking; its tradition of common law; its def-
erential, Protestant, and patriotic society; and its "Germanic" affiliation with the
states of the Confederation.

Elements of such identification and imitation persisted into the Wilhelmine era,
not least in the classic works of "old liberals" such as the constitutional lawyer Rudolf
von Gneist, who continued to look to "England"—albeit critically—as a progenitor
of the law-governed state (*Rechtsstaat*).[17] Although a younger generation of liberals,
including Friedrich Naumann, Theodor Barth, and Max Weber, paid less attention
to the "legal," "constitutional," and "parliamentary" pillars of liberalism examined by
Gneist, partly because of the new political challenges posed by industrialization,
nationalism, and imperialism, it nevertheless continued to look to Britain as a model
of parliamentary government that seemed to guarantee traditional political freedoms
at the same time as tackling more modern political problems, such as the selection of

elites. This is what Naumann meant when he wrote, in 1910, that "the goal of German development" was the transition "from absolutism to the English system," for Britain appeared to have dealt relatively well with the "simultaneous rise of both imperialist and democratic forces."[18] It had conserved a liberal heritage, while governing, adapting, and expanding a powerful empire.

By the Wilhelmine period, despite continuing cross-party admiration of the British Empire, the liberal, "English" paradigm of government had been undermined by three overlapping sets of arguments. First, and least significantly, Britain had increasingly been associated with images of decadence in German commentaries, even though it still constituted a strong financial, maritime, and diplomatic force that quickly became the Reich's principal enemy after August 1914. Some elements of such alleged decadence continued to be disputed, with certain liberal and left-wing Catholic critics of Wilhelminism such as Max Weber and Matthias Erzberger applauding the caliber of Britain's political leaders and the single-mindedness of its foreign policy, even if they also pointed to what the conservative academic Wilhelm Hasbach termed the "dark sides" of the country's parliamentary system of government.[19] Other aspects of British decadence—most notably, economic ones—were widely accepted. The overall indices of the two countries' changing fortunes are now well known, with Britain's share of world trade dropping from 23 to 17 percent and that of Germany rising from 10 to 13 percent between 1880 and 1913. At the time, more attention was paid to gross figures for foreign trade, but these statistics, too, showed that the Reich had rapidly caught up with its neighbor. Thus, between 1890 and 1913, British exports had risen from £264 million per annum to £525 million, whereas those of Germany had jumped from £166 million to £505 million. Even more strikingly, by 1905, the United Kingdom's exports and reexports to the Reich amounted to less than the value of the goods imported from it.[20] From such a perspective, which was presented to readers of the press on a regular basis, the historian Otto Hintze's claim that Britain was in decline appeared to be justified. The country had, he wrote, become a cautious, uncompetitive "pensioners' state" (*Rentnerstaat*), attaining "a satisfied, stationary condition" that was "not favorable to the needs of a national and political extension of power, to the striving for Anglo-Saxon domination of the world." Revisionist social imperialists in the SPD and left-liberal imperialists around Friedrich Naumann expressed similar points of view.[21] Compared to Britain and France, Germany seemed, in the decades before World War I, to have grown stronger. "If anyone is to be first among equals, then it will be he [the German] and not the Frenchman or the Briton," boasted Adolph Wagner.[22]

Second, increasing national antagonism after 1871—and especially after the inauguration of *Weltpolitik* in 1896—prompted German academics, journalists, and politicians to treat British policies simply as the arrogant and hypocritical expression of self-interest and power politics. Thus, Treitschke, who as a national-minded liberal had assured his readers in the 1850s and 1860s that admiration was "the first feeling which the study of English history calls forth in everyone," had given up the idea of transferring British political institutions to Germany by the late 1860s, and had come to contrast the two countries, making a distinction between "Anglo-Saxon" and "Teutonic" cultures by the mid 1870s. "In the halls of Parliament," he declared, "one heard only shameless British commercial morality, which, with the Bible in the right hand and the opium pipe in the left, spreads the benefits of civilization around the world."[23] Treitschke's assumption was that Britain's success rested on a ruthless foreign policy, rather than on an effective state machine. In the 1900s, a long line of liberal and conservative successors to Treitschke, including historians and economists such as Dietrich Schäfer, Hermann Oncken, Friedrich Meinecke, and Gerhard von Schulze-Gävernitz, went on to claim that the expansion of the British Empire had been the fortuitous consequence of Britain's advantageous trading position as an island and of its duplicitous policy of "divide and rule" toward the European mainland, which allowed it to acquire colonies in the eighteenth and nineteenth centuries with little opposition from other powers. All tended to overlook the industrial and administrative underpinnings of British imperialism.

Third, political conditions in Britain and Germany were widely perceived to be essentially different by the Wilhelmine era, much more so than previously had been the case. Right-wing commentators, in particular, pointed to the geopolitical gulf that separated the two countries' histories. To Hintze, Treitschke, and others, the German state inevitably bore the imprint of its military origins. By contrast, "the historical pillars, on which Continental constitutional monarchy rests—absolutism, militarism, bureaucracy—have never come into being in England, because there was no political need to push the island state in that direction, since it enjoyed relative military security and early political centralization."[24] Others on the right, such as Hasbach, went even further, arguing that parliamentary government had prospered in the United Kingdom only "because the bureaucracy was undeveloped, because state administration was carried out to an extensive degree through honorary offices, because thoroughgoing self-government made the interference of the state impossible, because liberal limitation of the state's goals made subsidies to electoral constituencies difficult, [and] because deputies were for the most part well off."[25] Left-wing observers were more reluctant to rule out comparisons with Britain, but the majority of them would probably have admitted, in the words of the revisionist socialist Karl Leuthner, that "English" parties—and, by implication, "England's" two-party system of government and type of state—constituted "a quite incomparable form," making it ill-advised "to transfer what had been said about English parties to Continental ones."[26] Even Naumann, although aspiring by 1908 to a broadly "English" type of parliamentarism, warned that "English history" was "different from German history," ruling out simple imitation of British institutions.[27] In short, the validity of the liberal British model, although still quite frequently referred to, was more open to question by the late Wilhelmine era than at any time since its inception during the early nineteenth century. Such German doubts about Britain's system of government tended to redound to the advantage of what Hintze called the "unique" polity of the Reich.

The *Kaiserreich* and the Continent

France seemed to constitute a more relevant point of reference than Britain. From a sample of the principal four foreign countries covered in the Wilhelmine press, the neighboring state was the subject of between 29 and 36 percent of reports during the decade and a half before World War I.[28] "Small" Continental states like the Nether-lands and Sweden, which even a liberal economist like Gustav Cohn believed to be dependent on the "great states," were routinely overlooked in such reportage.[29] By contrast, France seemed to have dominated Germany and Europe for most of the nineteenth century, doing more than any other power to initiate or spread the ideas— such as absolutism, revolution, and socialism—that had underpinned processes of state building. "Whatever occurs in France always concerns humanity as a whole, and the newspapers of all countries are well informed of what is happening there," wrote one observer on the eve of the war.[30] As the product of revolution, Bonapartist mili-tary levies, and comparatively early industrialization, the French state had been con-sidered the most modern in Europe. With the Third Republic usually portrayed in the German press as the successor to the revolution of 1789, this notion of French modernity proved surprisingly tenacious, lasting—in most political quarters—well into the Wilhelmine era.

The French state appeared to have faced the same problems as its German coun-terpart. Thus, it had been forced to confront the existence of bitter class conflicts and the rise of apparently militant socialist parties, which were set—though rarely explic-itly—against the background of a common revolutionary past. Despite the more grad-ual impact of industrialization in the neighboring state, the socialist vote there had risen twice as quickly as that in Germany between the mid 1890s and the mid 1900s, reach-ing one hundred seats, or 16.6 percent, by 1914. Newspapers of all parties reported this movement throughout the prewar period, comparing its implications with those in the Reich.[31] Younger academics within the Verein für Sozialpolitik such as the allegedly "socialist" Sombart, whose 1896 work *Sozialismus und soziale Bewegung im 19. Jahrhundert* had helped to raise the question in scholarly circles, as well as older conservative opponents, such as Schmoller, made similar sets of comparisons.[32]

Social conflicts, along with regional and confessional disputes, were linked by Wilhelmine observers to the existence of political fragmentation in France and Ger-many. Neither country, it was widely believed, possessed the unusual social and polit-ical conditions that would allow the creation of a British-type two-party system. Even Naumann, who later became a proponent of the system, believed before 1907 that its introduction would be impossible in Germany.[33] Consequently, the question for both apologists and critics of the French Third Republic and the German Empire was how to combine the politics of representation with the need for effective state intervention, or, to put it another way, how to reconcile the state with the competing interests of civil society, for Continental countries were believed to lack the prerequisites of self-gov-ernment and organic unity typical of Britain. It was held to be crucial that principles of state neutrality remained credible because the Reich and the Third Republic not only had to intervene more than the British state, since the institutions of civil society could not administer their own affairs, but also had to accommodate much larger armies and, consequently, bureaucracies. As military costs mounted during the 1900s and 1910s, and as political criticism of expanding armies and navies increased, commentators such as Hintze asked themselves how such armed forces could best be integrated within a representative and effective system of civilian government.[34]

In the opinion of most Wilhelmine observers, the leaders of the Third Republic had not found plausible answers to such questions. "The domestic political life of France shows no progress," wrote the author of the main history of France. "The republic has been consolidated not through love and the republican virtue of the French, but through the fear that they might be faced with still worse conditions and new unrest under a different form of government."[35] The basis of the French form of government was widely held to be parliamentarism (*Parlamentarismus*), that is, the appointment and dismissal of ministries by a popularly elected assembly. France's revolutionary and republican traditions had been pushed, by the time of the Dreyfus affair at the turn of the century, to the margins of German accounts of French decline. Instead, defects were linked to the inability of a dominant but divided parliament to run the affairs of the country. To right-wing newspapers such as the *Dresdner Nachrichten*, this inability was obvious: "Wherever you look, *reforms* are *needed urgently*. But the deputies care far too much about their parliamentary seat for them to be able to do anything for the country. This, however, is less their fault than that of the *parliamentary system*, which is dominant in France."[36] Yet similar reports could also be found, in growing numbers in the center and on the left, denouncing— in the words of the liberal *Vossische Zeitung*—"all the dear traditions of parliamentarism—of parliamentary anarchy."[37] By 1908, in the midst of vociferous debates about the reform of the political system of the *Kaiserreich*, it had become commonplace to compare German constitutionalism (*Konstitutionalismus*), in which ministers were nominated by the Kaiser and protected to a certain extent from parliamentary interference, with the perceived failure of French parliamentarism.

Under Continental conditions, the parliamentarization of government under the Third Republic appeared to a broad range of Wilhelmine onlookers to have had profound effects. The most immediate were ministerial instability and corruption, as a consequence of the merging of executive, legislative, and even judicial functions. "In England, France, and America," wrote the moderate-conservative historian Hans Delbrück, representative institutions had "achieved power by forcing aside or completely toppling the existing government." In effect, by seizing control of executive power, parliaments had nullified their own controlling function, since the major parties came to dominate government, administration, and legislature. "Here, the gap between, for example, Germany and France appears to be infinite. Here there is a professional government with a popular assembly as a sort of organ of control [*Kontrollstation*], there an elected popular government."[38] Only a parliament that was formally separate from the government seemed capable of ensuring the accountability and responsibility of ministers. Because French faction leaders controlled the assembly, senate, ministries, and, as a result, administration, there were no adequate safe-guards within the Third Republic for the probity or efficacy of governance. Popular checks, namely, occasional elections or press scrutiny, were widely held to be com-pletely inadequate. Newspapers from all political quarters concentrated instead on election fixing, the bribing of editors, ministerial incompetence, factional infighting and deal making, political corruption, favoritism, and governmental instability.[39] Like France, Germany was believed to be too socially and politically fragmented to allow aristocratic self-government and the alternation of two great parties, which alone could guarantee political competition and check corruption. "Here, too," concluded Hasbach, equating the political circumstances of the two countries, "parliamentary government would probably create conditions akin to those in France; perhaps we would approach a 'spoils system.'"[40]

Such a system of corruption under France's parliamentary republic not only seemed to impair the actions of the bureaucracy, with newspapers from across the party spectrum reporting at length on the misdemeanors of civil servants in the "scan-dals"—Panama, Dreyfus, Humbert, Edgar Combes, Rochette, and Duez—that punctuated the decades before World War I; it also appeared to accelerate the process of bureaucratization itself, as sinecures were created for the purposes of political patronage and nepotism.[41] In the absence of any orthodox academic theory of bureau-cratization, which scholars such as Max Weber, Robert Michels, and Otto Hintze were beginning to analyze for the first time, newspapers regularly treated its manifes-tation in France as the corollary of corruption. One typical report in the Center Party organ, *Germania*, stated: "Government and parliament compete with one another to create as many new civil service posts as possible and thereby to provide and care for their creatures. At present, France has 608,511 state and 262,078 communal func-tionaries .... Whoever gains power and a reputation in France wants to dispose, as 'Patronus,' of as numerous a 'Clientela' as possible ... and this goal is best achieved when clients are placed at the state trough, where possible in the most sought-after feeding places. That is what one calls serving the republic!"[42]

Conservative newspapers such as the *Neue Preussische Zeitung* confirmed such inflated figures, which were twice as high as those in textbooks on France, and repeated the explanation: "People push their way to the state trough in order to earn an assured, albeit scarcely adequate, income. The government accommodates this tendency and unrelentingly creates new legions of officials."[43] Both the article's find-ings and its conclusion—that "this French civil service, which cannot be compared to the German one, has become a real menace for the life of the French people"—were shared by liberal publications such as the *Hannoverscher Courier*: "Why should one send one's only son to the hard school of independent struggle, into the world, when one can shelter him in a civil service career by the proved and rarely, if ever, failing means of nepotism."[44] The implication throughout such reportage, as the *Courier* pointed out, was that "however bad it might be" in Germany, "there is a much big-ger and richer harvest of official pen pushers in France" as a direct result of unchecked parliamentarism, which undermined the efficiency and neutrality of administration.

Most academic observers believed that the integrity of the German state should be maintained—or increased—since its functions, jurisdictions, and bureaucracy seemed bound to expand. This belief in the inevitable social and economic expansion of the state was held even by an innovative historian such as Hintze and a rare scholarly critic of bureaucratization such as Weber.[45] To most other academics, such as the economist Gustav Schmoller and the historian Martin Spahn, the growth of the German state presented few problems, as long as its neutrality could be preserved. Parliamentarism seemed to pose the greatest threat. Both Spahn and Schmoller agreed that the attempt in France and Britain to award political liberties and establish parliamentary powers before solving the social question had led to unequal taxation, unregulated industries, inadequate social insurance, and inferior schools.[46] In the neighboring state, wrote the economist, "party bickering, personal ambition, and the restless struggle for ministerial positions do not allow the realization of great reforms."[47] Most of the general literature and press coverage on France, such as that of the *Tag* correspondent Karl Eugen Schmidt, whose main work was sarcastically entitled *Im Lande der Freiheit, Gleichheit und Brüderlichkeit*, added lurid details to such academic argument, chronicling the effects of political corruption on daily life. Thus, in Schmidt's opinion, the blatant partiality of the parliamentary state, which manifested itself in the class-specific repression of strikers' demonstrations or in the muzzling, imprisoning, and torturing of political enemies, had made it an object of suspicion and contempt among the French population, creating a damaging mixture of fatalism and occasional revolutionary anger.[48] For its part, the state, because of the political bias of its organization and policymaking, had failed to put forward modern social reforms, such as had been implemented in Germany. "Compared with the German Reich," Schmidt argued, "social welfare does not exist at all in the land of *fraternité*."[49] Political, social, and economic interest groups used their powers within the parliamentary state to block measures that were designed to benefit the nation as a whole and "that had been introduced long ago in most monarchies."[50] Consequently, successive governments had neglected to introduce or reform old-age pensions, unemployment insurance, public assistance, housing regulations, a nationalized system of railways, and income tax.[51] During the years before World War I, this alleged failure came to constitute a point of agreement in the German press, after previously Francophile liberal publications had become disenchanted with the record of Radical governments in France between 1906 and 1909.[52]

Uncontrolled bureaucratization, a backward system of taxation, and a failing public infrastructure seemed to have caused—not exclusively, but to a considerable extent—the decline of the French economy. By the turn of the century, even the most indifferent observers, such as Germany's most famous art critic, Julius Meier-Graefe, had come to accept the fact that France "did not take part in those enormous changes, which commerce and industry created in other countries, especially in its constantly dangerous neighbors, England and Germany."[53] Some of the reasons for the relative economic decline of the neighboring state—especially demographic stagnation—were still disputed. Virtually all German observers, however, concurred that the corruption, inefficiency, and indebtedness of the French state were a major cause of decline, threatening to bring about the collapse of the country's entire economy. France, it was well-known from reports in the press, had the largest national debt in the world, amounting to an estimated total of 32,000 million francs in 1914 or more than 1,000 million francs per annum—about a fifth of the national budget—in interest payments.[54] Its annual expenditure, the second largest in the world, was known to have surpassed 4,000 million francs by 1906 and 5,000 million francs by 1912. Such expenditures, it was held, could only be met by illicit loans and imprudent budgetary deficits.

To many commentators, it appeared that this practice of deficit financing, which made the state dependent on the confidence of stockholders (*rentiers*), might lead to financial ruin, since there would come a point at which the size of the national debt lowered the price of government-issued bonds (*rentes*). "The financial straits of the republic have already become a prolonged calamity, which, it appears, can only end in catastrophe," warned a writer in the *Münchner Neueste Nachrichten* as early as 1902.[55] By 1914, after state *rentes* had allegedly lost 4,000 million francs of their value in the preceding five years, the collapse of the state's finances seemed imminent. This, in turn, endangered the economy as a whole, since a reported 4.5 million French citizens possessed government bonds.[56] By contrast, the German Reich's budgetary deficits were minimized by much of the press, with one newspaper reporting erroneously that the German national debt was only 7 percent of the French one, and its economic growth was exaggerated.[57] At the very least, the *Kaiserreich*, unlike the parliamentary Third Republic, appeared not to have hindered German growth.

Even more significantly, the Reich was credited with having created Germany's supposed military superiority over its Continental neighbors. After the turn of the century, this fact had become so commonplace, partly as a result of Russia's defeat in the Russo-Japanese War in 1905, that journalists such as Käthe Schirmacher assumed without further comment that the German Empire had been mainland Europe's principal military power since 1871.[58] The Third Republic, by contrast, appeared to have damaged its army and destroyed its navy through political interference and mismanagement. After the Dreyfus affair, which came to a head between 1898 and 1900, and the subsequent "*affaire des fiches*" in 1904, which hinged on the French war minister's use of Freemasons' files—or *fiches*—on clerical, royalist, and Bonapartist officers, the presses of all parties except the SPD concluded that parliamentary republican government in the neighboring state had divided the officer corps, damaged morale, permitted anti-militarism within army ranks, and provided the military with substandard equipment. In the words of one left-liberal publication, the French army, which "should remain above politics," had instead become one of the "main fields of political conflict".[59] Another declared that it lacked "even that cohesion which is absolutely necessary for the maintenance of discipline."[60] As was to be expected, conservative, Catholic, and National Liberal newspapers concurred wholeheartedly, regularly reiterating Hintze's conclusion that peoples under arms—as the Germans of necessity, given their geopolitical position, were—had to be organized hierarchically, according to monarchical principles of authority and power. "Because the war constitution [*Kriegsverfassung*] forms the backbone of state organization," he declared, "the representatives of civil society, that is, the Assembly, can never become the dominant influence within the state."[61] In France, this lesson had been ignored, at the expense of military preparedness. Although many on the left continued to disagree with conservative assumptions that the army, on the one hand, and a parliamentary republic, on the other, were "as incompatible as fire and water," since the former derived "most of its force from the principle of authority and the latter from a denial of this principle of authority," most nonsocialists—and some imperialists and revisionists within the SPD—did accept that the French regime had failed according to the most significant yardstick of a state's success, endorsed alike by right-wingers such as Treitschke and left liberals such as Naumann—that of military power.[62]

By most significant contemporary criteria—military, economic, social, and political—the French state seemed, by the early 1900s, to have failed. Accordingly, parties from across the German political spectrum had come to reject the parliamentary republic as a suitable model for the reform of the Reich's institutions. For most parties, this definitive rejection of a French model came much later than is generally assumed: the majority of liberals, although increasingly skeptical from the Dreyfus affair onward, criticized the republic consistently only after the perceived failure of Georges Clemenceau and the Radicals during the years before World War I; Catholics, who had supported a less militantly anti-clerical republic under Jules Méline during the 1890s, distanced themselves from both republicans and clerical-conservatives during the Dreyfus affair, associating the deplorable tactics of all parties with the corruption of France's parliamentary regime; and socialists, who had been divided about whether to support the entry of their French "brother," Alexandre Millerand, into a "progressive" republican government in 1899, came to attack the allegedly opportunistic cooperation of moderate brethren such as Jean Jaurès under the Radical ministries of Emile Combes during the early 1900s.[63] Even conservatives, who had always been contemptuous of the democratic aspirations and revolutionary traditions of the Third Republic, were not convinced that the neighboring state had failed militarily and economically—as well as politically—until the turn of the century. For them, as for the other parties, it was the Universal Exhibition in Paris in 1900—visited by millions of Germans and covered by daily press reports—that brought about the unexpected realization—"one of the greatest surprises of the contemporary world," in the words of one journalist—that the German economy had overtaken that of France.[64] Similarly, it was the Dreyfus affair and subsequent military scandals that persuaded most conservatives, who had clearly feared the reconstructed military power of the Third Republic during the 1890s, that the French army no longer posed a threat to German national security.[65] This late realization that the neighboring state had failed effectively destroyed the idea of a credible, relevant, foreign alternative to the institutions of the *Kaiserreich* during the prewar crisis of the German state between 1908 and 1914.[66] There was, it seemed, no obvious foreign template for the reform of the Wilhelmine regime.

Conclusion: Domestic Reform and International Comparison

The perceived failure of modern parliamentary states and European Great Powers such as France and Britain served to reinforce many Germans' prior belief, dating back to the 1890s and beyond, that the *Kaiserreich* was a legitimate and modern regime in its own right. Such belief, together with a concern to meet the overwhelming challenges of demographic growth, industrialization, and social conflict, had pushed politicians and commentators such as Naumann to concentrate in the 1890s and early 1900s on the innovation of Germany's existing system of government rather than seeking to imitate a foreign alternative. In the opinion of the editor of *Die Hilfe*, the "social Kaiser" became both the pivot and the symbol of this new era of what has subsequently been termed "Wilhelminism." During the decade before World War I, all parties except the Free Conservatives had come to question the Kaiser's symbolic function and pivotal role, partly because of the monarch's mistakes in the critical realm of foreign policy, on which the necessary "extension of economic opportunities"—in the words of Weber and the minds of most nonsocialist Wilhelmine onlookers—was "absolutely dependent."[67] Yet this criticism of Wilhelm II did not lead to a rejection of the Wilhelmine system as a whole. Thus, Naumann continued to speculate, in a famous article of 1910, about the development of a modern type of functional hierarchy and leadership, which he termed "kingship" (*Königtum*), in the complex organizations of the industrialized world, from electricity companies to the "corporate" state.[68] Even Weber, who was much more disparaging about the constitutional system, refrained before 1914 from making unambiguous or public calls for the replacement of the Wilhelmine regime. In this sense, Wilhelminism—or the new "system" of the 1890s—had been dissociated in the minds of critics from Wilhelm himself. Such persistent support for the system during the crisis-ridden years between 1905 and 1914 derived in large part from the common belief that it had served Germany better than a parliamentary state had served Britain or France.

The lack of a relevant, successful foreign alternative to the *Kaiserreich* did not, of course, rule out criticism of Wilhelmine institutions on the eve of World War I. Indeed, opponents of the regime became so vociferous that a moderate politician such as Georg von Hertling began to fear a revolution.[69] The reasons for such criticism were manifold, arising out of debates about democratization, social reform, national identity, and the conduct of foreign policy. Unsurprisingly, contemporaries' depictions of neighboring states were themselves partly the product of these domestic party disputes and unprecedented discussions of national interests. They were not, however, merely the product of domestic politics and national conflict, for their autonomy was guaranteed by the tension between reformism, which pushed some Wilhelmine Germans to overstate the successes of foreign regimes so that change at home appeared less daunting, and nationalism, which seems to have led many contemporaries to emphasize the failings of neighboring states in order to underline the particularity of their own nation. More importantly, depictions of foreign regimes during the Wilhelmine era were related to an increasing mediation of politics resulting from an expansion of the press, the development of news agencies and networks of foreign correspondents, the spread of photographic journalism and the invention of newsreels. Studies of the press—the new "Great Power," as it was labeled at the time—suggested that reporting of foreign affairs had doubled since the mid 1880s, when compared with coverage of domestic news.[70] Consequently, assessments of other states became at once more immediate and more disparate, influenced by a constant flow of new evidence and statistics, self-representations in the presses of this or that country, and existing sets of images of other nations in Germany itself, as well as by the pressures of domestic politics and the imperatives of identity construction. In this context, agreement among Wilhelmine observers about the failure or decline of neighboring European states, especially France, was far from inevitable, relying on a precarious negotiation between established prejudices, national aspirations, cultural insecurities, foreign opinion, and accepted facts.

The perceived failure of the French and, to a lesser degree, British states helped to muffle, but not to silence, calls for the complete replacement of the Wilhelmine regime. In turn, this had an impact on the cause of reform more generally, since separate questions—against the background of constitutional crisis and a debate about the nation—were frequently portrayed, in the phrase of one observer, as "episodes" in a single, overarching "struggle."[71] The absence of a viable foreign alternative to the *Kaiserreich* served not to preclude questions of reform but rather to inhibit any thoroughgoing solutions that seemed to threaten the integrity of an increasingly well-defined regime. Such use of "news from abroad" did not prevent a crisis of the German state before World War I. It did, however, help to ensure that neither comprehensive reform nor a major upheaval resulted from that crisis.

Notes

1. Friedrich Naumann, *Demokratie und Kaisertum*, 3rd ed. (Berlin, 1905), 150, 166.
2. The argument here supplements those put forward in Mark Hewitson, *National Identity and Political Thought in Germany* (Oxford, 2000); idem, "The *Kaiserreich* in Question: Constitutional Crisis in Germany before the First World War," *Journal of Modern History* 73 (2001): 725-80; idem, "German Public Opinion and the Question of Industrial Modernity: Wilhelmine Depictions of the French Economy," *European Review of History* 7 (2000); and idem, "*Nation* and *Nationalismus*: Representation and National Identity in Imperial Germany," in *Representing the German Nation*, ed. Mary Fulbrook and Martin Swales (Manchester, 2000), 19-62.
3. Cited in Wolfgang J. Mommsen, *Max Weber and German Politics, 1890-1920* (Chicago, 1984), 142, 145, 148. Emphasis in the original.
4. Cited in Dieter Krüger, *Nationalökonomen im wilhelminischen Deutschland* (Göttingen, 1983), 78.
5. Friedrich Naumann, "Die Umwandlung der deutschen Reichsverfassung," *Patria* (1908): 84.

6. See Hans-Ulrich Wehler, *Deutsche Gesellschaftsgeschichte*, vol. 3, *1849-1914* (Munich, 1995), and Dieter Langewiesche, *Nation, Nationalismus, Nationalstaat in Deutschland und Europa* (Munich, 2000), for further literature.

7. *Simplicissimus* 10 (23 May 1905).

8. Mechthild Keller, ed., *Russen und Russland aus deutscher Sicht* (Munich, 2000).

9. Georg Jellinek, *Allgemeine Staatslehre*, 3rd ed. (Berlin, 1914), 732-35; Max Weber in *Gesamtausgabe*, ed. Horst Baier et al. (Tübingen, 1990), vol. 5, 693-98. Hermann Wellenreuther, ed., *German and American Constitutional Thought* (New York, 1990).

10. Andreas Etges, *Wirtschaftsnationalismus* (Frankfurt, 1999).

11. Dan Diner, *America in the Eyes of the Germans* (Princeton, 1996); Hans-Jürgen Schröder, ed., *Confrontation and Cooperation: Germany and the United States in the Era of World War I* (Oxford, 1993).

12. Cited in Schröder, *Confrontation*, 113. David E. Barclay and Elisabeth Glaser-Schmidt, eds., *Transatlantic Images and Perceptions: Germany and America since 1776* (Cambridge, 1997).

13. Mommsen, *Max Weber*, 109-10; Wilhelm Roscher, *Politik* (Stuttgart, 1892), 439-53.

14. Heinrich von Treitschke, *Politik*, vol. 2 (Leipzig, 1898), 276, 278-81.

15. Schröder, *Confrontation*, 80-81; Robert Weiner, *Das Amerikabild von Karl Marx* (Bonn, 1982).

16. Hewitson, *National Identity*, 9-10.

17. Rudolf von Gneist, *Der Rechtsstaat und die Verwaltungsgerichte in Deutschland*, 3rd ed. (Darmstadt, 1966), 38-64.

18. Friedrich Naumann, "Das Königtum," *Hilfe* 15 (10 Jan. 1910): 15.

19. Wilhelm Hasbach, "Parlamentarismus," *Zukunft* 68 (10 Sept. 1909): 403.

20. Paul M. Kennedy, *The Rise of the Anglo-German Antagonism* (London, 1980), 291-93.

21. Otto Hintze, cited in W. Schenk, *Die deutsch-englische Rivalität* (Aarau, 1967), 77.

22. Adolph Wagner, cited in Kennedy, *Anglo-German Antagonism*, 310.

23. Heinrich von Treitschke, cited in Charles E. McLelland, *The German Historians and England* (Cambridge, 1971), 168, 184.

24. Otto Hintze, "Das monarchische Prinzip und die konstitutionelle Verfassung" (1911), in *Staat und Verfassung*, ed. Gerhard Oestreich, 2nd rev. ed. (Göttingen, 1962), 364-65.

25. Hasbach, "Parlamentarismus," 403.

26. Karl Leuthner, "Parlament und Demokratie," *Sozialistische Monatshefte* 16 (2 June 1910): 683.

27. Friedrich Naumann, *Verhandlungen des Reichstags* (3 Dec. 1908), vol. 233, 5945-49.

28. Hewitson, *National Identity*, 8-11.

29. Gustav Cohn, *Grundlegung der Nationalökonomie*, vol. 1 (Stuttgart, 1885), 447-49.

30. Oskar A. H. Schmitz, *Das Land der Wirklichkeit*, 5th ed. (Munich, 1914), 43-44.

31. See Hewitson, *National Identity*, 178-82, 199-200, 207-12.

32. Werner Sombart, *Sozialismus und soziale Bewegung im 19. Jahrhundert* (Jena, 1896); Gustav von Schmoller, "Demokratie und soziale Zukunft," *Soziale Praxis* 22 (7 Nov. 1912): 145-51.

33. Friedrich Naumann, *Demokratie und Kaisertum*, 4th rev. ed. (Berlin, 1905), 42, 54.

34. Hintze, "Das monarchische Prinzip," 360-77.

35. Richard Sternfeld, *Französische Geschichte*, 2nd ed. (Leipzig, 1908): 188-89.

36. *Dresdner Nachrichten* (23 Apr. 1910). Emphasis in the original.

37. *Vossische Zeitung* (7 Apr. 1909).

38. Hans Delbrück, *Regierung und Volkswille* (Berlin, 1914), 59, 66.

39. See Hewitson, *National Identity*, 66-212.

40. Hasbach, "Parlamentarismus," 403.

41. On Rochette alone, see, for example, *Vossische Zeitung* (14 Mar. 1914), *Freisinnige Zeitung* (12 July 1914), *Kölnische Zeitung* (13 July 1914), *Vorwärts* (12 July 1914), *Neue Preussische Zeitung* (21-22, 24-25, 28 Mar, 2 Apr. 1914), *Deutsche Tageszeitung* (1 Apr. 1914), *Fränkische Volksfreund* (26 Mar. 1914), *Germania* (28 Mar. and 2 Apr. 1914).

42. *Germania* (28 Mar. 1908).

43. *Neue Preussische Zeitung* (12 Sept. 1906). Richard Mahrenholtz, *Frankreich* (Leipzig, 1897), 311-12, gave a figure of 350,000.

44. *Hannoverscher Courier* (24 Sept. 1907).
45. Otto Hintze, "Der Beamtenstand" (1911), in *Soziologie und Geschichte*, ed. Gerhard Oestreich, 2nd rev. ed. (Göttingen, 1962), 68-70, 121. Max Weber, *Wirtschaft und Gesellschaft*, 5th ed. (Tübingen, 1972), 541-868.
46. Martin Spahn, "Was ist Demokratie?" *Hochland* 11 (1913): 78-79, 83; idem, *Der Kampf um die Schule in Frankreich und Deutschland* (Kempten and Munich, 1907). Gustav von Schmoller, "Demokratie und soziale Zukunft," *Soziale Praxis*, 22 (n.d.), no. 6: 145-51; idem, *Skizze einer Finanzgeschichte* (Leipzig, 1909).
47. Schmoller, *Skizze*, 19.
48. Karl E. Schmidt, *Im Lande der Freiheit, Gleichheit und Brüderlichkeit* (Berlin, 1908), 119, 125, 24-25, 42-44, 47-49, 73-75.
49. Ibid., 119, 125.
50. Ibid., 119.
51. Ibid., 119, 125.
52. Hewitson, *National Identity*, 202-12.
53. Julius Meier-Graefe in *Zukunft* 8 (9 June 1900).
54. See, for example, *Hamburger Nachrichten* (26 Sept. 1899); *Tag* (3 Dec. 1913); *Magdeburgischer Zeitung* (22 June 1914); *Frankfurter Zeitung* (22 June 1901); *National-Zeitung* (29 Mar. 1904); *Germania* (10 July 1906).
55. *Münchner Neueste Nachrichten* (15 Sept. 1902).
56. *Vossische Zeitung* (23 Feb. 1914).
57. *Berliner Neueste Nachrichten* (20 Aug. 1900).
58. Käthe Schirmacher, *Deutschland und Frankreich seit 35 Jahren* (Berlin, 1906), 23. Mark Hewitson, "Images of the Enemy: German Depictions of the French Military, 1890-1914" (forthcoming).
59. *Berliner Tageblatt* (26 June 1907).
60. *Freisinnige Zeitung* (27 June 1907).
61. Hintze, "Das Monarchische Prinzip," 377.
62. *Neue Preußische Zeitung* (1 Dec. 1898).
63. Hewitson, *National Identity*, 182-212; Ernst-Otto Czempiel, *Das deutsche Dreyfus-Geheimnis* (Munich, 1966); Gerd Krumeich, "Die Resonanz der Dreyfus-Affäre im Deutschen Reich," in *Intellektuelle im Deutschen Kaiserreich*, ed. Gangolf Hubinger and Wolfgang J. Mommsen (Frankfurt a.M., 1993), 13-32.
64. Schirmacher, *Deutschland und Frankreich*, 81.
65. Gerd Krumeich, "La puissance militaire française vue de l'Allemagne autour de 1900," in *La puissance française à la belle époque*, ed. Pierre Milza and Raymond Poidevin (Brussels, 1992), 199-210.
66. See, above all, Dieter Grosser, *Vom monarchischen Konstitutionalismus zur parlamentarischen Demokratie* (The Hague, 1970).
67. David Beetham, *Max Weber and the Theory of Modern Politics*, 2nd ed. (Oxford, 1985), 134.
68. Naumann, "Das Königtum," *Hilfe* 15 (10-24 Jan. 1910): 15-18, 31-33, 48-50.
69. Wilfried Loth, *Katholiken im Kaiserreich* (Düsseldorf, 1984), 146.
70. Paul Stocklossa, "Der Inhalt der Zeitung," *Zeitschrift für die gesamte Staatswissenschaft* 66 (1910): 555-65.
71. Anonymous, "Gedanken über Parlamentarismus in Deutschland," *Deutsche Revue* 35 (July 1910): 2.

Lebensreform
A Middle-Class Antidote to Wilhelminism?

⇒•◊•⇐

MATTHEW JEFFERIES

Introduction

As a scholarly term "Wilhelminism" leaves much to be desired. Its meaning is vague; its usage, inconsistent. Nevertheless, its regular appearance in recent works of political and cultural history would seem to indicate that many find it indispensable. Two principal uses stand out. It is often employed to denote the apparent congruence between Wilhelm II as an individual and the age to which he gave his name. In this reading, which is usually to be found in works of cultural history, Wilhelminism stands for operatic gesture and sentimental yearning, for pomp and pathos, for "romantic modernity" and "nervous idealism."[1] However, as the title of the present volume suggests, it is also used more broadly to highlight the distinctive configuration of social, economic, and political developments after 1890, which together marked out a specific Wilhelmine era within the wider history of Imperial Germany. In either usage, the concept of Wilhelminism has its dangers, and any attempt to subsume such a complex and contradictory period under a single heading clearly runs the risk of cliché and generalization. Few, for instance, would agree with Nicolaus Sombart's bold assertion that "for all the variety, clash and confusion of Wilhelmine Germany, the era was also exceptionally unified in its physiognomy, in its style, in the variety of its expressions, as are few periods in history."[2]

On first impression, the main focus of this essay—the movement for the "reform of life" (*Lebensreformbewegung*) in Imperial Germany—would appear to highlight the shortcomings of the Wilhelminism paradigm all too well. Here was a substantial body of men and women, predominantly Protestant and *bürgerlich* in background, who explicitly rejected the aesthetic values, authoritarian rituals, and "hurrah patrio-

---

tism" of the *Kaiserreich*'s official culture; who favored a simple, more honest life of "self-control, moderation, simplicity in everything one does, in short inner freedom" (Gustav Struve);[3] and who attacked vulgar display and ostentation wherever they could find it. Indeed, their rhetoric suggested that nothing less than a fundamental reorientation of Wilhelmine values was required, if a healthy equilibrium was to be restored to society. Despite this, most historical treatments of *Lebensreform* have tended to see it as a symptom of Wilhelminism, rather than a cure. Critics, then and now, have been quick to dismiss the *Lebensreform* agenda for being too preoccupied with the individual at the expense of the societal, for failing to address the root causes of society's ills, and for seeking aesthetic answers to political problems.[4] The *Lebensreformer* are usually portrayed as sharing many of the pious dreams and prejudices of their age (and of their Kaiser), and as offering uncomfortable lines of continuity to the twentieth century's most infamous *Lebensreformer*, Adolf Hitler.[5]

In recent years, however, a more sensitive and nuanced approach to *Lebensreform* has begun to emerge, as part of an important reassessment of turn-of-the-century reform movements as a whole.[6] This historiographical development can be viewed in a wider context. The collapse of the Soviet model, and growing unease about the social and ecological costs of globalization, have led many to seek more sustainable and ethical patterns of life that may not pose a serious threat to capitalism's worldwide preeminence but might help to ameliorate its worst effects. Environmentalism, vegetarianism, animal rights, homeopathy, and countless health fads—not to mention forms of "new age" spirituality—have experienced a surge in popularity, as have locally grown organic foods. It is no longer so easy to caricature the Wilhelmine *Lebensreformer* as "casualties" of modernization or "enemies of progress," when such ideas are anchored in today's social and political mainstream.

In 1902 the eugenicist Heinrich Driesmans wrote: 'Innumerable are those who seek to reform our circumstances. Reform is the catchword of our age'.[7] Three-quarters of a century later, the historian Thomas Nipperdey concurred: "Wilhelmine society was a society of reform movements and of reforms."[8] Even so, comprehensive studies of the reform milieu—Diethart Kerbs's and Jürgen Reulecke's excellent *Handbuch der deutschen Reformbewegungen* notwithstanding[9]—remain comparatively rare.[10] One reason for this is undoubtedly the bewildering variety and diversity of causes that came together under this broad banner. Historians have generally preferred to focus on individual organizations or specific areas of reform—diet, medicine, clothing, cremation, religion, education, sexuality, ecology, conservation, animal rights, land ownership, architecture, and town planning—rather than undertake the much more difficult task of overall synthesis and interpretation. Moreover, among those who have attempted the broad overview, there is little consensus as to which of the various reformist strands actually belonged under the common umbrella—just as all efforts to create a single *Lebensreform* organization in Wilhelmine Germany ended in abject failure. What we are left with, then, is a host of autonomous leagues (*Bünde*), each with their own recipe for personal and social renewal.

Even so, a number of common characteristics can be identified. The reform leagues founded in the decades either side of 1900 were composed predominantly, but not solely, of urban, middle-class Germans from Protestant communities. They had more members in the north than in the south of the Empire, with particular strongholds in Dresden, Leipzig, Jena, and, above all, Berlin. Their leaders were often hailed as prophets, and their discourse could exude a fervent religiosity. They were pained by the excesses of capitalism, but firmly rejected Marxism, too. Under the influence of cultural pessimism and the late-nineteenth-century reaction against materialism, positivism, and historicism, the reform leagues therefore favored an elusive "third way" between capitalism and communism, or, in the words of the land reformer Adolf Damaschke: "Not Mammonism and not Communism, but instead social justice and personal freedom!"[11] In practice, this could mean anything from a broadly progressive German Fabianism[12] to a *völkisch* protofascism, but always with a pronounced tendency to seek individual, aesthetic, or cultural answers to what were essentially social, economic, or political questions. This does not mean, however, that the reformers can be dismissed as politically irrelevant. As Nipperdey noted: "Revolutions and reforms began in the sciences, in the arts, in lifestyles, rather than in politics. But politics was not left untouched."[13]

The Evolution of the Movement

The politics of *Lebensreform*, its attitude to modernity, and its relationship to Wilhelminism are all aspects worthy of further exploration. This chapter must begin, however, by outlining the evolution of the movement, focusing in particular on the years around 1900. It is generally agreed that the origins of *Lebensreform* lay in the numerous closely related strategies for self-improvement that emerged in Europe during the nineteenth century: abstinence, dietary reform, vegetarianism, natural health, and homeopathy. The reformers therefore began with the idea of reforming society through the individual, and as such reflected the enduring influence of both the Reformation and of German idealism, with its notion of the perfectibility of the individual through self-cultivation (*Bildung*). As one Wilhelmine reformer, Friedrich Landmann, put it: "Lifestyle reform is above all reform of the self; it has to begin with one's own body and in one's own home."[14]

In the particular German context, this is often portrayed as an acknowledgment of the difficulties of achieving reform through the political system, and as part of the *Bürgertum*'s withdrawal into the personal sphere. The fact that three of 1848's failed revolutionaries—Gustav Struve, Eduard Baltzer, and the composer Richard Wagner—were later all prominent advocates of vegetarianism would seem to lend weight to this case. This should not blind one to the fact, however, that the pioneers of modern vegetarianism and natural health came from a wide variety of national backgrounds. The ascetic Russian Leo Tolstoy and the British ethical socialist Edward Carpenter[15] were just as much role models for German reformers as Wagner, and key impulses came from France and Switzerland, too. The latter, for instance, produced the "sun doctor," Arnold Rikli, and Max Bircher-Benner, the inventor of muesli. In any case, since the Wilhelmine reformers ultimately went well beyond the sphere of the individual, the "retreat of the *Bürgertum*" argument should not be pursued too far.

In 1867 Baltzer had established a vegetarian association and journal; a year later, the first conference of German vegetarians took place in Nordhausen, Baltzer's hometown. Wagner wrote a famous pro-vegetarian tract and dined at one of Europe's first vegetarian restaurants, allegedly established in Bayreuth in 1871.[16] He also spoke in support of the anti-vivisection cause—vegetarians and natural health activists were often involved in the campaigns against the "twin evils" of vaccination and vivisection[17]—and posthumously became something of a role model for the Wilhelmine reformers (especially since his hero Tannhäuser wore sandals). In fact, by twenty-first-century standards, Wagner was no vegetarian, but paradoxically, a strictly meat-free diet was seldom the priority for early vegetarians. What was most important was the ability to lead—and display—a self-disciplined and ethical lifestyle, in which the intake of meat, coffee, alcohol, and tobacco were all subject to self-control.[18]

Such symbols of luxury and excess, which were often beyond the means of the poor, were seen to exacerbate divisions in society. Vegetarianism was therefore promoted as a means of achieving social integration and of solving the *soziale Frage*, correctly identified by Struve, Baltzer, and Hahn as the central issue of the day.[19] However, since most converts to vegetarianism came from the upwardly mobile new *Mittelstand*, they may also have adopted that lifestyle specifically to strengthen their own fragile class identity. As Eva Barlösius notes, the reformist way of life, with its emphasis on self-cultivation and its disdain for base materialism, offered an "off-the-peg" middle-class identity to people whose income was often perilously close to proletarian levels.[20]

Early German *Lebensreformer*—the term itself did not appear until the 1890s—also included the poet Johannes Guttzeit, who combined his vegetarian diet with a wardrobe of simple peasant clothes, and who in 1884 founded one of the first lifestyle reform leagues; Gustav Jäger, who propagated all-woolen clothing as a way to better health; Sebastian Kneipp, the Catholic priest whose herbal water cures are still on sale today; and Adolf Just, who chose to spend several years living in a wooden hut near Brunswick. Just, who also authored the influential tract *Turn Back To Nature!* (1896), founded the natural health spa "Jungborn" in the Harz Mountains, one of many establishments offering "sunlight and fresh air" cures, which, despite the much-touted achievements of scientific medicine, sprang up across Central Europe during the second half of the nineteenth century.

More than a decade earlier, Carl Braun, a keen supporter of homeopathy, had opened in 1887 a shop and mail-order business supplying organic food and vegetable oil to the middle classes of Berlin. This was in many ways the prototype *Reformhaus*, although that name did not come into use until the businessman Karl August Heynen opened the Reformhaus Jungbrunnen in Wuppertal in 1900. By 1925 there were about two hundred *Reformhäuser* in Germany and they remain a familiar sight in German cities today. In 1893 the vegetarian restaurant Ceres in Berlin was the venue for the founding of the Vegetarische Obstbau-Kolonie Eden at Oranienburg.[21] This large-scale orchard and market garden enterprise was set up on a cooperative basis: the Eden logo featured three trees, standing for lifestyle reform, land reform, and social reform. To discourage property speculation, all of Eden's 440 hectares were held in common ownership. Individual growers leased their plots and houses from the colony, and their produce was packaged and marketed collectively. The settlers and their families were expected to lead healthy lifestyles: the sale or serving of alcohol and tobacco was banned, as were gaming halls, brothels and betting shops.

In May 1901 one of the Eden settlers, Karl Mann, opened Berlin's first "sunlight and fresh air sport baths," offering lawn tennis, sand baths, and a massage room. Mann, who also published the "body beautiful" journal *Kraft und Schönheit*, was convinced of the health benefits of nakedness, but stressed its moral value too. It would, he argued, combat hypocrisy and prudery, and reduce the need for pornography and prostitution. The police were not fully convinced, however, and refused to allow permission for a "ladies section" on the site. At around the same time, naked bathing became popular in secluded spots on the North Sea and Baltic coasts, and authors like Heinrich Pudor and Richard Ungewitter began to celebrate a new "naked culture" (*Nacktkultur*) in numerous papers and pamphlets. These stressed the aesthetic as well as health benefits of nudity, but also explored notions of "racial hygiene" and purity: Ungewitter's Loge für aufsteigendes Leben (1910) was a particularly unpleasant forum for such ideas. A more erotic charge was carried by the journal *Die Schönheit*, published by Karl Vanselow from 1903 to 1932, which was shunned by many naturists as "pornographic." Undeterred, Vanselow set up the "Garden of Beauty" at Werder on the Havel and staged "Beauty Evenings" at which his future wife, the London-born Olga Desmond, performed naked dances. However, like all early naturist societies, Vanselow's enterprises suffered from a gender imbalance: there were too many men and simply not enough women.[22]

The distinction of being Imperial Germany's best-known naturist, however, probably belongs jointly to the Munich painter Karl Wilhelm Diefenbach and his loyal disciple "Fidus."[23] After many years of ill health, the longhaired Diefenbach had become a virtual hermit in a tumbledown cottage at Höllriegelskreuth in Bavaria. Here he experimented with a variety of alternative treatments, including a vegetarian diet and prolonged spells of nudity, and was dubbed by skeptical locals the "kohlrabi apostle." In 1887 he was visited by a young art student, Hugo Höppener, who had gone to study at the Munich Academy. Höppener, who had also endured a youth scarred by illness and had benefited little from conventional medicine, was persuaded to abandon Jäger's "wool cure" and live the Diefenbach way instead. In November 1888, however, the two men were observed walking naked near Diefenbach's house, and were charged with immoral behavior. Diefenbach was sentenced to six months, and his young follower, whom Diefenbach christened "Fidus," to three months.[24] The court case gave the painter and his young disciple cult status in avant-garde circles. Indeed, Fidus went on to become one of Wilhelmine Germany's best-known

lifestyle reformers, whose rather fey illustrations of naked androgynous youths and
Jugendstil angels were to adorn numerous reformist tracts, and some important literary works as well. First painted in 1890, his most famous work, the *Lichtgebet*—
which depicts a naked blonde-haired figure with upstretched arms, as if in communion
with the sun—was repeated in eight different versions over the following decades, one
of which is said to have ended up on the wall of Martin Bormann's Munich apart-
ment during World War II.

The popularity of the *Lichtgebet* motif—reproduced as a postcard, it became an
icon of the German youth movement—reflects the importance with which Wilhelmine
reformers regarded the sun and its rays as a metaphor for life and health. In fact, while
the notion of a "place in the sun" is generally associated with the Empire's colonial
aspirations, it was an equally important preoccupation among domestic reformers,
and featured prominently in the art and literature of the time. For the poet Otto Ernst,
sunshine was the "last human happiness";[25] while Cäsar Flaischlen proclaimed
'Have sun in your heart!' in a collection of poems entitled *Of Everyday Life and the
Sun* (1898); and another poet, Georg Heym, wrote in his diary in 1906: "I find
myself believing more and more firmly in Helios, in the light, the sun, the holiness of
the whole natural order."[26] The naturist organization Freyabund (1908) called its
journal *Der Lichtfreund*, while the lifestyle bible *House in the Sun* (1895), by the
Swedish artist-designer Carl Larsson, was also immensely popular in Germany, as
people attempted to break free from the gloomy interiors of the *Gründerzeit*. Inspired
by the same notion, reformist architects such as Walter Gropius propagated what
became known as the glass "curtain-wall," flooding factories, department stores, and
schools with "healthy" sunlight.

In some cases, the Wilhelmine sun worship took on a cultic and pseudoreligious
character. The midsummer solstice, for instance, was once again celebrated as a
major festival, with bonfires and parties across Central Germany sponsored by the
Lebensreform publisher Eugen Diederichs and his Sera Circle.'[27] Fidus, who was
introduced to the occult and theosophical ideas by Wilhelm Hübbe-Schleiden in the
1890s, produced many plans for temples and stone circles. The purpose of these fantasy structures, with their eclectic mix of Egyptian, Indian, and prehistoric forms, was
never spelled out and none were built, even though Fidus was always prepared to
adapt them to the demands of the time. In the 1890s, for instance, they stood for the
"regeneration of mankind" and the "sacred spring" of *Jugendstil*; in the 1910s he
offered them to Rudolf Steiner and the anthroposophists; and by the 1940s he was
still trying to get them accepted as crematoria for fallen Nazi heroes. One is reminded
of Heinrich Hart's retrospective observation on his fellow Wilhelmine reformers:
"The object of our longing was unclear, as is all springtime longing (*Frühlingssehn-
sucht*), but it was in a sense of spring that we lived and worked."[28]

Of course, not all *Lebensreformer* were prepared to eschew clothing altogether.
Some, inspired by the nineteenth-century natural health campaigners, such as the
aforementioned Gustav Jäger and Heinrich Lahmann, founder of the 'Weisser
Hirsch' sanatorium in Dresden and author of *The Reform of Clothing* (1889), merely

sought a better kind of clothing. Early clothing reform publications, aimed predominantly at men, polemicized against the stand-up collar, the frock coat, and the top hat. In the 1890s, however, the focus shifted toward female dress. Here, the demand was for dresses without stays and the abolition of the corset, which not only restricted movement and made breathing difficult, but could even damage internal organs. The medical discourse against the corset was given a *völkisch* spin in publications like Paul Schultze-Naumburg's *The Culture of the Female Body as a Basis for Women's Clothing* (1901) and Heinrich Pudor's *Reform Clothing* (1903), which claimed that the fertility of the German race was being threatened by the disfiguring dictates of French fashion houses. The women's movement also addressed the issue of crinolines and the corset. At the International Congress of Women's Organizations in Berlin (1896), there were several debates on clothing issues, resulting in the establishment of the General Association for an Improvement in Women's Clothing later that year and an exhibition in Berlin attracted over eight thousand visitors in 1897.

The first "reform dresses" were coarse and unshapely (*Reformsäcke*), but around 1900 a number of *Jugendstil* artists began to develop their own designer dresses. Fidus, Paul Schultze-Naumburg, Henry van de Velde, and Peter Behrens all came up with designs, many of which went on show at Krefeld in 1900.[29] Van de Velde's wife, Maria Sethe, wrote a preface for the exhibition catalogue and modeled many of the dresses herself. Curiously, the wife of another leading architectural reformer of the time, Hermann Muthesius's wife Anna, was also prominent in the dress reform movement. Indeed, the links between the reform movements in architecture and clothing at the turn of the century—both stressed the importance of hygiene, functional "honesty," sobriety, and material quality—represent a fascinating and largely unexplored chapter in the history of early German modernism.

The General Association split in 1903, but one of its successors—the Free Union for an Improvement in Women's Clothing—soon had over three thousand members in twenty branches and its own journal. Further splits followed,[30] but the simple linen or cotton reform dress gained steadily in popularity, especially among the first female professionals, the wives of vicars and professors, and bourgeois women's rights activists such as Gertrud Bäumer. In the 1900s, under the influence of the youthful hiking societies (*Wandervogel*), a distinctive "alternative look" also became well established amongst reform-minded German males. It involved sandals, long woolen socks, cotton knee breeches or *Lederhosen*, and loose tunics or nightshirts, often worn with a neckerchief. At the youth movement's famous 1913 gathering on the Hohe Meissner near Kassel, one of the organizers, Christian Schneehagen, distributed copies of a pamphlet that suggested that the new partnership between the sexes also required a common approach to questions of clothing. In fact, it was already apparent that, even without official coordination, the dress of male and female hikers was becoming steadily more similar.

A focal point for all kinds of *Lebensreform* activity was Friedrichshagen, the small town on the banks of the Müggelsee southeast of Berlin, which had become home to a colorful collection of literary and political "refugees" in the 1890s—people seeking

an alternative lifestyle, but one that was within easy reach of the comforts and attrac-
tions of modern urban civilization. Here they led comfortable middle-class lives, even
if their naturalist works were often critical of just such circumstances. The émigrés
from inner-city Berlin included Heinrich Hart, who published six editions of the
short-lived but influential literary journal *Kritische Waffengänge* with his brother
Julius; Wilhelm Bölsche, editor of the *Freie Bühne* and a self-styled scientist who
helped to popularize Darwin and the study of nature by lecturing to workers' groups
and writing books; Bruno Wille, a poet, preacher, and utopian anarchist; and the
three Kampffmeyer brothers, who were later to play leading roles in the German Garden City Association and who were the first to settle in Friedrichshagen after inher-
iting a villa in the town. These core members were joined from time to time by friends
and associates such as the dramatist Gerhart Hauptmann, who lived in the nearby village of Erkner and who parodied the Friedrichshagen circle in his 1890 play *Einsame
Menschen*; the anarchist writers Gustav Landauer and Erich Mühsam; the ubiqui-
tous Fidus; the Swedish dramatist August Strindberg; and the monocled but penni-
less cultural pessimist Arthur Moeller-Bruck.[31] The "Müggelsee Republic," as
Friedrichshagen was dubbed, also attracted political activists with no literary ambitions, such as the SPD Reichstag members Max Schippel and Georg Ledebour, and
the editors of the radical journal *Der Sozialist*.

    Arguably the best known of the many Friedrichshagen enterprises was the Neue
Gemeinschaft (New Community) established by the Hart brothers in 1900. The
New Community began as a loose and informal group meeting in local pubs, but in
1902 it took over a former sanatorium in nearby Schlachtensee. This was to be transformed into an earthly paradise: a place with a "genuinely humanitarian culture,"
offering "a life in the light." Appropriately, the New Community's symbol was a rising sun. The fifty or sixty members, predominantly writers and artists, paid a nomi-
nal monthly subscription. This entitled them to use the accommodations, partake in
communal meals, and to avail themselves of the other facilities, which included a
library, artists' studios, and an outdoor theatre. Within the community they were also
expected to contribute in some way to the provision of meals and accommodations.
The members were encouraged to address each other with the informal *Du*, and to
treat each other as brothers and sisters. The New Community published its own journal; staged lectures, and organized regular excursions and festive events on a variety
of themes. It attracted hundreds of curious visitors. One of them, the painter Paula
Modersohn-Becker, noted after her visit: "There seems to me to be a lot of vanity:
longhaired artists, powder, and excessive corsetlessness [*Korsettlosigkeit*]."[32]

    Julius Hart, the New Community's cofounder, had published an anthology of
poems under the title *Die Insel der Seligen* (The Isle of the Blessed), and the same
title was used by Max Halbe for a comic play loosely based on the New Community
and the wider Wihelmine reform movement. The play was set in a "back to nature"
commune, in which both naturism and Buddhism were practiced zealously, but where
the vegetables failed to grow. The commune ultimately fails because it has "too many
philosophers and insufficient potato-diggers," and the New Community met with

much the same fate. After a dispiriting succession of squabbles, intrigues, and accusations, the undertaking came to an end in 1904. Not only had the members failed to do their share of digging, but also most had taken advantage of the community's facilities without paying. Despite generous donations from well-wishers, the New Community was a financial disaster.

In his autobiography Max Halbe wrote that Friedrichshagen was a state of mind rather than a place.[33] If this was so, then Ascona, a tiny community on the Swiss side of Lake Maggiore, must also be considered as part of the Friedrichshagen mindscape. Ascona offered Wilhelmine reformers a lakeland idyll even more attractive than the Müggelsee, and a much better climate, but in the 1900s its transient population were still recognizably Friedrichshagener. Some, such as Landauer, Mühsam, and Elsa Lasker-Schüler, flitted between the two. For others, such as Henri Oedenkoven and Ida Hofmann, Ascona became a home for some twenty years. Oedenkoven, a wealthy Belgian, and Hofmann established a natural health sanatorium, Monte Verità, near the village in 1900. Their regime was strictly vegetarian and abstinent, with plenty of sun, fresh air and water, together with generous helpings of Wagner's *Parsifal*. At various times it attracted the likes of Hermann Hesse, D. H. Lawrence, Max Weber, and C. G. Jung, as well as a succession of *Naturmenschen*—longhaired, barelegged, sandal-wearing '"seekers after truth"—who passed through the small community, which became the "semi-official meeting place for all Europe's spiritual rebels."[34]

The Wilhelmine period also threw up three or four dozen less famous model communities and colonies, many of which survived well into the 1920s.[35] Some were anarcho-socialist in character, inspired by the likes of Peter Kropotkin, William Morris or Gustav Landauer. Others—such as the Siedlungsgemeinschaft Heimland, established in 1909 by readers of Theodor Fritsch's anti-Semitic *Hammer*; or Willibald Hentschel's Mittgard colony—were openly racist, and refused to allow "non-Aryan" members. There were also, of course, communities based on religion, and several women-only communities. Despite their philosophical differences, however, these undertakings all had much in common. Each sought to reestablish communitarian values in rural locations at a time of rapid social atomization, on the basis of a more natural and self-sufficient lifestyle that embraced organic farming, vegetarianism, naturism, and homeopathy. Each was anti-capitalist and anti-materialist in its rhetoric, stressed youth as a value in itself, and developed a calendar of celebratory rituals. Moreover, the problem of "too many philosophers, insufficient potato-diggers" was common to all such communities, whether left or right.

For many other *Lebensreform* organizations we must return to Friedrichshagen, since as Kevin Repp correctly notes, by "[c]reating more than 13 different associations and circles at the end of the nineteenth century, the Berlin Naturalists... stood near the center of the Wilhelmine reform milieu."[36] Arguably, the most important contribution of the Friedrichshagener to the cause of *Lebensreform* was in helping to shift the movement's focus from the individual to society at large. They played a key role, for instance, in the establishment of both the League of German Land Reformers (Bund Deutscher Bodenreformer, 1898) and the German Garden City Association (Deutsche Gartenstadtgesellschaft, 1902). Although German land reformers drew important inspiration from abroad, their principal motivation came from the crisis on their own doorstep. Reformers argued that the housing crisis in the Empire's cities would not be solved until land ceased to be treated as a speculative commercial commodity. They disagreed, however, on how this was to be achieved. Some, such as Michael Flürscheim, favored the nationalization of all land, and its subsequent leasing back to the highest bidder. Others called for a tax on profits made from land or property sales, which should be reinvested in cooperative housing schemes and in the employment of more housing inspectors. This more moderate course was advocated by the best known of the Wilhelmine land reformers, Adolf Damaschke, who came to land reform from an initial involvement in the abstinence and natural health movements (another indication of the growing willingness of *Lebensreformer* to look beyond the individual to the societal).[37]

Damaschke became a popular figure in reformist circles, not least because his work appeared to give credibility to the notion of a "third way" between capitalism and communism. In a cover design for the land reform movement's journal, Fidus attempted to express this in graphic terms. He depicted a country crossroads with three possible routes. To the right, a path with a signpost marked "capitalism" heads straight to the cliff's edge; to the left, a path marked "communism" follows a long and winding road to some distant hills; only the "third way," that of " reform," heads straight to a sunlit paradise. This uncharacteristically clear statement from the wooly-headed Fidus may have lacked sophistication, but it captured perfectly the essence of the land reform movement's appeal to middle-class Germans.[38]

A consistent feature of the land reform movement's program in the 1900s was its call for the establishment of cooperatively owned "garden cities." The German Garden City Association was founded in the autumn of 1902, with the Harts, the Kampffmeyers, Fidus, Bölsche, and Landauer all signing its first declaration.[39] The visionary literati soon fell by the wayside, however, and the pragmatists took over. Alongside founder member and revisionist Social Democrat Hans Kampffmeyer, a group of progressive architects and town planners soon set the tone in the Garden City Association. Despite much press coverage, however, the association failed to create a "German Letchworth," and Howard's original conception—an economically independent settlement of thirty-two thousand souls, built on a cooperatively owned green field site—was realized nowhere in Germany before 1918. Nevertheless, the garden city activists could draw some consolation from seeing at least some of their ideas put into practice at the model community of Hellerau near Dresden, planned between 1906-8, and built in 1909-12.

The simple but homely architecture to be found in Hellerau was also championed by Wilhelmine Germany's growing army of conservationists and environmental activists organized in the Bund Heimatschutz, which was founded as an umbrella organization for a host of smaller associations in 1904, and which claimed over one hundred thousand individual and affiliated members by 1906.[40] *Heimatschutz* was, of course, just one strand of a broad and disparate *Heimat* movement, which has been the subject of growing historiographical interest in recent years.[41] While it is clear that some of the initial promoters of *Heimatschutz* and *Heimatkunst* (an earthy new German literature and art, rooted in the diversity of regional cultures and dialects) held deeply conservative views, motivated by a blind and undifferentiated hatred of Germany's evolving modern urban culture, one must be careful not to fall into a similar trap by tarring all *Heimat* activists with the same "anti-modern" brush. In fact, as Martin Green points out, it is salutary to compare the reputation of turn-of-the-century German *Heimatkunst* writers with their equivalents in other national contexts.[42] In *Selections from Scrutiny*, for instance, the influential British literary critic F. R. Leavis highlighted the contribution made by unfashionable writers who had celebrated village life and arts, and argued that some in "The English Tradition"—such as the rural romanticist Richard Jefferies—had been important in paving the way for modernism.[43] In Germany, however, writers who worked very similar themes are portrayed as reactionary or even "cryptofascist." As Green puts it: "As we move from the English Department floor to the German Department floor of the language and literature building, we find that these ideas change colour, looking acid in one context, alkali in the other."[44]

The Berlin professor of music Ernst Rudorff, who coined the term *Heimatschutz* in 1897, was undoubtedly a died-in-the-wool reactionary, who had attacked the coming of the railways because it made it more difficult to find stable boys. However, the threat to the natural world posed by industrialization and urbanization was very real, and not all of the solutions pursued by the *Heimatschützer* were escapist or romantic. In any case, once the Bund Heimatschutz had been established, the likes of Rudorff took a back seat and were quickly eclipsed by more pragmatic figures, such as Paul Schultze-Naumburg and Hugo Conwentz. Unlike Rudorff and other nineteenth-century cultural pessimists who could see only decadence and decay on the horizon, Schultze-Naumburg's prewar writing was characterized by a genuine, if rather naive, optimism that his pedagogic efforts could really make a difference.[45] Of course, his attitude to the natural world was aesthetic and sentimental, rather than ecological, and historians have generally viewed this aesthetic approach as the *Heimatschutz* movement's fatal weakness. However, in a recent study William Rollins has argued that "a strongly aesthetic attitude toward the land was in some ways the most radical and effective form that environmentalism in Wilhelmine Germany could take," not least because at the turn of the century scattered scientific findings "stood little chance of overturning the immense cultural consensus in favour of industrial expansionism."[46] For Rollins, aestheticism "constituted a central ground of perception and discussion from which real problems could be addressed."[47] Moreover, since the emotional concept of *Heimat* is a more powerful rhetorical tool than the rather sterile notion of the "ecosystem," even contemporary scientific environmentalists should take note. The latter point may be debatable, but the Wilhelmine *Heimatschützer* are today no longer dismissed as blind reactionaries. It was, after all, largely their achievement that Article 150 of the 1919 Weimar constitution proclaimed: "The monuments of art, history, nature and the landscape enjoy the protection and the care of the state."

Conclusion

This brief survey of *Lebensreform* activity has inevitably left much untouched, but it does illustrate the impressive breadth of reformist concerns and, by implication, the pluralism and diversity of Wilhelmine Germany's bourgeois culture as a whole. It also suggests that while the reformers may have begun with the individual, they did not flinch from addressing fundamental social and political questions, too. A willingness to engage in political activity—lobbying officials, writing pamphlets, organizing public meetings—is not a characteristic frequently associated with the Wilhelmine middle classes, but the reformers did all that and more. Even if relatively few became involved in electoral politics, and fewer still posed a direct challenge to the power structures of the Empire, the stereotype of the apolitical German aesthete, seeking introspection instead of social engagement, is surely in need of revision.

While influence is a notoriously difficult commodity to measure, the frequency with which *Lebensreformer* appeared in the literature of the day gives some indication of their impact. Several examples have already been cited, and one could add to these Arno Holz's entertaining comedy *Sozialaristokraten*, Gerhart Hauptmann's *Der Apostel* (in which the main character was based on Johannes Guttzeit), Emil Strauss's *Riesenspielzeug*, Hermann Hesse's *Doktor Knölges Ende*, and many more. Another way of gauging their influence is to trace the way in which *Lebensreform* became instrumentalized "as an advertising gimmick for commercial enterprises with little interest in social or cultural reform."[48] The word began to appear with remarkable regularity in the advertising pages of Germany's *Illustrierten* after 1900, and continued to do so right through to World War II. Perhaps the best indication of its influence, however, is the way in which so many aspects of Wilhelmine *Lebensreform*—from naturism to the garden city—blossomed in the Weimar Republic.

With this in mind, it may seem surprising that the Wilhelmine reformers have not received a more sympathetic press. It must be acknowledged, however, that their impact was much greater in the "marginal" sphere of culture than in politics, where the illusions and evasions of the reformist discourse were easily and cruelly exposed. Thus, while the reformers' relatively enlightened approach to issues of personal health, diet, and education; their sensitivity to the natural environment; and their concern for habitable cities might win grudging respect, their political naiveté and elitist attitude toward the "masses" count against them. Certainly, their view of the labor movement was patronizing and often disdainful. The reformers were not, of course, solely responsible for the deep divide that existed between Germany's middle and working classes, nor was that divide wholly insurmountable: individual SPD members did work alongside bourgeois reformers in the Garden City Association, the League of German Land Reformers, and the Association for Natural Health Care, to name but three. Nevertheless, the relative lack of cooperation between bourgeois and proletarian *Lebensreformer* undoubtedly lessened the prospects of success.

This was just one of the reform movement's "dark sides" (Geoff Eley) or "dark strands" (Thomas Nipperdey). If the vulgar social Darwinism of much of the *Lebens-*

reform discourse makes for unsettling reading today, then the racial preoccupations of a small—but nevertheless significant—section of the reform milieu seems darker still. It took many forms, from the crude Aryan mysticism and anti-Semitism of the "General German Cultural League" (1906) to the comparatively sober and scientific approach of the Society for Racial Hygiene (1905), which counted Gerhart Hauptmann among its members. Even so, it is important to emphasize that not everyone who sought social or cultural renewal on the basis of the *Volk* ended up in the arms of Hitler. Moreover, just as the progressive and emancipatory energies contained within the *Lebensreform* or *Heimat* movements have often been obscured by the casual application of an "anti-modern" label, so the very real dangers inherent in the "rational" pursuit of scientific solutions are frequently underestimated or ignored. As Eley, Herf, and others have pointed out, there is nothing innately liberal or democratic about technological progress.[49] Indeed, the darkest side of the reform milieu arguably lay in its modernism, rather than its anti-modernism: the fascination with technocratic panaceas—including the new science of eugenics—had far more serious long-term implications than any amount of "back to nature" posturing.

In the increasingly polarized cultural conflicts of the 1920s, prominent Wilhelmine reformers were to be found in both camps: international and *völkisch*, pro- and anti-modernist. In reality, of course, Weimar cultural politics was never a simple clash of polar opposites; indeed, one of the most welcome features of the recent historiography on Wilhelmine reformism has been its desire to move away from a simplistic modern/ anti-modern schema. Both Rohrkrämer and Repp, for instance, have used the phrase "alternative modernity" (or "modernities"), in an attempt to capture the contradictions and ambivalences of Germany's turn-of-the-century reformers. Certainly, the "third way" did not have to lead to the political extremes—many Wilhelmine reformers participated in the founding of the left-liberal DDP in 1918-19— but it often did, whether to the utopian socialism of the Munich *Räterepublik*, or to the mythic *Volksgemeinschaft* of the Third Reich.

One of the most prominent *Lebensreform* figures attracted to National Socialism was Fidus, who joined the Nazi party on 1 May 1932. His illustrations had always promoted a Nordic rather than classical aesthetic of beauty, and his fascination for Germanic runes, myths, and legends was long-standing. But he had also designed the cover of the 1905 May Day supplement of the SPD newspaper *Vorwärts*, and remained a popular figure in the labor movement's youth organizations until after 1918.[50] Fidus met with a predictable fate in the Third Reich. The new masters regarded him as a historic relic, and—Bormann's liking for the *Lichtgebet* notwithstanding—showed little interest in his art. He spent the rest of his days as a rather forlorn figure, living a reclusive life in the Berlin suburbs. However, as Martin Green has noted, "in intellectual history the cranks and the fools are important too,"[51] and Fidus's story does have an interesting postscript. In his diary entry for 28 September 1946, the artist revealed that he had voted for the Christian Democratic Union (CDU) in Berlin's first postwar elections.[52] The newly formed party was launched under the slogan: "The CDU overcomes Capitalism and Marxism."

For the 78-year-old Fidus, the dream of the "third way" had apparently lost none of its seductive power.

Subsequently, of course, the "Third Way" also made a comeback in the Anglo-American political discourse of the late twentieth century, when—as vague and enticing as ever, but now with capital letters—it sought to give capitalism a more human face. Arguably, a more interesting parallel between the 1990s and the 1890s, however, was the way in which the looming prospect of a new century (and, indeed, a new millennium) not only sparked exaggerated hopes and apocalyptic fears once more, but also gave fresh impetus to lifestyle reformers of every description. Despite the momentous changes that had occurred in the intervening century, there were striking similarities in the solutions propounded by the reformers then and now. This leads one to conclude that although there were dimensions to *Lebensreform* that might be described as typically "Wilhelminist"—its attitude toward organized labor and its nationalism, pathos, and aestheticism—there was much more that should be viewed instead as part of a common Western heritage. Like their counterparts elsewhere in late-nineteenth-century Europe, the German *Lebensreformer* were not pursuing a self-serving, escapist dream, but rather wrestling with very real problems. Their solutions to the effects of capitalism—destruction of the natural world, social fragmentation, alienation, and the loss of community—may have been unconvincing, but as we bask in the golden light of a new century, there are precious few grounds for complacency.

Notes

1. Rüdiger vom Bruch, "Kaiser und Bürger. Wilhelminismus als Ausdruck kulturellen Umbruchs um 1900," in *Bürgertum, Adel und Monarchie*, ed. Adolf M. Birke and Lothar Kettenacker (Munich and London, 1989). See also Wolfgang J. Mommsen, "Kultur und Wissenschaft im kulturellen System des Wilhelminismus," in *Kultur und Kulturwissenschaften um 1900*, vol. 2, ed. Gangolf Hübinger, Rüdiger vom Bruch, and Friedrich W. Graf (Stuttgart, 1997).
2. Nicolaus Sombart in *Kaiser Wilhelm II: New Interpretations*, ed. John C. G. Röhl and Nicolaus Sombart (Cambridge, 1982), 287. For a general introduction to Wilhelmine culture, see Matthew Jefferies, *Imperial Culture in Germany, 1871-1918* (Basingstoke, 2003), from which much of the material in this chapter is taken.
3. Eva Barlösius, *Naturgemässe Lebensführung. Zur Geschichte der Lebensreform um die Jahrhundertwende* (Frankfurt and New York, 1997), 56.
4. Wolfgang Krabbe, *Gesellschaftsveränderung durch Lebensreform* (Göttingen, 1974); Janos Frecot, "Die Lebensreformbewegung," in *Das wilhelminische Bildungsbürgertum. Zur Sozialgeschichte seiner Ideen*, ed. Klaus Vondung (Göttingen, 1976); Janos Frecot, Johann F. Geist, and Diethart Kerbs, *Fidus 1868-1948. Zur ästhethischen Praxis bürgerlicher Fluchtbewegungen* (Munich, 1972); and Christoph Conti, *Abschied vom Bürgertum. Alternative Bewegungen in Deutschland von 1890 bis heute* (Reinbek, 1984).

5. For Hitler's alleged vegetarianism, see Ian Kershaw, *Hitler 1889-1936: Hubris* (London, 1998), 261-62; 343-45; also Ernst G. Schenk, *Patient Hitler. Eine medizinische Biographie* (Düsseldorf, 1989); Barlösius, *Naturgemässe Lebensführung*, 14.

6. See Thomas Rohkrämer, *Eine andere Moderne? Zivilisationskritik, Natur und Technik in Deutschland, 1880-1933* (Paderborn, 1999); and Kevin Repp, *Reformers, Critics and the Paths of German Modernity* (Cambridge, Mass., 2000).

7. Quoted by Gerhard Kratzsch in *Ideengeschichte und Kunstwissenschaft*, ed. Ekkehard Mai, Stephan Waetzold, and Gerd Wolandt (Berlin, 1983), 373.

8. Thomas Nipperdey, "War die Wilhelminische Gesellschaft eine Untertanen-Gesellschaft?" in idem, *Nachdenken über die deutsche Geschichte* (Munich, 1986), 178.

9. Diethart Kerbs and Jürgen Reulecke, eds., *Handbuch der deutschen Reformbewegungen 1880-1933* (Wuppertal, 1998).

10. In addition to the titles already cited, see also Karl Rothschuh, *Naturheilkundebewegung – Reformbewegung – Alternativbewegung* (Stuttgart, 1983); and Corona Hepp, *Avantgarde. Moderne Kunst, Kulturkritik und Reformbewegungen nach der Jahrhundertwende* (Munich, 1987).

11. Quoted by Repp, *Reformers, Critics and the Paths of German Modernity*, 100.

12. It is interesting to note that the Fabian Society in Britain evolved out of the Fellowship of the New Life, which had more than just a semantic affinity with German *Lebensreform*.

13. Thomas Nipperdey, *Deutsche Geschichte 1866-1918*, vol. 1 (Munich, 1991), 822.

14. Quoted in Frecot, Geist and Kerbs, *Fidus*, 56.

15. For Carpenter's influence in Germany see Keith Nield, "Edward Carpenter: The Uses of Utopia," in *Prose Studies* 13 (May 1990): 20. Also, Sheila Rowbotham, *Socialism and the New Life: The Personal and Sexual Politics of Edward Carpenter* (London, 1977); and Chushichi Tsuzuki, *Edward Carpenter 1844-1929: Prophet of Human Fellowship* (Cambridge, 1980).

16. Barlösius (*Naturgemässe Lebensfuhrung*, 183) notes that although the Bayreuth restaurant is frequently referred to in the secondary literature, it was not mentioned in contemporary vegetarian publications.

17. See Miriam Zerbel, *Tierschutz im Kaiserreich. Ein Beitrag zur Geschichte des Vereinswesens* (Frankfurt, 1993).

18. Barlösius, *Naturgemässe Lebensführung*, 12.

19. The notion that self-help strategies could solve deep-seated social problems had, of course, a long tradition within nineteenth-century liberal discourse. See Rita Aldenhoff, "Das Selbsthilfemodell als liberale Antwort auf die soziale Frage im 19. Jahrhundert," in *Sozialer Liberalismus*, ed. Karl Holl et al. (Göttingen, 1986).

20. Barlösius, *Naturgemässe Lebensführung*, 169-70.

21. See Judith Baumgartner, *Ernährungsreform - Antwort auf Industrialisierung und Ernährungswandel. Ernährungsreform als Teil der Lebensreformbewegung am Beispiel der Siedlung und des Unternehmens Eden seit 1893* (Frankfurt, 1992).

22. See Michael Grisko, ed., *Freikörperkultur und Lebenswelt. Studien zur Vor- und Frühgeschichte der Freikörperkultur in Deutschland* (Kassel, 1999); *"Wir sind nackt und nennen uns Du". Von Lichtfreunden und Sonnenkämpfern*, ed. Michael Andritzky and Thomas Rautenberg (Giessen, 1989); Rolf Koerber, "Freikörperkultur," in *Handbuch der deutschen Reformbewegungen*, ed. Kerbs and Reulecke, 103-14.

23. See Frecot, Geist, and Kerbs, *Fidus*.

24. A successful appeal meant that they had to serve only a few days.

25. The last line of his poem "Resignation" is "Sonnenschein, du letztes Menschenglück."

26. Quoted by Patrick Bridgwater in *Poet of Expressionist Berlin: The Life and Work of Georg Heym* (London, 1991), 173.

27. See Gangolf Hübinger, *Versammlungsort moderner Geister. Der Eugen-Diederichs-Verlag* (Munich, 1996); also, Erich Viehöfer, *Der Verleger als Organisator. Eugen Diederichs und die bürgerlichen Reformbewegungen der Jahrhundertwende* (Frankfurt, 1988).

28. Quoted by Rolf Kauffeldt and Gertrude Cepl-Kaufmann, *Berlin-Friedrichshagen. Literaturhauptstadt um die Jahrhundertwende* (Munich, 1994), 109.

29. See Karen Ellwanger and Elisabeth Meyer-Renschhausen, "Kleidungsreform," in *Handbuch der deutschen Reformbewegungen*, ed. Kerbs and Reulecke, 87-102. Also, Brigitte Stamm, "Auf dem Weg zum Reformkleid," in *Kunst und Alltag um 1900*, ed. Eckhard Siepmann (Giessen, 1978).
30. See Ellwanger and Meyer-Renschhausen, "Kleidungsreform."
31. Before he aristocratized his name to "Moeller van den Bruck."
32. Quoted by Ulrich Linse, *Zurück o Mensch zur Mutter Erde. Landkommunen in Deutschland 1890-1933* (Munich, 1983), 73.
33. Quoted by Herbert Scherer, *Bürgerlich-oppositionelle Literaten und sozial-demokratische Arbeiterbewegung nach 1890* (Stuttgart, 1974), 27-28.
34. Martin Green, *Mountain of Truth: The Counterculture Begins. Ascona, 1900-1920* (Hanover, N.H., and London, 1986), 3.
35. See Linse, *Zurück o Mensch.*
36. Repp, *Reformers, Critics and the Paths of German Modernity*, 262.
37. For Damaschke, see Repp, *Reformers, Critics and the Paths of German Modernity.*
38. See Elisabeth Meyer-Renschhausen and Hartwig Berger, "Bodenreform," in *Handbuch der deutschen Reformbewegungen*, ed. Kerbs and Reulecke, 265-76.
39. See Kristiana Hartmann, *Die deutsche Gartenstadtbewegung. Kulturpolitik und Gesellschaftsreform* (Munich, 1976); Nicholas Bullock and James Read, *The Movement for Housing Reform in Germany and France, 1840-1914* (Cambridge, 1985); Brian Ladd, *Urban Planning and Civic Order in Germany 1860-1914* (Cambridge, Mass., 1990).
40. See William Rollins, *A Greener Vision of Home: Cultural Politics and Environmental Reform in the German Heimatschutz Movement, 1904-1918* (Ann Arbor, 1997); Matthew Jefferies, *Politics and Culture in Wilhelmine Germany. The Case of Industrial Architecture* (Oxford, 1995).
41. For the *Heimat* movement in general, see Celia Applegate, *A Nation of Provincials: The German Idea of Heimat*; Elizabeth Boa and Rachel Palfreyman, *Heimat—A German Dream: Regional Loyalties and National Identity in German Culture 1890-1990* (Oxford, 2000); Edeltraud Klueting, ed., *Antimodernismus und Reform. Zur Geschichte des deutschen Heimatbewegung* (Darmstadt, 1991).
42. Green, *Mountain of Truth*, 227-30.
43. Cited by Green, *Mountain of Truth*, 230.
44. Green, *Mountain of Truth*, 227.
45. See Norbert Borrmann, *Paul Schultze-Naumburg 1869-1949* (Essen, 1989).
46. Rollins, *A Greener Vision of Home*, 155. There is a rapidly growing body of literature on early German environmentalism, including Franz-Josef Brüggemeier and Thomas Rommelspacher, *Besiegte Natur. Geschichte der Umwelt im 19. und 20. Jahrhundert* (Munich, 1989); Jost Hermand, *Grüne Utopien in Deutschland. Zur Geschichte des ökologischen Bewusstseins* (Frankfurt, 1991); Andreas Knaut, *Zurück zur Natur! Die Wurzeln der Ökologiebewegung* (Greven, 1993). The best introduction in English is Raymond H. Dominick's *The Environmental Movement in Germany: Prophets and Pioneers, 1871-1971* (Bloomington, 1992).
47. Rollins, *A Greener Vision of Home*, 171.
48. Repp, *Reformers, Critics and the Paths of German Modernity*, 256.
49. See Geoff Eley, "German History and the Contradictions of Modernity," in *Society, Culture, and the State in Germany, 1870-1930*, ed. Geoff Eley (Ann Arbor, 1996); Jeffrey Herf, *Reactionary Modernism: Technology, Culture and Politics in Weimar and the Third Reich* (Cambridge, 1984).
50. Frecot, Geist, and Kerbs, *Fidus*, 177.
51. Green, *The Mountain of Truth*, 256.
52. Frecot, Geist, and Kerbs, *Fidus*, 210.

– 6 –

Imperialist Socialism of the Chair
Gustav Schmoller and German Weltpolitik, 1897-1905

ERIK GRIMMER-SOLEM

Introduction

The intense involvement of Wilhelmine academics on behalf of the German navy has always been both fascinating and troubling—fascinating because of the sophisticated organization and broad influence of this activity, and troubling given these policies' undoubted contribution to the rising tide of international tensions before July 1914. The involvement of university teachers as "agitators" for the German high seas fleet has been perceptively investigated.[1] Yet the specific motivations and activities of a leading "Navy professor" and colonial enthusiast, the economist and social reformer Gustav Schmoller, have not been explored, and the dense and fascinating web of domestic and international contacts in which he was enmeshed during this activity has remained obscure. This gap in the historiography is surprising, given that a prominent "socialist of the chair" such as Schmoller would seem an ideal candidate for testing the concept of Wilhelmine "social imperialism."

The historian Eckart Kehr was himself well aware of Schmoller's importance in shaping public opinion on behalf of the fleet. Yet Kehr's analysis of his specific role remained both superficial and ambiguous, in effect asserting that men such as Schmoller had supported the fleet for vague and poorly considered reasons. Schmoller, according to Kehr, had consequently been blinded to the social imperialistic domestic agenda of those classes benefiting from and pressing for the high seas fleet.[2] While Wolfgang Marienfeld warned against interpreting academic involvement on behalf of the fleet as a political tactic or outcome of manipulation,[3] the Kehrite interpretation of social imperialism facilitated by bourgeois apologists such as Schmoller has found a

Notes for this section begin on page 120.

firm place in Hans-Ulrich Wehler's *Deutsche Gesellschaftsgeschichte*, and hence has become something of a permanent fixture in German historiography.[4]

The question that this chapter addresses is whether or not it can be said that Gustav Schmoller acted as cog in the machinery of social imperialism. More specifically, did he directly or indirectly instrumentalize *Weltpolitik* for a domestic social and political agenda, a palliative to ongoing socialist agitation, thereby distracting from the backlog of overdue social and political reforms? Moreover, can it be said that he was manipulated to placate powerful material interests and lend credibility to the existing regime? These are intriguing questions, given that it is beyond dispute that fear of socialist revolution was an important impulse for the social reform activities Schmoller had organized and directed since the early 1870s, the most prominent example being the Verein für Sozialpolitik.[5] Equally, the policy writings and activities of Schmoller before 1895 were focused almost entirely on domestic social policy, in particular, factory legislation, trade unionism, vocational training, social insurance schemes, and agricultural reform.[6] We would therefore come to expect a continuation of these themes in his activities as a German imperialist. Yet, as this essay will demonstrate, this does not turn out to be the case.

The following pages seek to illuminate the specific involvement of Gustav Schmoller in German *Weltpolitik* during the years 1897-1905, when a new German policy of naval power and assertive imperialism took shape. I will argue that Schmoller was not manipulated into becoming a naval and imperial advocate, that there is a remarkably consistent theme of international power politics and economic competition that permeates his *Weltpolitik*, that there is an absence of the themes social reform and social imperialism in his writings and activities in these years, and that his views were consistent with his historical interpretations of mercantilism and his position on the strategic use of trade. Concluding remarks address how we might assess Schmoller's *Weltpolitik* and what this might tell us about German imperialism.

Schmoller and the High Seas Fleet

Schmoller's active involvement on behalf of the German navy began in late July 1897, following a visit from Commander Heeringen of the newly created Information Bureau of the Imperial Naval Office. Heeringen had been sent by Alfred Tirpitz to discuss the longer-term involvement of leading academics on behalf of the expansion of the German fleet. As is known, Tirpitz had a very high estimation of professors and their capacity to influence the *Bürgertum* and had especially added Schmoller's name to Heeringen's list.[7] A letter from Schmoller to his colleague Lujo Brentano in Munich seeking Brentano's involvement for the fleet shortly after the visit from Heeringen shows that Schmoller had already known Tirpitz for some time and was on friendly terms with him. It also indicates that Schmoller hardly needed persuading. This letter and two others sent to him are worth citing at length because of the revealing detail they contain about the motivations for involvement on behalf of expanding the high sees fleet:

Through his deceased father-in-law Siepke I have known Secretary of State Tirpitz since old times. He recently sent Lieutenant Commander von Heeringen to me to discuss how one could, and better than hitherto, awaken in broader circles an understanding not so much for fleet plans as for the German colonies, exports, the significance of international power struggles with England, etc. Since on the whole I am on the same standpoint as he is and also have found in previous conversations with Tirpitz that he has clear and sensible views about our trade policy, etc., I therefore gladly declared my willingness to be helpful, yet I did not conceal that under the current government all efforts to quickly gain something for the fleet would be futile. Cap. v. H agreed completely and repeated his intention with precision: voting in the next budget years is less the aim than constantly producing a change in views about the significance of our external trade, German exports, the colonies, the power questions. Only a permanent change in the whole of public opinion can guarantee us the sort of fleet building [that] is needed and so spread itself over a generation.[8]

As this letter makes clear, from the very beginning, and at least as far back as Schmoller's first discussions with Tirpitz , the matter of the fleet was linked very closely to colonial policy, German exports, and an international power struggle with England. Indeed, these appear very much the ends of any expansion of the fleet (at least, as was presented to Schmoller by Tirpitz and Heeringen) and therefore also seem to be the basis for consensus with Schmoller. The response from Brentano is as interesting as this letter from Schmoller. Brentano was a passionate Anglophile and a left-liberal free trader, yet this did not stop him from lending his assent to Schmoller's request for support:

Every policy that effectively works toward raising our exports is assured my support. For—whether one may view it as a fortune or misfortune—it is nevertheless a fact that Germany is now an industrial state. Since this is how things are, the most important concern is to find sales markets for its products, and particularly the export of its industrial products. On this the sales will now depend, namely, even the domestic sales market of our agricultural products. For our domestic sales market is dependent upon whether we have a solvent working population. The solvency of the industrial working population has replaced the old [saying]: "if the farmer has money, so does everybody." The future of agriculture lies in the purchasing power of our industrial working population, the development of its necessities, the increase of its efficiency, and the adjustment of agricultural production to its needs. Yet the solvency of our working population has as a precondition the development of our exports.

The future of our exports is, however, currently very threatened. The development of the relationship between England and its colonies could become very detrimental to us. Similarly, our senseless bounty policy has given us the American Dingley Bill, whose horrors will likely be felt even sooner. Decades of work of our businesspeople could be endangered by it. Under such conditions it is natural that one looks about for alternatives. To expect this from our colonies would be childish. But in Asia and South America there may still be very much to be had. From this viewpoint, an increase in the German fleet appears justified.[9]

While Brentano was acutely aware of the dangers of a confrontation with Britain arising from an expanded German high seas fleet, he nevertheless felt that a larger navy was justified as a consequence of Germany's growing reliance on exports as an industrial power and, as importantly, the threats he saw to German exports emanating from a possible British imperial preferential tariff and American protectionist legislation. The larger fleet was to seek out and open alternative markets in Asia and South America. Later in this letter, Brentano admitted to Schmoller what a hindrance the southern German Center Party was to any of these plans, mentioning particularly the hostility to trade and exports growing out of the extreme protectionism then current in Bavaria.

Interestingly, very similar themes and justifications were given in a letter Schmoller received from Tirpitz, thanking Schmoller for his willingness to take up the task of popularizing the necessity of a larger fleet as part of Germany's broader international economic interests:

> Since the [18]80s I have been fighting for our fleet to be understood as a function of our maritime interests and to be constructed accordingly. This opinion has finally prevailed. Over the last year in Asia I have once again been able to convince myself of what influence this 'agency' of the German Empire is in the preservation of Germandom abroad and in the assertion of our economic interests, once it is sufficiently powerful and properly handled. I could give you countless reports about this. I have been able to observe the ruthless advance of Pan-Americanism, the tremendous successes of Russia, and the entirely astonishing growth in strength of the British Empire idea from close proximity with alarm. How depressing and alienating by comparison is the effect made by our political situation in general, and the position of our Reichstag majorities on the question of the fleet in particular. Daily detailed reports by telegraph come to Hong Kong on the position of the Reichstag regarding the development of the fleet; such interest and such understanding is compelled for this question by the English in Asia. I may have the pleasure to discuss these things and the economic prospects in Asia over the course of the winter. Since I am known everywhere and have first-rate contacts, a post as admiral is incomparably favorable for gaining a certain overview of these things.[10]

While these letters do not prove anything, they are suggestive about the set of motivations that drove Schmoller and his colleagues to lend their support for an enlarged fleet. There is not much evidence of having been "goaded" by Heeringen and Tirpitz, and little, if any, discussion of social reform, let alone evidence of "social-imperialist imperatives," which is quite surprising, given that Schmoller and Brentano were two of the leading social reformers in Imperial Germany.[11] The focus is squarely on Germany in the international arena, jostling for export markets and spheres of influence vis-à-vis the other powers in a climate of rising protectionism. One also finds an explicit understanding that Germany, as a major industrial power and exporter, would need a larger fleet to protect its interests and that this would mean reducing or challenging British hegemony. In short, there was a clear assertion of German power. Schmoller did not inadvertently wobble into this position as a consequence of illusions entertained about the purpose of the fleet, nor did he take this stand as an extension of his social imperialism. Real and imagined economic interests were linked closely to political and military power interests. In any case, it becomes easier to view the fleet and *Weltpolitik* as projects independent of domestic social reform or social imperialism in Schmoller's case.

The speeches and writings Schmoller subsequently produced on behalf of the navy are remarkably consistent with the picture we get of his motivations from these early letters. Schmoller began writing articles on the theme of German *Weltpolitik* and the role of the German fleet in 1898, contributing to such newspapers and journals as *Die Jugend, Tägliche Rundschau,* and *Die Woche,* and he was solicited for many more.[12] The activities of the "Navy professors" (*Flottenprofessoren*), as well their relationship to Tirpitz via Heeringen in the Information Bureau of the Imperial Naval Office, have been investigated and need not be explored here, but it is worth mentioning that Schmoller recommended one of his students, Ernst Levy von Halle, to direct the research and publishing activities of the Information Bureau.[13] Von Halle was an immensely bright and ambitious young economist whose direct knowledge of American economic conditions had contributed greatly to Schmoller's 1894 Verein für Sozialpolitik investigation of the controversial trust and cartels issue.[14]

An important theme that comes through in this early pro-fleet activity, despite the basis of agreement between Tirpitz, Heeringen, and Schmoller, is the utter inability of either the Imperial Naval Office or the Navy League—an organization comprised mainly of merchants, heavy industry, and banking—to bring under their aegis (let alone control or direct) the activities of the *Flottenprofessoren.* As is known, Schmoller and other academics were invited to join the Navy League in June 1898. They stipulated that they would join only on condition that the composition of its managing board be broadened to include opinions besides those of industrialists.[15] The refusal of the Navy League to meet this condition led Schmoller and his colleagues to organize their own body in November 1899, the Free Union for Naval Lectures (Freie Vereinigung für Flottenvorträge), to organize popular lectures on behalf of the fleet throughout Germany.[16] A loose association of academics, writers, and artists, the Free Union was nevertheless quite a sophisticated and effective pressure group because of the broad range of expertise from which it drew, its apparent disinterestedness and independence, and the academic authority of many of its participants.

The success of individual professors as well as the Free Union in influencing public opinion on behalf of the first two navy bills between 1898 and 1900 meant that the Navy League was initially eclipsed as the organizational locus of fleet advocacy coordinated by the Imperial Naval Office.[17] What is more, Schmoller and his colleagues succeeded in imposing fundamental changes on the Navy League's managing board to include liberals and social reformers. Pressure was put on its secretary, Victor Schweinburg, to resign, and Schmoller played a key role in forcing the resignation of Octavio von Zedlitz-Neukirch.[18] This had much to do with Schmoller's own personal hostility toward Zedlitz, because the latter had subjected Schmoller and other "socialists of the chair" to withering criticism in the debates over university expenditures in the Prussian Diet. Zedlitz, along with the industrialist Karl von Stumm, not only had attacked the commitment to social reform and supposed softness on socialism of Schmoller and other academics, but also had questioned their very competence as scholars.[19] With Zedlitz and Schweinburg gone, the basis for closer cooperation between the Navy League and the professors was finally established, and the Free Union disappeared.

Schmoller's broadening out of the Navy League to include Naumannite liberals and social reformers would suggest that social reform and social imperialism
would be themes in Schmoller's own writings on the navy, yet remarkably this was
not the case. Schmoller's speeches for the Free Union for Naval Lectures were in fact
particularly revealing for how consistently they emphasized the importance of the battle fleet to Germany's international power struggles with the United States, Russia,
and especially, England; the struggle for export markets in a rising climate of protectionism; and the role of the fleet in sustaining and expanding German commercial
and colonial interests.

In his capacity as a member of the Free Union, Schmoller himself crisscrossed
Germany in late 1899 and early 1900 on a lecture tour that generated extensive
German and international press attention.[20] The speech Schmoller gave in Berlin,
Strasbourg, and Hanover was later published in a separate collected volume by the
Free Union under the appropriate title *Handels- und Machtpolitik* (Trade and Power
Politics).[21] In it, Schmoller begins his discussion under the pall of the disappointing
economic upswing of 1894-1900 and the admonition that Germany had better accus-
tom itself to a more difficult international economic climate or else broaden its economic horizons and secure a sufficient economic basis, particularly in light of its
rapidly growing population. With growth of 1 percent yearly, Schmoller projected no
fewer than 104 million souls by 1965, and as many as 208 million by 2135, a demographic expansion that demanded an international outlet, given the European territorial strictures of the Reich. More fearsome than these figures were those he cited of
the French demographer Leroy-Beaulieu, who predicted no fewer than 200 million
Germans by 1999. Interestingly, Schmoller was positively enthusiastic about this
population surplus as it assured Germany's place in the international "*Wasserwan-
derung*" for new settlements, a development that had yet to reach its climax and
would ultimately determine the rank of nations.[22] In light of the vast size of the populations of the three great world empires, growth in the German population to 100-
150 million was "neither a fantasy nor undesired. It should, it will, it must come, if
we want to remain a great and powerful people. And it cannot be accommodated
exclusively in the old homeland. We must have farmer colonies and territories of cultivation that can absorb this surplus. Let us see to it if and by how much we can
increase our home population."[23] There is not much hand wringing here about demographic time bombs and their social implications for Germany.

Equally interesting about this speech is that Schmoller was resigned to the fact
that German agricultural productivity had strict limits and that therefore Germany
would remain a country that imports a substantial portion of its food grains. Unlike
agriculture, however, he noted that industry had no such strictures, encouragingly
mentioning that the latest economic upswing was based much more on a boost in
domestic consumption than on exports of industrial goods. Nevertheless, with rising
population density, exports needed to expand to ensure the importation of foodstuffs,
raw materials, and colonial goods (*Kolonialwaaren*). The fact was, he asserted, that
no large nation could exist and progress without vast imports and exports, without

being interwoven into the world economy, and the threats posed by this dependence on the world market receded to the degree that a state had colonies and naval power. Germany's "impotence on the seas" would therefore have to end. With the stagnation of exports over the last twenty-five years, only the highest degree of technical, intellectual, organizational, and social political progress would lead to export expansion, but only on the basis of a far-sighted trade policy and good trade treaties, so that the production of food and colonial goods, as well as the importation of German industrial goods in the colonies, were secured. All of these things necessitated a larger fleet. Aided by the fleet, colonial development could also retain for Germany the twenty million emigrants projected for the twentieth century.[24]

Schmoller's speech was predicated upon an interpretation of mercantilism that emerged from his historical research on the economic policy of Prussia in the eighteenth century published in the mid 1880s, excerpts of which he had republished in 1898 as "The Mercantile System in its Historical Significance."[25] In it, he had defined mercantilism as a doctrine neither of money nor of trade balances or protectionism, but as "in its innermost core nothing but state building—not simply state building but instead simultaneous state and economy building, state building in the modern sense, which creates out of a political society an economic society."[26] In other words, seventeenth- and eighteenth-century states had created larger consolidated economic units—national economies. Much of the remainder of Schmoller's speech was based upon this insight, one used in refuting those who would believe that trade policy could still be pursued independently of the power politics of states. Only by following the most ruthless piracy, destruction of rival shipping, seizure of colonies, and fraudulent trade treaties, through harsh navigation laws, steep tariffs, and import-export prohibitions, he recalled, had England emerged following the Napoleonic wars with a consolidated economy and an unchallenged international position. This had facilitated the spread of the liberal economic doctrine that became the basis for the long era of peace from 1815 to 1870 that had so benefited Germany, providing the conditions for the humane commercial interaction of states in the modern world economy.[27] This, he reminded, was possible as long as Cobden's ideas held sway and Gladstone led Britain. Had Britain abandoned its fleet and colonies as Cobden and Gladstone had proposed, Schmoller noted, Germany would not have any "*Flottensorgen.*"[28]

Schmoller believed that rising international competition and growing populations after 1870, combined with a new scramble for colonial possessions and protected spheres of influence, demonstrated that international competitive struggles remained power struggles. Britain under Disraeli helped to initiate an era in which prohibitions, tariffs, blockades, search and seizure of shipping, and prohibitions on the use of sea cables and coaling stations had become the order of the day. While announcing in 1876 that Britain was satiated and not an aggressive power, Disraeli had seized Natal, Cyprus, Egypt, and Burma. The territory of Great Britain between 1866 and 1899, Schmoller mentioned, had grown from 12.6 to 27.8 million square kilometers, thirty times that of the German Empire. The United States between 1800 and 1900 grew from over 2 to 9.3, and Russia between 1866 and 1899 from 12.9 to 22.4 million square kilometers. He believed that events over the last generation had created a wholly changed world and a different foundation for international economic relations. In place of a community of equal and peaceful states, three conquering world empires emerged against which all other smaller states paled. Only France and Germany had a position in between these three "conquering and colonizing empires" and the smaller states.[29] And it was in the freest states, Britain and the U.S., that tendencies to conquest, plans for imperialism, and hostility to up-and-coming economic competitors had emerged out of popular sentiment fanned by unscrupulous plutocratic leaders. The conquest by the United States of Cuba and the Philippines and its tendency to seek to exclude the Europeans from North and South American markets, as well as Britain's war against the Boers and its plans to dominate sub-Saharan Africa and bring the British Empire into a closer union to the exclusion of others, all necessarily led to greater conflicts with other states.[30]

In the final sections of his speech, Schmoller asserted that the dangers to Germany's trade and colonies by a "relapse to mercantilism" had long been there and were hardly created by plans for a larger fleet. But Germany, he claimed, did not aspire to a chauvinistic *Weltmachtspolitik*; it did not wish to become a naval and colonial power of the rank of Britain but only to expand its trade and industry, support a growing population, defend its colonies, and acquire a farmer colony somewhere. It was Germany's aim, he asserted, to oppose the exaggerated "robber mercantilism" and division of the earth by the three great world empires. To do so, a larger fleet was needed; the larger fleet would deter attack from these powers and at the same time win over the smaller and medium-sized states of Europe, who by joining into peaceful economic union with Germany could have their own colonies protected. In any case, according to Schmoller, Germany had become too large and powerful, and its competition too uncomfortable to the great world empires, to allow the competitive struggle to be conducted without proper naval armaments.[31]

Some of Schmoller's concluding proposals were not without Pan-German accents, such as his call to establish a large German settler colony in southern Brazil and to forge a customs union with Switzerland, Austria, Scandinavia, and Holland.[32] Closer customs, trade, and colonial ties to Holland were particularly enticing to Schmoller; Germany could gain access to colonial ports, coaling stations, and sea cables in return for guaranteeing Holland's political independence and colonial possessions. More broadly, Schmoller asserted, it was only through a fleet and with treaty ports such as Kiautschou in China that the East Asian and Middle and South American markets, with such promise for the future, could be held open.[33]

We see, then, that Schmoller's speech is noteworthy for the degree to which it remains focused on international economic competition and tensions, particularly on the strategic threats of the new imperialism for Germany, which he saw increasingly squeezed by the United States, Russia, and, especially, Great Britain. Schmoller envisioned Germany as a player in this international big league, and it was implicit, if not always explicit, that he sought to establish Germany as the fourth great world empire. There is no mention of what such *Weltpolitik* would contribute to social reform, nor is there much, if anything, that could be construed as social imperialism. The striking consistency with the themes outlined in the letters between Schmoller, Brentano, and Tirpitz above should be noted once again. Just as importantly, the justifications for *Weltpolitik* and the fleet were neither vague nor had they been quickly cooked up to serve a naval agenda; they were based upon scholarly convictions that had emerged out of research that predated considerably the proposals for the high seas fleet.

Schmoller and the New Mercantilism

The prospect of a protectionist and imperialist United States excluding Europe from North and South American markets as well as a neomercantilist Britain carving up the lion's share of what remained of the earth for itself was, as I have just outlined, a major theme in Schmoller's justifications for a larger fleet. As also suggested, Schmoller's contributions as a scholar of mercantilism undoubtedly played an important role in his assessments of the international situation and his proposals for remedies—in particular, that states had a role to play in securing and consolidating world markets, and that trade was to be seen in strategic terms. This next section will explore the extent to which this logic figured in Schmoller's subsequent writings and activities and their possible lines of influence.

The history of the emergence of heightened international economic tensions over the course of the nineteenth century remained a topic on which Schmoller wrote after the turn of the century, and in these pieces many of the themes that had been mentioned in his historical analysis of mercantilism and his Free Union speech were reiterated.[34] Schmoller described this new era as one in which a synthesis between mercantilism and free trade had been established. Indeed, he even wrote as if such a rebalance between national special interests and an international division of labor had been bound to develop and was therefore quite normal.[35] Schmoller here could speak from authority, as he had himself played a role in both free trade and protectionism, pressing for the free trade treaty between the Zollverein and France in the early 1860s (an act that had ended all prospects for a career in his native Württemberg), as well as participating in the passage of protective tariffs in the late 1870s.[36] Indeed, he had come to occupy a pragmatic middle ground in between doctrinaire free trade and ruthless mercantilism, justifying moderate protective tariffs for agriculture on the grounds of preserving and modernizing German farming in the face of fierce international competition—thereby avoiding massive foreclosures and the sort of dire rural poverty he knew of in Britain—yet mindful that such tariffs could and should be used as a negotiating tool to secure beneficial trade treaties, as they had been in signing the Caprivi treaties.[37] As far back as the early 1880s, Schmoller had also been advocating the strategic trade goal of creating a Central European customs union.[38]

Just such a position was staked out by Schmoller in 1901 during a Verein für Sozialpolitik debate over the Bülow tariff bill. In it, he clearly articulated that trade policy was a tool of power in an international competitive struggle, which, when applied correctly and moderately, could foster a national economy. While trade often benefited both parties, the formation of prices and distribution of the share of gains could be determined by the relative power of the trading parties, and here the weaker party, particularly the "undeveloped nation," as he put it, had a right and duty to protect itself.[39] Schmoller continued by noting that while in 1879 he had supported a position in favor of moderate industrial and agrarian tariffs because of the "agrarian and industrial crisis," his primary motivation for supporting them was his hope that they would be used as a negotiating chip to arrive at favorable trade treaties. He noted that he had warned of the dangers posed by escalating protectionism driven by interested parties—that tariffs were a cumbersome instrument to be used with great care and discretion. He recalled that he had become very skeptical when higher tariffs were negotiated than he had wanted, especially with subsequent increases in the rates, which he saw as an excessive burden on consumers and industry. As in the more democratic states, France and the U.S., the tariffs had been exploited in Germany to forge parliamentary majorities. For this reason, the Caprivi trade treaties had had his hearty support.[40]

While he could support moderate increases as a preparation for a trade treaty, he viewed the current bill with increasing concern. The official organs of the Reich had for years now taken a narrowly protectionist position and privileged the opinions of iron industrialists and large estate owners; worse, the preparations for the bill had been shrouded in bureaucratic secrecy.[41] Following the bad French example, German tariffs had become so extensive and complex that they delayed and obstructed cross-border trade. Schmoller noted that he had tried to understand the logic of the current bill but had failed—it remained "a book with seven seals."[42] As such, he concluded, it was an attempt by the government to win "all voices outside and within the Reichstag."[43]

At this point Schmoller reiterated his interpretation of mercantilism and the origins of what he called "*Neomerkantilismus.*" While protectionism, deployed felicitously, could be beneficial, Russia, France, and the United States had regressed into a "*Hochschutzzollsystem,*" and indeed "to a trade policy of raw power and violence of the worst kind." Under such circumstances, Germany had to employ certain trade "countermeasures," which he hoped could then be used to secure better trade treaties. Neomercantilism, he emphasized, would have to be fought by means of trade treaties "to bring about a reasonable measure of equitable and just trade policy in the entire international commerce of the civilized world."[44]

One might be excused for seeing a double standard underlying Schmoller's argument: only the protectionism of the U.S., France, and Russia was neomercantilism, not that of Germany. The possibility of a retaliatory cycle of tariffs and escalating trade wars was also clear. Recall also that Schmoller had explicitly asserted in his Free Union speech that it was one of the purposes of the high seas fleet to help secure trade treaties for Germany. Just how Schmoller imagined it being deployed to secure treaties with these countries is an interesting question. Yet despite these inconsistencies, the set of arguments presented on the issue of trade policy meshed seamlessly with those developed earlier on behalf of the fleet. The common thread here, if worn a little thin in places, was Schmoller's interpretation of mercantilism, particularly that states and state power could be used to secure and consolidate markets on terms more beneficial than would otherwise be possible. And here it is important to emphasize that in Schmoller's mind protectionism was not an end in itself but only a means—a means to international treaties.

In forming his opinions about trade and its relationship to German *Weltpolitik* early in the century, Schmoller was privy to an extensive international set of contacts that he maintained throughout his life. One of Schmoller's former students from the U.S., Henry W. Farnam, a professor of economics at Yale University and a Progressive who had written a doctorate on French *dirigisme* at Strasbourg University under Schmoller's supervision in the late 1870s,[45] frequently related his interpretation of events in America to Schmoller. Farnam wrote in September 1898 of his pleasure at the successful completion of the Spanish-American War and his view that Puerto Rico and Cuba should be linked to the union, given the close economic ties, yet he could not fail to add his displeasure with the widespread and extreme imperialist and jingoistic sentiments in America.[46] Three years later Farnam wrote of America's "bad example" with respect to protective tariffs and his belief that "the world is surely large enough for both peoples [Americans and Germans], and each can advance without necessarily harming the other."[47] Intriguingly, Farnam, who was under the influence of the theories of state administration Schmoller had developed from his historical writings on Prussia, was also a strong advocate of civil service reform and the expansion of the jurisdiction of the federal government in the United States. Farnam later wrote that he strongly supported Theodore Roosevelt on those very grounds.[48] As is known, Schmoller had some influence on the development of American Progressivism through the many future American university teachers he trained, and Progressives were, with some exceptions, supporters of an expanded American navy, protectionism, and imperialism.[49] This is not to claim that Schmoller necessarily acted as a catalyst for these developments in the U.S.; while that possibility exists, the lines of influence were reciprocal and complex. One can certainly imagine Farnam's letters having an impact on Schmoller's views on trade and Germany's relations with the United States.

Similar lines of contact and influence existed between Schmoller and the British economist William Ashley, a former student of Arnold Toynbee's at Oxford.[50] Ashley had been an admirer of Schmoller's work since the 1880s.[51] In particular, he was intimately familiar with Schmoller's oeuvre; indeed, he was so impressed with Schmoller's work on the history of mercantilism that he actually took the trouble to translate and publish this piece in English in 1896.[52] Schmoller himself later wrote a letter of reference for Ashley, which enabled him to secure a new professorship at the Faculty of Commerce at the University of Birmingham, which had been founded by Joseph Chamberlain.[53] As letters to Schmoller reveal, in his capacity as a professor at Brimingham, Ashley sought to defuse growing tensions between Britain and

Germany. He wrote: "I do hope that in my new position I may do something to draw England & Germany more closely together. They are natural allies—if we look at the large tendencies of economic development and away from the pressing causes of friction." Yet in the very next line Ashley went on to observe: "I have learnt very much of late from your paper in *Macht und Handelspolitik* [*sic*]," a reference to Schmoller's speech for the Free Union.[54] How much he would have learned in this tract about peace and understanding between Germany and Britain is of course questionable. Nevertheless, Ashley seems to have been a very good student of both Schmoller's writings on mercantilism and his new *Weltpolitik*: two years later Ashley would write that his own sympathies were strongly with Chamberlain.[55]

Just how strongly was revealed in Ashley's 1903 book *The Tariff Problem*, which promoted an imperial system of preferential tariffs to draw the British Empire into closer economic union, just the thing Schmoller had fretted about in his speeches for the Free Union only three years prior.[56] The irony is capped by what Ashley wrote to Schmoller in April 1904, just as the Entente Cordiale between Britain and France was being signed and Schmoller was penning a review of Ashley's book for his own *Jahrbuch für Gesetzgebung*:[57]

> You will find many indications of the way in which I have been affected by German methods of thought. Unlucky I do not find much *direct* assistance in dealing with our problems in current German writing. German literature deals mainly with the desirability of agricultural protection in Germany & in a lesser degree with the question of industrial protection in its relation to a given state. Our problem here—or so I conceive it—is that of binding together the very loosely connected members of a world empire by economic links.
>
> You will be glad to hear that there is now very little averse reference to Germany in the public discussion of fiscal policy....
>
> PS: You may, perhaps, have noticed that the well known sociological writer, Mr. Benjamin Kidd, has been referring to your essay on *Mercantilism*; & at Mr. Kidd's request I sent a copy of my translation to the Prime Minister. But I do not know whether he has read it.[58]

Certainly, Ashley had learned much from Schmoller, and Prime Minister Balfour might have read the book Ashley sent him with interest and instruction. This of course raises the intriguing question to what extent Schmoller the scholar of mercantilism might have contributed to the very problems that Schmoller the *Weltpolitiker* confronted. Nevertheless, caution is called for. Schmoller's scholarly influence in rehabilitating the reputation of mercantilism does not suffice to make Schmoller a neomercantilist or, as has been claimed, a "spokesman for neomercantilist ideas of world empire."[59] Writing about mercantilism, even acknowledging the contributions of mercantilism to state building and the creation of national economies, is one thing, advocating such policies, another, and it is to his credit that Schmoller repeatedly denounced the practices of the mercantilist age as unsuited to the modern era.[60] Nor, as we have seen, was he blind to the nefarious potential of German *Sammlungspolitik* to precipitate a regression to mercantilism.

That being said, Schmoller clearly had something analogous to mercantilism in mind when justifying German power politics to negotiate trade treaties, to create a Central European customs union, and to secure a German *Weltwirtschaft* within the context of the heightened tensions of the new imperialism. Schmoller did not create those tensions, but he did not do much to lessen them, either. I would nevertheless suggest that what is most striking about Schmoller's trade policy as it related to *Weltpolitik* is not its German peculiarity but rather its thoroughgoing conventionality— that is, its direct comparability with prevailing European and American thinking on the relationship between navies, empire, and trade around the turn of the century.

Conclusion

A study of Schmoller's *Weltpolitik* reveals a picture at odds with some of the core assumptions underlying the concept of social imperialism. There is little evidence that Gustav Schmoller was manipulated to lend his hand to the fleet-building campaign. Despite his status as a leading Wilhelmine social reformer, there is a striking absence of any discussion of how the fleet and German *Weltpolitik* would further social policy or provide specific social or political benefits to the German people. Neither is there evidence that stabilizing and legitimating the existing regime or placating influential material interests played an appreciable role in motivating him to lend his scholarly weight to the campaign for the fleet, nor does this play an explicit role in his arguments. Instead, there is every reason to believe that this involvement was born of strong personal convictions and a view of the world gleaned from his own scholarship. Schmoller's *Weltpolitik* was nothing more and nothing less than an international assertion of German economic and political power. The two were closely intermeshed.

This view is supported by considering the remarkable consistency between Schmoller's letter to Brentano of 1897, the speeches for the Free Association of 1899-1900, and his comments on the Bülow tariff bill of 1901. Indeed, what emerges is a picture of surprising consistency and clarity, certainly at odds with the view of Kehr and others that men like Schmoller supported the fleet for vague and ill-considered reasons. This hardly means that the views expressed by Schmoller were nonproblematic or always consistent; indeed, the contradictions and ironies in Schmoller's *Weltpolitik* have been highlighted. Nevertheless, a consistent logic informed these policies. We have good reason, then, not to attach the label "irrational" to the campaign to build the fleet and German *Weltpolitik*.

While not irrational, Schmoller's economic *Weltpolitik* was certainly dangerous: it was an assertion of power that assumed from the outset that British hegemony would be challenged. Schmoller did not unknowingly drift into this position. If we assume that hegemony is a zero-sum game, this assertion of German power was bound to antagonize Britain, and it is hard to imagine a policy of accommodation on mutually agreeable terms, given the prevailing strategic assumptions and attitudes about naval power. Indeed, the case of Gustav Schmoller's *Weltpolitik* lends weight to the argument that by the very first years of the twentieth century a course had likely already been set for some kind of future conflict between Germany and Britain.[61]

Notes

1. Wolfgang Marienfeld, "Wissenschaft und Schlachtflottenbau in Deutschland 1897-1906," *Marine Rundschau Beiheft* 2 (April 1957): 1-125.
2. Eckart Kehr, *Schlachtflottenbau und Partei-Politik 1894-1901. Versuch eines Querschnitts durch die innenpolitischen, sozialen und ideologischen Voraussetzungen des deutschen Imperialismus* (Berlin, 1930), 415-23.
3. Marienfeld, "Wissenschaft und Schlachtflottenbau," 8, 57. Reiterated more recently by Konrad Canis, *Von Bismarck zur Weltpolitik. Deutsche Außenpolitik 1890 bis 1902* (Berlin, 1997), 335.
4. Hans-Ulrich Wehler, *Deutsche Gesellschaftsgeschichte*, vol. 3, *Von der "Deutschen Doppelrevolution" bis zum Beginn des Ersten Weltkriegs 1849-1914* (Munich, 1995), 1129-1145, especially 1131ff.
5. For example, Gustav Schmoller, "Die Soziale Frage und der Preussische Staat" [1874], in *Zur Social- und Gewerbepolitik der Gegenwart. Reden und Aufsätze* (Leipzig, 1890), 37-63.
6. See Erik Grimmer-Solem, *The Rise of Historical Economics and Social Reform in Germany, 1864-1894* (Oxford, 2003).
7. Wilhelm Deist, *Flottenpolitik und Flottenpropaganda. Das Nachrichtenbureau des Reichs-marineamtes 1897-1914* (Stuttgart, 1976), 102.
8. Schmoller to Brentano, 23 July 1897, Bundesarchiv Koblenz (hereafter BAK), N 1001 Nl Brentano, Nr. 57, Bl. 107-8.
9. Brentano to Schmoller, 27 July 1897, Geheimes Staatsarchiv Preußischer Kulturbesitz (hereafter GStA PK), VI. HA Nl Schmoller, Nr. 114, Bl. 275-76. A short excerpt of this letter was quoted by James J. Sheehan, *The Career of Lujo Brentano: A Study of Liberalism and Social Reform in Imperial Germany* (Chicago and London, 1966), 180.
10. Tirpitz to Schmoller, 28 July 1897, GStA PK, VI. HA Nl Schmoller, Nr. 189a, Bl. 83-84.
11. Geoff Eley, *Reshaping the German Right: Radical Nationalism and Political Change after Bismarck* (New Haven, 1980; reprint, Ann Arbor, 1991), 85.
12. For example, "Was lehren uns die Vorgänge in Samoa?" *Die Woche* 1, no. 5 (1899). Schmoller was asked in January 1898 to write an article in the *Neueste Nachrichten* by the editor, Otto Friedrich Koch, under the heading "Was ist uns China?" Koch to Schmoller, 4 Jan. 1898, GStA PK, VI. HA Nl Schmoller, Nr. 190a, Bl. 216-17.
13. Kehr, *Schlachtflottenbau*, 101-2; Deist, *Flottenpolitik*, 113.
14. Gustav Schmoller, ed., "Über wirtschaftliche Kartelle in Deutschland und im Auslande," *Schriften des Vereins für Socialpolitik* 60 (1894). Von Halle's contribution on American trusts is on 93-322.
15. Schmoller to Schweinburg [draft], 15 June 1898, GStA PK, VI. HA Nl Schmoller, Nr. 190c, Bl. 171. See also Kehr, *Schlachtflottenbau*, 171; Deist, *Flottenpolitik*, 153; Eley, *Reshaping the German Right*, 85-86.
16. Marienfeld, "Wissenschaft und Schlachtflottenbau," 86.
17. Deist, *Flottenpolitik*, 103.
18. Secretariat of the German Navy League to Schmoller, 14 Dec. 1899, GStA PK, VI. HA Nl Schmoller, Nr. 191b, Bl. 170-71: "Regarding the retirement from the managing committee of Frei-herr Zedlitz, negotiations are still pending about the form in which his voluntary resignation should

be urged—in any case, however, I can only emphasize my assurances of yesterday that this resignation will be secured under all circumstances."

19. Prussian Landtag, Stenographische Berichte, Haus der Abgeordneten, vol. 3, 75th session (4 May 1897), 2380-83; Prussian Landtag, Stenographische Berichte, Herrenhaus, vol. 1, 19th session (28 May 1897), 382-88. These and other attacks in the press were motivated by the opposition of the socialists of the chair to repressive legislation against striking workers, support of the Hamburg dockworkers' strike in 1896, and Schmoller's defense as rector of Berlin University of the Social Democratic physicist Leo Arons in 1897.

20. "Professor Schmoller über die Flotte," *Hamburgerischer Correspondent*, no. 560 Abend-Ausgabe (29 Nov. 1899); "Eine Flottenrede von Gustav Schmoller," *Breslauer Zeitung*, no. 841 Morgen-Ausgabe (30 Nov. 1899); Die deutschen Universitäten und die Flottenbewegung," *Hamburgerischer Correspondent*, no. 280, Morgen-Ausgabe (10 June 1900); "Talk of German Future," *The Chicago Tribune* 59, no. 195 (14 July 1900).

21. Gustav Schmoller, Max Sering, and Adolf Wagner, eds., *Freie Vereinigung für Flottenvorträge. Handels- und Machtpolitik. Reden und Aufsätze* (Stuttgart, 1900).

22. Gustav Schmoller, "Die wirtschaftliche Zukunft Deutschlands und die Flottenvorlage" [1900], in *Zwanzig Jahre Deutscher Politik (1897-1917). Aufsätze und Vorträge von Gustav Schmoller*, ed. Lucie Schmoller (Munich and Leipzig, 1920), 1-6.

23. Ibid., 6.

24. Ibid., 6-9.

25. Gustav Schmoller, "Studien über die wirtschaftliche Politik Friedrichs des Großen und Preußens überhaupt von 1680-1786," *Jahrbuch für Gesetzgebung, Verwaltung und Volkswirtschaft im Deutschen Reiche* (hereafter cited as *JbfGVV*) 8 (1884): 1-61, 345-421, 999-1091; idem, "Das Merkantilsystem in seiner historischen Bedeutung," in *Umrisse und Untersuchungen zur Verfassungs-, Verwaltungs- und Wirtschaftsgeschichte* (Leipzig, 1898), 1-60.

26. Schmoller, "Das Merkantilsystem," 37.

27. Schmoller, "Die wirtschaftliche Zukunft Deutschlands," 9-12.

28. Ibid., 12.

29. Ibid., 13.

30. Ibid., 14.

31. Ibid., 14-19.

32. Ibid., 19.

33. Ibid., 20.

34. Gustav Schmoller, "Die Wandlungen in der europäischen Handelspolitik des 19. Jahrhunderts. Eine Säkularbetrachtung," *JbfGVV* 24 (1900): 373-82.

35. Ibid., 378.

36. [Gustav Schmoller], *Der französische Handelsvertrag und seine Gegner. Ein Wort der Verständigung von einem Süddeutschen* (Frankfurt a.M., 1862); Gustav Schmoller, "Korreferat über die Zolltarifvorlage," *Schriften des Vereins für Socialpolitik* 16 (1879): 19-29.

37. Gustav Schmoller, "Neuere Litteratur über unsere handelspolitische Zukunft," *JbfGVV* 15 (1891): 275-82.

38. Gustav Schmoller, "Die amerikanische Konkurrenz und die Lage der mitteleuropäischen, besonders der deutschen Landwirtschaft," *JbfGVV* 6 (1882): 247-84, here 283.

39. Ständiger Ausschuß des Vereins für Socialpolitik, ed., "Verhandlungen der Generalversammlung in München, 23., 24., und 25. September 1901," *Schriften des Vereins für Socialpolitik* 98 (1902): 264-65.

40. Ibid., 265-66.

41. Ibid., 267.

42. Ibid., 268.

43. Ibid., 269.

44. Ibid., 271.

45. Henry W. Farnam, "Die Innere französische Gewerbepolitik von Colbert bis Turgot," *Staats- und socialwissenschaftliche Forschungen* 1, no. 4 (1878).

46. Farnam to Schmoller, 7 Sept. 1898, GstA PK, VI. HA Nl Schmoller, Nr. 190b, Bl. 184-85.

47. Farnam to Schmoller, 4 Aug. 1901, GStA PK, VI. HA Nl Schmoller, Nr. 194a, Bl. 3-6.

48. Farnam to Schmoller, 19 July 1904, GStA PK, VI. HA Nl Schmoller, Nr. 196b, Bl. 35-39; see also Gustav Schmoller, "Die Amerikaner," *JbfGVV* 28 (1904): 1477-94.

49. William E. Leuchtenberg, "Progressivism and Imperialism: The Progressive Movement and American Foreign Policy 1898-1916," *The Mississippi Valley Historical Review* 39 (December 1952): 483-504; Jurgen Herbst, *The German Historical School in American Scholarship: A Study in the Transfer of Culture* (Ithaca, 1965); Daniel T. Rodgers, *Atlantic Crossings: Social Politics in a Progressive Age* (Cambridge, Mass. and London, 1998); Axel R. Schäfer, *American Progressives and German Social Reform, 1875-1920: Social Ethics, Moral Control, and the Regulatory State in a Transatlantic Context* (Stuttgart, 2000).

50. On Ashley and Toynbee, see Alon Kadish, *The Oxford Economists in the Late Nineteenth Century* (Oxford, 1982); on historical economics in England more generally, see Gerard M. Koot, *English Historical Economics, 1870-1926: The Rise of Economic History and Neomercantilism* (Cambridge, 1987).

51. Ashley to Schmoller, 24 Nov. 1887, GStA PK, VI. HA Nl Schmoller, Nr. 153, Bl. 25-26.

52. Gustav Schmoller, *The Mercantile System and Its Historical Significance illustrated Chiefly from Prussian History*, trans. William J. Ashley (New York and London, 1896).

53. Ashley to Schmoller, 31 July 1901, GStA PK, VI. HA Nl Schmoller, Nr. 193, Bl. 109.

54. Ibid.

55. Ashley to Schmoller, 19 Sept. 1903, GStA PK, VI. HA Nl Schmoller, Nr. 195b, Bl. 58-59.

56. William J. Ashley, *The Tariff Problem* (London, 1903).

57. Gustav Schmoller, "Die künftige englische Handelspolitik, Chamberlain und der Imperialismus," *JbfGVV* 28 (1904): 829-52. Schmoller was very kind in his review and went some way to try to defuse tensions between the two countries by playing down the threat posed to Germany of an imperial customs union. See especially 850-52.

58. Ashley to Schmoller, 9 Apr. 1904, GStA PK, VI. HA Nl Schmoller, Nr. 196a, Bl. 17-18.

59. Canis, *Von Bismarck zur Weltpolitik*, 333.

60. Schmoller, *The Mercantile System*, 79; idem, "Die Wirtschaftliche Zukunft Deutschlands," 10-12.

61. Canis, *Von Bismarck zur Weltpolitik*, 396-401.

– 7 –

"Our natural ally"

Anglo-German Relations and the Contradictory Agendas of Wilhelmine Socialism, 1897-1900

<del>>>·<<</del>

PAUL PROBERT

I

Without the growth of hostility between Great Britain and Germany, the crisis of late July and early August 1914 would have remained a Continental conflict rather than developing into a world war. One might even contend that, but for the presence of the British Expeditionary Force, the "knockout blow" called for by the Schlieffen Plan might have been successfully delivered, thus allowing the German High Command to turn its full attention to the campaign in Russia. In recent years, it has been argued that without British interference, Germany could have achieved the continental hegemony it desired, Britain's finances and Great Power status would have remained sound, and Europe would have been spared four years of war.[1]

The problem with such an analysis is that it tends to ignore the key factor in pre-1914 European diplomacy: the growth of Anglo-German antagonism. Although some blame for unleashing a world war can be laid on Whitehall, the responsibility for creating an international environment in which war came to be seen as a risk worth taking must rest with those in the Wilhelmstraße.

The perceived and actual deterioration in relations between London and Berlin was particularly galling for the German Social Democratic Party (SPD). The party had long looked to Britain as a model society and as late as 1914 argued that there was no real conflict of interest between the two states.[2] Yet between 1897 and 1900—years that constituted a turning point in Wilhelmine foreign and domestic affairs—the SPD criticized German policy in general, and the navy bills of 1898 and 1900 in particular, for their anti-English tone.

Notes for this section begin on page 134.

Of course, with Wilhelmine elections increasingly being decided on "fairness issues,"[3] it was to be expected that the SPD would use the controversy over naval expansion for domestic purposes. Yet criticism of proposed legislation because of the accompanying tax increases played a much smaller role than might be imagined. While the claim that "we Germans are not rich enough to throw millions into the water"[4] would appear to be "ideal type" opposition, the stance adopted by the SPD's leading newspaper, *Vorwärts*, was not, in fact, so dogmatic. The paper argued that the pace of technological change, coupled with the response from other Great Powers, would militate against Germany being able to create a fleet in isolation.[5] Moreover, the Social Democratic press suggested that Germany's interests would be better served by addressing its internal political problems rather than building new warships—warships that, if used to pursue "a policy [of] very dangerous foreign adventures," would only serve to damage Germany's international standing further.[6] When economic concerns were raised, they focused much less on the problem of "unfair" indirect taxation than on the inability of navy increases to affect Germany's economic development in any positive way. Bruno Schoenlank, Reichstag deputy and editor of the *Leipziger Volkszeitung*, argued that the strengthening of the North Sea fleet would hardly help to expand and protect trade—indeed, given that a third of Germany's trade was with either Great Britain or the United States, he questioned the need for protecting the merchant fleet at all.[7]

More common was criticism grounded in a desire to uphold what the SPD felt was Germany's constitutional system. The 1898 edition of the *Handbuch für Sozialdemokratische Wähler* (Handbook for Social Democratic Voters)—a manifesto of sorts—contained a substantial section on "navalism" that focused on the constitutional implications of Alfred von Tirpitz's policy. Like Bruno Schoenlank, the Handbuch equated Wilhelm II's accession with the beginning of "the great era of navalism"—a conclusion to which Friedrich Naumann later came in his *Demokratie und Kaisertum*.[8] The party executive believed that naval increases were not only intrinsically undemocratic and unconstitutional but a result of the "personal rule" that was "winning ever greater significance in Prussian Germany."[9] This line of argument allowed the party to portray itself as the upholder of Germany's interests, leaving it less vulnerable to the anti-national charge that would accompany criticism of the fleet from a military perspective.

The 1898 navy bill, then, was attacked primarily as an unconstitutional device to limit the Reichstag's powers; secondary criticism, as we shall see, focused on the bill as a piece of flawed strategic thinking and an unnecessary barrier to economic development. The "classic" complaint of unfair taxation figured only as a tertiary concern, although it did feature more regularly in public meetings held by the SPD—as meetings held in Hamburg and Cologne in early 1898 demonstrate.

On 7 January 1898, thirteen meetings were held in Hamburg to discuss the effect of naval expansion on the German people. The meetings drew reasonable crowds, reportedly numbering between 7,650 and 13,600—augmented in part by Hamburg's undercover political police.[10] During the course of one speech, Carl

Frohme, a Reichstag deputy, ranged widely over the naval issue and highlighted a variety of criticisms. Increased taxation was duly mentioned, as was the claim that the interference of the military and navy in business affairs was unwarranted and dangerous. Frohme also refuted the government's belief that a strong navy could protect German citizens abroad: with fewer than fifteen hundred German subjects resident in Africa and Asia—areas deemed to be less "free" than Germany—there was little need to expand the fleet to offer them protection. The cost of the navy bill was also said to be far in excess of what could be justified as reasonable spending levels to protect Germans living abroad from maltreatment.[11] The resolution adopted at the end of the meeting attacked the limitation of the Reichstag's budgetary rights, opposed any increase in taxation, condemned the idea of *Weltpolitik* (felt to be the reason for naval increases and offering nothing to the German people),[12] and called for attention to be focused instead on domestic political questions.

Protest meetings in working-class districts of Cologne adopted similar resolutions.[13] Carl Meist, a former Düsseldorf Reichstag deputy, spoke before a capacity crowd in a Nippes public house. It appears that Meist believed his audience would be more concerned about a possible rise in the cost of pork to fund naval expansion than about the navy's role in *Weltpolitik*; accordingly, he gave priority in his speech to economic concerns over foreign affairs.[14]

While both Frohme and Meist highlighted the increase in the cost of living that navy plans would mean for the working man, attacks on "unfair" taxation were a sure vote-winner for the SPD. Correspondingly, the issue was given more prominence in Cologne, a city that the SPD was by no means guaranteed to win in the next Reichstag election. The party's dominance in Hamburg allowed the party more latitude to address a wider variety of issues. In other locations, simple electioneering was much more important. Certainly, the campaign against unfair taxation was given more prominence in the popular party press than it was in the legislature, and impending Reichstag elections meant that it was all the more important to highlight the key issue—indirect taxation—that stood at the fulcrum where the building of a fleet and the interests of the German people met.[15]

The party's opposition to naval expansion was also based on strategic, power politics concerns. Those concerns were almost exclusively based on the SPD's pro-English stance and its desire for close Anglo-German relations. From the German wars of unification until Bismarck's dismissal in 1890, Social Democratic opposition to Prusso-German foreign policy amounted to little more than bemoaning the lost opportunity—thanks to the annexation of Alsace-Lorraine—of a Franco-German alliance directed against Russia (although Bismarck's policies were also attacked as Prussocentric and reactionary). The early 1890s saw a certain improvement in relations between the SPD and the authoritarian state now freed of the Bismarckian yoke: Chancellor Leo von Caprivi's "New Course" appeared to presage a more pro-English and anti-Russian tone in foreign affairs. Georg von Vollmar's famous "El Dorado" speech highlighted the willingness of reformist sections of the SPD to operate within the national sphere. And SPD leader August Bebel told the 1891 SPD congress that in the event of an attack from the East: "[W]e would then stand beside those who are presently our opponents, not to save them and their social order, but to save Germany."[16] By 1891, both Caprivi and the SPD's leadership recognized the likelihood of a concrete Franco-Russian alliance.[17] German first and socialist second, the SPD found itself unable to maintain a purely negative stance toward Imperial foreign policy. In 1892, Bebel summed up the international situation thus: "For an unforeseeable time to come, France will be the natural ally of Russia and Russia the logical ally of France. From this derives the danger that Germany may be crushed between two mighty foes and eliminated from the ranks of the Great Powers. Accordingly, this prospect generates the need to find, at any price, allies who in case of mobilization will be able to enter the war with the greatest possible chance of victory."[18] Austria-Hungary and Italy, however, were dismissed by the SPD as unlikely to fill the role of allies as outlined by Bebel.[19] Hence, with France bound to Russia, the only alternative that the party was willing to countenance was Britain.

Britain occupied a special place in the hearts and minds of many leading German Social Democrats. For socialists as ideologically disparate as Eduard Bernstein, Georg Ledebour, and Wilhelm Liebknecht, Victorian Britain had at one time or another offered sanctuary from the forces of Prussian law and order.[20] Moreover, even those Social Democrats who had not experienced firsthand the hotbed of revolution that was the Reading Room of the British Library were impressed by the strength of the British parliamentary government. Karl Kautsky saw an English-style monarchy and parliament as the basis upon which a socialist society could be built.[21] Both Liebknecht and Bebel placed British parliamentarism upon a pedestal: the latter wished that the Reichstag "had done even a tenth as much as the English Parliament" in fighting for parliamentary power, and claimed that Britain was the standard against which all European parliaments should be judged.[22] All this served an obvious domestic purpose. The British situation could be used to highlight the detrimental influence of the Prussian monarchy and the German bourgeoisie on Germany's political culture—criticism that seemed well and truly grounded in the domestic arena.

The Social Democrats were able to focus on this internal aspect because Anglo-German relations were relatively trouble free. Indeed, before the introduction of the first navy bill, the party believed there was no legitimate reason for the two Great Powers to come to blows, and even claimed that conflict was "simply impossible."[23] Nevertheless, the further improvement of relations between the two nations would be better still. In early 1896, Bebel explained why an Anglo-German alliance was so desirable: "Germany has the best army on the European mainland; England the largest navy in the world. An England and a Germany allied with each other would be a combination against which no other power or group of powers could prevail."[24]

This, then, was the trajectory of relations between London and Berlin desired by the SPD in the years leading up to the appointments of Alfred von Tirpitz and Bernhard von Bülow in 1897. While neither Whitehall nor the Wilhelmstraße wanted an alliance,[25] it is doubtful whether the goal of German policy after 1897 was, in fact, to move Britain from benevolent neutrality to open hostility. Cooperation at the periphery, in the Balkans, or in Africa was not enough to overcome the mutual mistrust that stemmed from Berlin's efforts to expand the Imperial navy and London's reaction to this.[26] Paul Kennedy has argued that British strategists did not acknowledge the German naval threat until 1902,[27] but the SPD had grasped the anti-British direction of Tirpitz's policy by 1898.

II

If the 1898 navy bill was opposed in the Reichstag primarily on constitutional grounds, its successor was criticized because of its strategic and foreign policy implications. However, the SPD's stance toward the bill was not the watershed that has been suggested by William H. Maehl,[28] who failed to see the embryonic beginnings of a move to assign primacy to foreign policy concerns in the opposition to the 1898 bill. Instead, the SPD's position was part of the continuing development of already extant views, ideas, and beliefs.

August Bebel's Reichstag speech of 24 March 1898 certainly paid attention to foreign policy issues; but Bebel was not alone in questioning the strategic and foreign policy thinking behind the earlier version of the navy bill. Alexander Helphand had also given the matter some thought in 1898 and had come to the conclusion that the best option for Germany would be an alliance with Britain, thus leaving only French seapower as a threat to the Reich.[29]

Helphand approached the matter by questioning the validity of the governmental claim that a fleet was necessary for the protection of German trade. He contended that the development of a fleet to protect the merchant marine was anachronistic, akin to building a wall around a town in order to keep out unwanted elements: if Great Britain wanted to damage German trade, it would use tariffs, not cruisers and cannon.[30] Thus, if the German government seriously wanted to protect German trade, it should look not toward the development of a battle fleet but rather the concluding of an agreement with Great Britain. The benefits of such a course were deemed by Helphand to be obvious. Thanks to its strategic locations on shipping lines, Britain could close Germany out of the world's oceans if she so desired; some sort of agreement—ideally, an alliance, but a trade agreement would suffice—would remove this threat. Then the French fleet would be prevented from passing the English Channel, thus at a stroke transferring the costs of naval expansion from Germany to Britain and allowing Germany to focus on preparing for land-based conflict. Britain would benefit from German military strength, which could act as a counterweight against Russia, while Germany would receive British protection against the French navy.[31] If Britain could be persuaded to join the *Dreibund*, the naval dominance of the alliance would obviate the need for Tirpitz's plans. Nevertheless, Helphand, like Friedrich von Holstein, felt there was a fly in the ointment: Germany's subservient stance toward Russia made British membership of this hypothetical *Vierbund* much less likely.[32]

To argue, then, that it was only in 1900 that foreign policy became a key component in the SPD's opposition to naval expansion is to miss the very real and relatively detailed thinking that occupied certain figures in the party. Bebel was not the only figure in the SPD to recognize the damage that Tirpitz's navy might cause. Moreover, he recognized the dangers earlier than he has been given credit for.[33] The importance of foreign policy as a determinant of party responses to official policy existed before the second navy bill. What did occur in 1900 was the adoption of this mode of reference by a greater section of the party and the recognition that the bill undoubtedly meant a change in the government's publicly stated policy from what had been euphemistically termed "coastal protection" to a much greater offensive capacity.[34] While Helphand had suggested that the 1898 program of expansion was strategically inappropriate because it failed to recognize either the maritime dominance of Britain or the importance of economic factors in limiting trade, the parliamentary caucus now proposed that the 1900 bill allow for the development of a fleet capable of repulsing the Royal Navy, a process guaranteed to seriously disrupt the very trade that the fleet had initially been intended to protect.[35]

While economic considerations were not completely jettisoned (particularly in materials targeted for the electorate),[36] the key factor in the SPD's parliamentary opposition to naval increases was now the strategic risk it entailed in completely alienating Great Britain. Bebel saw in the new bill an attempt to produce a fleet "that is strong and powerful enough to be a match in offensive action for the first navy of the world, the English navy."[37] This, he argued, ran counter to the intentions of policy in the 1880s and 1890s. The fleet had begun as a simple mechanism for coastal defense, in 1898 it had been increased to defend the North Sea and the Baltic, and the new bill would mean a doubling of naval strength with the guarantee of additional bills to follow.

Again, Bebel suggested that a large fleet would be of no use whatsoever, should Germany find itself faced with repulsing a Franco-Russian force—"in which the decision would be reached on land"[38]—and it would be financially impossible for Germany to maintain its army while expanding its navy. Britain, and, for that matter, other Great Powers as well, would counter German naval increases by expanding their own fleets, thus leaving Germany in the same relative position as it was at present.[39] If German naval expansion led to conflict with Britain, Bebel was convinced that France and Russia, the "natural opponents of Germany,"[40] would be quick to make the most of the situation and attack Germany.[41]

That any future Anglo-German conflict would come as the result of German aggression appears to have been accepted by Wilhelm Liebknecht as well. During his famous "*Flottenschwindel*" speech, in which he branded the navy bills "a campaign of robbery against the German people,"[42] Liebknecht asked rhetorically: "[W]hich nation threatens us? At present England ... cannot come into conflict with us."[43] He went on to suggest that if war came, Germany would be the guilty party and would reap a terrible reward for its actions: "if we started a war with England, the result would be that after twenty-four hours there would no longer be a German ship on the seas and the couple of colonies that we have would have gone for a burton [*flöten gegangen*]."[44] Echoing Helphand's comments of two years previously, Liebknecht highlighted the financial and strategic advantages to be gained from an alliance of sorts between Britain and Germany. While Britain needed a fleet to survive, Germany had "a small coast [and] a second-rate fleet, which is quite enough—and the largest standing army in the world." To become the greatest seapower as well was "simply impossible—just as it is impossible for England to have an army as large as ours."[45] Bebel had already gone further when he suggested that the entire concept of expanding the fleet was unnecessary: "[W]e do not need this fleet at all because England is our natural ally."[46] By joining forces, the Royal Navy could control the seas, and the German army, the land, each offering the other something it was unable to provide for itself, namely, the securing of a weak flank.

The growth of the fleet was not, however, viewed as a foreign policy issue by some on the left of the SPD. Franz Mehring saw naval expansion as part of the push toward *Weltpolitik*—a policy he felt was inextricably linked to the demands of big business. Although many Social Democrats blamed Wilhelm II for the growth in the fleet, Mehring viewed the Kaiser less as a prime mover than simply as an enthusiastic supporter of heavy industry's demand for a strong fleet. Like Friedrich Naumann, Mehring felt that the Kaiser's modernity meant that he was much more impressed by heavy industry than he was by agrarian conservatism, and this view was reflected in his enthusiasm for the navy and his dislike of the labor movement.[47]

Mehring did, however, depart from Naumann's thesis. Wilhelm needed a non-conservative government, Naumann argued—and a non-conservative government could be achieved only with the assistance of a national-thinking working class. As long as the working class failed to think nationally, the Imperial regime would have to remain conservative. By way of contrast, Mehring contended that the working class would have no interest in a *Weltpolitik* that he believed existed to open up new colonies to German goods.[48] Moreover, a heavy industrialist *Weltpolitik* meant little more than heavy levels of taxation to be levied upon those who were least able to afford them. Borrowing from Marx and Lassalle, Mehring claimed that if Germany wanted to improve its productivity, it would do better to emancipate its working class than to try to seek out new markets for its products. The world was already divided among European powers, and, more importantly, the quest for colonies would not be able to maintain the tottering capitalist system for long.[49]

Such a view was to become increasingly common among the far left of the party. Rosa Luxemburg's famous attack on Bernstein's Anglophilia, "*Die englische Brille,*" was also a criticism of a new trend in English policy, which, Luxemburg argued, was becoming increasingly bellicose as Britain sought to maintain and expand its empire. Kautsky, who in 1893 had looked on Britain in a positive light, also took a more critical view of late Victorian and Edwardian policy for the same reason.[50] The problem for these SPD leaders, however, was that imperialism is not foreign policy. By focusing on imperialism and developing theories with which to explain colonialism, the left not only misjudged the motives behind Tirpitz's naval policy but also failed to develop meaningful critiques of foreign policy.[51] The knife Tirpitz intended to hold to Britain's jugular was to create freedom for Germany to maneuver within Europe, not farther afield.[52] Although they may have developed theoretical frameworks with which to analyze the scramble for African colonies or the division of the Balkans, the theories of imperialism advanced by the SPD's left wing were singularly ill suited to understanding an Anglo-German antagonism grounded in geographical proximity and power politics.

III

Although the SPD's left and center approached Tirpitz's efforts from different perspectives, they were united in their hostility to his proposals for naval expansion. Opposition to the navy bills, however, was not quite universal. In matters relating to foreign policy, the extreme right of the party proved to be more troublesome than the left in promoting views that caused the dominant center a certain embarrassment. In the December 1899 edition of Joseph Bloch's *Sozialistische Monatshefte*, an article by Eric Rother managed to stir up debate within the party. *"Zur Theorie der Flottenfrage"* was one of the earliest examples of the more national frame of mind that existed within sections of the SPD and would reach its zenith in the writings of Richard Calwer, Max Schippel, and Karl Leuthner.[53]

Rother was unknown within the party, as Bebel told the Reichstag before reiterating that the revisionist *Sozialistische Monatshefte* was independent of the SPD.[54] Given that the article flatly contradicted the stance put forward by the parliamentary party, Bebel's willingness to distance himself from it is readily understandable. Beginning with the assertion that questions of naval policy had important meaning for the working class, Rother ignored the unfair taxation slogan and instead suggested that the proletariat had vital interests that a fleet would protect and uphold. Rother argued that naval expansion was necessary and desirable, regardless of whether the environment was capitalist or post-capitalist.

As part of his argument, Rother emphasized the need to develop a new economic system for the period following the collapse of capitalism and the beginning of the dictatorship of the proletariat. This new economic system (which appeared in Rother's mind to be a form of autarkic socialism)[55] could not be based in Germany alone—at least, not if current living standards were to be maintained. As Germany imported more than a third of its goods from abroad, it would be logical to assume that any future German state would need to do the same. It was therefore of the greatest importance that a socialist Germany be capable of securing minerals and food supplies, without which it would surely collapse. The necessary imports would come from German colonies. While suggesting that the colonial policy he had in mind was far removed from that pursued by the Imperial government, Rother claimed that a colonial policy was both necessary and in the best interests of the working class. A strong battle fleet was a prerequisite for more than just a colonial empire: "If warship after warship were built today, they would be—purely theoretically and grounded in the given premises—for us the most important means of power in our hands for the founding and securing of the future socialist polity [*Gemeinwesen*]."[56]

Looked at objectively, it is only a question of degree that differentiates colonial policy as advocated by Rother and the use of foreign policy implied by Paul Singer's claim that the party would concern itself with external affairs after it took power.[57] Both suggested ways in which the security of a socialist *Zukunftsstaat* could be maintained, even though Rother's stance was more pro-active than that of his party chairman.

The real problem occurred in the second part of Rother's article. Here he moved away from the safety of the *Zukunftsstaat* and looked instead at contemporary Germany. More importantly, he claimed that the pro-navy hypothesis he adopted was just as valid within a capitalist society. With the fate of the working class inextricably linked to that of capitalism, Rother believed that a powerful state was paramount if Germany was to be able to hold its own among other Great Powers. He felt that it was of the "utmost importance for the German working class" that Germany should be "armed to the teeth" and in possession of "the most important instrument of any future trade war—a strong fleet."[58] In fact, a powerful fleet was even more important for Germany than for the likes of Britain, France, Russia, or the U.S., since Germany lacked an overseas empire or other areas suitable for the large-scale production of goods.

It was common for the SPD to echo Bismarck's claim that Germany's lack of colonies was the result of its arriving too late on the world stage and then to suggest that, as the globe had already been parceled out among the other Great Powers, Germany did not require a fleet to gain nonexistent virgin territory.[59] It was unusual, however, to propose, as Rother did, that Germany should compete not just on an economic level but also on a military one in order to win new markets and—implicit within this argument—to take markets away from other countries. Rother claimed that the only safe market was one protected by cannon: as capitalism developed further, both the German export industry and the German working class could be faced with the choice of either capitulating or fighting for their existence. The working class, in short, had a stake in the development of capitalism, a developmental process that required a strong battle fleet.[60]

If this line of argument was not enough to upset the majority of the party, the tenor of the piece also made it clear that Rother envisioned the possibility of engaging in conflict with nations that could be reached only by sea. Hence, he demanded a strong fleet in order to wage such conflicts successfully.[61] Given his insistence on the importance of colonies and trade for the present and future health of the nation, there can be little doubt that the opponent he had in mind was Great Britain, which at that point was embroiled in the military conflict in South Africa and was thus seen by some commentators as being in danger of imperial collapse.[62] The explicit approval of colonialism would have been enough to upset mainstream opinion within much of the party, but the additional call for an aggressive naval policy directly contradicted the view put forward by the SPD's parliamentary caucus, as did the willingness to come to blows with Britain, seen by most of the party as an obvious ally. Even in the camp associated with the *Sozialistische Monatshefte*, there were those who believed that Rother was simply wrong.

In the next edition of the journal, Ernst Frei responded to Rother's article. Although he admitted that exporting goods was essential to a capitalist society, Frei disagreed with Rother's analysis that a strong navy would be able to protect such exports, and he refused to believe that a socialist society would or could be founded by means of cannons, ships, and torpedoes. The success or failure of a nation's export industry was determined by the cost and quality of the goods it produced, not the size of the navy it possessed. Cannon, remarked Frei, were of little use in combating cheaper products. American protectionism had harmed German exports far more than an unsuccessful war could ever have done—inflicting damage that a German navy, of whatever size, would have been completely unable to prevent.[63] Whereas Rother suggested a strong fleet as a means by which to combat Britain's economic power, Frei felt that trade agreements would be more beneficial.

Rother's emphasis on colonies was also criticized. The dream of a large empire that could be secured by a navy was dismissed out of hand: with the world already divided, there was no space for Germany's future empire. Although he felt that there was no sign of the Boer War signaling the demise of the British Empire, Frei maintained that if the collapse took place, most of Britain's territories would become independent states (he gave the examples of Australia, South Africa, and Canada), while India would fall to Russia.[64]

Frei conceded that the use of a navy to protect colonies was valid and recognized why the British working class supported British naval expansion. He appears to have agreed with the sentiment printed in *Vorwärts* that "England is a world empire and, as such, must have a world policy."[65] Germany, however, did not need to protect her inconsequential overseas possessions. As Frei put it: "[W]ho envies us for our couple of little islands and deserts? They're happy to leave them to us."[66] The German people, moreover, had "nothing to gain, but much to lose" from supporting naval expansion—a point not fully acknowledged by those social imperialists who advocated an aggressive, and expensive, foreign policy but chose to ignore the electoral repercussions of championing the increased taxation that such a policy would necessitate.[67] Frei suggested that looking to the oceans for Germany's future was a wrongheaded policy. Germany's geographic location dictated a land-based strategy, and the Balkans and Asia Minor offered numerous export opportunities—none of which would require a fleet. The incorporation of German Austria into Germany and the development of a rail network through the Habsburg and Ottoman Empires were of much greater significance for Germany than any overseas policy.[68]

As an alternative to Rother's colonial empire, then, Frei had proposed what amounted to a *Mitteleuropa* economic area. (While Frei did not use the term, it would later appear within the pages of the *Sozialistische Monatshefte*.) If Germany needed to travel down the road to autarky—and Frei was not convinced that it did—it had better look toward its European neighbors than to envision a future on the water.

Although Eric Rother's article seems to have presented the viewpoint of a very small minority, it merits the historian's attention in that it highlights differences of opinion that existed within the party, and because it is an early example of the socialist imperialism that many contributors to the *Sozialistische Monatshefte* promoted. The members of the party's Reichstag caucus were opposed to naval expansion, seeing it as either too costly or strategically flawed. While many on the party's left—particularly Helphand, Kautsky, Luxemburg, and Mehring—saw imperialism as the driving factor behind Tirpitz's naval expansion, the dominant party center tended to dismiss the colonial aspect, arguing along with Molkenbuhr that the concept of *Weltpolitik* was nothing more than a façade and that the growth of the fleet could only be directed against Great Britain.[69]

IV

More than ever before, foreign policy concerns were the prime motivation behind the SPD's opposition to government legislation. While extraparliamentary action once again complemented the party's parliamentary critiques, economic concerns were pushed to the fore only when it was necessary to elucidate party policy for the benefit of the people.[70] With the passing of the second navy bill in June 1900, the issue of naval expansion assumed a position of secondary, or even tertiary, importance in the political life of the Empire. The SPD, however, continued to look at the growth of the fleet, but through a wider lens that took in Germany's diplomatic position. August Bebel, the leading figure in the SPD at that moment and representative of the bulk of the party, was not immune to using fiscal arguments or the unfair tax burden when it came to criticizing the Imperial government. Yet in 1898, and more vehemently in 1900, his opposition to naval expansion was grounded in the belief that it would seriously damage Germany's security and freedom of maneuver in the international sphere.

In 1915, Eduard Bernstein suggested that "it was German naval policy that drove Britain into the arms of France."[71] This was a claim that would be echoed by other Social Democrats. In a draft of an article written for *The Times* in the mid 1930s, Max Beer, who replaced Bernstein as the London correspondent for *Vorwärts* upon the latter's return to Germany, highlighted what he thought was the most pertinent foreign policy issue in the years prior to World War I:

> In those days the difficulties were relatively simple because transparent. There was a Power which—owing to its maritime ambitions, engendered by the rapid expansion of its manufacturing and trading activities, and owing to its formidable naval preparations directed against the most vulnerable flank of British home communications—threatened the existence of Britain. The policy of the Foreign Office was dictated by that simple fact and it sought *ententes* with Powers that for one reason or another feared the territorial expansion of that Power.[72]

Social Democratic opposition to naval expansion ranged far beyond a simple hostility toward the building of more ships. To the SPD, naval expansion was less an

Imperial panacea than a foreign policy risk. By the turn of the century, the party press was already questioning the efficacy of Germany's alliances with Italy and Austria. The *Dreibund* was perceived to be dead in the water: Germany could "hardly expect much" from Rome, and the Habsburg regime was "scarcely a better ally."[73] The regeneration of Germany's diplomatic fortunes, ideally in a more democratic direction, was important to the party.

In 1898, there had been an embryonic fear that the development of a large German fleet would estrange England and leave Germany isolated. By 1900, this kernel of thought had developed to the point that the SPD could believe that in the event of a major European conflict, England's neutrality alone would not suffice. Germany had lost one ally in 1871; it could not afford to lose another. The possibility of German naval expansion resulting in the alienation of England was unfortunate enough. The vision of German policy provoking England into an alliance with France and Russia (the countries alluded to by Beer in his 1936 article), thus bringing about the encirclement of Germany, was nothing less than a nightmare—one the SPD sought at all costs to avoid.

The stance adopted by the SPD stands in manifest contrast to that of the British left, whose members were markedly reluctant to criticize foreign affairs and were only temporarily brought out of their stupor by the Boer War. In 1895, the Independent Labour Party's manifesto did not even mention foreign policy, and by 1906 the ILP had progressed no further than telling the electorate that "wars are fought to make the rich richer."[74] In the same period, the SPD had developed a foreign policy concept based on strategic and geopolitical concerns. Affirming its loyalty to the parliamentary process, the party agitated within the Reichstag for a foreign policy that stood in stark contrast to the one adopted by Bülow. Although the SPD failed to see its foreign policy agenda implemented, Social Democratic efforts in this sphere deserve to be recognized.

Notes

1. See Niall Ferguson, *The Pity of War* (London, 1998); John Charmley, *Splendid Isolation? Britain and the Balance of Power, 1871-1914* (London, 1999).
2. "Der deutsch-englische Interessengegensatz," *Hamburger Echo*, 11 Mar. 1914.
3. Brett Fairbairn, "Interpreting Wilhelmine Elections: National Issues, Fairness Issues, and Electoral Mobilization," in *Elections, Mass Politics, and Social Change in Modern Germany: New Perspectives*, ed. Larry Eugene Jones and James Retallack (Cambridge and New York, 1992), 17-48; idem, *Democracy in the Undemocratic State: The German Reichstag Elections of 1898 and 1903* (Toronto, 1997).
4. "Kannonfieber und Flottenkoller," *Vorwärts*, 13 Feb. 1897, and "Demagogie," *Hamburger Echo* (hereafter *HE*), 4 Dec. 1897.

5. "Die Marineleichen," *Vorwärts*, 19 Mar. 1897.

6. "Kannonfieber und Flottenkoller," *Vorwärts*, 13 Feb. 1897; the citation is from "Die Marinevorlage," *HE*, 2 Dec. 1897.

7. Bruno Schoenlank, *Stenographische Berichte, über die Verhandlungen des Deutschen Reichstages*, vol. 159, 6 Dec. 1897, 50.

8. Sozialdemokratische Parteivorstand, ed., *Handbuch für Sozialdemokratische Wähler. Der Reichstag 1893-98* (Berlin, 1898), 201; Friedrich Naumann, *Demokratie und Kaisertum. Ein Handbuch für innere Politik*, 4th ed. (Berlin, 1905), 212-20; Bruno Schoenlank, *Stenographische Berichte*, vol. 159, 6 Dec. 1897, 52; see also Franz Mehring, "Weltpolitik," *Die Neue Zeit* (hereafter *DNZ*) 15, no. 1 (1896-97): 801-4.

9. *Handbuch 1898*, 202.

10. Staatsarchiv Hamburg, Politische Polizei S2493 - 6UA11, Sozialdemokratische öffentliche Versammlungen am 7.1.1898. Thema: Die Flottenvermehrung und das Volk. On Hamburg's political police, see Richard J. Evans, *Kneipengespräche im Kaiserreich. Stimmungsberichte der Hamburger Politischen Polizei 1892-1914* (Hamburg, 1989), 7-33.

11. The government's argument that the navy could be used to defend German citizens from injustice was used against it by the *Leipziger Volkszeitung* (hereafter *LVZ*), 3 Dec. 1897, which mockingly called for a navy to protect Germans *within* Germany. A similar argument was used by Molkenbuhr in his Reichstag speech of 8 Dec. 1897: "Do we not have injuries to justice in Germany? I had to spend five months in custody awaiting trial because of the quirks of a public prosecutor. No cruisers came to Altona!" Hermann Molkenbuhr, *Stenographische Berichte*, vol. 159, 8 Dec. 1897, 103. See also Parvus, *Marineforderungen, Kolonialpolitik und Arbeiterinteressen* (Dresden, 1898), 24, for the view that most German emigrants lived in countries that had greater political freedom than Germany itself and went on to become citizens of their new homeland; also Staatsarchiv Hamburg, Politische Polizei S-2493 - 6UA1, and Politische Polizei S733, Bd. 1, Carl Frohme, 1884-1904.

12. See also "Das Flottengesetz," *LVZ*, 29 Nov. 1897.

13. Regrettably, the North-Rhine Westphalia *Hauptstaatsarchiv* in Düsseldorf has no files relating to these protests. Meetings were advertized in the 10, 11, 13 and 14 Jan. 1898 editions of the *Rheinische Zeitung*. On the history of the SPD in Cologne, see Gerhard Brunn, "Vom politischen Kellerkind zur Mehrheitspartei. Die SPD in Köln 1875 bis 1914," in *Sozialdemokratie in Köln. Ein Beitrag zur Stadt- und Parteiengeschichte*, ed. Gerhard Brunn (Cologne, 1986), 49-82.

14. *Rheinische Zeitung*, 18 Jan. 1898; Bruno Schoenlank, *Stenographische Berichte*, vol. 159, 6 Dec. 1897, 46-48.

15. For the suggestion that the 1898 navy bill was the main theme of the SPD's electoral campaign, see Jürgen Lampe, "Das Flottengesetz von 1900 und der Kampf der revolutionären deutschen Sozialdemokratie gegen das maritime Wettrüsten," *Militärgeschichte* 20 (1981): 41-50. It is, however, difficult to imagine that the party's electoral success in that year was a direct result of criticism of the fleet from either a constitutional or a strategic perspective; economic factors appear to have been more important in deciding the party's share of the vote, and in this respect, the party's tactic of publicly linking naval expansion with increased indirect taxation seems to have paid off.

16. August Bebel, *Protokoll Über die Verhandlungen des Parteitages der Sozialdemokratischen Partei Deutschlands*, (Berlin, 1891), 285.

17. Dieter Groh and Peter Brandt, *'Vaterlandslose Gesellen'. Sozialdemokratie und Nation 1860-1990* (Munich, 1992), 60-4; Ivo N. Lambi, *The Navy and German Power Politics, 1862-1914* (Boston, 1984), 57-9.

18. Cited in William H. Maehl, *August Bebel: Shadow Emperor of the German Workers* (Philadelphia, 1980), 339.

19. "Die Dreibund Krisis," *Vorwärts*, 5 July 1896.

20. Francis L. Carsten, *Eduard Bernstein 1850-1932. Eine politische Biographie* (Munich, 1993), 123-42; Ursula Ratz, *Georg Ledebour 1850-1947. Weg und Wirken eines sozialistischen Politikers* (Berlin, 1969), 117; Utz Haltern, *Liebknecht und England. Zur Publizistik Wilhelm Liebknechts während seines Londoner Exils (1850-1862)* (Trier, 1977); Rosemary Ashton, *Little Germany: Exile and Asylum in Victorian England* (Oxford, 1986), 97-138.

21. Karl Kautsky to Franz Mehring, 15 July 1893, cited in William J. Greenwald, "England in the Political Thought of the German Left, 1890-1914" (Ph.D. diss., University of North Carolina, Chapel Hill, 1972), 43.

22. August Bebel, *Stenographische Berichte*, vol. 150, 12 May 1897, 5859-68, here 5867.

23. "Im Spiegel des Auslandes," *Vorwärts*, 11 Dec. 1895.

24. August Bebel, *Stenographische Berichte*, vol. 144, 13 Feb. 1896, 938-45, here 940.

25. H. W. Koch, "The Anglo-German Alliance Negotiations: Missed Opportunity or Myth?" *History* 54 (1969): 378-92; Paul M. Kennedy, "German World Policy and the Alliance Negotiations with England, 1897-1900," *Journal of Modern History* 45 (1973): 605-25.

26. There is a voluminous literature focusing on German naval expansion and Anglo-German relations before the Great War. Given that this is not a historiographical essay, the reader is directed to the classic work by Volker R. Berghahn, *Der Tirpitz-Plan. Genesis und Verfall einer innenpolitischen Krisenstrategie unter Wilhelm II.* (Düsseldorf, 1971); Holger H. Herwig, *"Luxury" Fleet: The Imperial German Navy 1888-1918* (London, 1980); Lambi, *Navy*; Michael Epkenhans, *Die wilhelminischen Flottenrüstung 1908-1914. Weltmachtstreben, industrieller Fortschritt, soziale Integration* (Munich, 1991); for Anglo-German relations, the best study remains Paul M. Kennedy, *The Rise of the Anglo-German Antagonism 1860-1914* (London, 1980).

27. Paul M. Kennedy, *The Realities Behind Diplomacy: Background Influences on British External Policy 1865-1980* (London, 1985), 120.

28. William H. Maehl, "Bebel's Fight against the *Schlachtflotte*, Nemesis to the Primacy of Foreign Policy," in *Proceedings of the American Philosophical Society* 121 (1977): 209-26, here 209. Maehl claims, rightly, that the 1900 navy law overtly threatened Great Britain and led it to seek alliances with potential enemies of Germany; however, his belief that 1900 saw the SPD adopt foreign policy concerns as their guiding principle ignores moves toward this end by the party in earlier years.

29. Parvus, *Marineforderungen*, 21.

30. Ibid., 21, 23.

31. Ibid., 21-23. See also the previously cited speech given by Bebel in Zurich in 1892 in Maehl, *Shadow Emperor*, 339.

32. Parvus, *Marineforderungen*, 22.

33. Maehl appears to have recognized this by the time he wrote Bebel's biography. See Maehl, *Shadow Emperor*, 343-48.

34. See Carl Frohme, *Stenographische Berichte*, vol. 169, 10 Feb. 1900, 3966. With hindsight, Rosa Luxemburg (writing under the pseudonym Junius) suggested that the second navy bill amounted to "a German declaration of war." See Junius, *Die Krise der Sozialdemokratie* (Zurich, 1916), 80. In reality, mere coastal protection was never on Tirpitz's agenda—in 1898 he had already claimed that he sought "as large a navy as England." Cited in Lambi, *Navy*, 156.

35. August Bebel, *Stenographische Berichte*, vol. 169, 10 Feb. 1900, 4011, and see his comments to the Reichstag Budget Committee, 28 Mar. 1900, in Bundesarchiv Berlin, R101 31136.

36. See, for example, "Neue Schiffe, neue Steuern," *Vorwärts*, 5 Dec. 1899, and the cartoon "Der Ansporn," *Der Wahre Jacob*, 2 Jan. 1900.

37. August Bebel, *Stenographische Berichte*, vol. 169, 10 Feb. 1900, 4010-23, here 4011.

38. August Bebel, *Stenographische Berichte*, vol. 171, 6 June 1900, 5815-21, here 5817.

39. See August Bebel's comments, *Stenographische Berichte*, vol. 169, 10 Feb. 1900, 4013-4; Reichstag Budget Committee, 28 Mar. 1900, in Bundesarchiv Berlin R101 31136; *Stenographische Berichte*, vol. 171, 6 June 1900, 5818.

40. August Bebel, *Stenographische Berichte*, vol. 171, 6 June 1900, 5817.

41. August Bebel, *Stenographische Berichte*, vol. 169, 10 Feb. 1900, 4012.

42. Wilhelm Liebknecht, *Stenographische Berichte*, vol. 171, 12 June 1900, 6025-28, here 6028.

43. Ibid., 6025.

44. Ibid.

45. Ibid., 6026.

46. August Bebel, *Stenographische Berichte*, vol. 169, 10 February 1900, 4012.

47. Naumann's article is quoted in Mehring, "Weltpolitik," 802-3.

48. Ibid., 803.
49. Ibid., 804.
50. "Die englische Brille," *LVZ*, 9-10 May 1899, which highlights many aspects Lenin would elaborate in his later work on imperialism. See also Dick Geary, "Perceptions of Britain in Wilhelmine Social Democracy," in *Britain in Europe*, ed. John Milfull (Aldershot, 1999), 49-65.
51. The best study of Social Democracy's response to imperialism remains Hans-Christoph Schröder, *Sozialismus und Imperialismus. Die Auseinandersetzung der deutschen Sozialdemokratie mit dem Imperialismusproblem und der "Weltpolitik" vor 1914* (Cologne, 1966).
52. See Paul M. Kennedy, "Tirpitz, England and the Second Navy Law of 1900: A Strategical Critique," *Militärgeschichtliche Mitteilungen* 2 (1970), 33-58.
53. Eric Rother, "Zur Theorie der Flottenfrage," *Sozialistische Monatshefte*, Dec. 1899, 639-44. See also Roger Fletcher, *Revisionism and Empire: Socialist Imperialism in Germany, 1897-1914* (London, 1984).
54. August Bebel, *Stenographische Berichte*, vol. 169, 10 Feb. 1900, 4022. See also Gerhard Schulz, "Die deutsche Sozialdemokratie und die Entwicklung der auswärtigen Bezeihungen vor 1914. Ein Beitrag zur Geschichte des politischen Denkens und des Parteiwesens" (Ph.D. diss., Free University Berlin, 1952), 216, note 616, and Lampe, "Das Flottengesetz," 48-49.
55. Rother, "Theorie," 641.
56. Ibid.
57. Paul Singer, *Protokoll Über die Verhandlungen des Parteitages der Sozialdemokratischen Partei Deutschlands*, (Berlin, 1900), 158.
58. Rother, "Theorie," 643.
59. Mehring, "Weltpolitik," 804 and "Die 'starke Flotte,'" *HE*, 21 Apr. 1899.
60. Rother, "Theorie," 643.
61. Ibid., 640.
62. For example, "Die Engländer in Südafrika" and "Der Boerenkrieg," both *HE*, 7 October 1899 and 14 Jan. 1900; by way of contrast, see "England am Scheideweg," *Vorwärts*, 3 Feb. 1900.
63. Ernst Frei, "Zur Flottenpolitik," *Sozialistische Monatshefte*, Jan. 1900, 36-38, 37.
64. Ibid., 37.
65. "Weltpolitik," *Vorwärts*, 16 July 1899.
66. Frei, "Zur Flottenpolitik," 37. See also "Weltpolitik," *Vorwärts*, 16 July 1899.
67. Frei, "Zur Flottenpolitik," 38.
68. Ibid.
69. Contrast Parvus, *Marineforderungen*, 24-35, with Hermann Molkenbuhr, *Stenographische Berichte*, vol. 159, 9 Dec. 1897, 105, and August Bebel, *Stenographische Berichte*, vol. 171, 6 June 1900, 5817.
70. See, for example, the cartoon contrasting a new battleship and a dilapidated schoolhouse in *Der Wahre Jacob*, 19 June 1900. That this motif was popular among the European left was attested to by the comment of the British socialist Philip Snowdon: "[A] beautiful school is a grander sight than a battleship." Cited in Kenneth E. Miller, *Socialism and Foreign Policy: Theory and Practice in Britain to 1931* (The Hague, 1967), 47.
71. Eduard Bernstein, *Die Wahrheit über die Einkreisung Deutschlands. Dem deutschen Volke dargelegt* (Berlin, 1919), 12-13. Bernstein wrote the pamphlet at Kautsky's behest in 1915; it was first published four years later.
72. Historicus (pseudonym for Beer), manuscript written in April 1936, Beer NL, 1. Personliche Unterlagen and 2. Korrespondenz, Archiv der sozialen Demokratie (AdsD), Friedrich Ebert Stiftung (FES), Bonn-Bad Godesberg; the initial draft was prepared in August 1935; see Beer NL, 3. Artikeln vom Max Beer, AdsD, FES.
73. "Der östliche Verbündete," *HE*, 6 May 1900.
74. Cited in Kenneth O. Morgan, *Kier Hardie: Radical and Socialist* (London, 1984), 178. See also Douglas J. Newton, *British Labour, European Socialism and the Struggle for Peace, 1889-1914* (Oxford, 1985), 58.

The "Malet Incident," October 1895

A Prelude to the Kaiser's "Krüger Telegram" in the Context of the Anglo-German Imperialist Rivalry

⇒⋅◇⋅⇐

WILLEM-ALEXANDER VAN'T PADJE

I

The last German emperor's impetuosity has been frequently described.[1] His impulsive comments, actions, and orders created misunderstandings, diplomatic crises, and personal insults, which in turn led to estrangement and suspicion in the relations between Germany and the Great Powers. The "Malet Incident" of October 1895—which revolved around the British ambassador's[2] threat that German action in the Transvaal might have "serious complications"—forms a significant example with regard to the growing Anglo-German imperialist rivalry. As such it might be described as one of the most deplorable legacies of the Wilhelmine age.[3]

Only two and a half months later, the Kaiser "responded" to the incident by sending his infamous congratulatory message—the "Krüger Telegram" of 3 January 1896—to the president of the South African Boer Republic.[4] He obviously felt inclined to give a clear signal to the British government that Germany was anything but a *quantité négligeable*. Its effect one might call "fatal,"[5] or even one of the "greatest blunders in the history of modern diplomacy,"[6] as Wilhelm II repeatedly had challenged Anglo-German relations with a quite ill-considered step.

The day after the telegram, the German ambassador at London, Count von Hatzfeldt,[7] informed Baron Friedrich von Holstein at the German Foreign Office that he had assured Lord Salisbury that Germany still had "legitimate interests" in the Transvaal, and that one of its main interests was to maintain the status quo in South Africa.[8] Holstein, however, retrospectively regarded the telegram as the real beginning of the Anglo-German antagonism, as he wrote in 1907: "England, that rich and placid nation, was goaded into her present defensive attitude toward Germany by continuous threats and insults on the part of the Germans. The Kruger [*sic*] telegram began it all."[9]

II

On 4 January 1896, Sir Frank Lascelles,[10] the newly appointed British ambassador to the Berlin Imperial Court, reported to Salisbury that "it would ... be impossible to exaggerate either the extent or the bitterness of the irritation which the Transvaal business has excited against us." In his "daily conversations" with the German foreign secretary, he had noticed that Baron von Marschall[11] had "more than once alluded to the difficulty of his position." Marschall complained that at present he sat in "a hole, ... into which his efforts to remain on friendly terms with us had led him." At that stage, it is interesting to note, Marschall did not mention the "Krüger Telegram" to Lascelles. The latter cautiously "avoided the subject," as he had not yet received instructions from London about what "line" he should take with regard to it.

Sir Frank's advice was not to overemphasize the telegram's significance, although he admitted that it "evidently [showed] a most unfriendly feeling towards us": "Personally[,] I should be inclined to take no notice of it much especially as I hope that the effect it will produce in the Transvaal, where we seem to be on good terms with Krüger, may be very slight. *It will be a serious matter if the Emperor becomes actively hostile towards us, and he is so impulsive and impetuous that this is a contingency which must be considered.*"

Lascelles justified his warning about the Kaiser's attitude with what he had heard from Marschall on New Year's Day. Despite the emperor's civil language to Sir Frank, the baron secretly admitted: "His Majesty was much displeased [*très mécontent*] at what had occurred in the Transvaal." *The Times*'s correspondent in Berlin, Sir Valentine Chirol,[12] had even heard a rumor that "the Emperor was so rabid when the news first reached him that he thought of sending back his English uniforms with the remark that they were only fit to be worn by South African bandits." In addition, Chirol, who recently had had interviews with Marschall and Holstein, told Lascelles that both politicians had given him to understand that "although there could be no question of war, the Germans would pay us out by making themselves as disagreeable as possible in every part of the world, and that The Emperor was reported to have said that there was at all events one part of Africa over which England could not claim Suzerainty and that was Egypt." Sir Frank closed with the promise to do his "best to smooth matters over." But he admitted that at present he could do nothing to alleviate a situation that was "most serious" and "far more unsatisfactory than I could have believed possible."[13]

Four days later, however, Lascelles had the impression that there was—at least on Marschall's part—"an evident desire ... to smooth things over"; but "it would be very difficult" for the German journalists "to refrain from answering the very violent

attacks of the 'Times', and the abuse of The Emperor in all the English Press." He
also observed "a feeling" that the German government thought it had gone "too far."
The Kaiser's telegram was now regarded as "unnecessary and perhaps impolitic,"
since the Germans had been "taken by surprise [at] the violence of the English
Press" and at the prospect—or "calamity," as Lascelles called it—that a possible war
"with Germany would not be unpopular ... in England." On the other hand, Jules
Herbette,[14] the French ambassador, had told his English colleague that he "was convinced the present trouble would blow over[,] and he declined to believe in the possibility of a war between Germany and England."[15]

On 8 January, the Kaiser explained his motives to Queen Victoria in reply to a
letter in which she had expressed her "deep regret" at the telegram. The telegram, he
had written, had made "a very painful impression" in England. Victoria had emphasized her disappointment at the impulsiveness of her grandson, as it had always been
"our great wish ... to keep on the best terms with Germany, trying to act together,"
but now she feared that the German "Agents in the Colonies do the very reverse,
which deeply grieves us."[16]

In his answer, Wilhelm regretted that the telegram had been "totally misunderstood by the British Press." He emphasized that it "never was ... intended as a step
against England or your Government." He emphasized that he "was standing up for
law, order and obedience to a Sovereign." He also alluded to Sir Frank's information
that "the men [involved in the Jameson raid] were acting in open disobedience" to the
queen's order, and therefore had to be regarded as "rebels." In accordance with his
grandmother's "glorious example," Wilhelm charmingly wrote, he had tried to maintain peace, "which had been suddenly violated," even as he also tried to protect the
Germans and the interests of the German bondholders in the Transvaal. He totally
agreed with the queen's wish for Anglo-German cooperation, as he thought it "simply nonsense that two great nations ... should stand aside and view each other askance
with the rest of Europe as lookers-on," while repeatedly blaming the British press,
whose "conjectures ... made people rather hot and rash .... What would the Duke of
Wellington and old Blücher say if they saw this?" the emperor emotively concluded.[17]
Thus, this letter gives evidence of Wilhelm's determination to respond to the British
press attacks and provocation.

Three days later, Lascelles reported that "nothing could have been more amiable
than Marschall's language," which had become "diametrically opposite in tone of his
conversations of last week." Apparently, the foreign secretary had underestimated the
telegram's effect and had truly been "taken aback by the outburst of popular feeling
in England." On the other hand, Marschall had presumably realized that no other
European power was "prepared to join him in making war upon England on account
of so[-]called German interests in the Transvaal." Sir Frank interpreted the foreign
secretary's behavior as a "decided inclination to 'climb down,'" imagining that "the
best thing" he could do was "to enable him to do so in a graceful manner." With
regard to Marschall's and Holstein's "serious friendly warnings" to Chirol, the
ambassador raised the hope that those might be regarded "as a bit of bluff," but he

still handled them quite carefully; he was "not quite convinced that they did not think that they could have united the rest of Europe against us and may even have attempted to do so."

Lascelles gave two possible explanations for the sending of the Kaiser's telegram. First, the emperor still felt insulted by a press attack in the *Standard*[18] that was published when he had visited Cowes the previous year; subsequently Wilhelm "had made up his mind to have hit at us on the first favourable opportunity which he thought he saw in the Transvaal question." Second, Marschall, who had "often been reproached with neglecting German Colonial Interests and of favouring ... England, thought he saw an opportunity of gaining a cheap diplomatic victory" over Britain, which would improve his position and power in the Reichstag (both of which had allegedly weakened in the past months).[19] Sir Frank, however, was sure that "the very strong expression of public opinion in England and the increase of the British fleet" had taken away the telegram's objectivity and put Germany in a passive position, a "termination" which Lascelles noted with relief, suggesting that, it would be "the wisest course ... to act as though it had never arisen."[20] The "Malet Incident," however, did not arise as a possible motive in Lascelles' considerations.

By the end of January, Salisbury told Sir Frank that he agreed with him that his "present business" was "to persuade the Emperor that the two nations are on very good terms, and that he has never made a bore of himself." With regard to the telegram, the prime minister thought the Kaiser's "*boutade*"[21] to be "singularly clumsy": "As a matter of fact," he wrote, "the impression produced by the events of the last month[22] has been very profound among all classes here. Among politicians and officials no one will listen to a good word for the Germans." Under those circumstances, Salisbury considered it "better to keep clear of colonial negotiations. We shall do no good at present." On the other hand, he believed that after matters had developed further, Britain might have "more chance to come to an agreement," though he was not sure in which direction the political mood in Germany would turn: "Either they [the Germans] will become more mad with the colonial idea, and will commit some patent folly, or they may drop it and then they may talk sense again."[23] In his reply, Sir Frank repeatedly underlined "the violent outburst of Anti[-]German feeling in England" that had certainly come as a surprise to the German people. He therefore hoped that it would "prevent for some time to come any further attempts to 'teach us a lesson.'" However, as long as the British press did not "calm down," he foresaw the danger of continuing counterattacks from the German side, "whether official or otherwise," because German journalists "cannot but reply to attacks on The Emperor."[24]

In a memorandum, Chirol expressed his surprise at Marschall's complaints about the British press. He justified the tone of his telegrams and reports by explaining: "Ever since my return to Berlin in November both he [Marschall] & Baron Holstein had prepared me for some impending demonstration of hostility towards England by their repeated warnings that the selfishness & arrogance of British policy were exhausting Germany's patience & good will. The Transvaal itself was mentioned to me incidentally as one of the points besides Egypt where retribution might overtake us." With regard to the Kaiser's telegram, he added, Marschall had pointed out that the emperor "had not taken this step on any mere personal impulse, but after consultation with his advisers & that it was intended as 'a lesson to England' that she could not with impunity play fast & loose with Germany's friendship."[25]

Chirol then alluded to his conversation with Holstein, who had appealed to "the friendly & confidential relations which had subsisted for some years between us." He quoted Holstein as follows: "Things look very black & I do not think you realize in England how black they look for you. In such critical circumstances there are of course many things I cannot disclose to you, but I want to impress upon you once more & through you upon your friends in England, before it is too late, that never since, perhaps, 1810 has England been in such a dangerous position as at the present hour."[26] Holstein had asked Chirol to use his influence in the higher quarters of society and government[27] and to do what he could for his country's sake. Holstein emphasized that he was "an old friend of England" and knew what he was talking about. Returning to the malicious newspaper campaigns in both countries, Chirol remarked that the German government's influence over the press might "not be so skilfully worked as in Prince Bismarck's time, but its ramifications are more extensive than ever."[28] As he had a quite close insight into the Foreign Office's Press Bureau— more than Marschall imagined, as Chirol underlined—he had "good reasons for believing that the recent anti-English campaign in the press was initiated and carried on under direct instructions from that Department." He also stressed that it was "most immediately responsible" for those utterances, which were produced "hardly anywhere with greater violence."[29]

Accordingly, Lascelles was not surprised when the German press began "to be unpleasant again," although he attributed the attack as a countermove to the recent tone of the British press. On the whole, Sir Frank held the view "that the [German] Government really wish to be on friendly terms with England, perhaps because they feel that they are likely to get the worst of it if they make themselves too disagreeable." Lascelles regarded the Kaiser's latest extraordinary civility to Swaine,[30] the well-experienced British military attaché, as an indication of Wilhelm's intention to seek "anything more than personal friendship."[31]

However, if the Kaiser was really seeking "anything more than personal friendship," what was the actual motive behind sending the telegram, especially in light of Marschall's explanation that it had not been the result of the Kaiser's impulsiveness? The Jameson raid was surely the occasion or, rather, the immediate cause, but there might have been another reason. Something must have disturbed the Kaiser's affection toward England, something that weighed heavily on his mind and was vented in the telegram. The message itself was clear: Germany could not accept being treated as a *quantité négligeable* or second-class power in Africa by the British government. Where and when had the Kaiser gained that impression? Or had he been told that this was Germany's situation?

Shortly after his arrival at Berlin in December 1895, Lascelles had written to Salisbury that he had "every reason to be satisfied" with his reception. He emphasized that "nothing could exceed the amiability of The Emperor and Empress[,] and both Hohenlohe and Marschall have been as civil and cordial as possible." However, the Austrian ambassador, Count Szoegyenyi,[32] had informed Sir Frank soon after his arrival that the emperor had told him "the whole story of the Malet incident" and that "he had been perfectly satisfied with Malet's explanations." The Kaiser himself had added only that "he was determined to remain friends with England whatever they might do to him." Thus, Lascelles was not surprised that no allusion had been made to the incident during his audience; on the contrary, the emperor had mentioned Malet's name more than once, apparently in a friendly manner. Wilhelm evidently tried to overlook the incident, but the insult, irritation, and distress it had caused him was not forgotten. Lascelles therefore concluded with an initial but carefully formulated impression: "On the whole I think I may consider that my mission has begun hopefully[,] although it is far too early for me to form an opinion worth expressing."[33] The main reason for his cautious judgment was the still strained situation between London and Berlin, caused by Malet's provoking remarks to Marschall about German intrigues in South Africa shortly before his final departure to London. Obviously, Lascelles was convinced that the Kaiser's exaggerated amiability was only a means to disguise his real emotional state.

One week later, Lascelles reported an interview with the foreign secretary that had taken place shortly after the emperor had spoken to Swaine about a possible Anglo-German agreement. Sir Frank described Marschall's manner as "perfectly friendly," but declared that he had played "the part of the candid friend who wished to point out the error of our ways." According to Lascelles, it was "evident from the similarity of language that the Foreign Secretary knew all about the Emperor's language to Swaine," suspecting he had expected his visit and accordingly had prepared this conversation. Sir Frank confessed that he was "rather at a loss to understand what it all means": he could not make out whether the Kaiser was "seriously alarmed and wants to frighten us," or whether he wished the British government to know that he was "so well informed of all that takes place." Lascelles thought it would be "impossible for us to come to an understanding with Russia or indeed any other Power without his knowledge." Nonetheless, he saw a certain insecurity in the Kaiser's behavior: "It is evident that it is a matter of the greatest importance to Germany to know what line England will take in the event of a European war, for as Marschall pointed out today, if a war broke out between the triple alliance [sic] and Russia, France would certainly take part in it, and Germany would find herself in the position of being obliged to fight for her very existence as a state."

Sir Frank, however, continued by writing that "the distrust of England" in Germany was "so great" that the German fear of being left in the lurch became more and more apparent. Even after the breakout of "hostilities," England "might be forced by public opinion to back out and leave the other Powers to fight the battle by themselves." For that very reason, "Germany must insist that England should bind herself by formal obligations," Lascelles explained, adding: "Marschall let drop the word 'Convention.'" Sir Frank admitted that he saw great difficulties for "any English Government" to undertake such commitments, but made no secret of his view that the failure of an Anglo-German agreement could have quite dangerous consequences: as long as London remained in "isolation," and as long as Berlin was not "absolutely sure" of British support, it "could only advise her Allies not to agree to English suggestions for active measures." In summary, Lascelles observed that there was "an impression" in Germany that Britain was "inclined to treat Germany as a 'quantité négligeable.'" In his opinion, this was the obvious reason for the emperor's latest remarks.[34]

But what had actually happened earlier in 1895 that set the stage for the "Malet Incident" in October?

In the first six months of the year, the Kaiser had repeatedly shown a most cordial manner toward Great Britain. At the annual ambassador's dinner in January, Malet presumed that "His Majesty desired to make a demonstration of friendliness towards me before the other Ambassadors" when he spoke entirely to him alone after dinner. The recent colonial disputes had apparently burdened the Kaiser's conscience: "He was at great pains to assure me of his constant desire that the cordial feeling between England and Germany should increase and not diminish. I thought it as well to assert as plainly as possible that, whatever might have gone wrong, the blame lay here and not with us."[35]

To Sir Edward, Wilhelm expressed quite frankly his concerns about, and his desire for, cordial Anglo-German relations. Obviously, he saw in the ambassador the last glimmer of hope for an understanding. By contrast, Wilhelm's present chancellor (Prince Chlodwig zu Hohenlohe-Schillingsfürst) seemed to be too aged and weak; his foreign secretary (Marschall) had just escaped political defeat; and his ambassador in London (Hatzfeldt) had not only failed to set up an agreement (despite having resided in London for a decade), but had also just faced "a rather sharp passage" with Kimberley, in which he had been assured by the foreign secretary that Britain would "speak the strongest word" in an Anglo-German imperialist conflict.[36]

Malet, however, was not able to contribute to any further improvement in relations or a reconciliation. Despite Salisbury's return after the fall of the Liberal government in June, Malet contemplated his retirement, though for "purely personal" reasons, as he emphasized.[37] Sir Edward begged Salisbury to inform the emperor about his leaving before it would be announced in the newspapers or he would "leak [it] out" himself, as the Kaiser was "susceptible" on that point. Malet thought it wise "to remove any idea that I am to be dismissed or removed for reasons of State."[38]

On 6 July, Sir Edward informed Salisbury that he did not believe "any great change has taken place in the relations between England and Germany from what they were when you left [in August 1892]." Malet explained that the Kaiser and the German government had "thoroughly distrusted" the late Liberal cabinet, and felt confirmed in their attitude when Germany was "really coquetting" with the Transvaal. Moreover, Kimberley "no doubt used very strong language" to Hatzfeldt: "There is, indeed[,] no doubt that he threatened war(!)." The German Foreign Office had been "furious," but Sir Edward thought it had been treated only "as it deserved" at that time. Malet made clear that he himself had "used language of a less minatory character but designed to induce them to understand that the national feeling in England was just as susceptible over *Delagoa Bay*[39] as over Egypt." In December 1894, when British support for Italy was in question and the latter's drift from the Triple Alliance toward France became likely, the emperor and the German government had been "profoundly mistrustful of us." This time, Malet thought that "things [had] at last smoothed down," though he frankly regretted that Dr. Kayser, the head of the Colonial Department, who had "fortunately" been "ill to death's door" during the winter, "unluckily now recovered and has begun to rear his venomous little serpent head again and will assuredly sooner or later give us trouble." Still, Sir Edward confidently believed that the German government as a whole was "sincerely desirous of taking the opportunity [of] your return to office to come to a general settlement of outstanding [colonial] questions."[40]

But did Malet really want to retire for "purely personal" reasons? Does his letter of 6 July not give evidence of his mental exhaustion? Do his remarks not show a certain type of disappointment, if not anger, which caused him to lose his diplomatic tact a few months later, resulting in the spectacular climax of his distinguished diplomatic career?[41]

III

On 14 October, on the occasion of Hohenlohe's farewell dinner for Sir Edward and his wife, Malet engaged in an after-dinner conversation with the chancellor and Marschall at the Wilhelmstrasse.[42] Malet pointed out that South Africa was the "black spot" in Anglo-German relations and that German encouragement of the Boers might lead to "serious complications."[43] This remark—or as Martin Gosselin, who was as first secretary in charge of the embassy before Lascelles's arrival, put it, this "friendly hint given by Sir Edward" with regard to the German "intrigues ... in the Transvaal"—caused significant "irritation." It had the consequence that no member of the emperor's immediate entourage subsequently said farewell to the Malets at the train station.[44] This made an "unpleasant impression," as Gosselin observed, and "was a fact which all present at the station noticed." Accordingly, it became the "talk of the town" and was "in everybody's mouth." The contrast was all the greater when compared with the sendoff given the Russian ambassador, Count Shouvalov,[45] and his wife only a month before. On their departure, the emperor had come to the station himself and had conducted the ambassador's wife to the carriage: "[I]f he could not do the same for the Doyen and Doyenne, & His Grandmother's Representative into the bargain, he might at least have sent some member of the household with a message," Gosselin complained. "In curious contrast to this behaviour was the presence of the whole Court at the Requiem Mass for Tsar Alexander III [who had been assassinated in October 1894] at the Russian Embassy yesterday." For Gosselin, this clearly indicated that "a hint" must have been conveyed from the Palace to stay away from the station.[46]

Colonel Swaine had already informed Barrington about the lack of appreciation and honor one day after Malet's departure. He emphasized that Sir Edward's "last utterances" to Marschall had "created the greatest astonishment, irritation, and discontent"—sentiments that were only increased by Salisbury's reply to Hatzfeldt.[47] Swaine, however, thought that "the warning" Malet had felt compelled to give the baron "was one which for his own name and for the sake of his Country he felt in justice bound to place on record; and the irritation which it has here caused is a proof that it was justified. Personally he did himself harm by it here, but that carries no weight with it in Malet[']s character, and he probably is laughing in his sleeve at the slight put upon him."[48]

Three weeks after Malet's outburst, the emperor, after spending some minutes in conversation with Hohenlohe in the foyer of the opera house during the interval of a gala presentation for the king of Portugal, sent for Gosselin. Wilhelm declared to him: "I cannot think what has happened to Sir Edward Malet: we always thought him so prudent, and anxious to keep things straight, and maintain good relations between the two countries; but the language he used, when taking leave at the Foreign Office, was very surprising: he actually talked of an 'ultimatum.'" Gosselin ventured to interrupt Wilhelm, replying that Malet had conveyed to him "a full account of all that had passed" and saying he was "quite sure he [Malet] never could have used [the] word 'ultimatum.'" The emperor, however, insisted on the point, declaring that the words "ultimatum," "difference of opinion," and even "war" had been used: "Don't you think that is a very dangerous term?" he asked Gosselin. He then continued: "I can't understand it: we have known him so long, and he has now left us in an atmosphere of sulphur and gunpowder. I instructed my Ambassador [Count Hatzfeldt] to enquire of Lord Salisbury whether Sir Edward had been told to use such language, and his answer was that no such instruction had been sent." Gosselin once again told the emperor that he must have been misinformed. He pointed out that he, the Kaiser, had known Sir Edward for many years; hence, he must have been aware that Malet was "not the man to make use of any such expression as 'ultimatum' unless [expressly] instructed to do so." The Kaiser, however, still not satisfied with Gosselin's portrayal of the affair, left him with the words: "Well,... I cannot make it out. Good night, but remember we are not Venezuelans."[49] Retrospectively, Gosselin thought it interesting that the emperor had carefully "refrained from making any mention of the Transvaal by name." Apart from that, it struck him that Wilhelm "was anxious to explain & excuse the marked coolness, which had been displayed by the Court" on Malet's departure. "The more so as the Empress was at pains" to explain to Gosselin's wife how very sorry she was to lose Malet's wife, Lady Ermyntrude, "an expression which was subsequently repeated by the Mistress of the Robes and other ladies of the Court."[50]

One day later, Swaine wrote to Malet to express his absolute loyalty and confidence in him:

> You are too well known to us and to the Foreign Office to warrant any idea that you could have said anything intended to convey or interpret an ultimatum. But you know what the Germans are. They are jealous of us everywhere and they wish at once to jump

into the position of a great Colonial Empire. They ... wish us to knuckle under to them in every part of the globe. In other words they would like to drive us into the arms of the Triple Alliance. That your *warning* was well timed is proved by the great irritation it has produced; and the inference is that they are intriguing against us in *those* parts at this moment.[51]

On 7 November, Malet sent his own detailed report to Salisbury, describing exactly what had transpired on that night at the Wilhelmstrasse and what had "produced so unfavourable an impression towards him on the part of the Emperor." Sir Edward stressed that "the fact that this language should have given umbrage" had filled him "with unfeigned surprise":

> What passed was this: I said to Prince Hohenlohe that now that I was leaving I should like to speak to him about the only matter which, as far as I could see, contained real germs of danger to the friendship of Germany and England and that this was the question of the Transvaal about which I had, in the past, had several conversations with Baron von Marschall[52] and that I was anxious on the subject, because I feared that it might not be known in Germany how intense the feeling was in England in regard to it. I was alarmed lest the Transvaal Government should take a false view of the friendly attitude towards it of Germany and should be encouraged to acts which would place England in great embarrassment.[53]

Hohenlohe replied that what Malet had told him had been very interesting. He had not gone into the matter himself, but he said that he would inquire about it. Sir Edward emphasized in his report that "the whole conversation was perfectly friendly."[54] He also stressed that he had been motivated only by a desire to avert a misunderstanding that might imperil the policy he had steadily pursued during the whole time he had been British ambassador at Berlin, that is, removing dangers to a firm friendship between Germany and Great Britain. With regard to the Kaiser's being "under the impression that he had used the word 'ultimatum,'" he could only assure Salisbury that neither the word nor such a thought had come from him. He had been careful to say nothing that would lead the prince to suppose that he had been conveying official sentiments of Her Majesty's government or that he was speaking other than academically about possible future contingencies: "I need hardly say that had I had such a communication to make from Her Majesty's Government, I should not have made it in an after dinner conversation when I was being entertained in the kindest manner by Prince Hohenlohe at a banquet on the occasion of my retirement."[55]

On the same day, Malet composed a memorandum detailing his farewell audience with the emperor, which took place ten days after the dinner hosted by Prince Hohenlohe. On this occasion, the Kaiser, who "must have been in possession of any report" of Sir Edward's language by then, showed the kindest manner toward him. Moreover, when Malet saw Marschall a week later—on the afternoon of the day he left—"no inkling of dissatisfaction passed the Foreign Secretary's lips. We parted with exchange of sincere expressions of friendship and esteem and His Excellency came to the station and conducted my wife to the railway carriage[.] My surprise at the *finale* is therefore natural." Thus, Malet had only one explanation as to how the whole incident could have occurred: "Prince Hohenlohe knew nothing about the Transvaal question. His natural course therefore was to send for the dossier. The stormy scenes between Count Hatzfeldt and Lord Kimberley would be recorded in it[56] and my language and Lord Kimberley[']s, if the Chancellor made a verbal report to The Emperor, may have got mixed or The Emperor might have thought that I had endeavoured to imitate Lord Kimberley[']s menacing attitude."[57]

In the meantime, Gosselin had also made further investigations. To his surprise, Marschall, whom he had seen twice that week, "never alluded to the subject."[58] He only heard from other quarters that the foreign secretary himself had handed to Holstein a memorandum of the conversation, "saying that he had omitted the word '*war*,'" which Malet had used, "as it looked so bad on paper!" Gosselin, however, still thought that the paper had been drawn up—or at all events inspired—by Hohenlohe.[59]

Salisbury sincerely regretted that the "misunderstanding" had produced such a "disagreeable impression" upon the emperor. He informed Gosselin that Malet's explanation had arrived. In that explanation, Malet had been "naturally anxious" to explain the intent of his words to Hohenlohe. Malet had also sought "to disclaim the use of one or two most unsuitable words which by some mistake he was understood to have used." However, the prime minister still had difficulty understanding how the incident could have occurred: "It is impossible to offer an explanation of the mode in which the misconception has arisen; but as it was practically confined to one or two words, the possibility of some confusion produced by accidental causes is evidently conceivable."

Salisbury also reemphasized that Malet had acted without his knowledge. He had "never" addressed to Sir Edward "any instructions whatever upon the special subject which was referred to in the conversation under discussion."[60] In a third meeting with Marschall, Gosselin referred to the emperor's astonishment at Malet's language when they had met at the opera. Marschall, however, did not know about the meeting and asked Gosselin for further details. Gosselin repeated their conversation. Upon his mention of the word "*ultimatum*," "the Baron observed he had never reported any such word as having been used by Sir Edward: 'the Ambassador referred to a possible *war*, but never said the word *ultimatum*: that must have been entirely the impression left on H.M.'s mind from a perusal of my minute of the conversation.'" In addition, the foreign secretary reconfirmed that he had modified the word "war" to the "the most '*serious complications*.'"[61] To that confession, Gosselin emphasized in a later report: "It is quite true the word 'Krieg' did not occur in the minute, but His Excellency must have verbally repeated it to the Emperor, as His Majesty used the very same word when speaking of the conversation to me at the Opera House."[62] He expressed his gladness about Marschall's confirmation, as it agreed with what Malet had written to him. Gosselin cleverly added that: "*if* indeed the word 'war' had been used by Sir Edward, ... he in no way referred to a war between England and Germany, but to the possibility of a war between the Cape and the Transvaal." To that explanation, Marschall had exclaimed: "Oh! That is quite a different matter." He had thought Malet had alluded to a European war. After Gosselin had read out Salisbury's clarifying letter and Malet's report to the prime minister of 7 November, Marschall declared he was "much pleased" to have learned the letter's content. He stated that he would like to submit them to the Kaiser "to put the matter … in its true light" and to "rectify [this] unfortunate error."

On 18 November, Marschall presented the two letters to the emperor and returned them four days later. On Salisbury's letter were written in pencil the words in the Kaiser's handwriting: "Read. 18/11.95 and satisfied [Gelesen und befriedigt] W." Marschall also delivered the emperor's apologetic explanation that he had not wished Gosselin "to understand that Sir Edward had used the word '*ultimatum*'; but merely that that was the impression left on the emperor's mind from a perusal of the report of the Ambassador's observations." Gosselin, however, wrote to Salisbury later—"in justice to himself"—to say that he felt certain the emperor "distinctly told him at the Opera house that the Ambassador had employed the word itself." On the other side, Marschall admitted: "I must say, quite between ourselves, that I think it was a misfortune that His Majesty did not Himself talk the matter over with the Ambassador, when he came to say goodbye." The emperor had avoided the opportunity of speaking to Malet on the subject at the farewell audience,[63] but a day later he complained to Swaine of the language of his chief—something the latter mentioned to Sir Edward only shortly before his departure.[64]

IV

Thus, Malet left Berlin with virtually no honors or signs of appreciation from the German side.[65] It was left to the Bismarcks in Friedrichsruh to regret (albeit prior to the incident) Malet's final departure. "It is a pity, that Malet will not stay: under present circumstances you could not possibly have a better man in Germany," Herbert wrote to Lord Rosebery.[66] But who would have expected that such a distinguished and experienced ambassador would destroy his diplomatic reputation by dropping such a bombshell on the eve of his resignation? This action is all the more remarkable when one considers that Malet was well aware of the Kaiser's sensitivity and his impetuosity.

The "Malet Incident," therefore, has to be regarded as an unintentional prelude to the "Krüger Telegram." Wilhelm II now had reason and motive enough (*Jetzt erst recht! Euch werde ich es zeigen!*) to demonstrate German power and determination.

Notes

*   The author wishes to extend his thanks to the Duke University Manuscript Department for allowing the reproduction of excerpts from the Malet Family Papers. He would also like to express his gratitude to Lord Salisbury for allowing the reproduction of texts obtained from the papers of the third Marquess.

1. Most recently by Giles MacDonogh, *The Last Kaiser: William the Impetuous* (London, 2000), passim, and John C. G. Röhl, *Wilhelm II. Der Aufbau der Persönlichen Monarchie, 1888-1900* (Munich, 2001), passim. Underscored text in cited documents is rendered throughout in italics. British spellings are preserved in direct quotations.

2. Sir Edward Baldwin Malet (1837-1908), ambassador at Berlin 1884-95.

3. Cf. Paul M. Kennedy, *The Rise of the Anglo-German Antagonism, 1860-1914* (London, 1980), 195-222.

4. John Gallagher, Ronald E. Robinson, and Alice Denny, *Africa and the Victorians: The Official Mind of Imperialism* (London, 1961), 343, 430-31; *Die Grosse Politik der Europäischen Kabinette 1871-1914* [hereafter cited as *GP*], ed. Johannes Lepsius, Albrecht Mendelssohn-Bartholdy, and Friedrich Thimme, vol. 11 (Berlin, 1923); no. 2610, Kaiser Wilhelm II to Paul Krüger, 3 Jan. 1896, tel. sent 11.20am: "I express my sincere congratulations that, supported by your people without appealing for the help of friendly Powers, you have succeeded by your own energetic action against armed bands which invaded your country as disturbers of the peace and have thus been enabled to restore peace and safeguard the independence of the country against attacks from the outside." Krüger's immediate reply to the Kaiser: "I express to Your Majesty my deepest gratitude for Your Majesty's congratulations. With God's help we hope to continue to do everything possible for the existence of the Republic." Both in S. Lee, *King Edward VII, A Biography, vol. 1: From Birth to Accession,* (London 1925), page 722.

5. Röhl, *Wilhelm II. 1888-1900,* 867; Harald Rosenbach, *Das Deutsche Reich, Großbritannien und der Transvaal* (Göttingen, 1993), 50.

6. William L. Langer, *The Diplomacy of Imperialism 1890-1902,* 2nd ed. (New York, 1968), vol. 1,254.

7. Paul Count von Hatzfeldt-Wildenburg (1831-1901), foreign secretary, 1881-85, ambassador at London, 1885-1901.

8. *GP* xi, no. 2613, 33-34; Hatzfeldt to German Foreign Office (hereafter FO), 4 Jan. 1896, tel., private c/o Holstein. See Hatfield House [hereafter HH] (Salisbury Papers), A/120/22; Lascelles to Salisbury, 8 Jan. 1896, tel., private: "What he [Hatzfeldt] had said was that Germany could not tolerate a change in the 'status quo' and demanded the maintenance of the South African Republic as settled by the [London] Convention of [Feb.] 1884."

9. Norman Rich and M. H. Fisher, eds., *The Holstein Papers: Memoirs* (Cambridge, 1955), 1:160.

10. Sir Frank Cavendish Lascelles (1841-1920), British ambassador at St. Petersburg 1894-95; at Berlin, Dec. 1895-1908.

11. Adolf Baron Marschall von Bieberstein (1842-1912), foreign secretary, 1890-97; ambassador at Constantinople, 1897-1912; and at London, 1912.

12. Sir (Ignatius) Valentine Chirol (1852-1929), *The Times* correspondent in Berlin, 1892-96.

13. HH (Salisbury Papers), A/120/21; Lascelles to Salisbury, 4 Jan. 1896, private.

14. Jules Gabriel Herbette (1839-1911), ambassador at Berlin, 1886-96.

15. HH (Salisbury Papers), A/120/24; Lascelles to Salisbury, 8 Jan. 1896, private.

16. G. E. Buckle, ed., *Letters of Queen Victoria: A Selection from Her Majesty's Correspondence and Journal between the Years 1886-1901,* 3rd series (London, 1932), 3:8-9, hereafter *LQV;* Queen Victoria to Kaiser Wilhelm II, *Osborne,* 5 Jan. 1896, copy.

17. Sidney Lee, *King Edward VII: A Biography. From Birth To Accession* (London, 1925), 1:726-27; Kaiser Wilhelm II to Queen Victoria, *Neues Palais,* 8 Jan. 1896. See *LQV,* 3rd ser., 3:17-18; extract from the queen's journal, *Osborne,* 10 January 1896.

18. A. Eubule Evans, "Germany under the Empire," *Contemporary Review* [hereafter cited as *CR*] 69 (1896): 170.

19. For the "Marschall Crisis," see John C. G. Röhl, *Germany without Bismarck: The Crisis of Government in the Second Reich, 1890-1900* (London, 1967), 132-36.

20. HH (Salisbury Papers), A/120/25; Lascelles to Salisbury, 11 Jan. 1896, private.

21. Brain wave or joke.

22. In December 1895, Swaine had sent alarming reports to London with regard to a possible Russo-German rapprochement: "There are grave political combinations on the 'tapis' which may escape the watchful eye *even* of the British Foreign Office.... Keep your powder dry & your barrels open & think not unkindly of y[ou]rs VL Swaine [P.S.] I am perfectly sober!" Swaine thought Wilhelm II was "ready" to let the Russians have Constantinople, and wanted "to be arbiter of European Politics, very much as Napoleon III fancied himself once to be," though on the other hand, the Kaiser was "very solicitous with respect to the Triple Alliance and anxious that nothing should occur to weaken the 'Entente' of the 3 Powers." HH (Salisbury Papers), A/122/98-99; Swaine to Barrington, Berlin, 1 and 6 Dec. 1895 [private], emphasis in the original.

23. Ibid., A/122/5; Salisbury to Lascelles, FO, 22 Jan. 1896, private, copy.

24. Ibid., A/120/26; Lascelles to Salisbury, 25 Jan. 1896, private. See also Evans, "Germany," 172-73: "The Kaiser means much more to the Germans than any ordinary sovereign does to his people. For the Kaiser is not only Kaiser, he is the centre and symbol of racial unity. If there were no Kaiser, Germany would lose her proud position among the nations and become once more a mere congeries of separate states. Therefore, the Emperor represents the national greatness in a way and degree quite unusual among monarchs."

25. For the genesis, course, and aftermath of the "Krüger Telegram," see Röhl, *Wilhelm II 1888-1900*, 871-87.

26. Cf. HH (Salisbury Papers), A/120/23; Lascelles to Salisbury, 7 Jan. 1896, tel., private.

27. Chirol was a clerk in the FO from 1872 to 1876, before he became a *Times* correspondent.

28. *Kölnische Zeitung* of 3 Jan. 1896; *Norddeutsche Allgemeine Zeitung* of 4 Jan. 1896. *The Times* of 4 Jan. 1896, 5: "The Transvaal Crisis: Serious Action of The German Emperor." An ex-diplomat, "The Parting of the Ways," *CR* 69 (1896): 190-203; William Greswell, "The Germans in South Africa," *Fortnightly Review* 59 (1896): 209-15; William R. Lawson, "German Intrigues in the Transvaal," *CR* 69 (1896): 292-304. See also Kennedy, *Rise*, 231; Michael Fröhlich, *Imperialismus. Deutsche Kolonial- und Weltpolitik 1880-1914* (Munich, 1994), 71.

29. HH (Salisbury Papers), A/120/27; memo. of Valentine Chirol, Berlin, 25 Jan. 1896, confidential.

30. Col., later Major-Gen., Leopold Victor Swaine (1840-1931), military attaché at Berlin, 1882-84; 1885-89; 1892-96.

31. HH (Salisbury Papers), A/120/28; Lascelles to Salisbury, 15 Feb. 1896, private.

32. Ladislaus Count von Szoegyényi-Marich (1841-1916), ambassador at Berlin 1892-1914.

33. HH (Salisbury Papers), A/120/19; Lascelles to Salisbury, 14 Dec. 1895, private.

34. HH (Salisbury Papers), A120/20; to Salisbury, 21 Dec. 1895, private. See also Gerhard Ebel and Michael Behnen, eds., *Botschafter Paul Graf von Hatzfeldt. Nachgelassene Papiere 1838-1901*, vol. 2 (Boppard a.R., 1976), no. 664, note 6; Holstein to Hatzfeldt, same date.

35. PRO/FO/343/13 (Malet Papers); Malet to Kimberley, 19 Jan. 1895, private. In May, on the occasion of the queen's birthday, Wilhelm invited Sir Edward to "a large banquet" at Potsdam and awarded Malet the place to his right hand. Ibid., 25 May 1895, private.

36. PRO/FO/343/3 (Malet Papers); Kimberley to Malet, 5 Dec. 1894, private, published in Theodor A. Bayer, *England und der neue Kurs, 1890-1895. Auf Grund unveröffentlichter Akten* (Tübingen, 1955), 122. See also Kennedy, *Rise*, 217; Gordon Martel, *Imperial Diplomacy: Rosebery and the Failure of Foreign Policy* (Kingston and Montreal, 1986), 227-28.

37. PRO/FO/343/13 (Malet Papers); Malet to Salisbury, 30 June 1895, confidential. Somerset Record Office [SRO] (Malet Papers), DD/MAL/523; diary entry, same date.

38. HH (Salisbury Papers), A/120/2; Malet to Salisbury, 13 July 1895, private and A/120/4; 31 July 1895, private and secret. SRO (Malet Papers), DD/MAL/523; diary entry, same date: "The Emperor pays me a visit at 8am(!) [-] regrets my departure."

39. Delagoa Bay, located at the coast of South-East Africa (today Mozambique).

40. HH (Salisbury Papers), A/120/1; Malet to Salisbury, 6 July 1895, private.

41. On 1 Oct. 1895, Malet officially retired from his post at Berlin. PRO/FO/244/524 (British embassy at Berlin, official correspondence); Malet to Salisbury, no. 217, same date. For the queen's acceptance of his resignation, ibid. and FO/343/3 (Malet Papers); Salisbury to Malet, no. 288, 11 Oct. 1895, copy. For the "Malet Incident," see also Röhl, *Wilhelm II. 1888-1900*, 867-71; John Charmley, *Splendid Isolation? Britain, the Balance of Power and the Origins of the First World War* (London, 1999), 238. Matthew S. Seligmann, *Rivalry in Southern Africa, 1893-99: The Transformation of German Colonial Policy* (Basingstoke and New York, 1998), 99; Kennedy, *Rise*, 219; Christopher H.D. Howard, *Splendid Isolation: A Study of Ideas Concerning Britain's International Position and Foreign Policy during the Later Years of the Third Marquis of Salisbury* (London, 1967), 6; Langer, *Diplomacy*, vol. 1, 228-29. Pauline R. Anderson, *The Background of Anti-English Feeling in Germany, 1890-1902* (Washington, D.C., 1939).

42. MacDonogh, *The Last Kaiser*, 215-16, gives the wrong place, claiming that the incident took place after a farewell shooting party at Schloss Hubertusstock. The incident, however, took place at the Wilhelmstrasse. Walter Goetz, ed., *Briefe Wilhelms II an den Zaren, 1894-1914* (Berlin, 1920), 299; Wilhelm II to Tsar Nicholas II, *Neues Palais Potsdam*, 25 Oct. 1895: "Two days ago, Malet on his farewell visit to our Foreign Office used very blustering words, about Germany behaving badly to England in Africa ... he even was so undiplomatic to utter the word 'war'! Saying that even England would not shrink from making war upon me if we did not knock down in Africa. I have made an answer to the effect that the British were making themselves ridiculous in this case, but obnoxious to everybody, and if they got into trouble with anybody else I would not move a Pomeranian Grenadier to help them. I suppose that will cool them." Note that the Kaiser mixes up the dates by giving the date of Malet's farewell audience at the palace. See also Röhl, *Wilhelm II 1888-1900*, 868-89.

43. SRO (Malet Papers), DD/MAL/523; diary entry of 14 Oct. 1895 and *GP* xi, no. 2578; report by Marschall of 15 Oct. 1895. Cf. note 40.

44. SRO (Malet Papers), DD/MAL/523; diary entry of 30 Oct. 1895.

45. Paul Andreievich Count Shouvalov (1830-1908), ambassador at Berlin, 1885-1895.

46. HH (Salisbury Papers), A/120/6; Gosselin to Barrington, 2 Nov. 1895, private. See also *GP* xi, no. 2582; Hatzfeldt to German FO, 1 Nov. 1895, tel.

47. *GP* xi, no. 2579; Wilhelm II to Marschall, 25 Oct. 1895, in copy to Hatzfeldt and Bülow (in Rome) and no. 2580; Hatzfeldt to German FO, 25 Oct. 1895, tel.

48. HH (Salisbury Papers), A/122/95; Swaine to Gosselin, 31 Oct. 1895, conf.

49. For the Anglo-German Venezuela crisis of 1895-96 over British claims to the Orinoco delta, see Holger H. Herwig, *Germany's Vision of Empire in Venezuela, 1871-1914* (Princeton, 1986), 212-13.

50. HH (Salisbury Papers), A/120/7; Gosselin to Salisbury, 4 Nov. 1895, tel. private and secret and A/120/8, ibid., private and secret. Duke University, Manuscript Department [DUMD] (Malet Family Papers), box 18; Gosselin's private letter to Malet of the same date reporting the conversation with the Kaiser at the opera.

51. Ibid.; Swaine to Malet, 5 Nov. 1895; emphasis in the original.

52. Since the beginning of 1895. PRO/FO/343/13 (Malet Papers); Malet to Kimberley, 2 Feb. 1895, private. Malet met Marschall once a week on Fridays.

53. HH (Salisbury Papers), A/120/9; Malet to Salisbury, 7 Nov. 1895. *GP* xi, no. 2583; Hatzfeldt to Hohenlohe, 2 Nov. 1895.

54. Marschall called it "lively but friendly." *GP* xi, no. 2578; report by Marschall of 15 Oct. 1895. See also Seligmann, *Rivalry*, 15.

55. HH (Salisbury Papers), A/120/9. See also Ebel, *Hatzfeldt-Papiere*, vol. 2, no. 658; Holstein to Hatzfeldt, 15 Oct. 1895.

56. Angus Hawkins, and John Powell (eds.), *The Journal of John Wodehouse, First Earl of Kimberley for 1862-1902* (1997), 484, diary entry of 24 Nov. 1901. See also Ebel and Behnen, *Hatzfeldt-Papiere*, vol. 2, no. 600; Hatzfeldt to Holstein, 28 Mar. 1894.

57. HH (Salisbury Papers), A/120/11; memo by Malet, 7 Nov. 1895.

58. Ibid., A/120/10; Gosselin to Barrington, 9 Nov. 1895, private.

59. DUMD (Malet Family Papers), box 18; Gosselin to Malet, 9 Nov. 1895, arrived 12 and 13 Nov. 1895.

60. HH (Salisbury Papers), A/122/1; Salisbury to Gosselin, 13 Nov. 1895, draft.

61. Ibid., A/120/13; Gosselin to Salisbury, 15 Nov. 1895, private and DUMD (Malet Family Papers), box 18; Gosselin's letter to Malet, 16 Nov. 1895; Gosselin's underlining.

62. HH (Salisbury Papers), A/120/12; "Summary [by Gosselin] of report, made to His Majesty by Baron von Marschall, of conversation with Sir Edward Malet *on* the relations of Germany to the Transvaal. (Written from memory)," [typed], 15 Nov. 1895, private and secret.

63. Malet's farewell audience took place on 23 Oct. 1895. PRO/FO/244/524 (British Embassy Berlin); Malet to Salisbury, no. 235.

64. HH (Salisbury Papers), A 120/17; Gosselin to Salisbury, 22 Nov. 1895, private and DUMD (Malet Family Papers), box 18; Swaine to Malet, 22 Nov. 1895, and Gosselin to Malet, 23 Nov. 1895.

65. HH (Salisbury Papers), A 122/95; Swaine to Barrington, 31 Oct. 1895, conf. The German side was represented only by Marschall and Wolfram Baron von Rotenhan (1845-1913), German under-secretary of state for foreign affairs 1890-7.

66. National Library of Scotland (Rosebery Papers), Mss. 10005, ff. 151-52; Herbert von Bismarck to Lord Rosebery, 26 Aug. 1895.

– 9 –

Colonial Agitation and the Bismarckian State

The Case of Carl Peters

ARNE PERRAS

All the lines of the movement always eventually came together in the person of the young *Führer*. Lucid and quick of perception, he was always determined and often dictatorial in his manner. Towards those who opposed his goals, he was sometimes self-consciously provocative and ruthless. He dominated his milieu, which was excited by the liveliest of stimuli.

– Friedrich Fabri, on Carl Peters[1]

I

Carl Peters (1856-1918) ranked among Germany's most prominent colonial agitators in the Bismarckian and Wilhelmine periods.[2] He became widely known as the founder of Deutsch-Ostafrika, a place that many Germans at the time saw as the pearl of their colonial possessions. In late 1884 Peters traveled to the Swahili coast, collecting a number of so-called treaties in which local leaders had allegedly transferred their sovereignty to the young German traveler. Only a few weeks later, in February 1885, Kaiser Wilhelm I issued an Imperial charter placing a territory estimated at 140,000 square kilometers under German protection.

No other figure could have better illustrated the peculiarities of German colonial expansion than Carl Peters. The man was only twenty-eight years when he went to Africa. He had never been in the tropics before, nor did he have any experience in overseas trade or any other commercial field. An academic who wrote about metaphysics and Schopenhauer, he had won an empire for Germany. The Reich was totally unprepared when it acquired its overseas possessions; it had no trained

Notes for this section begin on page 167.

personnel to handle colonial affairs, and there were no legal provisions that could be applied to the new territories. The Germans, one could say, became a colonial power overnight. Their case thus contrasted sharply with that of Britain or France, who looked back over a long period of imperial activity overseas. In less than a year, between April 1884 and February 1885, Bismarck staked out a colonial empire in Africa and the Pacific that was many times larger than the mother country itself. The chancellor placed Angra Pequena, Togoland, and the Cameroons under German protection. He established a protectorate on the East African mainland and seized the northeastern part of New Guinea, plus a number of islands in Melanesia and Micronesia.

Germany's sudden appearance on the colonial stage raises important questions about the forces behind that expansion. Carl Peters's coup appears particularly puzzling in this context. How was it possible that Bismarck acted upon a few dubious documents produced by a young adventurer? What was the link between the colonial pioneer Peters and Bismarck's overseas policy? This chapter argues that earlier works have failed to grasp the real nature of German imperialism, partly because they have neglected Peters's role and the forces behind him. A case in point is Hans-Ulrich Wehler's *Bismarck und der Imperialismus*,[3] the first in-depth study of Bismarck's colonial policy since a very early monograph dating from 1923.[4] Although Wehler's interpretation came to influence a number of studies in the field of German imperial expansion,[5] there were also some critical voices that doubted its overall validity.[6] What was the core of Wehler's thesis? Essentially, he argued that the major cause of German colonial expansion was a domestic economic crisis. Bismarck, it was held, pursued a countercyclical economic strategy intended to offset the effects of depression. His policy is described as "manipulative social imperialism." It allegedly functioned as an instrument to divert internal tension and thus to maintain the political status quo. For this purpose, Bismarck adopted a technique of pragmatic expansion, leading to a series of colonial acquisitions in 1884-85.

As far as the economic aspect of the model is concerned, we are faced with a number of problems. First, politicians in the late nineteenth century did not have the instruments and the knowledge to pursue a sophisticated countercyclical policy.[7] This economic theory was a product of the twentieth century, and it could not possibly have formed the basis of Bismarck's policy. Second, Africa was by no means capable of absorbing a great quantity of export products. Figures for the early 1890s show that the exchange of goods with *all* German protectorates amounted to less than 0.2 percent.[8] Nor is there sufficient evidence to suggest that German industrialists had great expectations in an African market.[9] Indeed, they seemed fairly skeptical as far as quick profits were concerned.[10]

It should also be noted that the tariff policy in the German colonies did not favor the importation of German goods as opposed to those from other countries.[11] The levying of customs was a major source of revenue for the colonies, and its purpose was to reduce German state subsidies and to make the colonies self-sufficient. In fact, the customs policy contradicted the idea of promoting German exports to the colonial periphery. It is thus unlikely that German policymakers regarded the acquisition of colonies as a short-term economic strategy to offset the effects of an economic crisis.

The other major component of Wehler's thesis is Bismarck's alleged manipulative social imperialism. It is held that the chancellor's colonial policy served to divert internal tensions to the periphery. Allegedly, Bismarck counted upon the integrative function of colonial policy in his attempts to hinder the rise of social democracy. However, as we will see in this chapter, there were plenty of occasions in the 1880s and 1890s on which colonial issues *divided* the nation rather than having an integrative effect. Peters's expedition to rescue Emin Pasha and the famous "Peters Scandal" in the Reichstag are cases in point.[12] In fact, colonies provided a welcome weapon for Social Democrats, left liberals, and (at times) the Center Party, to attack the government. Moreover, they even began to cause friction within the right-wing political spectrum. Therefore, it is not very convincing to argue that colonial policy was an instrument to reduce internal tension. In fact, there is insufficient evidence to suggest that such a belief influenced Bismarck's decision at all.

On the other hand, the domestic context is still crucial to understanding the timing of Bismarck's colonial coup. Since 1884 was an election year, it therefore seems possible that the chancellor hoped to exploit the colonial issue for short-term political ends.[13] More precisely, he sought to regain a working majority in the Reichstag. Above all, he hoped that the colonial cause would improve the standing of the National Liberals in the new Reichstag, and in this sense his policy certainly displayed a manipulative tendency. But there is a danger of overemphasizing this point. Obviously, Bismarck sought to exploit the enthusiasm for colonial policy for his own ends, but there had to be an affinity among potential voters in the first place. It could not simply be generated and imposed from above; rather, the government itself rode a wave of popular feeling, which it perceived as being advantageous to its larger strategy.

However, the colonial movement was not easily controlled. When conflict arose between colonial interest groups and the government over colonial issues, Bismarck did not fully succeed in unifying these circles behind his own goals; instead, they continued to turn against him. Thus, the relationship between the colonial movement and the government could not have been a simple pattern of mobilizers at the top and willing followers below. It is important to recognize in this context that colonial demands had been popular in bourgeois circles since before 1848. In their close connection with the national question, they formed an important drive for expansion in their own right.[14]

Historians have also neglected another crucial point about Bismarck's colonial policy: the task of supervising colonization had been written into the Imperial Constitution of 1871.[15] The relevant passage was taken over from the previous constitution of the North German Confederation. If the expansionist needs of the German Reich had really already been satisfied, as is often emphasized, such a section would hardly have been necessary.[16] Against this backdrop, Bismarck was perhaps not as hostile toward colonial projects as some of his utterances in the 1870s seem to suggest.[17] He may not have been a colonial enthusiast, but he obviously felt obliged to keep the path open for the future. After the foundation of the Reich, colonial demands were expressed publicly more and more often. The Foreign Office was confronted with an increasing number of colonial plans submitted by private individuals who asked for annexation.[18] When Bismarck decided to go ahead and acquire colonial territories in 1884 and 1885, he could count on a good deal of public enthusiasm, especially in bourgeois circles.

It seems, then, that Wehler and his followers have put far too much importance on manipulation from above. What Marilyn Coetzee has written about the patriotic societies in the Wilhelmine period is also true for the colonial activists in the Bismarckian period: they were not "marionettes on a string that could be forced to perform perfunctory rituals of support."[19] Above all, the pioneering work by Geoff Eley has demonstrated the dynamics of nationalist forces in Wilhelmine Germany and the limits of official manipulation.[20] The colonial movement of the 1880s may be seen in a similar light. If we accept that Bismarck was reacting to mounting colonial demands, then his policy appears more opportunist and tactical than guided by a grand design. This also suggests that the colonial movement as such, together with the ideas that underpinned it, needs to be taken seriously.

It seems that the premises of Wehler's model have also led to a distorted picture of what he called the "ideological consensus" for colonization. Wehler has portrayed the question of exports as the overriding element of colonial ideology. Klaus Bade, on the other hand, has demonstrated that this analysis fails to recognize the significance of emigration in the debate about overseas possessions.[21] Woodruff D. Smith has focused on both aspects—trade *and* emigration. His interpretation, however, encounters another problem. According to Smith, colonial ideology since the mid 1870s displayed two major tendencies: "economic imperialism" and "migrationist colonialism."[22] These are viewed as "two distinct varieties of thought" or "idea-sets," which later developed into two different "ideological aggregations": *Weltpolitik* and *Lebensraum*. In fact, this separation is artificial and misleading, as economic aspects and the question of emigration were often closely intertwined in colonial literature. In general, existing studies of the colonial movement have one point in common: none of them has sufficiently examined the nationalist dimension of colonial ideology. Only rarely have historians focused on the nationalist drive in the context of Imperial policy under Bismarck.[23]

II

The tendency to neglect the relevance of nationalist forces in Imperial expansion is particularly evident in the way that scholars have dealt (or rather not dealt) with Carl Peters.[24] Historians have paid scant attention to his role as a leading colonial propagandist. In general, Friedrich Fabri, Wilhelm Hübbe-Schleiden, and Ernst von Weber have been presented as the most prominent colonial writers of the Bismarckian period.[25] Peters, on the other hand, is often viewed as a pathological case. Wehler calls him a criminal psychopath,[26] while Roger Chickering suspects that he may have been mentally ill.[27] For a historical analysis, however, these assessments are of limited value, quite apart from the problem that a psychiatric opinion is hard to verify in historical retrospect. It is striking that contemporaries had quite a different perception of the man. Heinrich Schnee, the last governor of East Africa, for instance, was well aware of Peters's brutalities, yet he wrote: "Peters was one of the sharpest-minded men and one of the most stimulating companions I ever met in my life. He was brimming with original and sometimes paradoxical ideas and arguments."[28] Whatever Peters's pathological features may have been, they should not obscure his political role in the colonial movement and his activities as an agitator. No less a historian than Friedrich Meinecke recalled that "we cheered our contemporaries Karl Peters, Jühlke and Count Pfeil as they boldly seized a part of Africa."[29] Peters's contemporaries were often fascinated by the young man and his agitational skills, not least because of his ability to carry away an audience during his public speeches. One of his early associates, Count Pfeil, made this point even after he had become an opponent of Peters: "I saw in him a man of unusual talent, a skillful man ..., with the power to move people, a thinker, but also a man of action. I also believed that I had recognized an organizer, a man of creative talent, the man who without regard for his personal interests would engage the power of his character and his intellectual skills for the task which he had taken up."[30]

According to Pfeil, Peters "had the gift of unifying people behind viewpoints, to promote those elements which were supportive, and defeat the hostile ones."[31] There were other people, too, who referred to Peters's specific charisma. Friedrich Fabri, another prominent figure of the colonial movement, discerned a similar appeal in his public appearances.[32] This did not mean that Fabri had great sympathy for Peters. On the contrary, he later saw in him "a degree of conceit which comes close to megalomania." In his eyes, this was rooted in "the devotion of the crowd" that followed Peters in those years.[33] Peters obviously had an excellent appreciation of the appeal of colonial ideas, and he gave them a strong voice. Thus, he came to ride the wave of public enthusiasm that formed a significant force behind Germany's colonial drive in 1884-85.

Peters produced a vast number of writings.[34] Essentially, his colonial ideology entailed a nationalist agenda for which the foundation of the Reich through war formed a central point of reference. In one of his early essays, he stated:[35] "The German colonial movement is the natural continuation of the German efforts for unification." It was natural, he continued, that the German *Volk*, after having established its European power position on the battlefields of Königgrätz and Sedan, felt the need to terminate its "miserable and almost contemptible position overseas." It had felt the necessity to "participate in the material advantages which the development of mastery on a large scale has always offered."

Significantly, Peters remained extremely vague as to what these material advantages would be. German exports to East Africa, for instance, were minimal, and the prospects for growth appeared dubious at best.[36] There was no large-scale market for

German goods, and as long as the financial foundation of the German East African Company was not secured, this would remain the case. "Overall this is a fairly sad picture," was how the German merchant Kurt Toeppen summed up the situation.[37] Hence, whenever Peters used economic arguments, they remained nonspecific and couched in stereotypes. However, it was difficult to oppose Peters's nationalist agitation, as one could quickly be accused of being hostile to the Reich. This weapon had been exploited by the parties loyal to Bismarck in the election campaign, and it seems that it had worked well to defeat the left liberals.

Peters usually argued on a very general political level. He tied colonial policy into a wider pan-German movement, whose final goal was Germany's mastery over the globe. On 16 May 1886, he published an article entitled "All-Deutschland,"[38] in which he observed that "a powerful struggle between nations runs through our epoch." All of these nations, argued Peters, sought to merge closely within the boundaries of their *Volkstum*. This idea would draw the east into the dangerous swirl of Pan-Slav appetite, for instance. However, Peters saw the most glorious manifestation of the idea in the pan-Anglo-Saxon concept encapsulated in Dilke's prophecy: "The world is rapidly becoming English."

"How radically different are all these wishes from the political and ideal cosmopolitanism that up until this century has mainly been sustained by *Deutschtum*," Peters continued. He referred to Goethe's works to show that the "best spirits" have constructed "something like an ideal *Weltbürgertum* instead of a universal empire." "It required deep humiliations and the greatest economic and political damage before our people woke up from such dangerous dreams." In Peters's eyes, the implementation of the "blood and iron" policy that had unified Germany was a decisive historical turning point. It led away from the theory of a nation of *Dichter und Denker*—a notion he dismissed as "airy spheres of weak abstraction and obscure humanitarian sentimentalism." With the victories of Königgrätz and Sedan, Germany had again joined the real struggle of peoples: "The German movement to unity has, of natural necessity, to be followed by a struggle for a position of power overseas. Our European position as a great power has to be followed by a position as a world power." Peters justified the German struggle for world power in terms of combatting the ongoing "Anglicization" of the world. Only through this policy would it be possible to guarantee that the Germans would not be completely overtaken by the Anglo-Saxons: "Every year of hesitation in the assumption of such a task upsets the relationship between both races to our disadvantage."

In another work, entitled "Nationalismus und Kosmopolitismus,"[39] Peters concentrated on two great ideas that, in his view, had determined the course of history: the cosmopolitan and the national. Medieval times had witnessed the rise of the national idea and had ended with the victory of nationalism over cosmopolitanism. In Peters's analysis, Oliver Cromwell and Richelieu are advanced as the victorious representatives of the national idea, Wallenstein and the Emperor Charles V as perhaps the last representatives of cosmopolitanism. As a result, Germany was pushed back from its European supremacy. While Western powers flourished and struggled for world supremacy, Germany dropped into a contemptible weakness. In Peters's eyes only the hard and pragmatic state building of the Hohenzollerns had turned the national idea into a reality. "Bismarck's tough and ingenious policy" had elevated Germany to the point at which Richelieu and Cromwell had brought their nations. Peters continued: "We are determined to fan and strengthen the German national spirit. What we know is this: for centuries, cosmopolitanism has brought our people humiliation and virtual ruin. For our nation, nationalism at the end of the nineteenth century means power, wealth, and blessing, and the more so, the more proudly and ruthlessly it is written on our banner."

Looking more broadly at Peters's ideology in the years 1883 to 1886, two points can be emphasized. First, the question of colonial expansion was dramatized as a matter of life and death. By employing a pseudo-Darwinian framework of a "struggle between nations," Peters claimed that the Anglicization of the world posed a threat to the survival of *Deutschtum*. Since he equated the German nation with the *Volk*, it was a scenario in which a lack of Imperial activity would allegedly result in the marginalization or even extinction of the Germans as a people. To counteract this threat, Germany had to give up its cosmopolitan attitudes and follow an energetic nationalist course, as reflected in the doctrine of Pan-Germanism. In this context, the experience of national unification through war was of central importance, encouraging the belief that the German state was powerful enough to achieve that agenda. The nationstate would provide the platform from which imperial activities had to operate; simultaneously, state power would guarantee the success of expansionist aspirations.

Second, the constant preoccupation with the British, both as a model and as a rival, suggests that Peters's colonial ideology was at its heart concerned with German national identity. He linked the issue of colonization to the question of what it meant to be a true German. As national identity can be seen as "fundamentally multidimensional,"[40] it is not static and immutable, thus allowing new elements to be integrated into it in certain circumstances. Peters portrayed the acquisition of an overseas empire as a vital prerequisite for Germany's self-perception on its path to becoming a leading world power. As the British Empire in the nineteenth century had gradually expanded, the perceived status gap between the two peoples had grown. The goal of German Imperial activity was to make sure that the Germans would at least draw level with the British. Pan-Germanism formed the doctrine for this projected identity, which was essentially Imperial. On the broader level of the nation-state, a colonial empire would provide a vital status symbol that would compensate for a kind of inferiority complex in relation to the British.

III

Nationalist pressure was an important factor guiding Bismarck's overseas policy. He sought to avoid antagonizing colonialist circles, and this is well reflected in the way he handled Peters's East African venture from 1885 onward. In fact, the Reich had chartered a venture that was on the verge of bankruptcy. By April Peters had formed the Deutsch-Ostafrikanische Gesellschaft. Carl Peters und Genossen (DOAG) for carrying out the task of colonial development under Imperial protection.[41] In the first three months of its existence, the company sold 310 shares with a total value of 270,000 marks[42]—a ridiculously meager amount to realize Peters's grand designs. The bulk of this money was spent on new expeditions into the African interior, so that by the middle of June only 63,000 marks were left.[43]

In this critical situation, one man saved Peters's venture from collapse: the young banker Carl von der Heydt from Elberfeld. In July 1885 he invested 100,000 marks in the company and became a member of the board.[44] His was not one of the big banking houses, but his contribution made it possible for current activities in Germany and Africa to continue. Heydt's step can hardly be explained on the basis of pure financial reasoning. If Peters's venture had really been attractive for German capital, one would have expected a much stronger response to his fundraising activities. But this was not the case. In fact, Heydt's enthusiasm for the venture seems to have been fueled by a strong nationalist zeal, which rivaled that of Peters himself.[45]

One month before Heydt invested in Peters's enterprise, Bismarck had already begun to look for ways of consolidating the financial basis of the venture. The early involvement of the state meant that Bismarck did precisely the opposite of what he had outlined as his colonial conception in the Reichstag in 1884; that is, the flag follows the merchant. With regard to East Africa, the chancellor's proclaimed colonial strategy existed only on paper.

Two factors were largely responsible for this gap between concept and reality. On the one hand, the chancellor lacked an understanding of how East African trade functioned in general, and how European merchants operated within the Zanzibari commercial empire in particular. On the other hand, his policy was not really designed to protect the established interests of the Hanseatic merchants. Quite the contrary, it concentrated on the rescue of the notoriously underfunded, but increasingly aggressive, venture under Peters.

Bismarck's initial idea was that he could bring about a fusion of interests. He sought an "association" between the Peters group and the main Hamburg merchant houses operating in Zanzibar.[46] In June 1885 the chancellor instructed Kusserow, his envoy to the Hansa cities, to approach the merchants for this purpose.[47] The two major German firms operating in Zanzibar were O'Swald and Hansing. Both had started their commercial activities more than a generation earlier, first engaging in the trade of cowrie shells from East to West Africa, where they were used as currency. When this trade broke down, the firms successfully modified their commercial activities, and now they imported cloth, firearms, gunpowder, and steamers to Zanzibar. Their exports comprised mainly ivory, skins, spices, and copal.[48] The Sultan of Zanzibar, Said Bargash, was himself a major customer of the merchants, but, more importantly, he had established a system of control and influence that secured long-distance trade on the major caravan routes to the interior. As a consequence, Hamburg commercial profits relied heavily on friendly relations with the sultan, as the merchants repeatedly pointed out. The relationship between European businessmen on the one hand and the sultan and Indian merchants on the other had secured mutual benefits: rising business profits for the traders meant increasing customs revenues for the sultan.

Peters, with his grand designs for Africa, did not fit into this picture at all. However obscure the eventual size of the German territory may still have been, the basic goal of the charter of protection was obvious: it had sanctioned Peters's colonial acquisitions and given the go-ahead for the company to establish control over the mainland. Since the territorial claims of the DOAG cut right across the major caravan routes to the interior, the sultan's protests were not surprising. He realized that the German protectorate threatened the fragile political and commercial balance in the region.

Peters's first memorandum about the future development of the German colony emphasized that the company must aim "at gaining the maritime coasts," maintaining that this was an "actual question of survival."[49] But most coastal towns lay under the influence of the sultan, so that DOAG priorities made a conflict with Said Bargash inevitable. There was no possible scenario that could have secured Bismarck's objective—fusing Peters's enterprise with the Hanseatic firms *and* securing friendly relations with the sultan. Kusserow may have regarded the prospects for an association of German interests as "not unfavorable,"[50] but he had a tendency to be overenthusiastic in colonial matters. The Hanseatic merchants themselves had no real interest in such an undertaking.

It is quite clear that the merchants distrusted Peters, who, in their eyes, lacked the commercial skill to run an enterprise.[51] However, this is only part of the story, and arguably not the most important one. In fact, the German protectorate as such raised vital questions about the future of Hamburg commerce. Early Hanseatic reactions to the *Schutzbrief* contain fierce criticism of Bismarck's colonial coup. O'Swald wrote in a memorandum of September 1885: "The pioneers of German trade have been entirely ignored." He added that the government had made its decision "without taking into account that such action would damage certain interests, in order to pave the way for a problematic and, even more so, a dubious future."[52] This was a clear statement, but it was not meant for publication. It may be argued that the merchants shied away from expressing their criticism openly because they feared that Bismarck might ignore their interests altogether. With the granting of the charter, Peters's East African venture had become a national undertaking, sanctioned by the Kaiser himself.

The merchants soon got a taste of how Bismarck handled those who dared to question the East African venture in public. In August 1885 the chancellor learned about newspaper reports critical of DOAG activities.[53] He immediately instructed Kusserow to issue a warning to Hamburg firms whom he suspected of having stood behind the criticism. The chancellor threatened that if no quick settlement between the interests involved was reached, he was determined "to drop the side that opposed an understanding." He stressed that "if this hit the merchants, existing trade relations would suffer seriously."[54] In other words, if the merchants did not give in, the Reich would no longer consider their interests and would support the DOAG at their expense.

The Hanseatic merchants were quick to deny that they had had anything to do with the respective articles. They agreed to continue negotiations,[55] fearing to be brushed aside if they did not comply with the policy of the government.[56] Peters suggested that Hansing and O'Swald should incorporate their businesses into the DOAG. Not surprisingly, this offer was not well received in Hamburg,[57] but Bismarck urged Kusserow to continue his efforts. The chancellor also made it clear that all of these negotiations had to be conducted under "official leadership."[58] It took until December 1885 for the parties to reach an understanding, which amounted to no more than a division of commercial activities in the region. By no means did it constitute a fusion of interests, as Bismarck had envisaged.[59]

Throughout 1885, Hanseatic concerns focused on maintaining good relations with the sultan. Hansing had already found that simply running financial operations for the DOAG on the spot had caused the sultan to become increasingly reserved toward the firm.[60] Any closer alliance with the declared enemy of the sultan would have endangered their businesses even further. In May 1886 the German consul in Zanzibar observed that "the strong antagonism between the Hanseatic firms and the representatives of the company [the DOAG] continues."[61] It is therefore misleading to say that the Hamburg merchants "supported the German colonial endeavors."[62]

Faced with enormous difficulties in financing the DOAG, Peters gradually increased his demands for state intervention. In a memorandum to the Foreign Office dated 3 April 1886, he asked for some "moral support from the state," in order to facilitate the financing of the company. He suggested that the Preussische Seehandlung, a state bank, should be chosen to issue DOAG shares in the future.[63] Bismarck instructed the Foreign Office to forward Peters's request to the Seehandlung. The chancellor proposed to the bank that they should arrange a meeting with Peters and seek to cooperate with him.[64] Eventually a commissioner from the Seehandlung was sent to attend consultations between the Foreign Office and the DOAG in Berlin. As a result, the bank agreed to Peters's proposal.[65]

Three months later, Peters modified his previous request. Now he proposed that the Seehandlung should actually approach potential financiers and seek to win them over for the East African venture.[66] The colonial expert in the Foreign Office, Krauel, noted: "This goes further than originally intended."[67] Nevertheless, Bismarck again supported Peters's proposal, which was quickly forwarded to the Seehandlung, with the approval of the chancellor.[68] Peters also reported on the results of his fundraising campaign.[69] He assured the Foreign Office that it would be easy to raise a million marks, once the government had approved the reorganization of the company. But Peters was bluffing. When the Seehandlung later asked him to supply more detailed information on potential investors, he did not send them anything.[70] At one point he stated that the Deutsche Bank would be willing to supply a quarter of a million marks, but bank director Siemens, when approached by the Seehandlung, said that he had never given such a promise.[71] On 4 November 1886, Peters eventually had to admit to the Foreign Office that prospective investment amounted to a mere 170,000 marks.[72]

This episode was important in so far as it triggered an eventual shift from Peters's fundraising activities toward an exclusive engagement by the state to secure the necessary funds. The DOAG was instructed to refrain from any further attempts to contact potential investors.[73] Bismarck, it may be argued, had by then drawn two major conclusions. First, the only way out of the problem was a stronger involvement of the Seehandlung in order to mobilize private capital. Second, Bismarck was now prepared to provide a sort of state guarantee for the East African venture, without which potential investors would not be attracted.

Eventually the Kaiser enabled the Seehandlung to invest 500,000 marks in the DOAG.[74] In an equally important step, the bank engaged in contacting potential financiers. A Foreign Office memorandum provides interesting insights in this respect. Leading representatives of the bank pointed out that they were faced with a difficult task. They had concluded that potential financiers were likely to invest only if they could expect other advantages, privileges, and benefits in return.[75] For this reason, it was seen as essential at the Seehandlung that the president of the bank should approach potential financiers.[76] The implication of this internal assessment is important: the mobilization of capital for East Africa involved an implicit deal. Investors who helped to finance the DOAG would be rewarded by the Seehandlung's support on other occasions. This suggests that the East African venture had no intrinsic attraction for most banks and industrialists.

The activities of the Seehandlung succeeded in enlisting a number of banking houses and industrialists to provide new capital for the reconstitution of the DOAG, amounting to a total sum of 2,080,000 marks. Apart from the *Seehandlung* (500,000 marks) and von der Heydt (who increased his share to 400,000 marks), the banking house Mendelssohn-Bartholdy (100,000 marks) was the next largest investor. The list of stockholders contained 102 names, who together had bought 208 shares at 10,000 marks each.[77] As F. F. Müller has rightly pointed out, most investors had bought only one share.[78] This again indicates that an investment in the DOAG was to demonstrate patriotism and loyalty to the state. It was not seen as a lucrative investment.

It is interesting to note that the leading investors themselves had proposed that the chancellor should appoint members to the board of directors.[79] They argued that a number of firms would make their contribution dependent on appointments being made by the chancellor.[80] Mendelssohn-Bartholdy, the third-largest shareholder, saw in such an arrangement a "guarantee ... for the operation of DOAG."[81] A ministerial note, probably from the Foreign Office, likewise concluded "that these were proposals which would strengthen the leadership and the prestige of the company, and would thus be also in the interests of this department."[82]

There is sufficient evidence to suggest that the reorganization of the DOAG marked another milestone on the road to formal colonial rule through the state, as it was eventually established in 1890. Müller's conclusion that the DOAG had become "the prey" of a pro-colonial "financial oligarchy"[83] is misleading, as it implies that capitalist circles had been the driving force behind the reorganization of the company. This, however, was not the case; rather, state intervention was crucial to bail the venture out of its trouble. The case of East Africa clearly supports the view that most German banks remained reserved toward colonial projects in the Bismarckian period.[84]

In the years 1885 to 1887, Bismarck made consistent efforts to prevent the DOAG from collapse. It is true that Bismarck once remarked in anger that he would watch the breakdown of Peters's venture in silence.[85] However, the foregoing analysis suggests that this statement is misleading. The chancellor's actual policy aimed at the opposite. The way in which the bankrupt DOAG was rescued through state intervention provides a valuable insight into the interaction between colonial agitation and Bismarckian imperial policy. The chancellor felt obliged to take that step because giving up East Africa would have meant too heavy a blow to his own and Germany's prestige. He acted as the custodian of national identity and fulfilled nationalist demands. Only a few years later, the chancellor was to experience fierce domestic opposition when he chose to resist increasingly aggressive demands for further colonial expansion. Again, Peters was the architect of such designs. He embarked on an expedition to rescue Emin Pasha in the African interior and hoped to use the opportunity to grab even more colonial territory. This time, Bismarck was not prepared to support such far-reaching demands, knowing that Germany had already taken more than it could possibly swallow.[86] However, Bismarck had to pay a high price for his resistance. The National Liberals turned increasingly against him. In fact, the Emin Pasha controversy provides further evidence for the view that growing dissatisfaction with a moderate colonial course contributed to the chancellor's final downfall.[87]

Therefore, the relationship between the colonial movement and the government cannot fittingly be described as "manipulation from above." German overseas expansion is still best explained by tracing its nationalist roots. Only by promoting colonial expansion as a truly national cause did the colonial movement achieve its full dynamism. Carl Peters emerged as a spearhead of this nationalist movement, and his rise would not have been possible without the backing of prominent figures in the National Liberal and Conservative parties, including Rudolf von Bennigsen, Count Mirbach-Sorquitten, Count Arnim-Muskau, and von Kardoff-Wabnitz. Peters was a useful drummer, serving the colonial and nationalist interests of his patrons. As one contemporary wrote in a letter to the National Liberal leader Rudolf von Bennigsen, Peters was an "eminent force of agitation."[88]

IV

Accepting the view that nationalist forces were decisive for Germany's colonial expansion carries some important implications for the general debate about the continuities of right-wing movements in the late nineteenth century. Geoff Eley, in his study *Reshaping the German Right*, drew attention to the "antagonism between old and new right" in the post-Bismarckian period.[89] "Old" here refers to the moderate national-ist forces, while "new" is attributed to the radicals. Eley argued that "the dominant ideologies of the Wilhelmine Right were actually generated by specific political con-flicts inside the Wilhelmine period itself."[90] 'The post-Bismarckian period—inaugu-rated by processes of accelerated capitalist development, the end of the depression and the passage to imperialism'—is conceived as "one of far-reaching political change in which the entire structure of the public domain was reordered. The particular history of the nationalist pressure groups makes only sense in the context of change."[91]

But how "new" was this radical Wilhelmine right, if we look at its ideology? Is it really sufficiently explained within a framework that limits itself to the time after 1890? Eley's study has been important in improving our understanding of the way in which right-wing dissidence operated in the particular setting of Wilhelmine poli-tics. He has also drawn our attention to the increasing mass mobilization from the 1890s onwards. However, the case of Carl Peters suggests that the substance of what the so-called radical nationalists wrote on their banner—further colonial expansion, Pan-Germanism, an energetic overseas policy—was already a feature of nationalist euphoria in the Bismarckian period. The case of Carl Peters makes this clear. The very fact that the Pan-German League sought to recruit Peters in the 1890s as their heroic figure (Eley) highlights continuity rather than change. In fact, Peters's career would not have been possible without the support of precisely those groups that, in Eley's model, would be part of the old moderate right. This casts some doubt on the idea of a principled antagonism between old and new nationalist forces. Conse-quently, if we seek to understand the origins of this nationalist dynamic, a wider focus may be required than is suggested by Eley's study.

Colonial aspirations had already flourished in the nationalist movement before 1848. In a pioneering article, Hans Fenske went so far as to argue that after 1870 the arguments for Imperial expansion were essentially the same as those expressed decades earlier.[92] However, Peters's ideology differed from older Imperial aspirations in at least two respects. First, his agenda was formulated in an unprecedentedly aggressive tone and, arguably, received a strong new impetus through pseudo-Darwinist ideas. Sec-ond, Peters placed great emphasis on the actual experience of German national unifi-cation, which had considerably changed the map of political power in Europe. The achievement of national unity through military victory was an impetus upon which writers in the 1840s could not yet draw. However, it bears emphasizing that Imperial aspirations had emerged hand in hand with the nationalist movement, and that this had occurred *before* unification. This is an important element of continuity, linking Bismarck's colonial policy and Wilhelmine *Weltpolitik* with the liberal nationalist movement at midcentury. Such continuity is not given its due by an explanation that seeks to locate the radical right within the Wilhelmine period exclusively.

Notes

1. "Deutsch-Ostafrika. I," *Kölnische Zeitung*, 16 July 1886, in Bundesarchiv Berlin (hereafter BA Berlin), Reichskolonialamt (hereafter RKolA) 360, 6. The articles had been published without the author's name; they were then reprinted as a pamphlet under Fabri's name: *Deutsch-Ostafrika. Eine colonialpolitische Skizze* (Cologne, 1886).
2. This chapter summarizes some of the major arguments laid out in detail in Arne Perras, "Carl Peters and German Imperialism, 1856-1918. A Political Biography" (D.Phil. diss., University of Oxford, 1998).
3. Hans-Ulrich Wehler, *Bismarck und der Imperialismus* (Frankfurt a.M., 1984), originally published in 1969. For a discussion of other interpretations of Bismarck's colonial policy, see Perras, "Peters," 1ff.
4. Maximilian von Hagen, *Bismarcks Kolonialpolitik* (Stuttgart, 1923).
5. See, for example, Elfi Bendikat, *Organisierte Kolonialbewegung in der Bismarck-Ära* (Heidelberg, 1984); H. P. Meritt, "Bismarck and the German Interest in East Africa, 1884-1885," *Historical Journal* 21 (1978): 97-116; Beatrix Wedi-Pascha, *Die deutsche Mittelafrika-Politik 1871-1914* (Pfaffenweiler, 1992).
6. The range of Wehler's critics includes Helmut Böhme, "Thesen zur Beurteilung der gesellschaftlichen, wirtschaftlichen u. politischen Ursachen des deutschen Imperialismus," in *Der Moderne Imperialismus*, ed. Wolfgang J. Mommsen (Stuttgart 1971), 31-59; H. Henning, "Bismarck's Kolonialpolitik — Export einer Krise?" in *Gegenwartsprobleme der Wirtschaft und der Wirtschaftswissenschaft*, ed. Karl Erich Born (Tübingen, 1978), 53-83; Hartmut Pogge von Strandmann, "Consequences of the Foundation of the German Empire: Colonial Expansion and the Process of Political-Economic Rationalization," in *Bismarck, Europe and Africa: The Berlin Africa Conference and the Onset of Partition*, ed. Stig Förster, Wolfgang J. Mommsen, and Ronald Robinson (Oxford, 1988), 105-20; Peter Hampe, *Die ökonomische Imperialismustheorie. Kritische Untersuchungen* (Munich, 1976).
7. See Pogge, "Consequences," 107.
8. See Hampe, *Ökonomische Imperialismustheorie*, 277.
9. See Böhme, "Thesen," 41.
10. See Pogge, "Consequences," 107.
11. See F. Schinzinger, "Die Rolle der Zölle in den Beziehungen zwischen dem Deutschen Reich und seinen Kolonien," in *Wirtschaftspolitik in weltoffener Wirtschaft*, ed. Manfred Feldsieper and Richard Groß (Berlin, 1983), 125-42.
12. For a detailed discussion, see Perras, "Peters," chaps. 4, 5, and 7.
13. Hartmut Pogge von Strandmann, "Domestic Origins of Germany's Colonial Expansion under Bismarck," *Past and Present* 42 (1969): 140-59.
14. Hans Fenske, "Imperialistische Tendenzen in Deutschland vor 1866. Auswanderung, überseeische Bestrebungen, Weltmachtträume," *Historisches Jahrbuch* 97/98 (1978): 337-83; Frank Lorenz Müller, " 'Der Traum von der Weltmacht.' Imperialistische Ziele in der deutschen Nationalbewegung von der Rheinkrise bis zum Ende der Paulskirche," *Jahrbuch der Hambach Gesellschaft* 6 (1996-97): 99-183.
15. Wedi-Pascha, *Deutsche Mittelafrika-Politik*, 29, seems to be the only scholar who has hitherto recognized this point.
16. See Ernst R. Huber, *Dokumente zur Deutschen Verfassungsgeschichte*, vol. 2 (Stuttgart, 1964), 289ff.
17. In 1871, for example, Bismarck is reported to have said that for Germany colonial possessions would be like the sables of a Polish nobleman who had no shirt to wear under them; see A. Zimmermann, *Geschichte der Deutschen Kolonialpolitik* (Berlin, 1914), 10.
18. BA Berlin, RKolA 7154-7161, contains these proposals (1860-1901).

19. Marilyn Shevin Coetzee, *The German Army League: Popular Nationalism in Wilhelmine Germany* (New York and Oxford, 1990).

20. Geoff Eley, *Reshaping the German Right*, 2nd ed. (New York, 1991).

21. Klaus Bade, *Friedrich Fabri und der Imperialismus in der Bismarckzeit. Revolution - Depression - Expansion* (Freiburg i. Br., 1975).

22. Woodruff D. Smith, *The Ideological Origins of Nazi Imperialism* (New York, 1986), 21; see also idem, "The Ideology of German Colonialism, 1840-1906," *Journal of Modern History* 46 (1974): 641-62.

23. See, for example, Pogge von Strandmann, "Domestic Origins," and idem, "Consequences"; see also the brief passage on "Nation and Power" in Klaus Bade, "Die 'Zweite Reichsgründung' in Übersee. Imperiale Visionen, Kolonialbewegung und Kolonialpolitik in der Bismarckzeit," in *Die Herausforderung des europäishen Staatensystems. Nationale Ideologie und staatliches Interesse zwischen Restauration und Imperialismus*, ed. Adolf M. Birke and Günter Heydemann (Göttingen and Zürich, 1989), 183-215.

24. A useful account of Peters's life is still Hermann Krätschell, "Karl Peters 1856-1918. Ein Beitrag zur Publizistik des imperialistischen Nationalismus in Deutschland" (D.Phil. diss., University of Berlin, 1959). H. M. Bair, "Carl Peters and German Colonialism: A Study in the Ideas and Actions of Imperialism" (Ph.D. diss., Stanford University, 1968), has not much to say about the nationalist dimension of Peters's writings.

25. See, for example, Horst Gründer, *Geschichte der deutschen Kolonien*, 3rd ed. (Paderborn, 1995); Jutta Bückendorf, *Schwarz-weiß-rot über Ostafrika. Deutsche Kolonialpläne und afrikanische Realität* (Münster, 1997), 162-64.

26. See Wehler, *Bismarck*, 338; for similar judgments see H. Stoecker, "The Annexations of 1884-1885," in *German Imperialism in Africa*, ed. H. Stoecker (London, 1986), 29; Winfried Baumgart, *Imperialism: The Idea and Reality of British and French Colonial Expansion, 1880-1914* (Oxford, 1982), 150.

27. Roger Chickering, *We Men Who Feel Most German: A Cultural Study of the Pan-German League, 1886-1914* (Boston, 1984), 125.

28. Schnee Papers, Rep. 92, vol. 22a (manuscript for his memoirs), 73, Geheimes Staatsarchiv Preußischer Kulturbesitz, Berlin-Dahlem.

29. Friedrich Meinecke, *Die deutsche Erhebung von 1914* (Stuttgart and Berlin, 1914), 21.

30. Joachim Pfeil, *Zur Erwerbung von Deutsch-Ostafrika* (Berlin, 1907), 43-44.

31. Pfeil, *Erwerbung*, 50.

32. See this chapter's epigraph.

33. Fabri's Promemoria to Bismarck, 5 July 1889, BA Berlin, RKolA 6925, 45.

34. See Perras, "Peters," for a list of works. Many of them have been reprinted in the three volumes by Walter Frank, ed., *Carl Peters. Gesammelte Schriften* (Munich and Berlin, 1943-44), hereafter cited as GS.

35. "Die deutsche Kolonialbewegung, die Gesellschaft für deutsche Kolonisation und die Deutsch-Ostafrikanische Gesellschaft," *Kolonial-Politische Korrespondenz* (hereafter cited as *KPK*), no. 1, 16 May 1885.

36. See Kurt Toeppen, "Einige Beobachtungen und Erkundigungen in den deutschen Schutzgebieten Ostafrikas," *Deutsche Kolonialzeitung* 3 (1886): 518-23.

37. Ibid., 523.

38. *KPK*, vol. 2, no. 20.

39. *KPK* vol. 2, no. 24, 12 June 1886.

40. A. D. Smith, *National Identity* (London, 1991), 14.

41. Carl Peters, *Die Gründung von Deutsch-Ostafrika* (Berlin, 1906), printed in GS, vol. 1, 185.

42. AA note, 26 June 1885, in BA Berlin, RKolA 392, 80.

43. Peters to Hermann, 14 June 1885, Frank Papers 2, Bundesarchiv Koblenz (hereafter BA Koblenz); Peters to Elli, 14 June 1885, ibid.

44. DOAG board meeting, minutes, 11 July 1885, in BA Berlin, DOAG Papers, vol. 1, 35.

45. See *KPK* leaders, nos. 1, 2, and 3, 1886; they were published anonymously, but Peters refers to von der Heydt as the author; see *GS*, vol. 3, 282 (note).

46. Bismarck's marginal comment on Keudell to Bismarck, 15 June 1885, in BA Berlin, RKolA 421, 1.

47. Ibid.

48. Helmut Washausen, *Hamburg und die Kolonialpolitik des Deutschen Reiches, 1880 bis 1890* (Hamburg, 1968), 85, 91.

49. Peters's memorandum, 2 May 1885, in BA Berlin, RKolA 391, 38.

50. Kusserow to Bismarck, 6 July 1885, in BA Berlin, RKolA 421, 2ff.

51. Kusserow to Bismarck, 4 Dec 1885, in BA Berlin, RKolA 421, 74; Kusserow to Bismarck, 26 Mar. 1886, RKolA 359, 114; O'Swald to Bismarck, 25 Sept. 1888, RKolA 360, 126ff.

52. O'Swald and Co., "Die Annexionen der Deutsch Ostafrikanischen Gesellschaft und die Wirkung auf die bestehenden Deutschen Handels Interessen" (note), 621-1, Firma O'Swald, vol. 71, Hauptstaatsarchiv (hereafter HStA) Hamburg.

53. Rantzau to [AA], 8 Aug. 1885 (copy), in BA Berlin, RKolA 393, 43-44.

54. Ibid.

55. Kusserow to Bismarck, 16 Aug. 1885, in BA Berlin, RKolA 393, 79-86.

56. O'Swald and Co., Annexionen, 621-1, Firma O'Swald, vol. 71, HStA Hamburg.

57. Kusserow to Bismarck, 16 Aug. 1885, in BA Berlin, RKolA 421, 19.

58. Marginal note on ibid., 21; Kusserow's report, in BA Berlin, RKolA 421, 49ff.

59. O'Swald and Hansing to DOAG, 19 Nov. 1885 (copy), O'Swald to DOAG, 5 Dec. 1885 (copy); O'Swald to Delbrück, 14 Feb 1887, 621-1, Firma Wm. O'Swald and Co., vol. 71, HStA Hamburg; contract of 16 Apr. 1887, copies in 621-1, Firma Wm. O'Swald and Co., vol. 71, HStA and BA Berlin, RKolA 421, 109-10.

60. See Washausen, *Hamburg*, 105.

61. Arendt to Kayser, 13 May 1886, Kayser Papers 3, Staats- und Universitätsbibliothek Hamburg.

62. Washausen, *Hamburg*, 96

63. Memorandum of 3 Apr., encl. in Peters to Foreign Office, 4 Apr. 1886, in BA Berlin, RKolA 359, 118ff.

64. Auswärtiges Amt to Seehandlung, 7 Apr. 1886, in BA Berlin, RKolA 359, 125.

65. Seehandlung [to AA?], 12 Apr. 1886, in BA Berlin, RKolA 359, 141.

66. Peters to Berchem, 26 July 1886, in BA Berlin, RKolA 360, 8.

67. Marginal note, ibid.

68. AA to von Scholz, 28 July 1886, in BA Berlin, RKolA 360, 9-11; von Lenz to Rötger, 31 July 1886 (copy), RKolA 360, 13; AA to Peters, 2 Aug. 1886, RKolA 360, 14.

69. Peters to Berchem, 3 June 1886, in BA Berlin, RKolA 359, 159-61.

70. Kayser's memo, 11 Oct. 1886, in BA Berlin, RKolA 360, 18ff.

71. Ibid.

72. Peters to Foreign Office, 4 Nov. 1886, in BA Berlin, RKolA 360, 27.

73. Foreign Office note, 29 Oct. 1886, in BA Berlin, RKolA 360, 25.

74. *Kölnische Zeitung*, 7 Feb. 1887, encl. in BA Berlin, RKolA 410, 54; *NAZ*, 7 Feb. 1887, evening edition; *NAZ*, 31 July 1887, encl. in BA Berlin, RKolA 360, 100; list of stockholders, RKolA 410, 131-39; Scholz to Caprivi, 3 May 1890, RKolA 361, 85ff; DOAG to Kaiser, 28 Sept. 1888, RKolA 360, 136ff. It should be noted that it is not entirely clear from the sources whether the invested sum was indeed Wilhelm's private money—this is assumed by Bair, *Peters*, 143, and F. F. Müller, *Deutschland-Zanzibar-Ostafrika* (Berlin, 1959), 165—or came from some other fund.

75. Kayser's memo, 11 Oct. 1886, in BA Berlin, RKolA 360, 19, BAB.

76. Ibid.

77. Seehandlung certificate, 7 March 1887, and list of stockholders, in BA Berlin, RKolA 410, 130-39.

78. Müller, *Deutschland*, 173.

79. Kayser's note, 11 Jan. 1887, in BA Berlin, RKolA 410, 28.

80. Ibid.

81. Ibid.
82. No date, in BA Berlin, RKolA 410, 34ff.
83. Müller, *Deutschland*, 174.
84. B. Barth, *Die deutsche Hochfinanz und die Imperialismen* (Stuttgart, 1995), 43.
85. Berchem's note, 18 July 1886, in BA Berlin, RKolA 360, 4ff.; see also Rantzau to Herbert von Bismarck, 12 Oct. 1886, Bismarck Papers, F3, Archiv der Otto-von-Bismarck-Stiftung, Friedrichsruh.
86. For an analysis of this aspect, see Perras, "Peters," chaps. 4 and 5.
87. Pogge von Strandmann, "Domestic Origins," 159; see also John C. G. Röhl, "The Disintegration of the Kartell and the Politics of Bismarck's Fall from Power, 1887-1890," *Historical Journal* 9 (1966): 75.
88. Irmer to Bennigsen, 2 Aug. 1890, note in Frank Papers 13, BA Koblenz.
89. Eley, *Reshaping*, 166.
90. Ibid., 186.
91. Ibid., 15.
92. Fenske, "Imperialistische Tendenzen," 379.

10

The Law and the Colonial State

Legal Codification versus Practice in a German Colony

⟫◆⟪

Nils Ole Oermann

Introduction

C olonial law has recently become a focus of extensive scholarly attention. Several authors have been concerned with the development of law in German colonies from a jurisdictional as well as a historical perspective.[1] A common methodological element of such studies is that they try to identify the significance of colonial law for German or international legal history by analyzing legal files and treaties from the perspective of what was happening at home in the Reich, even though they claim to describe how Germany's administration and legal systems functioned in the colonies.[2] This chapter has a different emphasis and a broader scope: it focuses on the actual application of colonial law in the case of South-West Africa and considers how that application was perceived by colonial administrators, by settlers, and—last but not least—by colonized Africans themselves.

The question as to how the rule of law was applied in South-West Africa raises important issues about the means and motives of Germany's colonial policy in general. South-West Africa serves as a useful case study because it illustrates the everyday application of law in a colony inhabited by more German citizens than any other German overseas territory. Those Germans interacted with an indigenous population that faced decimation after the Herero and Nama wars of 1904-6. Germany's first colonial war began literally overnight, when 123 German settlers were killed in a desperate surprise attack by the Herero. Subsequently, over 60,000 Herero died during the fighting. More than 12,000 African prisoners of war died in German camps, where catastrophic conditions prevailed. In October 1904 the Nama, under Hendrik Witbooi, also decided to revolt against German rule, an uprising that ended with the death of Witbooi in 1905. By one estimate, 80 percent of the Herero and 50 percent of the Nama population was killed, whereas 1,765 military and civilian casualties were counted on the German side.[3]

It is difficult to overestimate the degree to which the Herero Wars[4] altered the application of law in the colony. No other colonial space was affected as directly by a colonizer that tried to export not only its soldiers, settlers, and culture, but also its laws and administration. The latter elements of rule, therefore, must be considered as part of the larger strategy undertaken by Germany to secure its "place in the sun." That being said, legal and constitutional issues in a technical sense are considered in the following analysis only insofar as they are relevant to a discussion of how the law influenced political life in the colony and vice versa. How did the codification of colonial law fit with the administrators' avowed aim of creating a colonial society in which the rule of law prevailed? How was German law applied—in theory and in practice? Did a discrepancy emerge between the codification of law and its application? If so, did this discrepancy increase during the course of German colonial rule (1884-1915)?

On the basis of government files, missionaries' reports, and personal letters, this chapter examines two selected issues—the execution of corporal punishment and the controversy around mixed marriages—that proved to be particularly controversial and which received special attention in the German press and in the Colonial Office in Berlin. Together, these sources and the controversies that they reflect can help us understand the conclusions drawn by a British administrator when he prepared a report on the application of German colonial law in 1918: "In German South-West Africa, the native was oppressed by a criminal law of medieval severity, administered not in the calm judicial atmosphere of a Court, but in the heat and turmoil of everyday administration by executive officials; and, if he came before a judicial tribunal, laboured under most serious disabilities."[5] At the same time, however, these sources reveal how colonial institutions left their mark on the German political landscape. In this sense, and in following lines of investigation first laid down by Hartmut Pogge von Strandmann in the 1960s,[6] this analysis considers how center-periphery tensions were reflected in a colony itself.

The Application of Corporal Punishment

On 22 April 1896, the Imperial Decree in Respect of the Jurisdiction over Natives was issued as the first legal codification that exclusively addressed jurisdictional issues relating to Africans.[7] Women, children, and "natives of better standing" were exempted from corporal punishment. Moreover, the health of the offender had to be evaluated before any punishment was applied. Nevertheless, this colonial legislation was already more strict than the Imperial German Criminal Code, which excluded corporal punishment.[8] In Prussia, corporal punishment had already been banned by 1848 as a legitimate method to punish offenders. The German Reich banned corporal punishment from 1901 onward, except for disciplinary purposes in schools and jails.[9]

Against this backdrop in 1900, Governor Theodor von Leutwein evaluated the practice of corporal punishment in German South-West Africa. From the colony's capital city of Windhoek, Leutwein solicited the opinion of his district commissioners and of German missionaries—those who were most closely involved with the African population. Yet the manner of that solicitation reveals that there were significant differences in the way that the governor in Windhoek and the German Colonial Office in Berlin thought about corporal punishment and its legal codification. Members of the Rhenish Missionary Society (RMS) had been asked by Governor Leutwein whether they regarded the corporal punishment of Africans as a necessary tool to guarantee order. Most of them replied to Leutwein that they were in agreement that corporal punishment was a sensible tool. Yet Leutwein implicitly expressed what he really thought about the position of the Colonial Office in Berlin when he told RMS missionary Berger at a private dinner party that he was glad to have the support of missionaries in the field in this matter. As he put it: "The Negrophiliacs in the Wilhelmstrasse [the location of the Colonial Office in Berlin] had asked that corporal punishment for Africans should be legally abolished. Now he [Governor Leutwein] would be able to quote the missionaries' opinion."[10] Given this attitude in the governor's office, it is hardly surprising to find that in South-West Africa corporal punishment became anything but the exception. District commissioners used it as the preferred alternative to jail sentences. Why? Because the offender would be able to rejoin the work force immediately after the execution of the punishment, and no taxpayers' money would be used. After the Herero Wars, this form of punishment, which was exercised with a cane or a *sjambok* (a large whip), became considerably more popular.

One is struck by the meticulousness with which German colonial administrators documented these many acts of punishment. Extensive tables were drawn up listing the number of strokes and instruments used.[11] These tables reveal that after 1907 a huge increase occurred in the application of corporal punishment. While the lists and records of those punishments were centrally compiled from 1897 to 1914, each District Office started its own statistics with constantly increasing numbers of cases. Two observations are critical for an assessment of how the gap between colonial law and its implementation dramatically increased.

First, the already significant gap between Berlin's and Windhoek's outlook on the frequency with which corporal punishment should be applied widened following the Herero Wars. This development can be ascribed in large part to the fact that surviving Herero and Nama prisoners, together with the Ovambos in the north, represented a crucial potential labor pool of the future. Thus, whereas German State Secretary Bernhard Dernburg informed Governor Bruno Schuckmann in 1907 that too many penalties were inflicted on Africans, District Offices in the colony regularly applied the maximum number of twenty-five *sjambok* lashes or fifty lashes overall as the usual minimum within the realm of their discretion.[12] Eventually, after several examples of excessive lashings became known in Germany, officials in Berlin demanded that careful records be maintained documenting the reason for the punishment whenever an accused was to receive more than fifteen strokes with the cane.

The governor of South-West Africa, however, believing himself to be in full agreement with most of the German colonial population, argued that officials in Berlin simply did not understand the situation locally: Africans, he believed, could not be disciplined with jail sentences or only a few strokes of the lash. Even RMS missionaries such as Carl Wandres shared this view in private letters to colonial officials. Wandres went so far as to support the infliction of corporal punishment on women— a measure that the previously cited Imperial Decree of 1896 explicitly prohibited.[13] Indeed, when Wandres proposed that the prohibition could be outflanked by entrusting the execution of corporal punishment to African foremen as proxies, Deputy Governor Oskar Hintrager scribbled the marginal remark: "Given the sentimental humanitarianism at home, this would cause a loud outcry."

These differences of outlook and practice between Berlin and Windhoek support the assertion that the codification and application of German law in the colonies diverged due to a combination of political and economic factors in the colonies themselves. After the 1905, excesses regarding the application of law were no longer the exception; de facto they changed the rule of law itself. Implementing a code of criminal law proved a necessary, but not sufficient, condition to ensure that the rule of law was guaranteed in a colony. The specific ways in which the law was applied depended upon administrators and judges who were themselves influenced by very different experiences and cultural or sociopolitical views in a territory 12,000 kilometers removed from Berlin; this largely explains why Africans suffered increasing corporal punishment after the Herero Wars. As everyday conflicts between Africans and Europeans escalated after 1905 and as Europeans became increasingly reliant on African labor, the number of lashes applied increased correspondingly.

Second, the colonial administration increased its efforts to administer and document its growing application of corporal punishment to prove its legitimacy and necessity to Berlin as well as to itself. In the colony itself, economic aspects—such as the protection of an African labor pool for mining operations—became increasingly relevant for the way in which colonial law was actually applied. Klaus Richter is certainly correct when he concludes in the case of German East Africa that political decisions were inextricably intertwined with the legal developments in the colony, but that colonial law and its application were shaped by actions that had already occurred on the ground and were in response to them.[14] African labor was always in high demand. Therefore, district commissioners used their discretion to expand rather than decrease the number of lashes to the maximum allowed. They also preferred corporal punishment to other sentences in order to serve the settlers' interest in protecting their labor pool. Settlers wanted their African workers severely disciplined, but full jails and a diminishing labor pool had to be avoided in order to ensure continued economic growth. Therefore, corporal punishment became the preferred tool to reach that goal, and the administration specified and tightened the regulations regarding corporal punishment in pursuit of the same end.

To be sure, even some colonial administrators regarded the physical punishment being meted out to African laborers after the Herero Wars as highly problematic.

When it came to maltreatment of Africans by their employers, the Imperial magistrate in Lüderitzbucht concluded in a letter to the Imperial government in Windhoek: "The courts are failing completely."[15] However, articles in colonial newspapers voiced the public sentiment: "We want no equality, no brotherliness with the black races."[16] Such sentiments reflected the overall hostile attitude of the colonizers toward the colonized, and they necessarily had a significant impact on how the existing laws were implemented. The execution of corporal punishment was supervised by colonial administrators who acted primarily in the interests of the German colonial population and may have shared the views of the society they lived in.

The quantity and severity of the application of corporal punishment was increased to the maximum allowed under the law: the longer the Germans ruled South-West Africa, the more that Africans were convicted and punished. The total number of Africans convicted of an offense by German courts from 1 January 1913 to 31 March 1914 was 4,356.[17] Of these offenders, 4,039 were male. A total of 841 sentences involved imprisonment with hard labor, 2,787 Africans were sentenced to the lash and 257 to cane strokes, and 507 received sentences that left them bound in chains. During that period, Windhoek led the tables with 721 male and 28 female offenders committing 958 offenses that included "negligence," "disobedience," and "laziness." Corporal punishment was the prescribed form of punishment in 697 cases in Windhoek alone.[18]

That the official court record includes names such as "Cognac," "Schnapps," or "Bread Roll" confirms the dismissive and condescending attitude of settlers who had chosen such names for their African laborers. But the more important point is that as time went on, more excessive sentences were meted out, and the discrepancy between codification and application of the law increased. By 1913 even minors were beaten and imprisoned. This practice clearly violated both the Imperial German Criminal Code, which excluded minors from criminal trials, and the more lenient Imperial Decree in Respect of the Jurisdiction over Natives. Yet in Windhoek, a fourteen-year-old African named Fritz and a ten-year old named Moritz were sentenced to six months of imprisonment in chains and forty lashes for cattle theft and desertion of their employer. The district commissioner commented that this judgment was rather lenient as it took into account the youth of the offenders.[19] More tellingly, perhaps, the imprisonment of Moritz and Fritz was postponed and the number of lashes reduced to twenty following a special request from their German employer: according to the employer's request, strict application of the code of law by means of imprisonment would destroy the Africans' economic value to their employer.

From this example, we can see how laws were bent, stretched, and broken in the German colonies in order to serve the interests of settlers. The special situation prevailing there allowed district commissioners, acting as officials of the Reich, to conclude tacit agreements with German employers in order to hand down more lenient or more harsh terms of punishment according to the economic or political interests of the settlers.

Mixed Marriages

Mixed marriages between colonizers and colonized can also be studied as a means to examine the relationship between the codification and application of colonial law. The conflict over the legal treatment of those relationships in Windhoek and Berlin illustrates nuances in the manner in which white settlers were treated in relation to Africans. It also reveals how the application of law was modified on a case-by-case basis to prevent friction among the European population.

Before the Herero Wars, mixed marriages were not a major issue in the political or legal debate about German colonies. Before 1 October 1905, only twenty-four legally declared relationships of this kind existed between whites and Africans.[20] The number of sexual relations between colonizers and colonized remained relatively low. This changed suddenly, however, when thousands of German soldiers arrived in the colony during and after the Herero Wars. [21] In 1905 Governor Friedrich von Lindequist decreed mixed marriages to be unlawful. Two years later, the High Court in Windhoek declared that mixed marriages which had been concluded before 1 October 1905 were invalid. This latter decree led to a major conflict with a number of German citizens—those who were directly affected by this decision, as well as the missionaries who tried to protect the rights of the Africans by discouraging concubine relationships.[22] But how did the legal arguments that led to this prohibition of mixed marriages turn into a political conflict?

Before the new *Schutzgebietsgesetz* was introduced on 10 September 1900, the Imperial Act of 8 November 1892 was exercised, under which the law of 4 May 1870 regulating marriages for Germans abroad was declared valid for German South-West Africa.[23] This meant in practice that the regulations of the *Bürgerliches Gesetzbuch* (BGB, the German Civil Code) about civil marriage (§§1303ff.) also applied to German citizens in South-West Africa. These regulations enabled German citizens to marry Africans if one part of the couple held German citizenship. Under the German *Indeginatsgesetz* of 1 June 1870, the wife and children became German citizens. The German codification of civil marriage was not altered, at least until the Herero Wars, when it was applied in South-West Africa. The increase in sexual relations between German soldiers and African women after 1905 and the consequent emergence of a significantly large colored population after 1905 provided the main motivation for changing the articles regarding civil marriage. That change was encapsulated in the internal instructions circulated by the governor to his administrators on 23 September 1905,[24] prohibiting the official declaration of mixed marriages when there was a danger that the number of mixed marriages would increase rapidly. The governor feared that the full application of German law in relation to all marriages within the colony did not take race relations in South-West Africa into account and would legitimize a developing colored population. This led him to order his administrators to prevent the further conclusion of mixed marriages. Although biological aspects of race and purity of culture were one motivation for introducing the prohibition—a motivation that is usually stressed in the secondary literature, to the exclusion of other factors—von Lindequist actually aimed at something different: he was primarily concerned with the fact that an increase of mixed marriages would enable a large number of Africans to claim their rights as German citizens. In this spirit he wrote to the Colonial Office on 23 October 1905:

> This result of the legal situation [legitimacy of the prohibition of mixed marriages on the basis of the interpretation of Article 7 of the Law of the Colony from 10 September 1900] of the case is in accordance with what the colonial administration has to regard as necessary.... The native woman and the children would not be treated under the special native legislation, for example, in regard to the consumption of alcohol, the obligation to carry a passport, the right to carry arms, or the administration of justice. These consequences are highly alarming and carry a great danger in them. Taking this into account, not only is the purity of the German race and German sense of morality threatened, but so is the influential position of the white man overall.[25]

In his letter to the Foreign Office, von Lindequist raised the issue of mixed marriages in the same fashion as missionaries and Social Democrats discussed it later: for him, as for them, it became a matter of principle. Mixed marriages were not only a local problem in a German colony, but carried the potential to become a national threat because of the legal consequences. Colored children claiming German citizenship would be able to become involved in colonial policy or even the military. In fact, the worst nightmare of government officials and local settlers who supported the prohibition of mixed marriages lay close at hand in a case that had occurred in northern Germany.[26] The children of a white man and an African woman had passed their grammar school exams in Kiel and Hamburg and were completing their military service in the German colonial army. For the majority of German farmers, it would have been intolerable that those two junior officers could serve as officers in South-West Africa.[27]

The governor did not want to introduce major changes in the law of the colony. Rather, he wished to deal with the issue out of the limelight by enforcing a rigid application of his internal circular from 1905 prohibiting mixed marriages. Governor von Lindequist chose to reinterpret the *Schutzgebietsgesetz*, the law of the colony written in 1900, by commenting on Article 7. According to his interpretation, this article's regulation of marriages only applied to non-Africans, although there was no clear indication of this in the *Schutzgebietsgesetz*.[28]

German judicial experts opened a legislative path justifying the prohibition in a way that was even more subtle and insidious. They degraded the African tribes to the legal level of young children, disallowing them from concluding legally valid marriages. Unlike von Lindequist, they did not argue that the *Schutzgebietsgesetz* did not allow a white man to practice the right to marry whomever he chose. In a letter to the *Deutsche Kolonialzeitung* on 16 January 1909, a state attorney named Fuchs conceded that "a state that propagates Christian moral law and is built upon the institutions and views of the Christian church cannot prevent its subjects who are willing and able from concluding a civil marriage—neither the white full citizens nor the coloured Christian. Each is a protected subject, regardless of his culture."[29] Fuchs also wanted to prevent mixed marriages—not by legally abolishing the right of the white men to marry Africans, but by declaring Africans as unable to formulate a valid statement of their will. In Fuchs's point of view, Africans could not understand the requirements and consequences of an official, monogamous marriage. The more general problem that Fuchs addressed, though, was that the practice of German law in the colony was vague: the legal term *Eingeborener* (native) was nowhere properly defined in German law. After 1905, this vagueness remained and the term *Eingeborener* remained legally unspecified as a subtle way to prohibit mixed marriage without introducing new Imperial orders, which were regarded as unnecessary because of the relatively small number of cases. That number rose massively after the Herero Wars when many soldiers established sexual relations with African women.

After 1905, the situation in South-West Africa changed dramatically in comparison to other German colonies in Africa or the South Pacific, simply because of the rapid increase of the white population caused by the arrival of German soldiers. While the advisory councils in German East Africa and Togo advised the colonial government to prevent mixed marriages, the colonial authorities in Cameroon announced that no legal action needed to be taken in the matter, as no mixed race appeared to be emerging.[30] The authorities in Samoa went so far as to formally validate existing mixed marriages concluded before 1906: there was no presence of German military personnel, which could have exacerbated the situation through the spread of venereal diseases or a rapid increase of mixed relations. The governor in Samoa even reserved the right to declare a Samoan as white to force a European in a mixed relationship to payment of alimony—a right that was not exercised in any other German colony. This example illustrates that the evolution and application of laws depended on sociopolitical and economic conditions specific to each colony.

In the case of South-West Africa, and parallel to our earlier discussion of corporal punishment, one finds an increasing gap in the perception of mixed relations by two groups: colonial authorities in Windhoek and the settlers on the one hand, and missionaries and the spokesmen of public opinion in Germany on the other hand. Again, specific practices at the local level reveal the changing contours of this polarization of views. In 1906, the Windhoek sports club and the farmers' association of the district refused membership to anyone who was married to an African woman. The farmers' association of the Gibeon district went even further and excluded every member who had an open sexual relationship with an African female.[31] In 1907, the High Court in Windhoek declared that even marriages concluded before the prohibition order of 1905 were invalid. This decision led to a storm of protest. Settlers who had married African women before 1905 wrote personal letters to Chancellor Bernhard von Bülow in which they argued that there had been hardly any white females in the colony before 1905, and the only way to prevent a concubine relationship with an African woman was to marry her.[32] Until the Herero Wars, missionaries had no explicit orders to refuse such marriage requests of settlers. Therefore the state should have no right to refuse official recognition or declare children out of those marriages as illegitimate.[33] The colonial authorities and courts disagreed with this view and refused official recognition, regardless of the level of racial mixture.[34]

It is by no means coincidental that the governor tried to introduce an even stricter order in 1911, which would have allowed the police to enforce the severance of a mixed relationship. One has to keep in mind how the whole issue of mixed relations developed after the end of the Herero Wars. While there was no increase in the number of mixed marriages after the prohibition, the number of concubine relationships and illegitimate children as a result of sexual relations between soldiers and African women increased rapidly; the same is true of the cases of syphilis and other sexually transmitted diseases.[35] As early as 1908, Governor Seitz cited the "incredible spread" of venereal diseases among the African population in a report to the Colonial Office.[36] This observation is corroborated by a reported 63 percent infection rate among single white males.[37]

These increases, which so troubled contemporaries, also correlated to an increase in the number of children born from relationships between Europeans and Africans in South-West Africa. From 1908 to 1909, the number of children from mixed relationships increased in Windhoek from 68 to 186, in Karibib from 12 to 107.[38] As the authorities confronted a rapidly expanding cohort of mixed-race children born outside of a stable relationship, they recognized that the problem was not merely demographic or medical, but political and legal as well. As early as 1905, von Lindequist had already painted a horrifying scenario of a society dominated arithmetically by coloreds. Many settlers regarded German soldiers as mainly responsible for this emerging nightmare, as contributions to a colonial newspaper suggested:

> If one assumes that the number of children of a couple is six, which is moderately estimated, then we will have from the sixteen couples ninety-six colored children; after two generations it will be several hundred; and after a few more generations it will be thousands. Additionally, the number of sexual relations between white men and native women has increased rapidly since the [Herero] uprising. And unfortunately, the quality of the relationship of the white man to the native woman has changed in comparison to the past. While the soldiers of the present day do not mind drinking with the native "comrade" out of the same rum bottle, or smoking the same pipe, they often also regard the native maid not only as the instrument of sexual satisfaction, but they are after her like their Berlin cook or German farmer's daughter.[39]

The increasing number of illegitimate children born of mixed-race relationships generated much hostility toward this new demographic group in colonial society. Therefore, the proposed order of the colonial governor in 1911 appeared natural to the colonists. It also appeared praiseworthy to missionaries, who strongly opposed sexual relations outside marriage. Yet the proposed order elicited strong opposition in Germany. According to the new proposal, every mixed-race birth had to be reported to the District Register.[40] The most controversial part of the order was Article 5: if a concubine relationship caused any public unrest, the police could ask for this relationship to be ended, using the threat of arrest. This clause is particularly important for the larger argument of this essay because it exemplifies why the amount of discretion given to local authorities is especially significant in colonial law. Depending on political circumstances, the definition of "public unrest" and the application of repressive sanctions was left solely to the legal authorities and the local police. This broad discretionary exercise of authority helps to explain why one would be misled to assume that the rule of law in the colonies was guaranteed by legal codification. Quite the contrary: a strict application of the above-mentioned clause, even though it might be based on practical considerations resulting from the influx of German soldiers into the colony, inherently risked undermining the basic rights of Africans and Europeans alike. Nonetheless, colonial authorities continued to decide whether any legal measure would be applied rigorously or leniently, with no need to justify their actions either in the colony or in Berlin.

In the case of the clauses prohibiting mixed marriages, Governor Seitz expected that his order would be confirmed by the Colonial Office, but he obviously did not anticipate the level of controversy his proposal would cause in Germany. On 7 June 1911, the Colonial Office wrote back acidly: "The intended legislation is in conflict with any legal regulation known in modern civilized nations."[41] The governor was told that the Colonial Office was politically sympathetic to his proposal, but could not confirm it for legal reasons. He replied that the Colonial Office might claim that his order did not fit into the system of the German Civil Code, but from his point of view: "It is the existence of colored people that does not fit into this system at all, but they are still there!"[42]

Opposition in Germany condemning such views culminated in a resolution accepted by the Reichstag on 8 May 1912, proposed by the Social Democrats and the Center Party.[43] In this resolution, both parties asked for the introduction of a law that would validate all mixed marriages in the colony and confirm the rights of children conceived in those relationships. The two parties supported the motion, but for different reasons. Whereas the Social Democrats argued that it would be inhuman and detrimental to German culture to oppress a colored population, Matthias Erzberger, the Center's young colonial expert, argued that it would be impossible and immoral to prohibit Christians, no matter of which race, from marrying each other.[44]

The authorities in the colony pointed out that a great majority of whites would be in favor of prohibiting sexual relations between Germans and Africans in general. Yet a number of politicians and also sections of the German press supported the abolition of the prohibition on mixed marriages. Both Social Democrats and members of the Center Party made it clear that mixed marriages in themselves were not desirable and should be neither supported nor promoted by the state. The colonial authorities recognized the balance of power and successfully acted to prevent the abolition of the prohibition by passing a resolution themselves on 24 May 1912, which declared as legitimate those marriages that had been officially concluded before 1 October 1905. This resolution still refused to permit mixed marriages after that date or in the future.[45]

The authorities in Windhoek succeeded in perpetuating a legal vacuum regarding the codification of the mixed-marriage legislation. At the same time, they applied the existing laws in a much more rigorous way than had the Colonial Government before 1905. Internal pressure was exercised by the governor to prevent clergy and missionaries from concluding mixed marriages. The authorities wanted to use the legislative tools they had brought over from Germany, together with their culture and moral views, to prevent any form of mixed-race relations, in order to build up the colonial government. After the 1912 resolution in the Reichstag, an act allowing mixed marriages was never drawn up. The missionaries as well as the Social Democrats and the Center Party in Germany were especially focused on how to prevent concubine relationships and the rising numbers of illegitimate children, while ensuring that the rule of law in the colony matched the rule of law in Germany. In the end, the colonial administration succeeded in preventing the conclusion of further mixed marriages in South-West Africa. The legal situation on the eve of World War I, then, was that mixed marriages were not permitted, but sexual relationships were not legally forbidden.

Conclusion

Colonial law was a tool to be applied by Germans in order to serve German, not African, interests. Liberties created by a code of law are inextricably linked to the liberties that the society which applies those laws wants to allow. The limit of what the German administration was prepared to allow in the largest German colony, serving as a *pars pro toto* in this essay, was clearly set by events on the colonial stage: when relations between Africans and settlers changed convulsively during the Herero Wars, attitudes toward the application of the law changed too. Mixed marriages were no longer allowed because a growing colored population was seen as a political threat to German supremacy in the colony. The use of corporal punishment rapidly increased after 1905: a diminished labor pool had to be disciplined without losing its value for the colonizer, and corporal punishment served the economic interests of the colonial population better than jail sentences for Africans. Colonial policy as well as colonial law may have been regulated and codified in Berlin, but it was applied on the ground by a colonial government aiming for political stability and economic profitability—if necessary, at the expense of the African population.

Colonial law gave the colonial government considerable flexibility in responding to the needs and interests of the settlers, while its application also led to serious abuse of the rights of Africans, who were increasingly subjected to corporal punishment and other excessive measures. The controversy regarding mixed-marriage legislation and its application thus also serves as a good illustration of how a relatively minor matter became a center-periphery power struggle with experiences and legal views in Windhoek differed significantly from those found in Berlin. The aims of colonial employers were often achieved not through openly breaking the law, but through reinterpreting the context in which events unfolded and through applying maximal personal discretion in the application of judicial procedures. The willingness of colonial administrators and employers to press this advantage increased after the Herero

Wars. In the last decade before the war, many settlers as well as the colonial government perceived many good reasons to maintain European standards of law and order, to the point that "negligence" and "disobedience" by native Africans were seen as sufficient reasons for severe physical abuse. Missionaries and other "experts in native affairs," who were often appointed to testify in that function during court cases against Africans, implicitly or explicitly helped to undermine the actual legal position of Africans in colonial courts. The rapid increase of the gap between the codification of law in order to safeguard law and order, on the one hand, and the application of law by courts or by the colonial government, on the other, widened to the point that the British administrator's report of 1918, cited previously, did not miss the mark in describing the breakdown of the rule of law in South-West Africa.[46]

To be sure, signs of this breakdown were evident to authorities in Berlin when complaints were registered by missionaries or settlers who documented the extent of corporal punishment or the treatment of mixed marriages. Between 1906 and 1914, the mistreatment of Africans and the increase in the number of colored children could not go completely unnoticed. However, the courts in the colony never attempted to address this gap between the rule of law for Africans in relation to Europeans. In their view, the colony was a political, economic, and military operation being run by Germans who were 12,000 kilometers away from any potential opposition. The law was applied as a critical instrument to run that operation smoothly.

Notes

1. Udo Wolter and Paul Kaller, "Deutsches Kolonialrecht – ein wenig erforschtes Rechtsgebiet, dargestellt anhand des Arbeitsrechts der Eingeborenen," in *Zeitschrift für Neuere Rechtsgeschichte* 17 (1995): 201-44; Jürgen Zimmerling, *Die Entwicklung der Strafrechtspflege für Afrikaner in Deutsch-Südwestafrika 1884-1914. Eine juristisch/historische Untersuchung* (Bochum, 1995); Harald Sippel, "Verwaltung und Recht in Deutsch-Ostafrika," in *Kolonialisierung des Rechts. Zur kolonialen Rechts- und Verwaltungsordnung*, ed. Rüdiger Voigt and Peter Sack (Baden-Baden, 2001), 271-92; Klaus Richter, *Deutsches Kolonialrecht in Ostafrika 1885-1891* (Frankfurt a.M., 2001).

2. Klaus Richter, "Deutsch-Ostafrika 1885 bis 1890: Auf dem Weg vom Schutzbriefsystem zur Reichskolonialverwaltung. Ein Beitrag zur Verfassungsgeschichte der deutschen Kolonien," in *Forum Historiae Juris*, January 2000.

3. Hermann Sinram, *Blaubuch Namibia* (Lusaka, 1988), 54.

4. Jan-Bart Gewald, *Towards Redemption: A Socio-Political history of the Herero in Namibia between 1890 and 1923* (Leiden, 1996); Gesine Krüger, *Kriegsbewältigung und Geschichtsbewußtsein. Zur Realität, Deutung und Bewältigung des Deutsch-Hererokriegs 1904-1907* (Hanover, 1995); Peter Katjavivi, *A History of Resistance in Namibia* (London, 1988); Brigitte Lau, "Uncertain Certainties: The Herero-German War of 1904," in *Migabus* 2 (1989): 4-8. For the genocide debate, see Tilman Dedering, "The German-Herero War of 1904: Revisionism of Genocide or Imaginary Historiography?" in *Journal of Southern African Studies* 19, no. 1 (1993): 80-88;

Lothar Engel, *Die Stellung der Rheinischen Missionsgesellschaft zu den politischen und gesellschaftlichen Verhältnissen Südwestafrikas und ihr Beitrag zur dortigen kirchlichen Entwicklung bis zum Nama-Herero-Aufstand 1904-1907* (Hamburg, 1972).

5. Union of South Africa, *Report on the Natives of South-West Africa and their treatment by Germany, prepared by the Administrator's Office*, Windhoek, South-West Africa, January 1918, 162, S.W. Africa Miscellaneous. Blue Books and Pamphlets 1884-1960, Rhodes House Library, Oxford, UK (hereafter cited as RL).

6. Hartmut Pogge von Strandmann, "The Kolonialrat: Its Significance and Influence on German Politics 1890 to 1906" (D.Phil diss., University of Oxford, 1969).

7. Imperial Decree in Respect of the Jurisdiction over Natives in the German Protectorates in East Africa and Togo; Decree of the Imperial Chancellor from 22 April 1896, ZBU F.I.cI. (605), National Archives Windhoek (hereafter cited as NA). For a broader perspective on issues raised in this section, see Nils Ole Oermann, *Mission, Church and State Relations in South West Africa under German Rule (1884-1915)* (Stuttgart, 1999), 172-77.

8. Union of South Africa, *Report on the Natives*, 151.

9. Hinrich Rüping, *Grundriss der Strafrechtsgeschichte*, 3rd ed. (Munich 1998); Jürgen Zimmerling, *Die Entwicklung der Strafrechtspflege für Afrikaner in Deutsch-Südwestafrika. Eine juristisch/historische Untersuchung* (Bochum, 1995).

10. RMS Missionary Berger, Drie Jare v Hendrik Witbooi, A541 Accession C. Berger diaries 1901-48, ZBU, NA.

11. Accessions A 41 Corporal Punishment of Natives, A41, NA; ZBU F.V.f1. Vollzug der Prügelstrafe, vol. 1, 1909 (694), NA and ZBU F.V.f2. Vollzug der Prügelstrafe, vol. 2, 1912-14 (694), NA. The German files were translated by the South African administration as a proof for severe maltreatment of the African population by Germans to provide material for Union of South Africa, *Report on the*, 151.

12. State Secretary Dernburg to Governor von Schuckmann, Berlin, 12 February 1907, ZBU F.V.d1. Disziplinarbefugnisse gegenüber Eingeborenen, generalia, vol. 1 (692), NA.

13. Missionary Wandres to Deputy Governor Hintrager, 24 May 1910, ZBU F.IV.r1. Mischehen und die daraus entstammenden Nachkommen, generalia, vol. 1, 1887 (666), NA.

14. Richter, "Deutsch-Ostafrika 1885 bis 1890," 251f.

15. Union of South Africa, *Report on the Natives*, 161-62.

16. *Lüderitzbuchter Zeitung*, 22 May 1914.

17. Union of South Africa, *Report on the Natives*, 119 ff.

18. ZBU F.V.k10. Strafverzeichnisse und Prügelkontrolle des Bezirksamts Windhoek, specialia, 1913-13, 2 vols. (699), NA; A 41, 133, NA.

19. Verdict of District Commissioner Todt, Windhoek on 2 November 1912, Eingeborenenkommissariat Windhoek, EKW F.V.k3. Strafprotokolle vol. 1, 1913, NA.

20. Deputy Governor Hintrager to the Colonial Office, Windhoek, 20 June 1910, R1001/5423, Bundesarchiv Berlin-Lichterfelde (hereafter cited as BA).

21. Colonial Department of the Foreign Office to Governor von Lindequist, Berlin, 21 June 1906, R1001/5423, BA.

22. Harald Sippel, "Die rechtliche Behandlung von ehelichen und nichtehelichen Beziehungen zwischen Kolonisten und Kolonisierten in Deutsch-Südwestafrika," in *Zwischen Waterberg und Sandfeld. Die Verantwortlichen am Schicksal der Herero*, ed. August Wilhelm Steffan (Windhoek and Wuppertal, 2001), 73-88; Oermann, *Mission*, 185-201; idem, "'Hochverehrter Herr Gouverneur' - Zum Verhältnis von Mission und deutschem Kolonialstaat im Zeitalter des Imperialismus," in Arthur Bogner, Bernd Holtwick, and Hartmann Tyrell, *Weltgesellschaft-Weltmission-Organisation* (Würzburg, forthcoming 2003).

23. Mr. Bornhaupt, "Zur Frage der Mischehen zwischen Reichsangehörigen und Eingeborenen in Deutsch-Südwestafrika vom Rechtsstandpunkte," in *Deutsche Kolonialzeitung*, 2 January 1909.

24. Judgment in the case of Cornelia Denk, Rehoboth on 27 April 1911, in Microfilm archive of the Central Bureau R 151 I, microfilm 5181, F.IV.R2., vol. 2, *Rechtspflege gegen Nichteingeborene*.

25. Governor von Lindequist to the Colonial Department of the Foreign Office, Windhoek, 23 October 1905, R1001/5423, BA.

26. Helmut Bley, *Kolonialherrschaft und Sozialstrukturin Deutsch-Südwestafrika 1894-1914* (Hamburg 1968), 250.

27. This case was reported in an undated article sent by the Colonial Department of the Foreign Office to Governor von Lindequist, Berlin, 21 June 1906, R1001/5423, BA.

28. Governor von Lindequist to Colonial Department of the Foreign Office, Windhoek, 23 October 1905, R1001/5423, BA. See also Verordnung betreffend der Rechtsverhältnisse in den deutschen Schutzgebieten vom 9. November 1900, *Reichsgesetzblatt 1005*.

29. Letter of State Attorney Fuchs to the *Deutsche Kolonialzeitung*, 16 January 1909.

30. Martha Mamozai, *Herrenmenschen. Frauen im deutschen Kolonialismus*, (Reinbek 1982), 132.

31. Der Aufstand in Deutsch-Südwestafrika, in *Leipziger Neueste Nachrichten*, 8 March 1906; Helmut Bley, *Namibia under German Rule* (Hamburg, 1996), 214.

32. Letter of farmer Wrede to Imperial Chancellor von Bülow, Gamis near Rehoboth, 25 June 1907, R1001/5423, BA; Wrede and other settlers had married women who belonged to the so called Rehoboth Bastards. Wrede was married by missionary Heidtmann in Rehoboth and had asked for official recognition in September 1905. His request was refused; technically, his marriage was invalid and his children were illegitimate.

33. District commissioner to colonial government Windhoek, Karibib, 1 September 1908 to the attention of the German Colonial Office, R1001/5423, BA; farmer Guthke had appealed to the Colonial Office in Berlin, which asked the district commissioner to arrange a compromise, but the district commissioner had refused this request based on the circular order of 23 September 1905 prohibiting official recognition of mixed marriages.

34. District Commissioner Brill to Imperial government Windhoek in the case of Denk vs. Denk, 29 April 1911, in Microfilm archive of the Central Bureau R 151 I, microfilm 5181, F.IV.R2., vol. 2, Rechtspflege gegen Nichteingeborene, BA.

35. Governor Seitz to the German Colonial Office, Windhoek, 12 June 1911, R1001/5423, BA.

36. Governor Seitz to the Colonial Office, Windhoek, on 8 January 1908, ZBU H.II.h1. (846), NA.

37. This infection rate was determined through a medical exam at the Tsumeb mine. Dr. Wohlgemuth to missionary Eich, Tsumeb, 30 September 1908, ELCRN II.1.13, Archives of the Evangelical Lutheran Church in Namibia (ELCRN).

38. Report of Deputy Governor Hintrager in the *Windhuker Nachrichten*, 27 April 1910.

39. Statements of Mr. Janson and Mr. Schlettwein in "Maßnahmen gegen Mischlinge," *Windhuker Nachrichten*, 27 April 1910.

40. Proposal of the Verordnung des Kaiserlichen Gouverneurs Seitz von Deutsch-Südwestafrika betreffend der Mischlingsbevölkerung, March 1911, R1001/5423, BA.

41. Colonial Office to Governor Seitz, 7 June 1911, R1001/5423, BA.

42. Governor to Colonial Office, Windhoek on 29 October 1911, R1001/5423, BA.

43. For the text of the resolution, see the stenographic minutes of the German Reichstag, vol. 299, Attachment IIa, 380. See also *Germania* on 1 October 1912; Bley, *Namibia*, 219.

44. Stenographic Minutes of the German *Reichstag*, vol. 285 on 7 May 1912.

45. Governor Seitz to Colonial Office, 24 May 1912, R1001/5423, BA.

46. Union of South Africa, *Report on the Natives*, 161-62.

11

Max Warburg and German Politics

The Limits of Financial Power in Wilhelmine Germany

Niall Ferguson

We are growing stronger every year; our enemies are getting weaker internally.

Max Warburg, 21 July 1914.

Introduction

The role of businessmen in the politics of Wilhelmine Germany has long been the subject of intense investigation. However, until relatively recently it tended to be industrialists who attracted most scholarly attention. Even before Hartmut Pogge von Strandmann's edition of Walther Rathenau's diaries,[1] several major studies on the power of industrial interest groups and "organized capitalism" in politics had appeared in the 1970s.[2] There was at one time vehement disagreement about the extent to which businessmen wielded effective political power, with approaches ranging from the pure Marxism-Leninism favored by historians in the German Democratic Republic,[3] to the skepticism of Volker Hentschel.[4] Business influence was assessed on a scale beginning with near impotence and rising through "corporatism" and "organized capitalism" to the maximum of "state monopoly capitalism." By comparison, less attention was paid until recently to the political role of Wilhelmine finance, despite the emphasis placed on "finance capital" by contemporary Marxist theorists such as Rudolf Hilferding, whose book of that name was published in 1910. Only in the last decade, with the publication of two major works on the subject, has the imbalance begun to be redressed.[5] In particular, historians are beginning to realize how lopsided Hilferding's account of German banking was. By focusing on the (undoubtedly large) proportion of the assets of the big joint-stock banks that took the form of industrial shares, Hilferding underestimated the role of merchant banks similar in their structure and function to the acceptance and issuance houses of the city of London. Even Deutsche Bank—usually thought of as the epitome of "finance capital"—was principally concerned before 1914 to compete with the big London and Paris banks for a share of the international bond market.[6]

In part, this neglect is not so surprising, in that the bankers—as Morten Reitmayer has shown—were simply less well organized than the industrialists. However, not all business politics took place in the easily investigated loci of the *Interessenverbände*. The merchant bankers of Hamburg took pride in acting discreetly, "behind the scenes." They saw themselves as "die Stillen im Lande," combining surreptitious political influence with studied self-effacement. Moreover, their reluctance to hold official posts has meant that historians have tended to underrate their contribution.[7] Of no individual is this more true than the banker Max Warburg.

Of course, Warburg is not unknown to historians. [8] He features prominently in histories of the Warburg firm and family.[9] He was one of the so-called *Kaiserjuden* who enjoyed relatively good relations with Wilhelm II.[10] Fritz Fischer identified him as a "firm believer in an active [German] foreign policy."[11] Warburg is also known to have played an influential role in the preparations for the Versailles peace conference and, along with his partner Carl Melchior, at the conference itself.[12] He was much involved in economic policy making during the early Weimar era.[13] And he was one of the many prominent Jewish businessmen to suffer discrimination, expropriation, and exile after 1933.[14] Yet none of this gives an adequate idea of the extent and nature of Warburg's importance. Although a less cerebral figure than Rathenau, he played as important a role in the economic and political life of Wilhelmine Germany. This chapter offers a brief account of his career to 1918. It also subjects Warburg's critique of German economic policy to empirical reexamination in the light of recent economic research. Warburg's writings lack the pseudoscientific jargon of Hilferding's and the philosophical trimmings of Rathenau's. Yet in many respects, he got rather closer to the truth than either of these more highly esteemed figures.

The Hanseatic Setting

The rapid expansion of Hamburg's economy before 1914 would not have been possible without corresponding developments in the city's financial sector.[15] Established merchant banks were principally concerned with discounting commercial bills. However, the later nineteenth century saw a widening of financial opportunities as the international bond market grew increasingly "globalized," and no private bank in Germany did more to exploit these opportunities than the house of M. M. Warburg & Co.

The Warburgs had established themselves in Altona in the late seventeenth century, but for four generations remained little more than minor moneychangers. In the wake of the Napoleonic Wars, however, the firm succeeded in establishing itself as one of the Rothschilds' correspondents in Hamburg, finally supplanting Salomon

Heine as their principal Hamburg agent in 1865.[16] This made the bank a satellite of what was by far the nineteenth century's biggest concentration of financial capital.[17] In the succeeding years, the Warburg bank's interests expanded to embrace straightforward commercial bill transactions, arbitrage, and foreign bond issues (for governments, banks, and railways). But it still remained a relatively inconsequential concern—one of hundreds of small firms around the world with whom Rothschilds had regular dealings.[18] It was only after 1900, under the inspired direction of Max Warburg, the second of Moritz Warburg's five sons, that the bank rose to national and international prominence.[19] Connected by the marriages of two of Max's younger brothers, Paul and Felix, to the powerful New York house of Kuhn, Loeb & Co., M. M. Warburg & Co. joined the international elite of banks capable of participating in the business of bond issuance for governments and big corporations.[20] Between 1895 and 1913, the firm's balance sheet grew nearly fourfold, from 30 million marks to 118 million marks.[21] In these terms, it is true, the three major joint-stock banks in Hamburg (the Norddeutsche Bank, the Commerz- und Diskonto Bank, and the Vereinsbank) were substantially bigger and played the leading role in the rapid industrial development of Hamburg and its environs after 1880.[22] But although M.M. Warburg remained a family-run concern, it was active in this field, too—particularly in financing the expansion of the Hanseatic merchant fleet and the associated shipbuilding industry—and it was firmly established as the leading North German house for international bond issues.[23]

Like so many members of the Wilhelmine Jewish business elite born around the time of German unification, Warburg was an ardent German nationalist. True, his was a cosmopolitan background. He had served his own banking apprenticeship in Frankfurt, Amsterdam, Paris, and London. Not only had two of his brothers emigrated to the United States, the family also had marital links to England, Sweden, and Russia. Warburg retained a strong sense of loyalty to Hamburg as his *Vaterstadt* and *-staat* and had a keen awareness that its economic interests were far from identical to those of the Reich as a whole. Yet—and in this his sense of identity was typically Wilhelmine—none of this struck him as incompatible with a strong sense of identification with the German Reich, which an enjoyable period of military service in the 3rd Bavarian Light Cavalry Regiment had only served to heighten.[24]

It is against this background that Warburg's contribution to Wilhelmine politics needs to be understood. Though he preferred to call himself a Free Conservative rather than a National Liberal, and sat among the "Rights" after his election to the Hamburg Bürgerschaft in 1903, there is no question that Warburg was fundamentally a liberal in his politics. He was not unsympathetic to Friedrich Naumann, for example,[25] and on one occasion he even referred to himself mischievously as "an old democrat." After the war, Warburg himself likened his support for Germany's colonial policy to party-political contributions of the sort that British and American bankers habitually made. But the historian Alfred Vagts believed that "it had more to do with the anti-Semitism abroad in the Reich. Alongside the unrealistic imperialism propagandized by often anti-Semitic Pan-Germans, the imperialism of banking capital found considerable favor in official circles. ... There was a tacit competition between the two imperialisms in the Second Reich. ..."[26] Though an oversimplification, this interpretation conveys more than a grain of truth.

Warburg and *Weltpolitik*

Max Warburg's involvement in the efforts of the German Foreign Office after 1900 to assert German influence entitled him to claim that "no banking house in Germany has interested itself so determinedly for Germany's activity in the colonies as ours"[27]—though he ought also to have mentioned Germany's activity in areas of informal imperial rivalry. True, the bulk of the bank's business remained of little political significance: discounting commercial bills, selling foreign railway bonds to German investors, issuing bonds for Central and Eastern European banks. Nevertheless, the extent to which he and his partners took account of political considerations at this time is quite striking. For example, before deciding to participate in a new Japanese bond issue in July 1905, Warburg "did what any sound banker must do in such cases: I went straight to the Foreign Office in Berlin."[28]

Warburg's activities in this area have been detailed elsewhere and need only be summarized here. In 1910, for example, he had a hand in the efforts to involve German banks in Chinese government finance.[29] Above all, he was heavily involved in the attempt by the German Foreign Minister Alfred von Kiderlen-Wächter to challenge the growing French dominance of the Moroccan economy. It was an employee of M. M. Warburg, Wilhelm Karl Regendanz, who furnished the German Foreign Office with the claim that there were valuable copper deposits in the south of Morocco, which—it was alleged—the French were seeking to monopolize. (Admittedly, Warburg was not aware of how far Kiderlen was exaggerating the extent of German interests in Morocco.)[30] In the last few years before the war, he and his partners also floated a loan for the West African state of Liberia, joined the Colonial Office's new syndicate for colonial loans, raised money for a number of German companies with colonial interests, negotiated with the British Bank of West Africa to establish a new Anglo-German Bank of North-West Africa, and participated in a "German-Portuguese Colonial Syndicate," set up by the Colonial Office to facilitate the German penetration, if not takeover, of Portugal's colonies in Africa.[31] In Hamburg Warburg also funded organizations including the Colonial Institute, the Institute for Tropical Medicine, and the Hamburg-Morocco Society. All of these efforts were clearly motivated by something other than economic self-interest. Indeed, Warburg himself admitted that his labors for *Weltpolitik* brought "little return [*wenig Verdienst*]—a phrase that could easily be applied to German colonial policy as a whole.[32]

Yet Warburg quite quickly came to have doubts about the viability of *Weltpolitik*. His critique was based on the identification of two basic structural weaknesses in Germany's position relative to her overseas rivals. The first was fiscal. Quite simply, the German Reich lacked a tax base large enough to match British, French, or Russian expenditures on armaments. As a result, according to Warburg, Germany had to rely too much on government borrowing, and this in turn led to problems of "crowding out" by pushing up German long-term interest rates. The second weakness Warburg detected lay with the German balance of payments. Late-nineteenth-century imperialism—broadly defined to include both "formal" and "informal" variants—rested above all on capital exports. But Warburg argued that Germany did not export sufficient capital to exert the kind of leverage in foreign markets that could be exerted by Britain and France.

As a member of the Reich Loan Consortium from 1905, Warburg was only too well aware of the high level of government borrowing necessitated by rising military spending and the growth of "social" expenditure at the state and local level. From the late 1890s, Tirpitz's plan to build a German battle fleet had enjoyed considerable support in Hamburg, not least because of the value of naval contracts to the city's shipyards.[33] In the years after 1908, however, Warburg and his friend the shipowner Albert Ballin became convinced that Germany could not (in Ballin's words) "afford a race in dreadnoughts against the much wealthier British."[34] In 1909 Warburg persuaded the Hamburg Chamber of Commerce to lend its support to the newly founded Hansabund's campaign for tax reform. At the time of the financial wrangles that helped topple Bülow from the Reich chancellorship, Warburg drafted a memorandum on Reich fiscal reform entitled "How can we avoid a solution to the Reich's financial crisis that simply gives rise to a financial crisis among the federal states?" This document denounced the fiscal stalemate in the Reichstag in remarkably prescient terms: "If we carry on our financial policy in this way, we will be guilty of financial asset-stripping; and, one fine day, we will find that we can only make good the damage with the greatest possible sacrifice—if we can make it good at all."[35] Like many of his contemporaries, Warburg saw the price of a government's bonds as an accurate measure of its fiscal health. Here, too, he saw cause for concern, prompting his 1912 address to the Central Association of German Banks and Bankers (CVDBB), entitled "Appropriate and Inappropriate Ways to Raise the Price of Government Bonds."[36] Unfortunately, these arguments fell on deaf ears in high places. When Warburg attempted to broach the subject of financial reform with the Kaiser, he merely provoked the shrill response that it was Russia, not Germany, which was "going bust."[37]

Yet it was not just Germany's fiscal weakness that perturbed Warburg. Also of concern were its comparatively weak balance of payments and, above all, the vulnerability of German financial markets to outflows of foreign capital in the event of political crises. This was a phenomenon Warburg noted as early as 1905, in the wake of the first Moroccan crisis.[38] It was, he later declared, "financial influence which supported French policy in Algeciras. ... The success [of that policy] was more a victory of French financial strength than a victory of French diplomacy."[39] In September 1907, at the annual conference of the CVDBB in Hamburg, Warburg asked his audience whether, in view of this vulnerability, Germany was adequately prepared to weather the financial consequences of a major European war.[40] Warburg provocatively entitled his speech "Financial Readiness for War" and startled his audience by estimating the annual cost of a major European war at 22 billion marks,[41] a higher figure than most other commentators anticipated (although still an underestimate, as it turned out).[42] One conclusion he reached was that the government should lift the remaining restrictions imposed on German financial markets by the 1896 Stock Exchange Law. This was less of a non sequitur than might at first appear. Ever since the passage of the Stock Exchange Law in 1896, he and other German bankers had waged a campaign to have the law amended, particularly the restrictions it placed on futures transactions (*Termingeschäfte*) in grain and industrial shares.[43] (It was indeed in response to this legislation that the CVDBB had been founded in 1901.) Warburg and other banking spokesmen had consistently argued that the effect of the restrictions was to drive business away from the German stock exchanges to the less regulated financial markets of London and Paris. It was a significant victory for the bankers' campaign when Bülow acknowledged in May 1906 that an amendment of the *Börsengesetz* would be "in the interests of state credit."[44] However, this was only part of Warburg's argument. He also insisted that it would be a mistake if Germany were to respond to the outbreak of war by imposing a moratorium on financial transactions, or some other kind of control on the capital and money markets. Rather, the aim should be to build up during peacetime a sufficiently large portfolio of foreign securities in German hands, which could be liquidated in the event of war to mitigate the effects of any capital flight out of Germany.

To many contemporaries, the events of 1911 seemed to expose the relative weakness of the German capital market compared to that of Britain or France. In Albert Ballin's view, it was the "collapse of the bourse" that was to blame for the failure of Kiderlen's coup. This was also the view of the German ambassador in Paris, who felt that "the self-confidence the French derive from their capital resources [had] been given new sustenance by the events on the German stock exchange."[45] According to Ballin, the crisis could have been averted if the government had consulted the German banks before sending the gunboat *Panther* to Agadir.[46] Warburg, however, was more positive in his assessment. True, there had been something close to a withdrawal of "all the deposits that Europe had in Germany" on 2 and 4 September.[47] But "Germany had withstood the test well in financial terms"; the real financial crisis, Warburg maintained, had been in Paris, not Berlin or Hamburg.[48] He had in fact written to the Foreign Office on 11 September, urging that a "support action" be organized by the main German banks to shore up the German stock exchange "in order to give the outside world a display of strength on the bourse."[49] When it proved possible to place 80 billion marks of Prussian Treasury bills in New York, the drain of capital out of the German markets had been effectively counteracted.[50] Warburg also praised the conduct of the Reichsbank in maintaining money market liquidity during the crisis—praise he reiterated at the time of the Balkan War in 1912.[51]

Anglo-German Relations and the Coming of War

The German financial markets might have been able to weather a storm over Morocco. Yet Warburg never had any doubt that they would not fare so well if Germany were to risk a confrontation with Great Britain. As early as 1912, he could see the possibility that an Austrian clash with Russia over the Balkans could lead to "further complications (Germany *contra* France and England)."[52] Despite the failure of Lord Haldane's "mission" to Germany (which they helped to arrange),[53] Warburg and Ballin continued to pin their hopes on small-scale colonial agreements as the basis for a broader Anglo-German entente. Indeed, Warburg's three visits to England in February, April, and June 1914 to discuss German involvement in Portuguese Angola and other overseas markets led him to hope that "an extraordinary amity between the Germans and England [had] broken out."[54]

Needless to say, none of this had a significant influence on Britain's Continental policy in July and August of that year, which was determined in the end by a complex of strategic and domestic political calculations.[55] Nor was Warburg able to make much headway in Berlin, where pessimistic estimates of the pace of Russian rearmament were increasing the pressure on the government to wage a "preventive war." He was dismayed when, at a gala dinner in Hamburg on 21 June 1914, the Kaiser outlined to him the case for a preventive war against, implicitly, all three Entente powers: "He [the Kaiser] was worried about the Russian armaments [program and] about the planned railway construction, and detected [in these] the preparations for a war against us in 1916. He complained about the inadequacy of the railway links that we had at the Western Front against France, and hinted [at] whether it would not be better to strike now, rather than wait." Warburg "advised decidedly against" this: "[I] sketched the domestic political situation in England for him (Home Rule), the difficulties for France of maintaining the three-year service period, the financial crisis in which France already found itself, and the probable unreliability of the Russian army. I strongly advised [him] to wait patiently, keeping our heads down for a few more years. 'We are growing stronger every year; our enemies are getting weaker internally.'"[56] This advice, as we know, was ignored in the wake of the assassinations at Sarajevo. On 18 July, the Kaiser requested that Ballin be informed about possible mobilization. Three days later, the Reich Chancellery wrote to the Senate about the need for regional labor exchanges to allocate manpower in the event of a war. On 23 July, the Foreign Office dispatched Langwerth von Simmern to Hamburg with a copy of the Austrian ultimatum, which had just been sent to Serbia.[57]

As it unfolded, the July crisis unleashed a severe financial crisis that spread from Vienna to the other European financial markets, including Hamburg. M. M. Warburg had already begun to "realize what could be sold, and reduce our engagements" immediately after the Sarajevo assassination, but by 20 July the main Hamburg banks had to take measures to counter a general panic on the stock exchange.[58] When news reached Hamburg on the evening of 28 July that the German government had rejected Sir Edward Grey's proposal for a conference of foreign ministers in London,

Warburg felt compelled to contact the Wilhelmstrasse. Arthur Zimmermann, the under-secretary at the Foreign Office, authorized him to announce that although the German government did not regard the proposed conference as "feasible," nevertheless "the negotiations from cabinet to cabinet, which had already been initiated with the utmost success, would be continued." Although this statement was greeted with applause, the bourse was not reopened that evening.[59] The subsequent entry of England into the war plunged the Hamburg economy into a profound slump, as overseas trade beyond the Baltic all but ceased.[60]

Unlike Albert Ballin, who was a pessimist from the outset,[61] and his brother Aby, who suffered a nervous breakdown as a result of the war,[62] Max Warburg was not immune to the febrile patriotism that swept through bourgeois Germany during World War I. For example, he argued repeatedly during the course of 1916 for the creation of German "colonies" in the Baltic territories of Latvia and Courland, employing language that was almost Pan-German.[63] However, the economic disadvantages under which Germany labored as a result of the sea blockade made him much less certain of victory against the Western powers. Early in the war, he and Ballin were driven to Berlin to discuss the question of food imports with officials of the Ministry of the Interior, the Treasury Office, the Foreign Office, and the Reichsbank. Both men were disconcerted by the officials' assumption that Germany would be able to make use of the American merchant marine.[64]

Warburg also had a clearer idea than most Treasury and Reichsbank officials of the financial difficulties facing Germany. Like Karl Helfferich, he assumed that the costs of the war would ultimately be defrayed by reparations from the vanquished foe. Indeed, in November 1914 he proposed 50 billion marks as an appropriate level of reparations, assuming a victorious war lasting just four months. Warburg acknowledged from the outset that "the longer the war progresses ... the greater will be the discrepancy between the demands that we will be justified in making and the ability of our enemies ... to meet these." But he continued to envisage reparations as high as 100 billion marks as late as May 1918.[65]

Warburg was well aware that until the moment of victory, Germany could fight the war only by running twin deficits: a balance of payments deficit with neutral trading partners, and a public sector deficit, funded by the German public and by the country's financial institutions. His bank played an important and profitable part in the financing of both: at the end of the war, its balance sheet (adjusted for inflation) showed a 50 percent increase on the 1913 figure.[66] But as Warburg noted with characteristic black humor: "If Germany should lose the war, and the Reichsbank finds itself unable to honor its obligations to us, we will have no alternative but to put an announcement in the papers saying: 'Payments suspended on the field of honor. M. M. Warburg & Co.'"[67]

Mounting pessimism about Germany's chances of victory explains Warburg's involvement in the efforts to win new allies for Germany (Italy, Romania, Bulgaria, Sweden) and his advocacy of a separate peace with England.[68] It also explains why—uniquely in the Hamburg business community—Warburg opposed the lifting of restrictions on submarine warfare, on the grounds that, however great the impact on British food supplies, the risk of alienating the United States was too grave. "If America is cut off from Germany," he argued in February 1916, "that means a 50 percent reduction in Germany's financial strength for the war, and an increase of 100 percent for England's and France's. ... Everything should ... be done to avoid a breach with America."[69] "The war is lost if it [unrestricted submarine warfare] goes ahead: financially, because our loans will no longer be bought; economically, because the masses of raw materials that we continue to get from abroad and which we cannot do without will be cut off."[70] For Warburg, the German response to Wilson's "peace without victory" note of 22 January 1917 was not conciliatory enough: "We cannot pay any heed to the dangerous views prevalent in our 'piazza.' The *Basser*-and *Stresemänner* are really less important than our relations with America. If we end up at war with America, we will face an enemy with such moral, financial and economic strength that we will have nothing more to hope for from the future; that is my firm conviction."[71] But the restrictions on submarine warfare were again lifted and, just over two months later, the United States declared war on Germany.

Of course, the collapse of Russia and the military victory on the eastern front gave fresh impetus to those who opposed negotiation. Indeed, it was the publication of the Treaty of Brest Litovsk in March 1918 that helped torpedo an attempt by Warburg (acting on Reich Chancellor Hertling's instructions) to hold unofficial talks about the postwar status of Belgium with the American ambassador in Holland.[72] But Warburg had little doubt that this victory in the East would prove illusory. He denounced the peace with Russia as "thinly veiled annexation, with an all too transparent façade provided by the right of national self-determination,"[73] and increasingly gravitated toward pacifist writers including Martin Hobohm and Walther Schücking.[74] As this might suggest, opposition to annexationism entailed some kind of shift on domestic politics. It was increasingly obvious that a negotiated end to the war could be achieved only if some form of domestic reform could increase the power of the Reichstag over the Reich chancellor, and that of the chancellor over the military.[75] Such views drew Warburg from July 1917 into the circle of men around the future chancellor, Prince Max of Baden; they also meant that he had little difficulty in finding common ground with the leader of the Majority Social Democrats, Friedrich Ebert, when the latter visited Hamburg in June 1918.[76] When it became clear that Ludendorff's spring offensive on the western front had failed to win the war, Warburg had little hesitation in advising Prince Max to "persuade the Kaiser to abdicate"[77] and in urging parliamentarization for the Reich and democratization for Prussia.

These domestic reforms were in fact largely achieved by the government of Prince Max in the course of October 1918. But Warburg's fear that Prince Max was coming to power "too late" had already been confirmed four days before his appointment as chancellor by Ludendorff's demand for an "immediate armistice to avoid catastrophe." Warburg's argument against this "panic" was a strong one: "Begging President Wilson for an armistice" would mean "the capitulation of Europe to America" if it was done before "the idea has taken root abroad that there had been a change in Germany."[78] Without the leverage of a defensible front, there was no sense in attempting to make a qualified acceptance of the Fourteen Points, as Warburg, Kurt Hahn, and Konrad Haussmann had intended, and nothing to prevent Wilson from demanding further political reforms within Germany—including the end of the monarchy—as a precondition for negotiation.[79] Exactly this happened, and when the navy then attempted to launch a last-ditch raid on Britain, the effect was to precipitate the Kiel mutiny and unleash the spontaneous revolution from below.

The Reckoning

The full extent of the catastrophe that had befallen Germany by the end of 1918 was not grasped by those who maintained that the German army remained "undefeated in the field." But to a man like Max Warburg, the truth was painfully apparent. Although Warburg later admitted that he had "labored under deep misapprehensions as to the terms that would be put to us," few of his circle had expected to be treated lightly.[80] He himself had demurred when asked by Prince Max to represent Germany at the peace negotiations because "the Entente conditions would doubtless be extremely hard."[81] Some officials talked of reparations demands of between 20 and 30 billion marks, but Warburg warned them to brace themselves for an "absurdly high" figure. As he put it to Count Brockdorff-Rantzau, the head of the German peace delegation, in early April: "We must be prepared for damned hard conditions."[82] Having once anticipated imposing reparations of up to 100 billion marks on the Allies in the event of a German victory, Warburg now assumed that Germany would be burdened with reparations for between twenty-five and forty years.[83]

The cost of the war to German—and especially Hanseatic—finance was already calamitous as a result of the wartime disruption of trade, the sequestration of overseas assets, and the seizure of German merchant vessels. Approximately 16.1 billion marks of German overseas investments had been seized, to say nothing of around 1.9 billion marks of short-term credits to foreign trading partners that had been frozen, and 1.3 million tons of shipping that had been sequestrated. Although it is not certain what proportion of the total overseas assets were Hamburg-owned, it was certainly not a trifling amount, judging by the vehemence with which Hamburg spokesmen insisted that "our overseas assets" must "fundamentally be exempted from any incursion aimed at the satisfaction of enemy financial demands on the Reich."[84] One of Warburg's principal preoccupations at the Versailles conference was therefore to press for the return of German private property that had been confiscated in markets controlled by the Allies. In his view, the combination of wholesale expropriation and the imposition of reparations would inevitably plunge Germany into a catastrophic balance of payments crisis.[85] It was on this basis that Warburg opposed efforts to stabilize postwar German monetary and financial policy: only after reparations had been revised would such steps be worth taking. The stage was set for the tragedy of Germany's descent into hyperinflation.

A Balance

Warburg's early doubt about the viability of Wilhelmine *Weltpolitik* was very much a banker's critique, and it needs to be set in its proper financial context to be appreciated. As he rightly said, Germany was "growing stronger every year" in the broadest macroeconomic terms. The country's per capita gross domestic product (GDP) grew at an average annual rate of 1.63 percent between 1870 and 1913—the highest growth rate in the world apart from Canada and the United States.[86] Admittedly, in absolute terms German per capita GDP was still less than British; indeed, it was lower than that of Belgium, Denmark, Holland, and Switzerland, too. But Germany was poised to overtake these smaller countries. In terms of total factor productivity, the German economy was rapidly gaining on the British, though—unlike the U.S.—it had not yet surpassed it.[87]

However (notwithstanding Paul Kennedy's contrary view), a simple growth in economic output does not automatically translate into an increase in power in the field of international relations.[88] Higher output does not yield greater power unless growth can be tapped by the government's fiscal system and channeled into military assets, and (or) unless some proportion of national savings can be made available for giving loans or subsidies to potential allies. These were precisely the points that Warburg was trying to make. First, there was the problem that the Reich lacked a broad enough tax base to finance its rising military and other expenditures. Between 1891 and 1913, Reich expenditure increased more than twofold, the expenditure of the federal states rose one and a half times and communal spending trebled.[89] But tax revenue did not keep pace because of the "gridlock" over tax reform in both the Reichstag and the Bundesrat.[90] As a result, total public sector debt rose by a factor of more than one and a half: the funded Reich debt trebled, the unfunded debt rose eighteenfold, while communal debts rose by a factor of more than six.[91] This rise in public sector debt clearly coincided with a fall in the price of German and Prussian bonds. To take a single but typical example, the price of German 3 percent bonds fell from 101 in September 1896 to 74 in August 1913.[92]

Secondly, Warburg's concerns about the limits of German overseas investment also seem legitimate. By the eve of World War I, German foreign investments amounted to roughly a third of the British total; moreover, the bulk of German foreign investment was in Europe rather than overseas.[93] The average value of capital exports from Germany in the period 1890 to 1913 was around 1.5 percent of gross domestic product compared with a British figure of 4.6 percent.[94] As a proportion of net national product (NNP), the German stock of overseas assets was in fact falling—from around 50 percent in 1891 to 38 percent in 1913.[95]

Still, the extent of the German Reich's economic weakness should not be exaggerated. In total, public sector expenditure rose from under 14 percent of NNP in 1891 to just over 18 percent in 1913—a modest proportion by late-twentieth-century standards.[96] Total public debt rose from just under 50 percent of NNP in 1890 to around 63 percent in 1913—again, hardly the onset of a debt crisis.[97] Although contemporaries tended to fixate on the quoted prices of government bonds, the correct measure of any change in the risk premium on a government bond is the spread between its yield and the yield of a comparable but effectively risk-free security. Relative to British "consols" (the perpetual government bonds that are conventionally regarded as risk-free in the pre-1914 period), the risk premium on German bonds tended to fall in this period, from in excess of one hundred basis points in early 1901 to little more than fifty basis points in 1913.[98]

Finally, we should put contemporary worries about the German balance of payments into perspective. There was nothing inherently bad about the fact that Germany exported a smaller proportion of its savings than Britain. On the contrary, it may well have been economically preferable that a larger proportion was being invested in the development of rapidly growing domestic industrial sectors such as electrical engineering and chemicals. Nor was Germany especially vulnerable to outflows of foreign "hot money" from its banking system. Such flows were an inevitable and even indispensable part of the prewar international gold standard.[99] Indeed, a cursory glance at financial indicators at the time of the second Moroccan crisis shows how successfully the Reichsbank was able to counteract the repatriation of foreign funds. In the period of the crisis (June–November 1911), the market discount rate rose from 2.46 percent to 4.51 per cent (205 basis points), but the German stock market fell by less than 4 percent.[100] At its lowest point, the price of Imperial 3 percent bonds fell to 80.5 marks, compared with 83.5 marks on the eve of the crisis, a decline of just 3.6 percent. The depreciation of the mark against sterling was at most 1.1 percent.[101] The Reichsbank responded to the crisis with only a modest increase in its official discount rate, from 4 to 5 percent. By simultaneously discounting commercial bills, increasing the volume of small denomination bank notes, and selling foreign currency, it was able to avert any danger of a liquidity crisis.[102] Nor did this policy create an exceptional imbalance between its gold reserve and its liabilities: the 24.4 percent low reached in September 1911 was somewhat higher than the nadirs of 1910 and 1912.[103] This was precisely Warburg's point when he insisted that Germany had financially "withstood the test [of the Agadir crisis] well."

What was undeniable, nevertheless, was that Germany lacked the resources to win a global war with the British Empire—and this was the real thrust of Warburg's advice to the Kaiser to be patient rather than gamble on a preventive war. In 1914 the British Empire remained a formidable antagonist. Not only did it have a larger stock of foreign assets available as a kind of financial strategic reserve, but its navy was roughly twice the size of Germany's, and its colonial empire was vastly larger: twelve times more extensive and thirty-six times more populous.[104] As a world war—and this was how the Germans themselves chose to regard the conflict—the war that broke out in 1914 was between profoundly unequal combatants.

Conclusion

Ever since Eckart Kehr, the political economy of Wilhelmine Germany has been misunderstood by historians too influenced by contemporary Social Democratic polemics. The *Kaiserreich* has been portrayed as excessively militaristic, yet the German defense budget accounted for a lower proportion of national income (3.9 percent) than that of Russia (5.1 percent) or France (4.8 percent).[105] It has been portrayed as protectionist, yet average tariffs on manufactures were just 13 percent, far less than the equivalent figures for Russia (84 percent) and the United States (44 percent), not to mention France (20 percent), Italy (18 percent), Spain (34 percent), and Sweden (20 percent).[106] Above all, it has been portrayed as having an economy dominated by "organized capitalism," when there were significantly more large companies in Britain (forty-one industrial companies with capital of £2 million or more, compared with just sixteen in Germany).[107]

The career of Max Warburg sheds new light on the relationship between business and politics in Wilhelmine Germany. A cosmopolitan nationalist, Warburg was keen to see Germany participate in the "globalization" of the world economy before 1914. He was sympathetic to the aspirations of *Weltpolitik*, yet he was a realist about what Germany could achieve in a world still dominated by British financial and naval power. He recognized that the real "Achilles heel" of the German political system was its decentralized fiscal system, which imposed real financial constraints on the Reich government. He also recognized that without larger net capital flows out of Germany to strategically contested markets, the Reich could aspire to little more than junior partner status overseas. Whether in China, Morocco, or Portuguese Angola, therefore, imperial partnership was what Warburg hoped to achieve. In many ways, his efforts were an attempt to translate into the sphere of diplomatic relations what had long been the norm in the world of the *haute banque*. Such a strategy would have allowed Germany to benefit from the opening up of new markets without diverting too many resources away from the economic development of German industry. As Warburg rightly said, Germany was growing economically stronger every day. The tragedy of the Wilhelmine era was that justified confidence in Germany's growth was trumped by the hysterical pessimism of those who wanted Germany to risk a European war sooner rather than later.

Notes

1. Hartmut Pogge von Strandmann, ed., *Walther Rathenau, Industrialist, Banker, Intellectual, and Politician: Notes and Diaries, 1907-1922* (Oxford, 1985).
2. Dirk Stegmann, *Die Erben Bismarcks. Parteien und Verbände in der Spätphase des Wilhelminischen Deutschlands. Sammlungspolitik 1897-1918 (Cologne, 1970)*; Klaus Saul, *Staat, Industrie und Arbeiterbewegung. Zur Innen- und Sozialpolitik des Wilhelminischen Deutschlands 1903-1914* (Düsseldorf, 1974). See also Heinrich August Winkler, ed., *Organisierter Kapitalismus* (Göttinger, 1974), and the comments in Geoff Eley, "Capitalism and the Industrial State: Industrial Growth and Political Backwardness, 1890-1918," *Historical Journal* 21 (1978): 737-50.
3. See, for example, Kurt Gossweiler, *Großbanken, Industriemonopol, Staat* (Berlin, 1971).
4. Volker Hentschel, *Wirtschaft und Wirtschaftspolitik im wilhelminischen Deutschland. Organisierter Kapitalismus und Interventionsstaat?* (Stuttgart, 1978).
5. Boris Barth, *Die deutsche Hochfinanz und die Imperialismen. Banken und Außenpolitik vor 1914* (Stuttgart, 1995); Morten Reitmayer, *Bankiers im Kaiserreich. Sozialprofil und Habitus der deutschen Hochfinanz* (Göttingen, 1999).
6. Lothar Gall, "The Deutsche Bank from Its Founding to the Great War, 1870-1914," in *The Deutsche Bank, 1870-1995*, ed. Lothar Gall, Gerald D. Feldman, Harold James, Carl-Ludwig Holtfrerich, and Hans E. Büschgen (London, 1995).
7. Compare the case of Karl Helfferich, the subject of a detailed and scholarly life: John G. Williamson, *Karl Helfferich, 1872-1924: Economist, Financier, Politician* (Princeton, 1971).
8. An early contribution was Alfred Vagts, "M. M. Warburg & Co. Ein Bankhaus in der deutschen Weltpolitik, 1905-1933," *Vierteljahreshefte für Sozial- und Wirtschaftsgeschichte* 45 (1958): 289-398.
9. For a general history of the firm, see Eduard Rosenbaum and A. J. Sherman, *M. M. Warburg & Co. 1798-1938: Merchant Bankers of Hamburg* (London, 1979). David Farrer, *The Warburgs: The Story of a Family* (New York, 1975), is journalistic and unreliable. Ron Chernow, *The Warburgs* (London, 1993), is somewhat better.
10. Werner E. Mosse, *The German-Jewish Economic Elite 1820-1935: A Socio-cultural Profile* (Oxford, 1989), 197ff.
11. Fritz Fischer, *War of Illusions: German Policies from 1911 to 1914* (London and New York, 1975), 457.
12. Niall Ferguson, *Paper and Iron: Hamburg Business and German Politics in the Era of Inflation, 1897-1927* (Cambridge, 1995), esp. chapter 4.
13. Charles S. Maier, *Recasting Bourgeois Europe: Stabilisation in France, Germany and Italy in the Decade after World War I* (Princeton, 1975), 247, 367-82.
14. Avraham Barkai, *From Boycott to Annihilation: The Economic Struggle of German Jews, 1933-1943* (Hanover and London, 1989), 53, 76f., 103f., 128.
15. In 1909 there were 258 banks in Hamburg, compared with 515 in Berlin and 135 in Frankfurt: Manfred Pohl, *Hamburger Bankengeschichte* (Mainz, 1986), 97.
16. Rosenbaum and Sherman, *M. M. Warburg & Co.*, 1-64.
17. Niall Ferguson, *The World's Banker: A History of the House of Rothschild* (London, 1998), 302f.
18. Rosenbaum and Sherman, *M. M. Warburg & Co.*, 84-90.
19. Max M. Warburg, *Aus meinen Aufzeichnungen* (Hamburg, 1952), 15ff.
20. Vagts, "M. M. Warburg & Co.," 300f., 336f.; Karl E. Born, *International Banking in the Nineteenth and Twentieth Centuries* (Leamington Spa, 1983), 127f.; Gustav Stolper, Karl Häuser, and Knut Borchardt, *The German Economy, 1870 to the Present* (London, 1967), 31.
21. Figures from Rosenbaum and Sherman, *M. M. Warburg & Co.*
22. Pohl, *Bankengeschichte*, 96-101; Born, *International Banking*, 87-92, 169.
23. Rosenbaum and Sherman, *M. M. Warburg & Co.*, 29-43. Cf. Mosse, *German-Jewish Economic Elite*, 161-85.
24. Warburg, *Aufzeichnungen*, 8-15. Cf. Chernow, *The Warburgs*, 38.

25. Lamar Cecil, *Albert Ballin: Business and Politics in Imperial Germany* (Princeton, 1967), 118.
26. Vagts, "M. M. Warburg & Co.," 330.
27. Warburg, *Aus meinen Aufzeichnungen*, 24. This was also the view of the diplomat Friedrich Rosen.
28. Ibid., 19.
29. Vagts, "M. M. Warburg & Co.," 336f.
30. Ibid., 311f., 320-7. Cf. Wolfgang J. Mommsen, "Die latente Krise des Deutsche Reiches," *Militärgeschichtliche Mitteilungen* 1 (1974): 29.
31. Archive of M. M. Warburg & Co., Hamburg [hereafter WA], various Jahresberichte; Vagts, "M. M. Warburg & Co.," 342ff.
32. WA, "Jahresbericht 1911."
33. Ekkehard Böhm, *Überseehandel und Flottenbau. Hanseatische Kaufmannschaft und deutsche Seerüstung, 1879-1902* (Hamburg, 1972).
34. Volker R. Berghahn, *Germany and the Approach of War in 1914* (London, 1973), 78.
35. Max M. Warburg, "Die geplante Reichsfinanzreform. Wie vermeiden wir, daß aus der Beseitigung der Reichsfinanznot eine Bundesstaatsfinanznot entsteht?" in Sterling Library, Yale University, Paul M. Warburg Papers, Ser. II, Box 8, Folder 118.
36. WA, Folder 19, Gesammelte Vorträge, Max M. Warburg, "Geeignete und ungeeignete Mittel zur Hebung des Kurses der Staatspapiere," 1912.
37. Warburg, *Aufzeichnungen*, 29-33.
38. WA, "Jahresbericht 1905."
39. Vagts, "M. M. Warburg & Co.," 318f.
40. Reitmayer, *Bankiers*, 334.
41. WA, Folder 19, Gesammelte Vorträge, Max M. Warburg, "Finanzielle Kriegsbereitschaft und Börsengesetz," 5 Aug. 1907.
42. Cf. H. Haller, "Die Rolle der Staatsfinanzen für den Inflationsprozeß," in *Währung und Wirtschaft in Deutschland, 1876-1975*, ed. Deutsche Bundesbank (Frankfurt a.M., 1976), 115f.
43. Reitmayer, *Bankiers*, 300-314.
44. Ibid., 315. It is worth noting how important futures markets were in the Hamburg economy. Not only were the bulk of registered futures transactions in Germany carried out in Hamburg, but Warburg was busily building up a copper futures market even as these debates were going on: see WA, "Jahresbericht 1910."
45. Rudolf Kroboth, *Die Finanzpolitik des Deutschen Reiches während der Reichskanzlerschaft Bethmann Hollwegs und die Geld- und Kapitalmarktverhältnisse (1909-1913/14)* (Frankfurt a.M., 1986), 57.
46. Ibid., 56. According to the well-informed British consul at Frankfurt, Sir Francis Oppenheimer, the big German banks had in fact welcomed the crisis as an opportunity to increase their influence over the Foreign Office, which they felt had failed to consult them adequately. See *British Documents on the Origins of the War, 1898-1914*, ed. G. P. Gooch and Harold Temperley, 11 vols. in 13 (London, 1926-38), 7:796-805.
47. WA, "Jahresbericht 1911." Cf. Vagts, "M. M. Warburg & Co.," 328f.
48. WA, "Jahresbericht 1911." This was also Karl Helfferich's view.
49. Kroboth, *Finanzpolitik*, 57.
50. WA, "Jahresbericht 1911."
51. Kroboth, *Finanzpolitik*, 62f.
52. Berghahn, *Germany and the Approach of War*, 68, 78. For Warburg's anxieties, see WA, "Jahresbericht 1908"; "Jahresbericht 1912."
53. Warburg, *Aufzeichnungen*, 27ff.; Cecil, *Ballin*, 161-65, 180-200. Cf. Jonathan Steinberg, "Diplomatie als Wille und Vorstellung. Die Berliner Mission Lord Haldanes im Februar 1912," in *Marine und Marinepolitik 1871-1914*, ed. Herbert Schottelius and Wilhelm Deist (Düsseldorf, 1972), 263-82.
54. Pohl, *Bankengeschichte*, 110.
55. Niall Ferguson, *The Pity of War* (London, 1998), chaps. 1-6. Cf. Zara S. Steiner, *Britain and the Origins of the First World War* (London, 1983), 94-109.

56. WA, "Jahresbericht 1914," 1f. This passage was crossed out in pen at a later date, probably when Warburg was compiling his *Aufzeichnungen* in the 1940s. See WA, "Jahresbericht 1920" (for Warburg's account of the meeting before the Weimar Untersuchungsausschuß); Warburg, *Aufzeichnungen*, 29.

57. WA, "Jahresbericht 1914," 3.

58. WA, "Jahresbericht 1914," 2ff.

59. Ibid.; *Hamburger Börsenhalle*, 28 July 1914.

60. Ferguson, *Paper and Iron*, chap. 2.

61. Cecil, *Ballin*, 210-14; Warburg, *Aufzeichnungen*, 34. By contrast, Warburg and the shipowner Richard Krogmann remained hopeful of a swift victory until, respectively, September and November.

62. Gombrich, *Aby Warburg*, 206.

63. WA, "Jahresbericht 1916," 13, Warburg to Ballin, 10 March 1916; Warburg to Wahnschaffe (under-state secretary at the Reich Chancellery), 19 May 1916.

64. WA, "Jahresbericht 1914," 6; Warburg, *Aufzeichnungen*, 34f.

65. WA, "Jahresbericht 1914," Anlage IV, "Gutachten über eine mögliche Kriegsentschädigung," 26 Nov. 1914; WA, "Jahresbericht 1918," Anlage 13, "Beemerkungen über die östlichen Friedensverträge und die deutschen Kriegsziele," 1 May 1918.

66. Calculated from figures in Rosenbaum, *M. M. Warburg & Co.*

67. Warburg, *Aufzeichnungen*, 44f.

68. WA, "Jahresbericht 1915," 2-5; "Jahresbericht 1916," Warburg to Ballin, 2 Feb. 1916; Warburg, *Aufzeichnungen*, 39-48; Cecil, *Ballin*, 272, 276-84, 295f., 307. See also Leo Haupts, *Deutsche Friedenspolitik. Eine Alternative zur Machtpolitik des Ersten Weltkrieges* (Düsseldorf, 1976), 113f.

69. WA, "Jahresbericht 1916," Warburg to Ballin, 2 Feb. 1916.

70. Haupts, *Friedenspolitik*, 119.

71. WA, "Jahresbericht 1917," Warburg to Langwerth von Simmern, 26 Jan. 1917.

72. WA, "Jahresbericht 1918," 3; Warburg, *Aufzeichnungen*, 58; Prince Max von Baden, *Erinnerungen und Dokumente* (Stuttgart, Berlin, and Leipzig, 1927), 248, 252, 660f.

73. WA, "Jahresbericht 1918," Anlage 13, Max M. Warburg, "Bemerkungen über die östlichen Friedensverträge und die deutschen Kriegsziele," 1 May 1918.

74. Haupts, *Friedenspolitik*, 103, 119f., 123, 132f. For Warburg's involvement with Walther Schücking and the German Association for International Law, see WA, "Jahresbericht 1916"; "Jahresbericht 1917," 12; "Jahresbericht 1918," 9.

75. WA, "Jahresbericht 1918," Anlage 21, Max M. Warburg, "Gedanken zur Fortbildung unserer auswärtige und innere Politik als Grundlage einer Verständigung der Völker" (undated), esp. points 15, 16, and 18.

76. WA, "Jahresbericht 1917"; "Jahresbericht 1918," 11, 11a; Warburg, *Aufzeichnungen*, 61ff.

77. Cecil, *Ballin*, 334ff.; WA, "Jahresbericht 1918," 4ff., Anlage 1, Warburg Angabe, 22 Sept. 1918; Anlage 8 [Warburg's account of Max of Baden's government]; Warburg, *Aufzeichnungen*, 65f. Warburg still hoped to be able to "retain the dynasty."

78. WA, "Jahresbericht 1918," Anlage 8; Warburg, *Aufzeichnungen*, 65; Vagts, "M. M. Warburg & Co.," 367; Baden, *Erinnerungen*, 329f., 476; Haupts, *Deutsche Friedenspolitik*, 144ff., 186-91, 196-99.

79. WA, "Jahresbericht 1918," Anlage 8; Baden, *Erinnerungen*, 329f.

80. Warburg, *Aufzeichnungen*, 75.

81. Ibid., 64.

82. Klaus Schwabe, *Deutsche Revolution und Wilson-Frieden. Die amerikanische und deutsche Friedensstrategie zwischen Ideologie und Machtpolitik, 1918/19* (Düsseldorf, 1971), 526.

83. WA, Warburg Diaries, 4 Jan. 1919. The position he took in a letter of 30 December 1918 to Count Bernstorff was admittedly less realistic: "For Germany, there can be never be any talk of war compensation.... Germany needs 50 to 100 years to restore its own land." *Akten zur deutschen auswärtigen Politik 1918-1945*, Serie A (Göttingen, 1982), vol. 1, 154f.

84. Warburg, *Aufzeichnungen*, 74. See also Staatsarchiv Hamburg, Firmenarchiv Arnold Otto Meyer 1, Bd. 10, 116, Franz Withoefft to the State Secretary at the Economics Ministry, 26 Nov. 1918. Cf. "Das Schicksal unserer Auslandseffekten," in *Wirtschaftsdienst*, 14 Apr. 1919, 275f.

85. Niall Ferguson, "The Balance of Payments Question: Versailles and After," in *The Treaty of Versailles: A Reassessment after 75 Years*, ed. Manfred F. Boemeke, Gerald D. Feldman, and Elisabeth Glaser (Cambridge, 1998), 401-40.

86. Angus Maddison, *The World Economy: A Millennial Perspective* (Paris, 2001), 186.

87. Stephen N. Broadberry, "How Did the United States and Germany Overtake Britain? A Sectoral Analysis of Comparative Productivity Levels, 1870–1990," *Journal of Economic History* 58 (2) (1998), 375-407.

88. See Paul M. Kennedy, *The Rise and Fall of the Great Powers: Economic Change and Military Conflict from 1500 to 2000* (London, 1988).

89. Calculated from figures in Suphan Andic and Jindrich Veverka, "The Growth of Government Expenditure in Germany since the Unification," *Finanzarchiv* 23, no. 2 (1964): 244.

90. Details in Niall Ferguson, "Public Finance and National Security: The Domestic Origins of the First World War Revisited," *Past and Present* 142 (1994): 141-68.

91. Kroboth, *Finanzpolitik*, 489.

92. Figures from *The Economist*.

93. Calculated from Maddison, *World Economy*, table 2-26a.

94. Alan M. Taylor, "International Capital Mobility in History: The Saving-Investment Relationship," *NBER Working Paper* 5743 (September 1996).

95. Calculated from the data in W. G. Hoffmann, F. Grumbach, and H. Hesse, *Das Wachstum der deutschen Wirtschaft seit der Mitte des 19. Jahrhunderts* (Berlin, 1965).

96. Calculated from figures in Andic and Veverka, "Growth of Government Expenditure," 244; and the net national product data in Hoffmann et al., *Wachstum*.

97. Calculated from Kroboth, *Finanzpolitik*, 489 and Hoffmann et al., *Wachstum*.

98. Calculated from data in the National Bureau of Economic Research data archive (http://www.nber.org/data/).

99. See, in general, Barry Eichengreen, *Golden Fetters: The Gold Standard and the Great Depression, 1919-1939* (New York and Oxford, 1992), chap. 1.

100. Calculated from the National Bureau of Economic Research dataset.

101. Calculated from the prices quoted in *The Economist*.

102. Kroboth, *Finanzpolitik*, 54f.

103. Ibid., 491-93.

104. Mary Evelyn Townsend, *European Colonial Expansion Since 1871* (Chicago, 1941), 19. Cf. Avner Offer, *The First World War: An Agrarian Interpretation* (Oxford, 1989).

105. John M. Hobson, "The Military-Extraction Gap and the Wary Titan: The Fiscal Sociology of British Defence Policy, 1870-1913," *Journal of European Economic History* 3 (1993): 465f., 478.

106. Richard E. Baldwin and Philippe Martin, "Two Waves of Globalisation: Superficial Similarities, Fundamental Differences," NBER Working Paper 6904 (Jan. 1999), 13.

107. Youssef Cassis, *Big Business: The European Experience in the Twentieth Century* (Oxford, 1997), 10f.

– 12 –

Continuity and Change in Post-Wilhelmine Germany

From the 1918 Revolution to the Ruhr Crisis

CONAN FISCHER

I

T he 1918 revolution marked the irrevocable demise of monarchical government in Germany, but the interwar Republic preserved intact much of the institutional and ideological substance of the Wilhelmine era. The grandees of the civil service and of the economy remained uncannily familiar by name, all of which helped to nourish fear and suspicion among Germany's former wartime adversaries. The French establishment in particular protested that beyond the Rhine democratic conviction ran only skin deep, with the institutions and the people who in 1914 had unleashed an unprovoked war on France still very much in control. Deprived of any meaningful security guarantees or economic support from their major allies and fearful that Berlin intended to renege on the 1921 London Reparations Agreement, French civil and military leaders resolved during the latter half of 1922 to revise the peace settlement on their own terms.[1] At the heart of this strategy lay the military and economic seizure of Germany's Ruhr district, already partially occupied in March 1921 and completely so, with Belgian support, in January 1923. Lacking any predetermined strategy for dealing with such an incursion, the German government latched on to and formalized a popular, mass campaign of passive resistance in the western occupied territories.[2]

Leaving aside the precise nature of France's objectives,[3] German opinion stood fully behind the passive resistance campaign, which was generally perceived as a peaceful response to French imperialism and militarism.[4] Soon enough, however, the

---

feeling grew that while the miners, railwaymen, and officials in the Rhineland and Westphalia could obstruct the invaders, they could hardly broker any settlement of this increasingly ruinous confrontation. Berlin would have to take the initiative and, if possible, secure British and American mediation.[5] The foreign minister of the day, Frederic von Rosenberg, appeared unequal to the task[6] and it was at this sensitive moment, on 1 April 1923, that the Social Democratic (SPD) newspaper, *Vorwärts*, launched a withering attack on the substance and tenor of German foreign policy. This questioned the very composition and ethos of the German Foreign Office, which, the paper claimed, was dominated by erstwhile members of university dueling fraternities, notably by Bonner Borussen. Of eighteen recent promotions to the rank of diplomatic councilor (*Legationsrat*), seventeen reportedly were former Bonner Borussen. The diplomatic corps allegedly had witnessed little if any democratization since the revolution, and *Vorwärts* dismissed the appointment of a handful of "left-oriented" people as ambassadors in the immediate aftermath of the revolution as a token gesture.[7]

Historians, too, have tended to regard negatively this continuity of personnel from the Empire into the Republic. Peter Krüger's study of the postwar reparations settlement, for example, argues that a realistic foreign policy based on domestic modernization and realizable goals was never really established during the Weimar era. Instead, conservatives instrumentalized foreign policy to further their reactionary domestic agenda.[8] All this notwithstanding, the Foreign Ministry reacted to the *Vorwärts* article by claiming the very opposite. Ago Count von Maltzan served at the Foreign Ministry as secretary of state during the Ruhr crisis, but has acquired a certain notoriety for having previously assisted Foreign Minister Walther Rathenau to broker the 1922 Rapallo Treaty between Germany and the Soviet Union.[9] However, during 1923 and 1924, he strove to realize an international settlement to the postwar reparations crisis, first, in the face of the Cuno cabinet's vacillation,[10] and then in tandem with Gustav Stresemann.[11] Maltzan was sufficiently exercised by *Vorwärts*'s claims to write in person to its editor, Friedrich Stampfer. Although the piece had appeared on April Fools' Day, he began, it was evidently meant seriously[12] and demanded a reply on several counts. For one thing it was inadmissible and even demeaning to write off diplomats who supported the Weimar coalition as "token appointments": "We have eleven gentlemen in senior positions abroad who have not risen up through the Foreign Office, yet have collaborated to outstanding effect with their colleagues at the Office on the basis of complete trust and, in some cases, on the basis of regular and amicable exchanges of view. Others, such as the late Center Party member Ambassador Mayer [Paris] have fulfilled their duties to the point of self-sacrifice."[13]

These eleven republican-minded gentlemen included the ambassadors to London, Prague, and Vienna, and Maltzan was uncomfortably aware that a week earlier, senior permanent officials within the Foreign Office had protested to the foreign minister that while the revolution had made external political appointments inevitable, their frequency was prejudicing normal career development.[14] The closure of some twenty consulates general and ten embassies since the war had done nothing to help, and rather than eighteen promotions to the position of diplomatic counsilor, Maltzan observed, the true figure was five. None were Bonner Borussen, and among appointments to the more junior post of attaché, he continued, no "Bonner Preuße" had featured for a year at least.[15] He conceded that former corps members were more prevalent in the higher reaches of the Foreign Office, himself among them, but protested that a former Social Democratic foreign minister, Hermann Müller, had restored him to high office after a brief period of semi-retirement. Former corps students, Maltzan asserted, were as determined to do their duty under the new constitution as any other citizen.[16] In June 1922 the "Bonner Preuße" had cancelled the celebration of their ninety-fifth anniversary out of respect for the assassinated foreign minister, Walther Rathenau[17] (as the miners of the Ruhr came out in protest against the same outrage).

Stampfer replied that he had never questioned the eligibility of former corps students for public service,[18] but, given the timing of this correspondence, Maltzan's protestations might be taken with a pinch of salt. He could not have wished to leave his department an easy target for German republicans, who were particularly exercised that erstwhile supporters of the monarchy seemed ready to exploit the Ruhr crisis to their advantage.[19] That said, Maltzan's accommodation with the republican order resurfaced more emphatically following the trial in 1924 of Adolf Hitler and his fellow putschists. The Hitler affair had already caused the Foreign Office considerable grief as France edged toward accepting international mediation of the reparations dispute with Germany. Foreign Office seniors and diplomats were thoroughly conversant with the fears France harbored toward Germany and had trodden a long and stony road to convince French Premier Poincaré and his colleagues of Weimar's bona fides.[20] The announcement of the verdicts on 1 April 1924, which included a derisory prison sentence for Hitler himself and the acquittal of General Ludendorff, prompted Maltzan to dispatch a withering aide mémoire to German embassies in Europe and the United States.[21] He repeated without qualification the press's condemnation of the fiasco, denounced as "a trial in name only," and the feeling that political expediency had prevailed over any concept of justice: "A trial of this nature could only end with a verdict which amounts to a catastrophe for the cause of justice. Not only should the acquittal of Ludendorff be regarded as misconceived, but also the light sentences imposed on the remaining accused. The granting of periods of probation is particularly disturbing, for this amounts to a bonus for high treason."[22]

Maltzan found it grotesque that the accused had had the opportunity to broadcast their views beyond the court to a wider public,[23] but was particularly exercised by the damage they had inflicted on foreign policy interests, days before the publication of the Dawes and McKenna reports promised to set in motion German diplomatic and economic rehabilitation,[24] yet while the disarmament question remained acute.[25] He concluded that the repeated humiliation of Germany since 1918 in matters of foreign policy had helped create the domestic preconditions for such a trial,[26] but there was no mistaking the fundamental differences in outlook and behavior that separated the post-Wilhelmine Foreign Office from the Republic's ultra-rightist enemies.

II

If the received wisdom of an unreconstructed and reactionary Foreign Office requires qualification, then the wider implications for the history of Weimar, often the plaything of external events and forces, are profound. The rarefied environment of Foreign Office diplomacy was hardly representative of the wider postrevolutionary settlement, but the very nature of Germany's defeat in 1918 had bound politics, both foreign and domestic, to the industrial economy with an unprecedented immediacy,[27] and at critical moments had left the young Republic's prospects in the hands of the gentlemen at the Foreign Office. Few in late 1918 nurtured illusions of any immediate postwar military revival, but the economy was another matter. Organized labor, industry, and the political world shared a perception that economic revival held the key to Germany's wider rehabilitation.[28] Accordingly, the German delegation at Versailles strove to limit reparations demands and territorial losses, while hoping (vainly) for a postwar economic order sufficiently liberal to allow Germany to compete on acceptable terms.[29]

Such a strategy, predicated on the rapid rehabilitation of a severely disrupted economy, would, beyond successful diplomacy, demand an unprecedented degree of cooperation between employers and labor. Intimations of such cooperation preceded the armistice. On the domestic front, employers and employees shared a mutual interest in ending the war before the economy and society collapsed in chaos or, worse, before fighting enveloped Germany's western industrial regions. Since confidence in the Imperial government had evaporated, industry agreed with the Social Democrats that the Kaiser would have to abdicate swiftly, even if a republican future was not yet anticipated.[30] Business organizations exchanged information with Social Democratic and labor leaders during the final weeks of the war, and agreed on 8 November 1918 to manage the process of demobilization in concert with the trade unions and civil service. Government approval of this extraordinary initiative followed retrospectively.[31] A week later, a committee representing both sides of the economy, headed by Hugo Stinnes for industry and Carl Legien for the trade unions, thrashed out a settlement of differences that accorded the unions wide-ranging negotiating rights and the promise of an eight-hour day, while recognizing implicitly shareholders' property rights. As Gerald Feldman remarked: "The industrialists were, in effect, abandoning their long-standing alliance with the Junkers and the authoritarian state for an alliance with organized labor".[32]

This might appear as a development of breathtaking proportions that anticipated many of the defining characteristics of contemporary European society, but Germany did not get the revolution many historians would have preferred. Any thoughts of nationalizing the economy were quickly put to rest,[33] but the undiluted misery of famine, disease, and the grimmest of working conditions combined with military defeat to provoke popular insurgency and more-or-less utopian demands for workplace or communal democratization based on emergent workers' and soldiers' councils. Such notions hardly constituted the settled will of the German people, nor in all likelihood the will of organized labor. Heavy industrial trade union leaders (admittedly uneasy with any grassroots challenge to their authority) were among the most savage critics of far-left utopianism and urged the framing of a parliamentary republican constitution, the conclusion of a definitive peace settlement, and the codification in law of the agreements forged with the employers during the traumas of defeat. Their mandate, they believed, lay in the surging membership of their own unions.[34] Academic debate once raged over the possible alternatives to a parliamentary republic that the council movement might have offered,[35] but of greater interest here is the reception of the actual revolutionary settlement in business and labor circles.

During 1919 and 1920 the outward signs were not encouraging. Wildcat strikes and low-level insurrection gripped Germany's heavy industrial heartlands, leaving managers and trade union officials to struggle desperately and sometimes vainly to enforce wages and working conditions agreements that had been collectively negotiated under the terms of the Stinnes-Legien Agreement.[36] In March 1920, an abortive coup d'état in Berlin by dissident military units (the Kapp Putsch) triggered an armed uprising by workers in the Ruhr district, which the republican government crushed with military force. For all this unrest, however, it has been argued that the radicalism of the majority embraced a trenchant republicanism, and that relatively few workers wished to subvert the political order.[37] The 1920 Ruhr uprising, for example, was aimed primarily against the anti-republican *Reaktion* and the Kapp Putsch. Most insurgents, Eliasberg claims, sought through their actions to defend "the admittedly questionable 'bourgeois' republic and the undoubtedly incomplete, yet certainly substantive 'achievements of the working class.'" When the SPD-led coalition government met their demands halfway, these "constitutional warriors" were ready to disengage from the struggle, but continued defiance from a utopian-radical minority precipitated the ensuing bloodshed.[38] Newer research has emphasized the deep suspicion harbored then by the miners of the Ruhr toward institutions they perceived, rightly or wrongly, as "anti-republican." Similarly, outrage and grief swept the Ruhr when anti-republicans murdered the nonsocialists Matthias Erzberger in 1921 and Walther Rathenau in 1922, just as it had after the killing of Rosa Luxemburg and Karl Liebknecht in 1919. All in all, Karin Hartewig concludes, the behavior and attitudes of these workers stemmed from "a loyal attitude toward the young Republic."[39]

The institutionalization of the revolution through the constitution and acts of parliament was vital in lending substance to these attitudes. Equal rights in the economy and society were granted to workers in principle by Article 165 of the Weimar Constitution[40] and in more concrete form by the Factory Council Act of 4 February 1920,[41] which created works councils (*Betriebsräte*) at workplaces with twenty or more on the payroll in order to improve lines of communication between management and employees.[42] The new law served to channel spontaneous radicalism and thereby raise efficiency and output, but left property relations untouched. Radical workers greeted this as a poor alternative to socialization, but union leaders hoped that the councils might eventually promote economic democracy in the workplace.[43] Furthermore, since the act incorporated key tenets of the Stinnes-Legien Agreement in law, republican workers regarded it as their formal stake in the new parliamentary order.[44] This settlement was lent greater robustness by the Company Board Act of November 1921, which granted works councils two seats on their company board, with rights identical to the shareholders' representatives,[45] even if both acts were circumvented on occasion by management, for instance, by putting sensitive business before special committees.[46]

The *Betriebsrätegesetz* had generated heated controversy during its passage through parliament, as business-oriented politicians sought to curtail its scope. The reactions in society at large were similarly intense, indicating that more was at stake than left radicals imagined.[47] However, the eventual settlement was not simply the outcome of a struggle between pro- and anti-republican forces, for more subtle dynamics were at play that drew on continuity as much as on change. Optional workers' committees, and compulsory committees in the Prussian mining industry had been introduced shortly before the war in an attempt to improve industrial relations, although employers were disinclined to take them too seriously. These committees saw their powers enhanced during the war and offered the Republic a template for postwar legislation and personnel with the expertise to take reform further.[48] The Works Council and Company Board Bills were drafted by the same civil servants at the National Labor Ministry—versed in a long-standing statist tradition of social reform—who had formulated the Wilhelmine legislation; among them was a known SPD sympathizer.[49] Beyond this, the employers' publicly expressed opposition to the works councils contrasted markedly with their behavior in the workplace. As a senior trade union official in the Rhenish metallurgical industry observed:

> On the whole, the entrepreneurs have come to terms quickly with the establishment of the works councils. Here one has to distinguish clearly between the pragmatic attitude of the factory owner or manager—that is, the actual employer—to the works council and the principled stance of the employers' federations or the business press. One cannot simply equate the typical, often of necessity dogmatic utterances and views of the latter with the views of employers, and especially individual factory managers themselves. The attitude of factory managers, of the real workplace politicians, is usually completely flexible and down to earth.[50]

We shall find in due course comparable attitudes reflected in the most unpromising of environments—the coal-mining companies of the Ruhr during the crisis of 1923.

III

First, however, we must examine the impact of reparations on the post-1918 domestic settlement. It took the European Allies several years to formulate comprehensive reparations demands, but with the principle of payment contained in the initial armistice agreement, the surrender of German property and the delivery of reparations in kind began without further ado. Total annual coal production in the French mining *départements* of Pas-de-Calais and Nord had fallen from 18.6 million tons in

1913 to 0.6 million tons in 1919,[51] and while France's acquisition of coal mines in the Saar district and Lorraine helped to make good this shortfall, the Ruhr delivered some 6 million tons of reparations coal to France in 1920 and 1921 and a further 4.5 million tons in 1922.[52] The dependence of France's metallurgical industry on Ruhr coke was even more critical. By 1922, reparations deliveries of coke had reached 5.65 million tons,[53] but officials at the Quai d'Orsay appreciated that should Germany choke off these deliveries, much of France's heavy industry would shut down within weeks. Such fears had been greatly strengthened in July 1920 during the Spa negotiations between Germany and the Allies on coal and coke deliveries. Hugo Stinnes attended as an official delegate, only to let fly at his Allied counterparts, who were left comforting themselves that, after all, he represented the vanquished party.[54]

However, the view from Berlin was bleaker still. Fulfillment of reparations deliveries in kind demanded the delivery of fifty trainloads of coal and coke daily from the Ruhr, containing about a fifth of the coalfield's output.[55] The Versailles settlement envisaged sanctions should Germany renege on her commitments, and in March 1921, as reparations negotiations faltered, France and Belgium occupied the western Ruhr and Düsseldorf without setting a withdrawal date, declaring them a "sanctions territory" (*Sanktionsgebiet*).[56] During 1922, the likelihood of further territorial seizures in the Ruhr increased, but each time workers went on strike at any mine or coke oven battery that was contracted to fulfill the reparations account and a train could not then be loaded, a 2 percent shortfall in daily reparations quotas was notched up. If a Reichsbahn locomotive failed or exhausted equipment at a mine gave up the ghost, the result was essentially the same[57] and hung like a sword of Damocles over the entire German polity.

Reparations policy had become inextricably intertwined with the fortunes of heavy industry and the revolutionary traumas of labor relations. Claims by the Ruhr's magnates that longer shift times or lower wages were essential to the longer-term viability of their operations could not be dismissed as matters of purely domestic concern, for the reparations regime left it only a short step from deepening pessimism in the domestic arena to unsolicited intervention by the same industrialists in foreign affairs. During the 1921 reparations crisis, for example, Paul Reusch of the Gutehoffnungshütte opined that an Allied occupation of all Germany "would leave us to endure several difficult years, but it would provide the fastest escape from this miserable situation."[58] Similarly, in October 1922, Peter Klöckner concluded that in comparison to the burdens of reparations, resistance and the "attendant misery" of a French invasion of the Ruhr were lesser evils.[59] Stinnes, never afraid to speak his mind, had provoked government fury when speculating openly in May 1922 on the possible advantages of a Ruhr occupation. Social Democratic Economics Minister Robert Schmidt raged that while he and his cabinet colleagues were struggling to maintain the very existence of Germany, Stinnes could afford the luxury of pursuing his personal interests.[60]

Confrontation, however, represented only half the story. Stinnes, for example, made repeated efforts at conciliation with France before 1923[61] and again during the winter of 1923-24 when, along with fellow industrialists Peter Klöckner and Paul Silverberg, he advocated a merging of French and German heavy industrial interests through an exchange of shares in selected companies.[62] This initiative complemented simultaneous efforts by Konrad Adenauer and others to create an autonomous Rhenish state, designed to serve as a bridgehead between Germany and France,[63] and reflected a realization on both sides of the Rhine that unless the constructive, pre-1914 relationship between French and German heavy industry was restored, neither side would have real peace.[64] Weeks before, France and Belgium had negotiated an agreement covering taxation and reparations provisions directly with the Ruhr's mining industry (the Micum Accord),[65] prompting the mine owners to concede that the time had, indeed, come to draw a line under the sterile and mutually destructive confrontation with their western neighbors. The accord was tough and in some regards open-ended, but: "Peace could only be achieved in Europe by linking together the respective major economic interests of France and Germany."[66] The German chargé d'affaires in Paris, Leopold von Hoesch, expressed comparable views at the beginning of 1924, when doubting that Germany would ever shake off France's grip on the western territories: "I ask myself whether … a solution … might instead be sought in an intimate combination of mutual interests."[67] If thereafter the Dawes and McKenna reports greatly strengthened Germany's position and left its industrialists and diplomats less accommodating than hitherto, the notion of a rapprochement with France was not abandoned.[68] While historians have found convincing premonitions of a darker future in the politics of Weimar's heavy industry and in the Republic's wider foreign policy, intimations of the post-1949 Franco-German settlement were also unmistakable.[69]

Heavy industry's attitude was similarly ambivalent in the domestic arena. Beyond the relatively accommodating attitude displayed by management on the shop floor, the captains of industry were not universally opposed to the postrevolutionary labor settlement. Paul Reusch, for example, warned his colleagues that "industry did not have the power to change the economic and social system of Weimar Germany," while Carl Duisberg of the Bayer chemical enterprise argued that opponents of the 1920 settlement "had completely lost sight of the advantages of state arbitration in labor disputes."[70] This helped the trade unions to operate constructively within the parameters of the domestic revolutionary and international peace settlements, collaborating, for example, with the Ruhr's magnates to defuse distributional conflicts within mining. In the postwar monetary climate, industry and unions were able to underwrite generous pay deals by voting together on the National Coal Council to hike coal prices,[71] although riding the inflationary tiger merely served to buy time. The trade unions agreed with the government that lasting recovery and the elimination of the burden of reparations demanded enhanced output, achieved through collectively negotiated rationalization and increased productivity. As their counterparts at the National Labor Ministry put it: "Taylorism could serve as 'an instrument of national liberation' under the democratic control of the new state."[72] Longer hours were also on the agenda. Miners worked two negotiated extra half-shifts weekly, whether to address the national energy shortage or to meet reparations targets, but at an appalling cost to their own health and that of the mining communities, despite bonus payments and extra food.[73]

However, in the minds of both labor leaders and ordinary republican workers, the domestic revolution and the international settlement constituted a single package that could not be unraveled. The SPD had proven itself a measured advocate of the national interest during and after the war,[74] as had the majority trade unions, who promoted the national cause within the context of international reconciliation. The postwar career of Otto Hué, who represented the mining unions at the Spa reparations conference, illustrates further the merging of prerepublican and republican interests. Like many labor leaders, Hué favored a degree of cooperation with government and employers and served after the revolution as national commissioner for the Ruhr coal field and as a councilor in the Prussian Ministry of Trade, from which perspective Communist or Syndicalist agitation posed a far greater threat than his workmanlike Wilhelmine colleagues. At Spa he declared that the miners were ready to deliver reparations in kind as a contribution to international rapprochement and the reconstruction of northern France, but he insisted that the Allies had to tailor their demands realistically to the physical capacities of the German miners themselves: "Gentlemen [he warned], you can pass whatever resolution you like, but in the final analysis the decision rests in the gnarled hands of the miners."[75] Hué was to die in 1922, but his successors and constituents regarded the 1923 Ruhr invasion as an outright betrayal of their support for the postwar international settlement, which had been delivered at great personal cost.

IV

It has been suggested here that the postwar revolution delivered a settlement more robust than conventional wisdom would allow, but this leaves the collapse of parliamentary government in 1930 and Hitler's seizure of power in 1933 begging an explanation. The Great Depression alone cannot be blamed, for there were longer-term factors at play, rooted in the Wilhelmine era or before. These continuities have informed the view that the compromise settlement of 1918-20 was inherently flawed. Epithets such as "the unfinished revolution" or "betrayal of the revolution" reveal a deeply pessimistic teleology, posited in models of continuity from "Bismarck to Hitler" or from the "Kaiserreich to the Third Reich,"[76] that threatens to reduce the story of Weimar to a doomed interlude within, or, a prelude to, a far darker history.[77] In defense of our contrary hypothesis, we must return to the early years of the Republic to ask how and when its prospects became fatally compromised.

The symbolic moment of truth may have come on 23 November 1923 when a bizarre combination of Communists, Social Democrats, German Nationalists, and protofascists supported a no confidence motion against Gustav Stresemann's second cabinet. Confronted by this inchoate but numerically superior opposition, Stresemann knew that his days as chancellor were over, but appealed to parliament and the country at large to work for German economic rehabilitation within the context of a prospering global economy. The crises of 1923, he hoped, represented nothing worse than the growing pains of the young Republic.[78] Leading Social Democrats, however, already feared otherwise. Beholden to their parliamentary fraction, Social Democratic ministers had resigned unwillingly from Stresemann's cabinet in protest over military intervention in Saxony, which was governed by a Socialist-Communist coalition. As Robert Schmidt conceded: "The whole business will not play so badly for the party, [but] the political consequences will be grave, and history will put us in the dock."[79] President Ebert echoed Schmidt's sentiments, warning his fellow Social Democrats: "Everything that induced you to overthrow the Chancellor will be forgotten in six weeks, but you will suffer the consequences of your stupidity in ten years."[80] Historians have remarked on the Social Democrats' unwillingness to assume governmental office during Weimar, but until the autumn of 1923, the reverse had often been the case. Social Democrats had not shirked their responsibilities during and after the revolution, and the trade unions also continued to shoulder the burdens of reparations and domestic upheaval. However, the unions walked out of the Zentral-Arbeitsgemeinschaft (ZAG), which had been formed with the employers in 1918 to institutionalize the Stinnes-Legien Agreement at subgovernmental level, just weeks after the SPD left government.[81] What had precipitated this sea change in attitudes and behavior?

An abortive attempt in early October 1923 by the mining industry unilaterally to revise statutory working times was vital in this regard, for republicans interpreted it as a direct assault on the substance of the postwar revolution. Historians have generally considered the magnates' démarche, issued after a meeting of the Mining Association at Unna-Königsborn, politically motivated, with the Ruhr crisis merely providing a pretext for rolling back the revolution.[82] Reactionary politics undoubtedly contributed to the disaster, but the combined effects of a structural crisis within German coal mining and the impact of the Ruhr crisis were vital in their own right. Structural problems had been deepening since the end of the war. By 1922 productivity had plunged well below 1918 levels, and, with profits pared to the bone, mining chiefs were finding meetings with their shareholders increasingly uncongenial.[83] The employers' mood was not improved when British coal entered the Ruhr during 1923 at two-thirds the price of the locally mined product,[84] and prospects darkened further once Stresemann abandoned passive resistance unconditionally on 26 September. Industry had endorsed this step, but Poincaré's refusal to negotiate a settlement of differences with Berlin left western Germany prey to whatever ambitions Paris might wish to pursue there.[85] The initial signs were ominous. France sought not merely to restore reparations deliveries, but also to reclaim an enormous backlog created by the passive resistance campaign between January and September. French officials also demanded the receipt of output taxes and customs duties in the occupied territories and backdated these claims to January 1923.[86] Meanwhile the German cabinet resolved to bring the budget into balance within months in order to conquer inflation.

Ministers warned appalled industrialists that the inflation-fueled torrent of subsidies that had supported company payrolls and balance sheets in the occupied territories would shortly cease.[87] Furthermore, the Treasury lacked funds to underwrite reparations deliveries, and all the government could do was to waive its own tax demands and chalk up the reparations tally for settlement at some point in the future.[88]

By comparison, the labor question appeared less intractable. The Social Democrats and trade unions accepted in September 1923 that miners would have to work longer, as had many miners themselves.[89] The mine owners, too, continued to seek a statutory solution to their economic problems until late September, understanding that a compromise settlement was available on the working hours question. Their sudden decision to circumvent the parliamentary process was certainly inflammatory in the extreme,[90] but rather than reflecting any considered strategy, seemed motivated more by naked panic in the aftermath of 26 September. Senior pit head managers ("directors") responded to the Unna-Königsborn resolution with incredulity, which again suggests that this extraparliamentary strategy was a bolt from the blue. The Gelsenkirchener Mining Company and its director general, Emil Kirdorf, for example, ranked among the most reactionary in the Ruhr district,[91] but the company's workplace directors were essentially pragmatic men who had worked closely with the unions and the works councils before and throughout the passive resistance campaign. Even Gelsenkirchener's head office acknowledged its debt to the unions during 1923 in maintaining workplace discipline[92] and knew that one mining director had forced everyone on his payroll into the official unions.[93]

Now, in early October, directors deluged the head office with protests against the Mining Association's ill-conceived and counterproductive attempt to take the extraparliamentary road. The young hotheads aside, their workers were reasonable men who appreciated the need for longer hours, with the understanding that changes would be properly negotiated.[94] Director Bruch of the Minister Stein and Prince Hardenberg mines continued: "Given that we constantly emphasized compliance with justice and the law during all [previous] negotiations, the attempt to introduce prewar working times, contrary to the law and to wage agreements, has gravely damaged the works management's position."[95] Director Scheulen at the Zollern mines remonstrated that he had maintained order and output by insisting on adherence to the law and existing wages agreements, and now the ground had been cut from under his feet,[96] while the director of the Hamburg and Franziska mines warned that publication of the Unna-Königsborn resolution had "exploded like a bomb in the midst of a depressed atmosphere and provoked the deepest fury."[97] These managers' anger and their willingness to speak their minds openly suggest that acceptance of the postwar labor settlement at Gelsenkirchener was more than a passing whim. To all appearances, the climate of reform noted previously in the metallurgical industry extended to coal mining, whose managers had staked their personal credibility on upholding the revolutionary labor accords.

Beyond precipitating an intemperate response by the mining barons, Germany's capitulation in September 1923 did little to improve the mood of organized labor. In their history of the Ruhr crisis, the trade unions laid claim to its conduct and ethos,[98] while the SPD presented 1923 as a struggle by republican Germany to uphold the values of the revolution and the international peace settlement.[99] A couple of examples must suffice to illustrate comparable perceptions among the industrial workers and blue-collar civil servants (notably railwaymen) of the Ruhr during the course of the passive resistance campaign. Works councilors from the mines around Wanne lambasted a French colonel:

> Since the war, they had worked four long years under utterly wretched conditions. Despite the fact that thousands of workers had had no meat on the table for a month at a time, that there wasn't even margarine for their bread, the miners' unions had accepted overtime agreements so as to maximize reparations deliveries to France. Their comrades in the German metal industry had made furious demands for more coal for their factories because a shortage of coal had forced production to cease. The German working class had starved, frozen, and toiled to meet the obligations to France as far as possible. In particular, they as miners knew that the German people had done its duty.[100]

Similarly, ordinary miners at the von der Heydt mine protested bitterly to the occupiers: "We didn't invite you, nor do we want you here. We have demonstrated through years of overtime that we support our government's fulfillment policy. You have substituted violence for justice, sanctions for fulfillment; our defensive struggle has flared up in response to this."[101]

These words were echoed in contemporary official trade union pronouncements,[102] and by Social Democratic members of parliament.[103] The Ruhr struggle came to be seen as republican-style patriotism, as a peaceful campaign to defend Germany against foreign invasion, which stood in complete contrast to Imperial Germany's military campaign of foreign conquest. However, if the Empire had staked its survival on victory in the Great War, the Republic found itself embroiled in a comparable elemental battle during 1923. By August, republican leaders accepted that capitulation was inevitable,[104] but when defeat in this perceived struggle for the Republic against foreign aggression was compounded by the mine owners' domestic assault on the revolutionary settlement, the sense of betrayal among republicans became acute. Although parliament eventually approved a compromise solution to the working hours question in December it could not prevent the strikes and lockouts that swept through the Ruhr shortly thereafter. Industrial relations in Germany's heavy industrial heartland had been undermined beyond repair, with neither side willing to grant the other the benefit of the doubt.[105]

We are left to speculate on what a more statesmanlike French response to Stresemann's overtures of August and September might have preserved of the republican settlement,[106] but key players in the French polity sensed the oncoming disaster. Marshal Foch and President Millerand urged Poincaré in August 1923 to abandon his *va banque* strategy and negotiate a compromise settlement with Stresemann, naturally on terms favorable to Paris.[107] Paul Cambon, scarcely a noted Germanophile, warned that Franco-German reconciliation had to come sooner or later, and better sooner and through a French initiative.[108] Appalled Socialist deputies in the French

National Assembly warned from the opposition benches that their government was
fighting the wrong enemy in Germany. It was not the German Empire that an outright French victory would destroy, but *"l'autre Allemagne,"* without whose survival
France's own prospects would be bleak.[109]

In fact, as we have seen, the destruction extended even further. Elements of the
Wilhelmine order had proven ready to compromise with the republicans and create
an environment in which the new Germany and the old could coexist. This is not to
ignore the powerful forces on the right and the frustrated radicals on the left, who
despised this very compromise. Given the plethora of challenges it faced, Weimar's
future was not assured and any single explanation for the Republic's demise would
scarcely hold water. However, the crisis of 1923, accentuated by the external shock
of French invasion, weakened significantly the prospects for pluralistic parliamentary
democracy in Germany. The Republic lived on and even enjoyed a period of remis-
sion during the later 1920s, but many already sensed that it was in no condition to
survive a further crisis. Too many of its original supporters lacked conviction, while
within the elites, including elements that had initially compromised with the republicans, planning for an alternative constitutional order that harked back to the Empire
became increasingly widespread and increasingly concrete. As heir to this process, the
Third Reich represented the disastrous end to one line of continuity, but Hitler's
regime might also be regarded as a brutal interruption to a parallel pattern of development. It is possible to see in the German revolution and its immediate aftermath
intimations of forces that were to shape the post-1945 order in (western) Germany
and Europe, even if these were only to blossom and bear fruit after a second, more
terrible European war.

Notes

1. Stanislas Jeannesson, *Poincaré, la France et la Ruhr (1922-1924). Histoire d'une occupation*
    (Strasbourg, 1998), 71-125.
2. On 7 January the German foreign minister assured the British ambassador to Berlin that strikes
    would not be used as a political weapon by the German government. The government did not antic-
    ipate significant disruption of the railways, although some grassroots action was to be expected:
    Akten zur deutschen auswärtigen Politik 1918-1945 (hereafter cited as *AP*), Serie A: *1918-1925.*
    Band VII, 1. Januar bis 31. Mai 1923 (Göttingen, 1989), no. 13, 963-64. On 10 January the
    railways were ordered to cooperate with the invaders: *Akten der Reichskanzlei. Weimarer Republik.*
    Das Kabinett Cuno. 22. November 1922 bis 12. August 1923 (Boppard am Rhein, 1968), no.
    38, 10 January 1923, 129. As grassroots unrest burgeoned, the reluctant decision to support pas-
    sive resistance on the railways was taken on 16 January: *Reichskanzlei Cuno*, no. 45, 16 January
    1923, 149. For a wider discussion see Barbara Müller, *Passiver Widerstand im Ruhrkampf* (Mün-
    ster, 1996), 97-99, 111-13, 467ff. A new history of the crisis is appearing in Conan Fischer, *The*
    Ruhr Crisis 1923-24 (Oxford University Press, 2003).

3. Jacques Bariéty, *Les relations franco-allemandes après la Première Guerre Mondiale. 10 Novembre 1918–10 Janvier 1925. De l'exécution à la négociation* (Paris, 1977) 139; for a discussion of France's postwar economic foreign policy, see Jacques Bariéty, "Le Traité de Versailles et l'ambition d'industrialiser la France," *Revue d'Allemagne et de pays de langue allemande* 30, no. 1 (1998): 41-52.

4. See, for example: Nordrhein-Westfälisches Hauptstaatsarchiv Düsseldorf (NWHStAD) Regierung Düsseldorf. Politische Akten: IV Besatzungsangelegenheiten (R Dü) 16535(5), 17 January 1923; Nordrhein-Westfälisches Staatsarchiv Münster (NWStAM) Kreis Recklinghausen (Kr Rhn) no. 269 (17/29), 26 February 1923, Anlage 9, Stimmung.

5. Examples include *AP* VII, no. 108, 24 February 1923, 245-46; *Reichskanzlei Cuno*, no. 109, 27 March 1923, 342-43; no. 120, 14 April 1923, 376-77.

6. Hermann J. Rupieper, *The Cuno Government and Reparations 1922-1923: Politics and Economics* (The Hague, 1979), 147-48. For later examples of Rosenberg's obstructiveness and truculence, see *Reichskanzlei Cuno*, no. 142, 28 April 1923, 433-35; no. 144, 30 April 1923, 441 note 7.

7. *AP* VII, no. 176, 3 April 1923, 429-30.

8. Peter Krüger, *Deutschland und die Reparationen 1918/19. Die Genesis des Reparationsproblems in Deutschland zwischen Waffenstillstand und Versailler Friedenschluß* (Stuttgart, 1973), 45-46.

9. Hartmut Pogge von Strandmann, "Rapallo – Strategy in Preventive Diplomacy: New Sources and Interpretations," in Volker R. Berghahn and Martin Kitchen, eds., *Germany in the Age of Total War* (London, 1981), 127-43.

10. Peter Krüger, *Die Außenpolitik der Republik von Weimar* (Darmstadt, 1985), 204.

11. Christian Baechler, *Gustave Stresemann (1878-1929). De l'impérialisme à la sécurité collective* (Strasbourg, 1996), 474-75.

12. *AP* VII, no. 176, 3 April 1923, 430.

13. Ibid.

14. Ibid., 430-31 note 2.

15. Ibid., 431.

16. Ibid., 431-3.

17. Ibid., 432.

18. Ibid., 432 note 3.

19. See, for example, *Reichskanzlei Cuno*, no. 109, 27 March 1923, 347. Cf. Deutsches Bergbau-Museum Bochum; Bergbau-Archiv (BBA)Bestand 32: Hibernia Bergwerksgesellschaft, Herne (32)/4364, "Das unmögliche Verlangen. Berliner Stimmen zum passiven Widerstand," *Kölnische Zeitung*, no. 296, 28 April 1923.

20. Typical are *AP* VIII, no. 138, 10 September 1923, 363; no. 177, 5 October 1923, 447-48; no. 179, 6 October 1923, 452.

21. *AP* X, no. 6, 9 April 1924, 15-17.

22. Ibid., 16.

23. Ibid., 17.

24. The Experts' Committees presented their reports to the Reparations Commission on the same day that Maltzan dispatched his aide mémoire.

25. *AP* X, no. 6, 9 April 1924, 15-17.

26. Ibid.

27. Richard Bessel, *Germany after the First World War* (Oxford, 1995), esp. 107-11; Krüger, *Reparationen*, 67-68, 80-82.

28. Krüger, *Reparationen*, 12, 26.

29. Krüger, *Aussenpolitik*, 110; Peter Krüger, *Versailles. Deutsche Außenpolitik zwischen Revisionismus und Friedenssicherung*, 2nd ed. (Munich, 1993), 58.

30. Krüger, *Reparationen*, 17, 33-34.

31. For a detailed account of this process, see Bessel, *Germany*, chap. 4; see also Krüger, *Reparationen*, 34.

32. Gerald D. Feldman, *Army, Industry and Labor in Germany, 1914-1918* (Princeton, 1966), 523; see also idem, "The Origins of the Stinnes-Legien Agreement: A Documentation," *Internationale wissenschaftliche Korrespondenz zur Geschichte der deutschen Arbeiterbewegung*, no. 9 (19-20) 1973, 45-103, and Heinrich August Winkler, *Weimar 1918-1933. Die Geschichte der ersten deutschen Demokratie*, 2nd ed. (Munich, 1994), 45-46.

33. Winkler, *Weimar*, 46-47.

34. Werner Abelshauser and Ralf Himmelmann, eds., *Revolution in Rheinland und Westfalen. Quellen zu Wirtschaft, Gesellschaft und Politik 1918-1923* (Essen, 1988), 114; no. 54, is representative. Cf. Bessel, *Germany*, 138-40.

35. Among notable exponents of the council movement were Francis L. Carsten, *Revolution in Central Europe, 1918-1919* (Berkeley, 1972), and Sebastien Haffner, *1918/19. Eine deutsche Revolution* (Hamburg, 1981). Compare with the very different views of Wolfgang Mommsen, "The German Revolution 1918-1920: Political Revolution and Social Protest Movement," in *Social Change and Political Development in Weimar Germany*, ed. Richard Bessel and E. J. Feuchtwanger (London, 1981), 21-54.

36. Werner Plumpe, *Betriebliche Mitbestimmung in der Weimarer Republik. Fallstudien zum Ruhrbergbau und zur Chemischen Industrie* (Munich, 1999), 299-300.

37. Mommsen, "Revolution."

38. George Eliasberg, *Der Ruhrkrieg von 1920* (Bonn-Bad Godesberg, 1974), 262. Cf. Heinrich August Winkler, *Von der Revolution zur Stabilisierung. Arbeiter und Arbeiterbewegung in der Weimarer Republik 1918 bis 1924* (Berlin and Bonn, 1984), 331-35.

39. Karin Hartewig, "Wie radikal waren die Bergarbeiter im Ruhrgebiet 1915/16-1924?" in *Sozialgeschichte des Bergbaus im 19. und 20. Jahrhundert*, ed. Klaus Tenfelde (Munich, 1992), 629.

40. Plumpe, *Mitbestimmung*, 45.

41. Ibid., 10-17, 37-56

42. Ibid., 10.

43. Benno König, "Interessenvertretung am Arbeitsplatz. Betriebsrätepraxis in der Metallindustrie 1920-1933," in *Arbeiter im 20. Jahrhundert*, ed. Klaus Tenfelde (Stuttgart, 1991), 74; Plumpe, *Mitbestimmung*, 41, 44.

44. Cf. König, "Interessenvertretung," 69-70.

45. Plumpe, *Mitbestimmung*, 53-55.

46. Ibid., 319-20, 325,

47. Ibid., 37.

48. Ibid., 37-38, 44, 50.

49. Ibid., 50, and 50 note 50.

50. Quoted in Werner Plumpe, "Die Betriebsräte in der Weimarer Republik. Eine Skizze zu ihrer Verbreitung, Zusammensetzung und Akzeptanz," in *Unternehmen zwischen Markt und Macht. Aspekte deutscher Unternehmensgeschichte im 20. Jahrhundert*, ed. Werner Plumpe and Christian Kleinschmidt (Essen, 1992), 52.

51. Alfred Baedeker, ed., *Jahrbuch für den Oberbergamtsbezirk Dortmund 1922/25* (Essen, 1925), 549, table 4.

52. Baedeker, *Jahrbuch*, 560, table 15.

53. Ibid.

54. This outburst is widely quoted, e.g., in Hans Mommsen, *Die Verspielte Freiheit. Der Weg der Republik von Weimar in den Untergang 1918 bis 1933* (Frankfurt a.M. and Berlin, 1990), 123.

55. Baedeker, *Jahrbuch*, 553, table 8 and 560, table 15.

56. Arnold Wolfers, *Britain and France between Two Wars: Conflicting Strategies of Peace since Versailles* (New York, 1940), 58 note 7.

57. Cf. Bessel, *Germany*, 95-97, 112-13.

58. Quoted in Rupieper, *Cuno*, 34.

59. Gerald D. Feldman, *The Great Disorder: Politics, Economics and Society in the German Inflation, 1914-1924* (New York, Oxford, 1997), 465.

60. Feldman, *Disorder*, 439-40.

61. Karl Dietrich Erdmann, *Adenauer in der Rheinlandpolitik nach dem Ersten Weltkrieg* (Stuttgart, 1966), 156-59; Wolfram Fischer, "Wirtschaftliche Rahmenbedingungen des Ruhrkonflikts", in Klaus Schwabe, ed., *Die Ruhrkrise 1923. Wendepunkt der internationalen Beziehungen nach dem Ersten Weltkrieg*, 2nd ed. (Paderborn, 1986), 97.

62. Erdmann, *Adenauer*, 159-61, 171-72, 180-84.

63. Erdmann, *Adenauer*, provides comprehensive coverage.

64. For example, Krüger, *Reparationen*, 136-37.

65. Mission Interalliée de Contrôle des Usines et des Mines.

66. Quoted in Conan Fischer, "Heavy Industry, Society and Aspects of Foreign Policy in the Weimar Republic," *Revue d'Allemagne et des pays de langue allemande* 30, no. 1 (1998): 60.

67. Quoted in Erdmann, *Adenauer*, 171.

68. *AP* IX, no. 177, 1 March 1924, 476-77; no. 177, 477 note 10; *Reichskanzlei Marx* I, no. 146, 15 March 1924, 466-68.

69. Cf. Fischer, "Heavy Industry", 60-61.

70. Quoted in Rupieper, *Cuno*, 41.

71. Berndt Weisbrod, "Arbeitgeberpolitik und Arbeitsbedingungen im Ruhrbergbau. Vom "Herr-im-Haus" zur Mitbestimmung," in *Arbeiter, Unternehmer und Staat im Bergbau. Industrielle Beziehungen im internationalen Vergleich*, ed. Gerald D. Feldman and Klaus Tenfelde (Munich, 1989), 136-37; Plumpe, *Mitbestimmung*, 315-16.

72. Gunther Mai, "Wenn der Mensch Hunger hat, hört alles auf." Wirtschaftliche und soziale Ausgangsbedingungen der Weimarer Republik (1919-1924)," in *Die Weimarer Republik als Wohlfahrtsstaat*, ed. Werner Abelshauser (= *Vierteljahresschrift für Sozial- und Wirtschaftsgeschichte*, Beiheft 81, 1986), 60 note 105.

73. Plumpe, *Mitbestimmung*, 315-16; Mai "Wenn der Mensch," 61-62.

74. See, for example, William Lee Blackwood, "German Hegemony and the Socialist International's Place in Interwar European Diplomacy," *European History Quarterly* 31, no. 1 (2001): 115-16.

75. BBA 32/4364, "Ein prophetisches Wort von Otto Hué," *Herner Zeitung*, no. 25, 30 January 1923.

76. Thus, Fritz Fischer, *Bündnis der Eliten. Zur Kontinuität der Machtstrukturen in Deutschland in Deutschland 1871-1945* (Düsseldorf, 1979); Mommsen, *Freiheit*.

77. The pessimists include Fischer, *Bündnis*, and Detlev Peukert, *The Weimar Republic: The Crisis of Classical Modernity*, trans. Richard Deveson (London, 1991). Cf. Marcus Gräser's comments in his positive review of David Crew, *Germans on Welfare: From Weimar to Hitler*, in German Historical Institute London, *Bulletin* 22, no. 1 (2000): 65-66.

78. Baechler, *Stresemann*, 453.

79. Quoted in *Reichskanzlei Stresemann* II, no. 216, 2 November 1923, 954 note 3.

80. Quoted in Baechler, *Stresemann*, 457; cf. Winkler, *Weimar*, 239-40.

81. Winkler, *Weimar*, 248-49. A full history of the ZAG is in Gerald D. Feldman and Irmgard Steinisch, *Industrie und Gewerkschaften 1918-1924. Die überforderte Zentralarbeitsgemeinschaft* (Stuttgart, 1985).

82. Thus, Charles Maier, *Recasting Bourgeois Europe: Stabilization in France, Germany and Italy in the Decade after World War I* (Princeton, 1975), 390, 419, 445-47; Mommsen, *Freiheit*, 155.

83. Baedeker, *Jahrbuch*, 553, table 8, 561-63, tables 16-18; J. Ronald Shearer, "The Social Consequences of Modernisation: Rationalisation and the Politics of the Labour Market in the Ruhr Coal Mines, 1918-1929," in *Sozialgeschichte des Bergbaus im 19. und 20. Jahrhundert*, ed. Klaus Tenfelde (Munich, 1992), 422; E Jüngst, "Zur Abwehr," *Glückauf. Berg- und Hüttenmännische Zeitschrift* 59, no. 9 (1923): 219-20.

84. Hans Spethmann, *Zwölf Jahre Ruhrbergbau. Aus seiner Geschichte von Kriegsanfang bis zum Franzosenabmarsch 1914 bis 1925. Band III: Der Ruhrkampf 1923 bis 1925 in seinen Leitlinien* (Berlin, 1929), 184, 378-79 Anlage 58. Cf. BBA 32/4365, "Ueber die Lage des Bergbaues," *Herner Zeitung*, no. 234, 5 October 1923.

85. *AP* VIII, no. 186, 10 October 1923, no. 473; cf. Baechler, *Stresemann*, 354-62; Krüger, *Versailles*, 116-17; Jeannesson, *Poincaré*, 293-303.

86. *Reichskanzlei Stresemann* I, no. 58, 14 September 1923, 270; *AP* VIII, no. 136, 10 September 1923, 350; Jeannesson, *Poincaré*, 298. But compare with J. F. V. Keiger, *Raymond Poincaré* (Cambridge, 1997), 303-4.

87. Mommsen, *Freiheit*, 159; Bariéty, *Relations*, 228 note 22. For subsequent business reaction, see NWHStAD Industrie- und Handelskammer, Düsseldorf. 2. Ruhrbesetzung. Passiver Widerstand (RW49)/69 I(92), 7 October 1923; BBA 32/4365, "Vorbedingungen der Arbeitsaufnahme," *Rheinisch-Westfälische Zeitung*, no. 569, 12 October 1923; BBA 32/4365, "Die Aufnahme der Kohlenförderung im Essener Bezirk," *Bochumer Zeitung*, no. 139, 6 October 1923.

88. Spethmann, *Ruhrbergbau* III, 198-209; *Reichskanzlei Stresemann* II, no. 155, 20 October 1923, 660; no. 156, 21 October 1923, 682.

89. *Reichskanzlei Str* I, no. 97, 1 October 1923, 429-30; Feldman, *Disorder*, 738, 745; Baechler, *Stresemann*, 373.

90. Cf. Conan Fischer, "Arbeitgeber, Arbeitnehmer und das Scheitern des passiven Widerstands 1923 im Ruhrgebiet," *Mitteilungsblatt des Instituts für soziale Bewegungen* 26 (2001): 101-2.

91. See, for example: BBA Bestand 55: Gelsenkirchener Bergwerks AG, Essen(55)/2866, Vertraulich! Herrn Arthur Dix, Berlin. 13 August 1923. A comprehensive analysis of industrial relations at Gelsenkirchener is found in Plumpe, *Mitbestimmung*, IV and V.

92. BBA 55/411, Betrifft: Allgemeine Lage bei der Bergwerks-Abteilung in der Woche vom 10. bis 17. August. Essen, 21 August 1923.

93. Fischer, "Arbeitgeber", 100.

94. Ibid., 102-4.

95. Ibid., 103.

96. Ibid.

97. BBA 55/411, Betrifft: Stimmungsbericht für ver. Hamburg und Franziska. Mitteilung an die Direktion. Schächte Franziska I/II, Witten, 10 October 1923.

98. Lothar Erdmann, *Die Gewerkschaften im Ruhrkampfe. Im Auftrage des Allgemeinen Deutschen Gewerkschaftsbundes* (Berlin, 1924), esp. 3-4, 23, 86-87.

99. Vorstand der Vereinigten Sozialdemokratischen Partei Deutschlands (VSPD), ed., *Handbuch für sozialdemokratische Wähler. Der Reichstag 1920 bis 1924* (Berlin, 1924), 30.

100. BBA 32/4371, Abschrift. Protokoll über die Besprechung der Arbeitervertreter der hiesigen 6 Schachtanlagen, mit dem Kommandeur der Besatzungstruppe, Oberst Homgie, vom Infant. Regiment 147 [23 January 1923].

101. BBA 32/4364, "Entschließung," quoted in "So reden Bergarbeiter," *Gelsenkirchener Allgemeine Zeitung*, 26 February 1923.

102. Quoted in BBA 32/4364, "Die deutsche Abwehr. Fortsetzung des passiven Widerstandes," *Kölnische Zeitung*, no. 155, 2 March 1923, and "Die Haltung der Arbeiterschaft," *Kölnische Zeitung*, no. 222, 29 March 1923.

103. See, for example, *Reichskanzlei Cuno*, no. 109, 27 March 1923, 342-43.

104. Michael Ruck, *Die Freien Gewerkschaften im Ruhrkampf 1923* (Frankfurt a.M., 1986), 441-44; *Reichskanzlei Stresemann* I, no. 18, 23 August 1923, 80.

105. See, for example, Abelshauser and Himmelmann, *Revolution*, 122, no. 58.

106. Cf. Fischer, "Arbeitgeber," 104.

107. Jeannesson, *Poincaré*, 300.

108. Ibid., 294.

109. Maier, *Recasting*, 405-6, 458; Blackwood, "German Hegemony," 118-20.

13

A Wilhelmine Legacy?

Coudenhove-Kalergi's Pan-Europe and the Crisis of European Modernity, 1922-1932

⎯⎯⧫⎯⎯

Katiana Orluc

Ethics is the soul of European culture—technology is its body.
– Richard N. Coudenhove-Kalergi (1922)[1]

Introduction

Can Count Richard Coudenhove-Kalergi (1894-1972)—an Austro-Hungarian noble who was only in his late twenties when he founded the Pan-European movement in 1923-24—be considered an heir of Wilhelminism? Did the retrospectively picturesque German Empire not vanish into historicity the moment it became politically extinct? Did this putatively backward regime in fact produce any intellectual or ideological phenomena strong enough to endure? Indeed, if anything remained from the prewar period, was it not the bitter memory of a failed project of modernity, in which social conditions had deteriorated and in which capitalism had finally shown its ugly face with the rise of inequality and a growing number of people living under conditions close to slavery? That, at least, was Coudenhove-Kalergi's perception of the Wilhelmine era.

From a perspective outside the established narrative of "political backwardness" or, in the newest catch phrase, of Germany's "long way toward the West," these questions are more relevant than they might seem at first sight. Choosing modernity—ambiguous as the category might be—as the guiding concept of analysis, and adopting Hartmut Pogge von Strandmann's definition of Wilhelminism as outlined in the introduction to this book, the following analysis argues that the Wilhelmine condition did persist in certain forms throughout the 1920s and early 1930s. In many ways Coudenhove-Kalergi's ideas—albeit with their fierce critique of pre-war times and strong advocacy of a particular kind of future society—echo those of the Wilhelmine era proper.

In 1923, Coudenhove-Kalergi delineated in his programmatic book *Paneuropa* his model of a future Europe. Europe should be united for three main reasons: politically, as guarantee of world peace; culturally, as a bulwark against the "non-Occidental culture of Bolshevism" and as the bedrock of European civilization; and economically in order to prevent American domination. He explained the reasons for his call for unity, on the one hand, with reference to his experiences in World War I, which had, in his view, been a civil war. On the other hand, he cited the new diplomacy of American President Woodrow Wilson. However, at the end of the Paris peace conferences in 1919, Coudenhove-Kalergi was deeply disappointed, since he could still see nationalism holding its ground. For him, the devastation of war was endowed with a dialectical sense: the struggle between aggressive nationalisms had led to an international reconciliation, and it was here that he laid his hopes for the future.[2]

In arguing consistently that the national perspective should be replaced with a European one, Coudenhove-Kalergi may be said to have been a Wilhelmine European. Believing as he did in the power of the technical age and the perfectibility of society, wishing to solve the social question, and relying on a strong and authoritative state organization, Coudenhove-Kalergi favored what can be called a "third way": an approach that denied the importance of parliamentarianism and party politics, whether Conservative or Social Democratic. Rather, he believed that through a combination of ethics and technology, the state could implement a social system for the good of all people: it should be built on a structure comparable to a well-run company.[3]

In fact, Coudenhove-Kalergi took the argument of the primacy of economics over politics—as outlined by Walther Rathenau is his famous dictum, "The economy shapes our destiny"[4]—one crucial step further.[5] After the cataclysmic experience of World War I, Coudenhove-Kalergi adapted the profoundly changed paradigms of his times to the development of his vision of a Pan-European state. That state was to be based on moral virtues and, above all, on the idea of individual freedom, and it was to be inaugurated through technological achievements. The debate about his ideas can be followed through his sociophilosophical works and his correspondence with those who joined or were commentators on his Pan-European Union.

The Way toward Pan-Europe: Organization and Aims of the Pan-European Union

The Pan-European Union was founded in 1924 and was dissolved by the Gestapo in March 1938. With the support of the Austrian government, it established its headquarters in the prestigious Viennese Hofburg. Its foundation had been secured by the German banker Max Warburg through a donation of 60,000 gold marks (approximately $14,000). It seems that German banks and industrialists provided the principal source of revenue for the Union. This was facilitated by the fact that several members of the Union were actually bankers themselves, such as Arthur von Gwinner, treasurer of the Paneuropean's German section and a member of Deutsche Bank's supervisory board, and the director of the Dresdner Bank, Geheimrat Frisch. In addition, the movement benefited from its membership fees. For the German section membership can be estimated at 2,300 members a year after its foundation.[6] Across Europe the Union was able to establish twenty-three national sections; it also founded a supporting committee in the United States in 1925.

The Pan-European Union was not the only pro-European organization in the inter-war period. The competing interest groups drained each other of energy and impetus, leaving many proponents of a common Europe puzzled as to which organization to support.[7] There existed, for example, several associations which took over Friedrich Naumann's concept of *Mitteleuropa*. Each sought to solve Germany's uncertain future by establishing a central European federation under German leadership as a first step towards a United States of Europe.[8] These were ideas which would later be adopted by the National Socialists, though of course in a very different way. *Mitteleuropa* and the concept of *Anschluss* were very successful and drew much support away from the Pan-European Union, at least in Germany. The German Foreign Ministry Office in particular followed a revisionist *Mitteleuropa* line and therefore supported these groups rather than Coudenhove-Kalergi. Having defended the Versailles Treaty—although his position on this question was quite ambiguous — Coudenhove-Kalergi opposed the *Anschluss* until 1932.[9]

As early as 1922, Coudenhove-Kalergi had started to publish in Austrian and German newspapers his ideas on a common European political structure. In 1923 his book *Paneuropa* appeared, its aim being to "create a great political movement that lies dormant in all European peoples."[10] In the same year he set up a publishing house, the Paneuropa Verlag, which edited the ideological linchpin of the movement, the journal *Paneuropa*.[11] The latter, founded in April 1924, was to become the official discussion platform of the Union until its last edition in March 1938. Coudenhove-Kalergi had thus in a very short time-span given his ideas an impressive propaganda apparatus, which—at least theoretically—was now able to influence both public opinion and politics. Seeking to remind Europeans of their common features—"the Occidental cultural community"—the Pan-European movement's ultimate goal was to forge the political integration of the Continent on the basis of this renewed consciousness.[12]

Coudenhove-Kalergi made the question of the extent of Europe the starting point of his observations. He did so by considering a variety of perspectives that might define Europe. He accordingly drew a distinction between the geographical, political, and cultural components. He recognized that in geographical terms Europe could not be strictly defined, and insisted that a demarcation existed only in accordance with the criteria inherent in what he called European culture—the "culture of the white race which has sprung from the soil of antiquity and Christianity," with its fundamental principles of "Hellenic individualism" and "Christian socialism."[13]

However, because he realized that this Occidental culture had been disseminated all over the world and was hence not sufficient as a basis for demarcation, a more refined criterion had to be adduced—the political one. Coudenhove-Kalergi broke this down into two components: first, the democratic system of governance, although he was never a fierce supporter of democracy, and, second, the subdivision of the world into political regions, of which Europe and its colonies were but one. Applying the geographical, political and cultural criteria, the resulting demarcation distinguished a smaller Europe, excluding Great Britain and Soviet Russia. These two states fell outside his definition, being independent world empires that constituted separate regions of power. In the case of Soviet Russia, its exclusion was additionally based on the fact that it was defined as a nondemocratic state. However, in order to keep Mussolini's Italy inside Europe, Coudenhove-Kalergi enlarged his definition of democracy. Consequently, Pan-Europe comprised all the "democratic and semi-democratic states of Continental Europe, including Iceland."[14] He envisioned a regional organization of the world around five federations: under the supervision of a modified League of Nations, a British, an East-Asian, a Pan-American, and a Russian federation should be organized beside Pan-Europe.

The unification of the Continent was to be accomplished, according to Coudenhove-Kalergi, in three steps. Initially, a European conference would be convoked, which would be followed by a treaty of federation; the last step was to be the establishment of a European tariff union. As a long-term goal he envisioned the creation of the European Union, though he was realistic enough to aim only at a federation of states.

The "Modern Dilemma" and the European Idea

Many proponents of European unity stressed the impact of modernity on the spread of the European idea. Here, I am less interested in following the project of modernity, understood as the expansion of socioeconomic processes, than its imaginary dimension, even though the development of modern technologies has been essential to the creation of a European consciousness in that it has facilitated communication between individuals and states. Whatever the individual understanding of modernity might be, it is certainly a common point of departure to state that its quality involved a break with traditional bases of both Western culture and art, of both Western economic conditions and social organization.[15]

Throughout the nineteenth century, human life was transformed by a modernization process that was constantly accelerating and was marked by individualization, differentiation, specialization, abstraction, mechanization, secularization, rationalization, and the advance of science.[16] Max Weber's exemplary model of the world—as a place that had lost its magic, from which the supernatural had disappeared and in which nature had been replaced by man-made, artificial, cultural production—was thus a very contemporary conception of the state of the world and an expression of modern self-doubt and cultural critique. Not only had God disappeared from the scene, but the verities of what were truth, beauty, and good had also dissolved.

The "crisis of modernity" could thus be encountered at all levels of society: it lay in the connection of subject and object, in the individual as well as the state, connected as they were by ethical values and the notion of individual freedom. However, on both levels, interior contradictions—or, rather, oppositions—were at work. On the one hand, the individual's will and right to freedom were constantly challenged by existential fear and the weight of self-responsibility. On the other hand, the state, or social organization in general, was put under constant scrutiny. While it was thought to have the power—thanks to technology—to shape and to guarantee the individual's freedom and general well-being, and would thus also be capable of designing the future, the state was constantly suspected of enslaving modern man. It could be accused of being a simple but all-determining machine that dehumanized its inhabitants instead of providing them with a secure basis for the development of essential human qualities. One of the qualitative control mechanisms in deciding whether or not freedom had been provided, thus guaranteeing the ends of human self-fulfillment, was ethical values, such as the possibility of choice, of a self-determined life.[17]

Thus, the idea that something fundamentally new could occur, and that new occurrences would continue to accrue faster and faster, is indeed characteristic of what has been retrospectively termed modernity. It is in this sense that modernity, as a material, psychological, and philosophical condition, is indispensable for understanding the formation and transformation of the European idea around World War I—a period that Peter Wagner has termed "the first crisis of modernity."[18]

Throughout the previous two centuries the vision of a united Europe had become part of a wider struggle for modernity and progress. By saying this I do not mean to imply that Europe represents something like the cradle of civilization, which has evolved in an unbroken line from antiquity to the present day, and which, through the modernization process, has continuously progressed. I surmise, however, that the European idea after World War I was a classic expression of the modern condition—although with an eschatological temporal dimension. This holds particularly true for the Weimar Republic, whose violent political and ideological struggles "can be understood as the convulsions of a society [coming] to terms with modernity in all its manifestations."[19]

Coudenhove-Kalergi himself had devoted his *Apologie der Technik* and its revised version of 1932, *Revolution durch Technik*, to the question of modernity. He continued to pay attention to modernity as the very kernel of his European vision. In his most famous book, *Paneuropa*, Coudenhove-Kalergi recognized that "the world is getting smaller every day: progress in transportation technologies brings cities and countries closer and closer together."[20] He did not let this seemingly banal statement stand on its own, however, even though it was an argument widely shared by his contemporaries.[21] He used it as an opening position from which to develop his conviction that the modernization process as such should not end at this point. Rather, it had to move on to the sphere of politics: "If the political technology does not adapt to

the transportation technology, the tension between the two will lead to terrible cata-
strophes. A political convergence must result from the temporal-spatial convergence
of neighboring countries if clashes are to be avoided."[22] Modernity was thus essential
for the European idea and was also thought to be a decisive element in bringing about
the advent of its realization. Following this line of thought, he regarded European
unity as historically inevitable on the grounds that the structural changes in the economy and society that were beginning to appear made adherence to nation-state sovereignty seem anachronistic.

Ethics and Technology as the Foundation of a European (Post-)Modernity

Coudenhove-Kalergi accepted the notion of the decline of Occidental culture. He
shared the widespread contemporary pessimism of the Wilhelmine generation and
adhered to a set of assumptions common to cultural critics and the "Conservative
Revolutionaries." Nevertheless, his conclusions differed from those of the latter.[23] He
rejected, for example, the restrictive notion of national community (*Volksgemeinschaft*)
advocated by the Conservative Revolutionaries, although the nation remained the
nucleus in his political understanding, as it did for his concept of a common Europe.
Yet he shared their faith in authoritarian leadership over parliamentary politics.

Coudenhove-Kalergi was thus filled with a quasi-religious conviction that
Europe could still rescue itself by uniting. He presented a way out of the perceived
decline of the European civilization, presuming that an age of reason—expressed
through a combination of ethics and technology—was dawning and elaborated a
long-term model through which a terminus of human history, a post-technical or postmodern society, might be reached.

To achieve what he termed "the second paradise," Coudenhove-Kalergi postulated a reformation of society via the revolutionary character of technology, which
would change the outside of society, the things, while the ethical reformation would
transform the inside, the people. At the end of this evolution would emerge "a community of wealth and saints."[24] His argument here is neither original nor very well
elaborated. But what makes it so interesting is that it echoes a whole range of contemporary interpretations of the state of society while, at the same time, proposing a
quite distinctive plan for solving contemporary problems.

Pondering the alternatives that confronted Europe, Coudenhove-Kalergi tried
to identify the main points of criticism. What exactly were the "modern dilemmas"?
How could the modern European escape from his disastrous living conditions? In
Coudenhove-Kalergi's words: "The modern average European is no longer a natural creature—nor is he yet a cultural being; no longer an animal—but not yet a
human being."[25]

Coudenhove-Kalergi identified a number of problems characteristic of the modern age. One of the most obvious was the problem of overpopulation, resulting in the

appalling living conditions of what he understood as the masses. The great majority of the population were controlled by a ruling "*Zwangsstaat*" (authoritarian state) and had to work under conditions of "*Zwangsarbeit*" (forced labor). According to Coudenhove-Kalergi, the ultimate goal of a society, however, was to reach a state of anarchy and leisure, which were the utmost expressions of a free and self-fulfilling individual. Yet the high road—which he regarded as a means as well as an end—leading to this state of social bliss in which certainty and stability reigned, had to pass through precisely this stage of slavery: "The way to ethical anarchy is reached after a period of totalitarian state organization—the way to technical leisure is reached after a period of forced labor."[26]

He described this evolution as a "turn of the cultural spiral" (*Kurve der Kultur-spirale*), which would lead from a past paradise to a future one. He thus developed a very schematic philosophy of history, which was deeply indebted to the tradition of German dialectics and seemed to be drawing on contemporary models of social evolution. His idea is strikingly close to Walther Rathenau's sketch of a path toward the future. As Hartmut Pogge von Strandmann has pointed out, Rathenau "saw industrial domination as a transitory phase to achieve a greater 'spiritualized' period in human history. Industrial growth was not to be seen as an end in itself, but the material basis for something like a 'spiritual elevation.'"[27]

In Coudenhove-Kalergi's philosophy of history, however, it was clear that what he called natural anarchy would lead to overpopulation. This, in turn, would result in a totalitarian state. This totalitarian state would again bring about the development of ethics, which would finally take history and mankind to its final stage, the stage of cultural anarchy. At the same time, there would be a parallel development in Europe. Natural leisure would lead to a migration toward northern parts of Europe, which would result in a situation of forced labor. The critical conditions of forced labor themselves would further the inauguration of a technical world to solve social misery, in particular, unemployment, and provide immediate necessities, finally liberating the masses by facilitating their lives to such a degree that a state of permanent cultural leisure would be reached.[28] This implied that, at the final stage, both the state and labor would have to dissolve themselves, the first by strongly supporting ethics and the latter by an implementation of technology.

Coudenhove-Kalergi's understanding of ethics was outlined in 1922, in his book *Ethik und Hyperethik*. For him, ethics were the foundation of every functioning society and it had to be possible for everybody to lead an ethical life. To provide this to each individual inhabitant of a society was one of the major tasks. Through virtuous, or decent behavior, sinful, or indecent behavior could be diminished. Human beings had to follow their ethical instincts to combat their equally naturally given indecent instincts.[29]

In a further step of reasoning, Coudenhove-Kalergi added an aesthetic level to his moral definition of ethics. In order to reach what he called "hyper-ethics," the notion of beauty had to be added to the principle of human action. Only then would human beings be able to reach a higher ethical status, a "hyper-ethical" quality.

Decency and a beauty of will, of action, of feeling, thinking and of personality would
generate a new human aesthetics. The final goals of hyper-ethics were: a harmonious
way of life, a development of life, and a development of personality,[30] while the major
virtues connected to hyper-ethics were greatness, strength, harmony, and most of all,
freedom. After a process of refinement, a perfect individual would arise. Coudenhove-Kalergi claimed that: "Personality is the greatest natural phenomenon and at the
same time the greatest work of art."[31]

He continued his reflection on ethics by transposing his deductions on the human
condition to the political sphere. He believed that hyper-ethical political ideals would
be: power, honor, truth, order, victory, glory, equality, renewal of the world as well as
freedom, and he did not hesitate to put Garibaldi and Lenin on an equal footing,
casting them as examples of hyper-ethical politicians who were convinced of what they
were doing and believed that they were bringing exactly the above-mentioned virtues
to their people.[32]

Coudenhove-Kalergi thus established freedom as the kernel of his ethical as well
as political world view. Freedom was the only ground on which personality could truly
blossom, leading to a refined individuality. However, he was aware of the problem
that "today freedom is practically a prerogative of the propertied class alone." Only
the rich were able to indulge in leisure, which again was the precondition for the
development of personality and the temporal correlate of freedom. From these
premises, Coudenhove-Kalergi deduced that one of the most pressing tasks of contemporary politics would be to provide leisure to everybody, to thus reduce the work-
load and, consequently, establish an ethical life for mankind. Only technology would
be able to do this.[33] He concluded: "Only when work and the state have been rendered superfluous by technology and ethics will humanity be able to achieve true freedom; only then will the possibilities of personal development cease to be confined to
a small number of privileged people, as they are today. To prepare and accelerate this
transformation is the most important task of society."[34]

Hyper-ethics would also unite the notions, or, for him, conditions, of civilization
and culture. Ethics were striving for civilization, hyper-ethics were striving for culture.
He concluded: "Civilization and culture are not mutually antagonistic, but reinforce
one another in the same way as education and cultivation [*Bildung*]; civilization
wants a tame humanity in a well organized state; culture wants a beautiful humanity
in a beautiful state."[35] The establishment of a hyper-ethical state following the ideals
of beauty and good moral attitudes[36] would enable true freedom of personality in a
quasisocialist framework. Coudenhove-Kalergi believed in the possibility of establishing such a society since he was convinced that all human beings were either consciously or unconsciously "hyper-ethical."[37]

Europe, itself, however, was not capable of generating a stimulus for a hyper-ethical development anymore. Rather, the ethical renewal itself would arrive from Asia,
from the experience of a vital and alien culture. Here, too, Coudenhove-Kalergi placed
himself in the tradition of Enlightenment self-criticism of European morals, contrasting the perceived decline and degeneration of European virtues and its rotten society

with the idealized fully functioning societies of the "Orient."[38] However, it was through the development of science and technology that Europe could again claim its superiority over other cultures: "[I]t was through technology that Europe would become master and leader of the world."[39]

At the same time, Coudenhove-Kalergi compared the two dominant ideologies of the time, communism and capitalism—which he believed to be engaged in a clash of cultures—only to dismiss both as inadequate tools for resolving Europe's immediate and pressing social problems.[40] The capitalist economy had failed the moment it had lost its moral core, the moment it was only installed for the egoism of individuals, when the support of the common good was asked for and needed desperately. Hence, instead of relieving modern society, which capitalism could potentially achieve, it had led to a growth of unemployment by displacing enormous amounts of technological and human resources, which could have been used more productively for the common good. As Coudenhove-Kalergi noted: "Capitalism will not fail due to its technical defects, but due to its ethical ones."[41] In his view: "[N]aked capitalism is doomed to die just as naked absolutism was doomed one hundred years ago. Civilized people can no longer tolerate that a minority owns almost everything and a majority almost nothing."[42]

In his general analysis, Coudenhove-Kalergi resembled the advocates of the so-called technocratic movement of the first half of the twentieth century. The reference to putatively neutral and objective solutions for the crisis of modern society was part of an international trend "between Taylorism and technocracy".[43] It was the common conviction among technocratic thinkers that professional politicians could not lead the world out of crisis and into a golden age; on the contrary, conventional politics would lead to a constant cultural and social decline. The contemporary political world was seen by the technocrats as simply not capable of facing the tasks of modernity—destroying instead of building, drawing borders instead of integrating countries. Instead, the dawning technological age had to be guided by a ruling elite, which Coudenhove-Kalergi called the new aristocracy. This idea of an international union of the best was in fact shared by many of his contemporaries. The intellectual and writer Fritz von Unruh, for example, wrote encouragingly to Coudenhove-Kalergi: "I also believe that it would not be too late, if not only economists, but particularly the spiritual minds of all countries, were to unite in order to put an end to the deeds of the incompetent people who are spreading a politics of fear throughout Europe."[44]

European integration could thus be seen as an idea to overcome short-term political and economic problems by proposing a federal organization and a customs union.[45] This seems a familiar enough program to us today. But there was also a startlingly imperialist dimension to Coudenhove-Kalergi's thought. For the advent of Pan-Europe, the European colonies on the African continent were needed as well. Africa was the space that would be given to the Europeans to resolve problems of overpopulation and dwindling natural resources.

Yet, a guiding, and for him essential, aim was the safeguarding of peace. How could an eternal peace be achieved and guaranteed? For him, fundamental elements of the international political setup had to be changed or redefined. Europe had to overcome petty nationalism. His belief in a latent though dormant "European national consciousness" constituted the core of his concept of Europe, and his understanding of national consciousness and nation building combined the models of the cultural nation and the nation-state. In his view, neither a common language nor an integrated idea of the state was sufficient to build a nation. Even a clearly defined geographical demarcation would not inevitably lead to the creation of a nation, nor would a putative community of blood. His experience of close ties between all European cultures led him to the conclusion that a European consciousness did exist. Transcending all the frontiers and all the differences in language and political constitution, the Continent was united by common historical experiences, which were tied together in the collective unconsciousness of all Europeans. Coudenhove-Kalergi made Europe, not the nation, the constituent sociocultural entity.

His reasoning was straightforward. Nations were always prone to wage war among themselves, and this was the fundamental reason for overcoming nationalism. After all, war was no longer a means of solving disputes; World War I had provided enough evidence for this. Now nations had to cooperate, integrate, and amalgamate. At the same time, the act of warfare had changed to such a degree that humans were becoming merely parts, mere soft tissue, of a rationalized machine built for destruction. Wars—this was clear to Coudenhove-Kalergi—could no longer constitute steps or caesuras in human history. Rather, human progress symbolized by eternal peace was to be achieved through technical inventions. The inventor, not the general, would be the new avant-garde hero of progress.[46]

Coudenhove-Kalergi thus returned to his central idea of technology as the kernel of social and human progress. Once the problems sketched out above were solved, the "second paradise" would be reached. Coudenhove-Kalergi called his Pan-European state of the future a second paradise because he assumed that humans had started from a pre-technical paradise in the first place, in a time when they still belonged to nature. In the second, post-technical paradise, human beings would reconstitute their natural qualities through the application of ethics and technology, and the machine itself would prepare a new idealism.[47]

Coudenhove-Kalergi used the image of purification to illustrate this coming paradise. Dirty and pestiferous cities would be clean and hygienic; rich and poor people would all have access to the new technology and share in a new cleanliness, health and joy of life. The second paradise would mean nothing less than the return to nature on a higher level. "With technical help, the whole globe will be changed into a garden of Eden: with canals and streets,... hygiene and engineering, central heating and central cooling ... men, women, and children will find the leisure to play, to fight, to dream, to think, and to create. The metropolis will disintegrate, and a garden city will arise in its place."[48]

Coudenhove-Kalergi believed that two influential European thinkers supported his case: Karl Marx and Friedrich Nietzsche. He regarded Marx as the prophet of the future state and Nietzsche as the prophet of the future human being.[49] The future state and the future human being would finally end the condition of revolution in which Europe and the world had lived ever since the Renaissance. They would also realize the ultimate goal of this world revolution: freedom. Indeed, Coudenhove-Kalergi envisaged the future of freedom as a freedom that was at last complete. It was complete because it was no longer an ambiguous category, as expressed in modernity, but a clear and certain liberty that no longer gave rise to uncertainties, doubts, or existential fear. Under the leadership of Europe, humanity would reach this new level of existence, this new level of freedom—a freedom without ideologies, without despotic constitutions and laws, without the constant pressure and threat of the forces of nature, without misery, forced labor, or slavery. But to reach this second paradise and to sustain it, technology had to play a vital part. Indeed, in achieving this new freedom, technology would find its meaning.[50]

Conclusions

Coudenhove-Kalergi's Pan-Europe clearly belonged to the category of envisioned societies that aimed at replacing the conflict-ridden systems of governance and social organization of the post- World War I period. Like socialism, communism, and fascism, Pan-Europeanism was a proposal for an ideal society. It was a model that offered a way out of the crisis of modernity, a way toward ethical certainties, lasting peace, and true individual freedom. Coudenhove-Kalergi's vision of a united Europe was thus part of a discourse within modernity, one that tried to unravel the dilemmas and find a way out of the perceived stagnation and decline of the postwar era. He designed a plan for a postmodern society, not as we think of postmodernity today, but in the sense that it would leave behind the disconcerting volatile conditions of modernity and instill new self-confidence and verities into the lives of Europeans.

How far, then, can Coudenhove-Kalergi's sociophilosophical model be aligned with the Wilhelmine period? The answer is that it can be aligned quite closely indeed. Together with truly liberal thinkers and actors such as Walther Rathenau, Coudenhove-Kalergi was deeply wary of the foundations of the existing social order. He did not believe in the inherent good of capitalism, nor in parliamentary politics nor in democracy as such. Capitalism had developed into a system for satisfying the egoism of the few while exploiting the masses; parliamentary politics was blocking the necessary reforms of society and at the same time mutating into an oligarchic system; and democracy was a system he simply did not believe in since it bore the seeds of tyranny.[51] Furthermore, Coudenhove-Kalergi shared with many Wilhelminians the conviction that the present they were living in could be nothing but a transitory period of social development. Modernity as such was perceived as a challenging phase of a change in paradigms, and it would be easier to bring about the coming technological age of leisure and freedom through more authoritarian structures of governance. It was not the lack of democracy, the seeming backwardness of German political conditions, that was defined as the obstacle, but rather the unfinished industrial and technological conversion of society.

Coudenhove-Kalergi also appears as an authentically "modern man" because his thoughts and theories are full of inherent contradictions. Whereas he proclaimed his concerns for the good of the masses, he proposed an aristocratic model of governance; whereas he attacked capitalism for its lack of morals, he accepted financial support from members of the economic elite. As Klaus Mann, a fervent supporter of Coudenhove-Kalergi in the 1920s, wrote in his memoirs, the Pan-European movement needed to make clear whom it was representing: "At the beginning, the Pan-European movement—despite certain flaws and uncertainties—found much support among the intellectual youth. It was only later, when bankers, cardinals, and industrialists made the Count their patron, that his liberal friends began to grow suspicious and slowly to withdraw from him. What was he aiming at? At a united continent or a crusade against Russia? Soon we could not rebuff this question anymore. Did we want a Pan-Europe under the rule of the Vatican, Monsieur Schneider-Creusot, and the IG-Farben?"[52]

Thus, although occasionally farsighted, Coudenhove-Kalergi did not provide original or practicable solutions for the supposed cul-de-sac of modernity. His publications as well as his model of a technological, anti-parliamentarian, and (in fact) nonpolitical society were, however, representative of his time and of the ideological crises of the interwar period.

However, in the end, an authoritarian system of governance based on a "new aristocracy of the mind," technology, rationalization, and ethics could not replace politics. As Thomas Mann came to see, political neutrality was doomed to turn into political vice: "Political neutrality is a scary thing; it does not remain a neutrality for long. Soon it no longer stands for nothing, but simply for the bad."[53] Coudenhove-Kalergi was a prominent representative of these discursive reactions to crisis and a social philosopher deeply connected to the Wilhelmine legacy, which was more complex and diverse than has traditionally been argued.

Coudenhove-Kalergi's ideas may not have achieved much success, but one should not be too dismissive of his efforts to take Europe beyond the crisis of modernity. Rather, he should be appreciated as one of those thinkers who criticized the post-war order without falling prey to National Socialism or communism. In the way he combined cultural pessimism about the recent past and present with technocratic optimism toward the future, he was as much a product of the Wilhelmine age as Walther Rathenau himself.

Notes

1. Motto of Richard N. Coudenhove-Kalergi's book *Apologie der Technik* (Leipzig, 1922). For comments on a draft of this chapter, I would like to thank Sandra Mass, Lubor Jilek, Prof. Niall Ferguson, and in particular Hagen Schulz-Forberg.

2. See Richard N. Coudenhove-Kalergi, *Ein Leben für Europa. Meine Lebenserinnerungen* (Cologne and Berlin, 1966), 82-104.

3. The idea of running a united Europe like a multinational company was shared by the German publisher Hermann Ullstein. Ullstein wrote to Coudenhove-Kalergi on 25 September 1932: "[S]hould the 'company' Europe join forces, it would last until eternity. As a continent, it would be economically as well as politically a great power, just like the British Empire and the United States of America are." Herman Ullstein to Richard Coudenhove-Kalergi, 25 September 1932, Berlin. Centr chranenja istoricesko-dokumental'nych kolekcij Moskva [Center for Conservation of Historical-Documentary Sources Moscow] CChIDK, record 554, inventory 4, file 164, folio 409-411, here 410b.

4. See Walther Rathenau's speech at the assembly of the Reichsverband der deutschen Industrie in Munich, 28 September 1921, cited in Hartmut Pogge von Strandmann, ed., *Walther Rathenau, Industrialist, Banker, Intellectual and Politician: Notes and Diaries, 1907-1922* (Oxford, 1985), 1.

5. Coudenhove-Kalergi had, in fact, thought of inviting Walther Rathenau to become the leader of the Pan-European movement. Yet he believed him as a German to be unacceptable to the Allies, and as a Jew to be unacceptable to the Germans. Richard N. Coudenhove-Kalergi, *Crusade for Pan-Europe. Autobiography of a Man and a Movement* (New York 1943), 71.

6. The numbers are from the beginning of 1927. See the report of the General Secretariat of the German section, in *Fondation Archives Européennes* (FAE), "Paneuropa Deutschland". The German section was founded on 1 July 1925 in Berlin, having as members, among others, Paul Loebe, president of the Reichstag; Georg Bernhard, director of the liberal *Vossische Zeitung*; Erich Koch-Weser, member of the German Democratic Party; the industrialist Robert Bosch; and the journalist Samuel Sänger, who wrote for the *Neue Rundschau*, a newspaper that supported Gustav Stresemann's politics. Other sections were opened in a dozen German cities. See "Statut der Paneuropäischen Union Deutschland," 31 July 1925, in FAE, "*Paneuropa Deutschland*".

7. For an insightful analysis of the different pro-European associations between the world wars, see Oliver Burgard, *Das gemeinsame Europa – von der politischen Utopie zum außenpolitischen Programm. Meinungsaustausch und Zusammenarbeit pro-europäischer Verbände in Deutschland und Frankreich, 1924-1933* (Frankfurt a.M., 2000).

8. The idea of a Central European Customs Union to foster German leadership in Europe was also propagated by Walther Rathenau. He legitimized Germany's call for hegemony by its industrial power. See Pogge von Strandmann, *Rathenau*, 163, and Wolfgang Michalka, "'Mitteleuropa geeinigt unter deutscher Führung'. Europäische Wirtschaftsgemeinschaft als Friedens- und Kriegsziel," in *Die Extreme berühren sich. Walther Rathenau 1867-1922*, ed. Hans Wilderotter (Berlin), 179-88. For the reception of Naumann's *Mitteleuropa* concept, see Henry Cord Meyer, *Mitteleuropa in German Thought and Action 1815-1945* (The Hague, 1955), 194-217, and Peter Stirk, ed., *Mitteleuropa: History and Prospects* (Edinburgh, 1994), 1-35.

9. See, for example, Peter Stirk, *A History of European Integration since 1914* (London, 1996), 18-50.

10. Richard N. Coudenhove-Kalergi, *Paneuropa*, 2nd edition (Vienna and Leipzig, 1926), 5.

11. For a detailed analysis of the journal *Paneuropa* in the 1930s, see Ina Ulrike Paul, "Die *Paneuropa* 1933-38 und Coudenhove-Kalergi: Ein 'getreues Spiegelbild seines Denkens und Wollens und Wirkens,'" in *Der Europadiskurs in den deutschen Zeitschriften (1933-1939)*, ed. Michel Grunewald and Hans Manfred Bock (Bern, 1999), 161-93.

12. See Coudenhove-Kalergi, *Paneuropa*, introduction.

13. Ibid., 32.

14. Ibid., 34.

15. Peter Wagner, *A Sociology of Modernity, Liberty and Discipline* (London and New York, 1994), 4.

16. For the acceleration of time, see, for example, Reinhart Koselleck et al., *Das Zeitalter der europäischen Revolution 1780-1848* (Frankfurt a.M., 1963), 303-6.

17. For the nexus of modernity, the metropolis, and relations between subjective perceptions and discursive narratives, see Hagen Schulz-Forberg, *London-Berlin: Authenticity, Modernity and the Metropolis in Urban Travel Writing, 1851-1939* (forthcoming 2003).

18. See Wagner, *Sociology*.

19. Alan S. Steinweis, "Conservatism, National Socialism, and the Cultural Crisis of the Weimar Republic," in *Between Reform, Reaction, and Resistance: Studies in the History of German Conservatism from 1789 to 1945*, ed. Larry Eugene Jones and James Retallack (Providence and Oxford, 1993), 329-46, here 329.

20. Coudenhove-Kalergi, *Paneuropa*, 16.

21. The German industrialist Edmund Stinnes, for example, wrote to Coudenhove-Kalergi on 8 May 1925: "The inconceivable technical progress of the last century has shrunk the world. Then, it was a pressing task to unite Potsdam with Magdeburg, which were only connected by an hours-long ride with the postal service, whereas today Berlin and Paris are connected by a few hours of flight." Edmund Stinnes to Richard Coudenhove-Kalergi, 8 May 1925. CChIDK, 554/4/296, ff. 32-40, here 37.

22. Coudenhove-Kalergi, *Paneuropa*, 17.

23. To associate Coudenhove-Kalergi in general with the "Conservative Revolutionaries," as some historians have done, is to oversimplify the question of his political affiliations, which were more ambiguous than it appears at first sight, as illustrated by his rejection of the Conservative Revolutionaries' negative ideals, such as anti-liberalism and anti-Semitism, as well as his distaste for the National Socialists.

24. Coudenhove-Kalergi, *Apologie der Technik*, 10-14.

25. Ibid., 13-14.

26. Ibid., 13.

27. Pogge von Strandmann, *Rathenau*, 16.

28. Coudenhove-Kalergi, *Apologie der Technik*, 13: "Naturanarchie – Überbevölkerung – Zwangsstaat – Ethik – Kulturanarchie; Naturmusse – Nordwanderung – Zwangsarbeit – Technik – Kulturmusse."

29. Richard N. Coudenhove-Kalergi, *Ethik und Hyperethik* (Leipzig, 1922), 3. Coudenhove-Kalergi defined the major virtues on which ethical behavior was based as belonging to four groups of ethics: Social Ethics (sympathy, community spirit, and justice); Individual Ethics (prudence and loyalty); Tribal Ethics (chastity and respect); Universal Ethics (truthfulness and humility). From these cardinal virtues all decency originated. (3 ff.) Coudenhove-Kalergi's philosophical publications were taken seiously by Pan-Europeans, especially by those supporters of which Coudenhove-Kalergi thought highly. *Ethik und Hyperethik* was sent, for example, to Max Warburg, one of his earliest supporters and with whom he was engaged in a constant intellectual dialogue. Warburg sent his notes to Vienna on 11 March 1925, when he had finally managed to read the book. In a very detailed discussion of Coudenhove-Kalergi's concepts, Warburg hinted at certain problems in the terms used. For example, he pointed out that Coudenhove-Kalergi misused the word humility, and that he would rather prefer the term reverence. See Max Warburg to Coudenhove-Kalergi. CChIDK, 554/4/74, ff. 338-41.

     Another intellectual partner of Coudenhove-Kalergi already in the early years was the writer Rudolf Pannwitz. Concerning *Ethik und Hyperethik*, for example, Pannwitz wanted Coudenhove-Kalergi to give more credit to Friedrich Nietzsche, whom he regarded as the obvious influence on Coudenhove-Kalergi's thinking. Despite his criticism in detail, Pannwitz was enthusiastic about Coudenhove-Kalergi's book and made this clear by writing on 30 April 1922: "I hope you understand from my letter that you do not feel different from myself, that we are striving for similar if not the same ideals and are fighting the same fight." Rudolf Pannwitz to Coudenhove-Kalergi, 23 January 1922. FAE, 'Union Paneuropéene,' dossier Rudolf Pannwitz; and letter from 30 April 1922, FAE, 'Union Paneuropéene,' dossier Rudolf Pannwitz.

30. Coudenhove-Kalergi, *Ethik und Huperethik*, 108 ff.
31. Coudenhove-Kalergi, *Ethik und Huperethik*, 118.
32. Coudenhove-Kalergi, *Ethik und Huperethik*, 149.
33. Coudenhove-Kalergi, *Ethik und Huperethik*, 152.
34. Coudenhove-Kalergi, *Ethik und Huperethik*, 153.
35. Coudenhove-Kalergi, *Ethik und Huperethik*, 155.
36. Coudenhove-Kalergi did not refer to Victorian values here. In fact, he was quite explicit that when he wrote on chastity and moral behavior he was not condemning sexuality. He believed that the erotic attraction of a human being would be equal to his or her biological value. (*Ethik und Huperethik*, 123)
37. Coudenhove-Kalergi, *Ethik und Huperethik*, 156.
38. A famous example is Charles de Montesquieu, who in his *Lettres Persanes* (1721) compared European absolutism with the Orient, although not to the advantage of Europe. Following this line of thought, Jean-Jacques Rousseau had also contrasted the "noble savage" with the decadent European, indicating that the goal of humanity was not to be found in the Parisian cafés of the Palais Royal but in the lands of exotic natives (*Discours sur l'origine de l'inégalité parmi les hommes*, 1755). See also Katiana Orluc, "Decline or Renaissance: The Transformation of European Consciousness after the First World War," in *Europe and the Other and Europe as the Other*, ed. Bo Stråth (Brussels, 2000), 123-55.
39. Coudenhove-Kalergi, *Apologie der Technik*, 23.
40. Richard N. Coudenhove-Kalergi, *Revolution durch Technik* (Vienna and Leipzig, 1932), 83-85, claimed that capitalism and communism, which he understood as state capitalism, were representatives of the "state based on work" that were two opposite forms of the same historical phase. For him, it was obvious that technology should be implemented to realize the final stage of historical state development, which was the "state based on culture."
41. Coudenhove-Kalergi, *Apologie der Technik*, 54.
42. Coudenhove-Kalergi, *Revolution durch Technik*, 89.
43. See Dirk van Laak, "Imperiale Infrastruktur. Deutsche Planungen für eine Erschließung Afrikas, 1880-1960" (Ph.D. diss., University of Jena, 2001), 227-307, here 278; and Charles S. Maier, "Zwischen Taylorismus und Technokratie. Gesellschaftspolitik im Zeichen industrieller Rationalität in den zwanziger Jahren in Europa," in *Die Weimarer Republik. Belagerte Civitas*, ed. Michael Stürmer (Königstein/Ts., 1980), 188-213. In fact, Coudenhove-Kalergi's *Apologie der Technik* belonged to the classics of the technocratic literature. See Stefan Willeke, *Die Technokratiebewegung in Nordamerika und Deutschland zwischen den Weltkriegen. Eine vergleichende Analyse* (Brussels, 1995), 171-72.
44. Fritz von Unruh to Richard Coudenhove-Kalergi, 6 February 1932, Frankfurt a.M. CChIDK, 554/4/92, f. 341.
45. Many of his followers shared his belief in the necessity of a European customs union. Economically active Paneuropeans especially put much weight on this point. See, for example, Carl F. von Siemens, commenting on the necessary propagandistic work to be done, who wrote to Coudenhove-Kalergi on 26 June 1928: "The problem of an elimination of all inner-European custom's borders had already fascinated my father.... Europe can only survive against the economical advances of America when we reach a European agreement.... That is why I believe the next immediate task should be to convince the governments of the impossibility of developing all branches of industry in all countries without taking heed of economic preconditions." Carl F. von Siemens to Richard Coudenhove-Kalergi, 26 June 1928, Berlin. CChIDK, 554/4/345, ff. 78-79.
46. Coudenhove-Kalergi, *Revolution durch Technik*, 36.
47. Ibid., 90-101.
48. Ibid., 101. In one of the more elaborate critical letters reaching Coudenhove-Kalergi after the publication of *Revolution durch Technik* in 1932, Heinrich Döll from Berlin wrote on 7 May 1933 that even though he shared Coudenhove-Kalergi's general belief in technology, he would be wary of relying too much on it, if Coudenhove-Kalergi wanted to protect it from turning into a mere superstition. CChIDK, 554/4/99, ff. 36-40, here 38.

49. Coudenhove-Kalergi, *Revolution durch Technik*, 98.

50. Ibid., 90.

51. In his envisaged European state, Coudenhove-Kalergi intended to even out the defects of universal suffrage, which he feared might lead to a regime of "demagogues, capitalists, and seducers," by the introduction of a two-chamber system in politics—a combination of a ruling house of the elite—a "social aristocracy of the mind"—with an elected second chamber. See Richard N. Coudenhove-Kalergi, "Die Zukunft des Neo-Aristokratischen Prinzips," in idem, *Krise der Weltanschauung* (Vienna, 1923), 74-75.

52. Klaus Mann, *Der Wendepunkt* (Munich, 1976, orig. 1942), 239.

53. Thomas Mann to Richard Coudenhove-Kalergi, 24 February 1943. *Fondation Archives Européennes* (FAE), fonds AP 2 (RCK), *Correspondance générale.*

14

Ideas into Politics

Meanings of "Stasis" in Wilhelmine Germany

JAMES RETALLACK

Of all civilized peoples, the German submits most readily and permanently to the regime under which he lives.... His character combines understanding with phlegma: he neither indulges in subtilizations about the established order nor devises one himself. ... [I]n keeping with their penchant for order and rule, [the Germans] will rather submit to despotism than venture on innovations (especially unauthorized reforms in government). — *That is their good side.*

– Immanuel Kant[1]

Introduction

Whole books could be filled citing Germans who felt that every dimension of their personal, communal, and political existence was in flux between 1890 and 1914. There is hardly another period in which German society, culture, and politics were allegedly more "turbulent," "tumultuous," or "disorienting." Historians concur that Germany in these years was also undergoing its definitive "transition to modernity." Nevertheless, debates about the nature of these changes continue to exercise scholars, as do disagreements about their magnitude and trajectory.[2] Hence there exists an opportunity to take stock of competing viewpoints and to consider whether the *Kaiserreich* was fundamentally transformed by 1918 or whether it remained a recognizably close approximation of the Empire founded in 1871.

Commonly, this problem has been approached as one of political dis/continuity: What lines of development do or do not extend across the divides of 1864–71, 1888–90, and 1918–23? In what follows, however, the focus is shifted slightly: away from the search for epochal thresholds, watersheds, and turning points;[3] away from

---

analyses of the "rise" or "decline" of Germany's Great Power status;[4] away from per-
sonalistic appraisals of distinctions between the Bismarckian and Wilhelmine eras;[5]
away from attempts to explain why life in the Empire was not so brutish or boring after
all;[6] away from questions about the regional diversity of the Empire (not because such
questions are uninteresting but because they have attracted growing attention elsewhere);[7] and *toward* the question of why the *Kaiserreich*'s basic political institutions
remained consonant with so many of its citizens' desires and expectations until the very
last weeks of its existence. Thus, this chapter will explore selected aspects of political
life in the Empire that were deemed by contemporaries to be closely enough aligned
to their own interests and ideals that they deserved to be defended (or at least not challenged openly). In this way I hope to grapple with the multiple meanings and varied
consequences of both "reform" and "stasis" in Imperial Germany.

How should we set about appraising contemporaries' alleged preference for
political "stasis"? Recent studies that examine centennial or millennial turning points
as representative of a distinctive *Zeitgeist* illustrate that an interdisciplinary approach
is the ideal toward which we should strive.[8] Only by taking stock of Germany's economic, social, and cultural development in these years can we hope to explore whether
Wilhelmine political culture can best be described in terms of its edginess or its immobility. Notwithstanding the impossibility of ranging across so many spheres of
endeavor in a single essay, it is arguably in the political sphere that historians of the
Kaiserreich can profit most directly from a new appraisal of the "blockages" to modernity that remained in place up to 1918. One strategy for beginning such a reappraisal
was offered in the introduction to this volume; a rather different one is presented here.
Indeed, this chapter is conceived as a think piece, in which I consciously play devil's
advocate by trying to set up a counter-argument to other essays in the volume.

In asking why so many aspects of Germany's political institutions and processes
did *not* fundamentally change during the Wilhelmine age—this is the thesis that I
defend in the first two-thirds of this chapter—it is patently unwise to proceed by cutting selected examples of political change from their historical context and fixing them
to the static conceptual backdrop encapsulated in the phrase "life goes on." To
address crises and continuities together, we must concern ourselves not only with aims
and ambitions, but also with underlying values; not only with strivings and successes,
but also with lingering regrets. This approach seems particularly useful when dealing with an age in which new motifs of liberation became tied to actual embodiments
of vitality. Hence, I build my historical analysis upon the twin observations that the
quest for emancipation often falls short of the act of rebellion, and that bodies gradually become less vital with the passage of time. Such analysis involves taking the
pulse of the German body politic in subjective as well as objective ways. Thus, we
want to determine why Wilhelminians did not *feel* compelled to rebel against their
government before 1918.

On the other hand, in this chapter's penultimate section—titled "Nemesis"—I
suggest that exploring elements of stasis and reform together in the post-1900 period
does in fact reveal compelling transitions to modernity. Precisely because preceding

acts of restraint were so successful, precisely because persistent political blockages had created a backlog of reforms too massive—too *embarrassing*—for "modern" Germans to ignore, stasis itself fueled and facilitated new ways of bringing "ideas into politics." It nevertheless bears emphasizing that, for the structure of my larger argument, the idea of nemesis does not make sense without its antecedent. Only once the dynamic, dialectical relationship between stasis and reform is established can we understand why contemporaries after 1900 came to accept certain means of crisis management (qua system stabilization) that they had previously considered unthinkable or unacceptable. Only then can we begin to determine why the solutions proposed to problems of political deadlock after 1909 were so radical. And only then can we discover a new meaning of reform in Wilhelmine Germany, namely, reform as a reluctant response to stasis rather than a ringing endorsement of change.

Economy, Society, Culture

We are told that Germans could not have been unaware of the accelerating pace of economic change in the Wilhelmine era. For example, the growth of giant cartels in German big business is generally taken as one feature of the "full-throttle capitalist transformation between the 1890s and 1914."[9] But cartels are meant primarily to stabilize things, not encourage change willy-nilly. They make forward planning easier, simplify industrial relations, and insulate both individual enterprises and larger economic sectors from shocks to the economic system.[10] Cartels, in other words, freeze economic advantages that are already in place. Much the same could be said of other "corporatist" features of the economy and society. Klaus Tenfelde has recently argued that these social aspects did not differ as much as we suppose from those of an earlier age. "The concept of [social] 'estate' [*das Ständische*] continued to have a virulent but real effect—even an increased one, possibly, but at the very least one that decisively conditioned perceptions well beyond its time…. It may be too much to claim that milieus can be conceived as surrogates for [social] estates, but arguably there was a certain functional equivalency nonetheless."[11] Thomas Kühne and Gerhard A. Ritter have demonstrated that corporatism also infused German political thought—and Prussian political practice—much longer than we have believed.[12] The Nazis were not the first to recognize the political dividends to be reaped from freezing labor relations and the organization of key industries in corporatist modes or extolling, however hypocritically, the virtues of a stable *Mittelstand* of peasants, artisans, and small shopkeepers. Even the role of banks in the Wilhelmine era tended in the same direction. Long-term financing gave bankers a tangible motive to prefer stability and security over upheaval and risk, and the investment of huge amounts of capital inclined bankers to opt instinctively for steady growth and continuity: "By tying up their capital, they tied their own hands."[13]

In short, although the Wilhelmine era can rightly be seen as an age in which the distance between economic interests and politics diminished, we should not identify the "modern" aspects of this relationship unequivocally with a tendency toward economic experimentation or accelerating change. It may be true that government ministers and party leaders asked themselves every day whether stability was "best served by traditional, paternalist nostrums, or by more modern policies geared to the new kind of society that had emerged."[14] However, it is equally important to note that even contemporaries who opted for modern policies were seeking to ensure steady economic growth, social harmony, and political stability.

Joachim Radkau has reminded us that many things took a lot longer during Wilhelm's reign than in previous decades.[15] Of course, time was controlled in many new ways—had been controlled since the advent of the first industrial revolution; but that did not change the rhythm of the seasons one whit. The "kinetic energy" of German society was increasing; but psychosomatic suffering hobbled more and more Germans. Radkau explains that his grandfather could date precisely the arrival of his own personal pathology of nervousness: it occurred on the morning of 28 January 1901, after which he acquired—nerves. But like the knotted *Zeitgeist* itself, personal "nervousness" was not necessarily channeled into excitable aggressiveness. It might foster a reaction akin to that of the proverbial deer caught in the headlights. Or it might foster new faith in an old adage: "The good things in life come to those who wait."

University education took longer than ever before in German history. So did the making of a career, the decision to marry, the planning of children, the path to death. More time than ever was needed to wring decisions from an expanding bureaucracy and increasingly complex industrial management. Even the new kinds of fast food and refreshments available on Wilhelmine street corners required greater time (and effort) to digest. So did the task of recuperating from things unwisely ingested, for instance, by bringing the daily alcohol-coffee drinking cycle into balance.[16] The German lifestyle reform movement (*Lebensreformbewegung*) focused on exactly these kinds of novelties and targeted them for criticism and study. However, that very criticism fueled a new dialectic between the changing pace of life and the confused, pragmatic, stubborn efforts of contemporaries to understand and deal with it. Often, lifestyle reformers' lobbying efforts merely fed a bad conscience or led to closer self-inspection. As reported in the records of a rehabilitative center in Ahrweiler, a corpulent pastor spent half a day reclining on a sofa, thinking of nothing but passing his next stool.[17]

Cramping and constipation: Are these the proper subjects of political history? Could reduced motility of the intestines possibly be relevant to the fate of political reform in Wilhelmine Germany, even metaphorically? Does stasiphobia—the fear of standing upright—lie on the same axis as the tugging of German forelocks identified by Immanuel Kant in this chapter's epigraph, or of German democracy's alleged self-abasement long before the Nazis or the GDR's secret police appeared on the scene? Could bacteriostasis be related to Germans' desire to inhibit the growth of (without destroying) foreign elements in their body politic? Were Wilhelminians more anal-retentive than their Victorian counterparts?

Notwithstanding their quixotic boldness, such leaps between personal and political pathologies do not require as much analytical athleticism as one might suppose.

After all, other chapters in this volume document the efforts of Wilhelmine reformers to draw linkages among the "modern" problems of unhealthy lifestyles, dysfunctions of class society, and bottlenecks in governmentality. The larger point, though, is that contemporaries eventually started to make the same linkages: They moved away from the "sterile equilibrium" or the "static balance among opposing tendencies" that are listed among definitions of the word "stasis," toward a new condition in which impediments to "the normal flow of fluids in an organ" could be progressively removed. As this process unfolded in late Wilhelmine Germany, previously unimagined strategies to overcome political immobility were considered plausible for the first time. Quiescence and stagnation gave way to new (or renewed) creative activity. Even then, though, anxiety and self-reflection were not removed entirely from the equation. Radkau has written illuminatingly about this:

> Social counter-reactions and stress effects of the modernization process do not as a rule follow promptly but rather are delayed.... It is precisely the hindrances that contribute to the fact that particular features of modernization, as soon as the hindrance is removed, proceed in reverse and give rise to severe upheavals. That was apparently the case in the "age of nervousness." And more: between the process and the reaction it elicits, there frequently occurs not a calm equilibrium but a knotting-up, which itself produces new tensions.[18]

What, then, of culture? The best discussions of both high- and low-brow culture in the Wilhelmine era stress its "extraordinary richness," creative energy, and diversity. Nor do the fluidity and indeterminacy of Wilhelmine high culture often go unmentioned. One recent account, for example, posits a "general identification by most Germans with the ideas of newness, regeneration, and change"[19] in late Imperial Germany. But only at their peril do historians forget that most of Wilhelm's subjects retained their conservative artistic tastes or that pre-war Germany's avant-garde actually generated only a tiny following before the war. Thus, Peter Jelavich has reminded us that "movements" within Wilhelmine Germany's modern artistic scene developed "against the backdrop of, and often in direct hostility to, a persistent tradition of idealized realism in literature and academic painting."[20]

Against this backdrop we can test reactions to the attack on German *Kultur* allegedly unleashed by the Allies in August 1914. Was German vitriol generated because Wilhelm's subjects wanted to defend change? Or did most of them believe instead that German *Kultur* was threatened by the same "superficiality, caprice, and ephemera" that they had ascribed to the works of their own avant-garde before 1914? Friedrich Nietzsche had predicted many years earlier that the European response to German "effervescence" would be to pronounce it "invariably *evil*, wanting as it does to break through the old limits and subvert the old pieties." But arguably, Germans themselves—whom Nietzsche also labeled "procrastinators [*Verzögerer*] par excellence"[21]—were at least as bloody-minded as their enemies when they declared that the Germany of Goethe and Schiller (not Nolde or Wedekind) had to be preserved and enshrined for the sake of "honesty and sincerity."[22] In any case, the victories that Expressionists won in the half-decade before 1914 or that German academics won (so rhetorically) in the first months of the war cannot be said to have contributed decisively or unambiguously to overcoming political stasis. Arguably, they did the exact opposite. Wolfgang J. Mommsen has written that the independence of German artists and writers may have helped resist the instrumentalizing intentions of Germany's rulers and political parties; nevertheless, he adds, the tendency toward "purely theoretical negation" of the existing order—for example, *against* large cities and other aspects of modernity—"accelerated the emergence of largely nonpolitical subsystems within Wilhelmine society and thereby contributed indirectly to the weakening of reformist forces" in the Empire.[23] In making much the same point, Modris Eksteins has stressed the darker irony in this:[24] "The modern temper had been forged; the avant-garde had won. It tried to fight new battles, but these turned out to be the same old battles, or in fact no battles at all because the infamous bourgeoisie now often bowed with polite, if silent, respect. The 'adversary culture' had become the dominant culture, irony and anxiety the mode and the mood, hallucination and neurosis the state of mind."

Le plus ça change ...

The list of political institutions that retained their contours between 1871 and 1918 is familiar to most scholars.[25] First to be mentioned is the federal structure of the German Empire. The constitutional arrangement devised by Bismarck left to the individual federal states considerable autonomy in the realms of culture, education, policing, religion, schools, and health. While a centralizing Reich government made inroads in some of these areas, federalism itself blocked many political initiatives that might otherwise have contributed to significant constitutional reform. Second, and related to this point, is the overwhelming dominance of Prussia within the Empire. Quite apart from the unchanging demographic and geographical preponderance of Prussia—constituting roughly two-thirds of the Empire—the Prusso-German dualism that was readily apparent to constitutional scholars and politicians alike in 1871 had diminished hardly at all by 1918. For that very reason, reformist efforts to devise a "new order" (*neue Ordnung*) during the last years of the war were directed against this anomaly of German national life. The Prussian state parliament (*Landtag*) and the Prussian bureaucracy remained such bastions of conservative interests that the wheels of state in the Reich seemed to turn—or more often stop—at the command of Prussian civil servants and Conservative *Landtag* deputies. Much the same conclusion arises when we consider the Kaiser's continuing influence as supreme warlord (his *Kommandogewalt*), the survival of the aristocracy, and other aspects of the existing constitutional order.

While recent studies of Wilhelmine elections acknowledge that ministerial responsibility and the formation of national governments on the basis of parliamentary majorities were never within the realm of practical possibility in Imperial Germany, they point to the increasing importance of national elections based on the principle of "one man, one vote." Arguably, however, they still direct their gaze too infrequently toward elements of political stasis in the Empire. As just one among many possible examples, historians tend to note only in passing that constituency boundaries for Reichstag elections were never redrawn between 1871 and 1918. Not only the government but the majority parties themselves refused to endorse legislation that would have made reapportionment a reality, even after population shifts made a mockery of the original principle behind such geometry. Over time, the relatively underpopulated constituencies of the rural east continued to send Conservative landowners into parliament, whereas the refusal to consider reapportionment effectively devalued the votes of Socialist supporters in the huge urban constituencies. This apparently mundane aspect of constitutional stasis set parameters of far-reaching importance for larger political contests.

I have argued elsewhere that it is helpful to differentiate between two kinds of continuity discernible within Wilhelmine politics: continuity of political alignments and continuity of political styles. These elements of continuity should be considered as two sides of a single coin. There is no opportunity here to review either earlier, groundbreaking studies that focused on the national plane, or recent accounts that consider local and state-level politics as a means to address questions of national importance. The latter kind of study, nevertheless, has proved particularly important in reminding us that liberals as well as conservatives changed their voting habits, party alignments, and styles of campaigning much more slowly at the state level than in national politics. The ingrained rituals of Prussian *Landtag* voting, for example—in which up to a week might be required to complete the complicated two-stage voting procedure—found their analogy in the parties' unwillingness to break with the face-to-face style of campaigning, the preference for home-grown candidates, and the perpetuation of time-honored party blocs at the local and regional level. Recent studies of state *Landtage* and their associated political cultures in Württemberg and Saxony also illustrate that the new tempo of national politics was not uniformly reflected at the subnational levels.[26]

Nor have studies of Wilhelmine political culture undermined an interlocking group of three hypotheses, each of which points not to dramatic changes in the political culture of Wilhelmine Germany but to the resiliency and longevity of political alignments that arose during the Reich's first decade. The first of these theses points to the remarkable degree of continuity within German social-moral milieus, from the dawn of the Imperial era until the Nazis' electoral breakthrough after 1928. Second, historians and political scientists continue to work through the significance of four persistent cleavages within Wilhelmine political society: between the center and the periphery, between state and church, between the agrarian and industrial sectors, and between employers and employees. Third and lastly, the concept of camps (*Lager*) focuses on sentiments that seemed at least as permanent, and sometimes more so, as milieus and cleavages. For example, the gulf between the working classes and *bürgerlich* society was reflected in the enduring political division between the socialist and nationalist camps. Two points are worth emphasizing here. On the one hand, historians continue to disagree about the function of these camps and the degree of flux within them. Nonetheless, most analyses recognize that changes in the nature of Wilhelmine elections had the effect of asserting and confirming the divisions between these camps. On the other hand, a camp is defined as something more than a convenient or momentary coalition: it is built on powerful historical, cultural, and emotional foundations. By definition, only political continuity lends it historical significance. It is predicated, in a word, on stasis.

Ideas into Politics: Real Men, Skirted Decisions

On Thursday, 25 July 1912, the man who has been called Wilhelmine Germany's "grand master of capitalism" dined with Chancellor Theobald von Bethmann Hollweg at his country estate. Later, in his diary, Walther Rathenau described the course of the evening's discussion. He did so in a way that speaks volumes: about the two men in conversation, about Germany's foreign and domestic political situation at that juncture, and about how the most fundamental and far-reaching reformist ideas concerning Germany's future were—and were not—translated into practice by those who had the power to do so.

> Dined at Hohen-Finow.... Chancellor [Bethmann Hollweg] ... asked what I meant by what I had called political goals. He saw no such goals for Germany. Long discussion on this after dinner. I put forward: (1) Economy ... (2) Foreign Policy ... (3) Domestic. Reform of parliament. Prussian franchise. Reich constituencies. Proportion. These are all ways to a full parliamentary system.
> Bethmann in overall agreement; arguing against 3 (*a*) inferiority of the Reichstag, lack of political personalities. Reply: No one wants to enter a mere debating machine. (*b*) [He]: we have the most perfect self-government (municipal, country, provincial). Reply: Only as far as the kitchen, not as far as the drawing-room.
> I went on to explain. He could not very well dispute that change would come. Answer: No (!). Hence: either it would come as a result of unfortunate circumstances, or "heroically" amid sunshine, through a new Hardenberg. ...
> Bethmann urged me three times, the last time as he accompanied me to the car, to elaborate my ideas regarding electoral reform for him. *Each time I declined: he has better people for that among his staff.* [27]

This diary entry can be taken as evidence of the complexity with which Rathenau and other moderate liberals regarded the meanings of reform. Those meanings clearly included the limits of reform, enthusiasm for reform, fear of reform, love and hatred of reform, and—not least—satisfaction with particular but not inconsequential aspects of the political status quo. Rathenau's words substantiate Mark Hewitson's observation that although the relationship between the nation and politics in the *Kaiserreich* was invariably close, it was also "brittle, opaque, and frequently taboo."[28] When Rathenau remarked that Bethmann Hollweg had "better people ... among his staff" to undertake the drafting of reforms—reforms for which he had just spent a full evening serving as impassioned advocate—both the brittleness and the taboo-like qualities of reform come into focus. For Rathenau, it was one thing to counsel "a full parliamentary system" or other equally far-reaching departures from the political status quo. It was quite another thing to carry those proposals to fruition in practice.

At this point we should also pause and consider how our perspective shifts when we convert the unexciting passive voice used so often in analyses of the *Kaiserreich* to the more affirmative active voice. Thus, rather than claiming that "skirted decisions" and "delaying compromises"[29] persisted from the beginning to the end of the Empire, it may be more helpful to say that particular groups and individuals actually wanted such things to "persist." Why? Because they believed that such elements of stasis—albeit in particular combinations—might accrue to their material or spiritual benefit. That is, stasis might increase their standing in the hierarchies of wealth, status, and power.

In practice, although real men might make political decisions to realize (or avoid) one or the other extreme of "stasis" or "reform," most commonly they sought to mediate between change and no change. Any future, no matter how boldly or timidly envisioned, could not be balanced, harmonized, or reconciled with the present except via the mediation of compromise or gradualism. Seen in this light, Rathenau displayed the idiosyncratic mixture of conflicted feelings, ranging from self-righteousness to self-contempt and everything in between, that was so typical of other Wilhelmine figures unwilling to make a leap of faith into an unknown political future. In fact, Rathenau was not very different from either the constitutional theorists about whom Mark Hewitson has written, or the left-liberal politicians whom Alastair Thompson has studied.

Hewitson has argued convincingly that support for the idea of German constitutionalism *as it existed* in Wilhelmine Germany "prevented the practice of parliamentarization from extending beyond certain critical thresholds." On the one hand, this debate signaled that "the meaning of 'parliamentarism' and 'constitutionalism' remained in flux and thus contributed for a time to a feeling of crisis." Nevertheless, writes Hewitson, the debate "eventually led to a stabilization of the German regime" by "serving to reinforce contemporary support for the *Kaiserreich*."[30] In this way, even such dedicated reformers as Friedrich Naumann acknowledged in 1908 that "the constitution, as it was fashioned by Bismarck's hand, was to be accepted as the fixed property of the German people."[31] Like many of his liberal contemporaries, Naumann "had accepted the institutional structure of the *Kaiserreich* as the invisible framework of his political thought."[32]

In his study of Wilhelmine left liberalism, Alastair Thompson rightly sidesteps the unpersuasive version of history that depicts liberalism as "a study in failure." Indeed, writes Thompson, on this point "there is even some danger of historians exaggerating those aspects of Imperial Germany which were successful and 'modern.'"[33] Nevertheless, he acknowledges that the pressure on liberal politicians to be pragmatic increased in the final peacetime years of the Reich: "[L]eft liberals increasingly identified with the Wilhelmine state and yearned for practical results after over two decades in opposition."[34] Although most left liberals in Prussia shared

Rathenau's support for electoral reform, responsible government, and the rule of law, they were also, like him, "visibly patriotic and not *insistent* on full parliamentary rule."[35] When these men added up the numbers, they saw that they did not need "to trouble their heads" about the imminent introduction of a system whereby shifting parliamentary majorities could force a change of government. As Friedrich von Payer declared in December 1908: "We can leave this question to future generations; for we lack the unavoidable prerequisite for it, namely a closed, capable, enduring majority, as in England."[36]

If we follow the liberals' preference for stability and pragmatism into the war years, are we correct to find "defeat in victory" and "victory in defeat," as Thompson suggests? Is Jan Palmowski correct in asserting that bourgeois liberals "came to appreciate the power of the state because of their inability to reconcile their own desire for social, cultural and political unity with the reality of ever-increasing social and confessional division"?[37] Such would appear to be Palmowski's conclusion when he assigns priority to questions about "*how* liberals combined opposition to state authoritarianism with trust in state reform [and] *how* liberals translated their political appeal from the local to the state and national levels." Palmowski has no wish to deny the liberal talent for organization he has uncovered in his own research into municipal liberalism in Frankfurt am Main.[38] But Palmowski also suggests that German liberalism was most important as a mediating factor within the "ruptured polity" of Imperial Germany:

> The studies reviewed here do not contradict the *Sonderweg*'s assumption of a society deeply divided along the lines of class and authority. Instead, they argue that superimposed upon these fissures were evolving frictions between town and countryside, rivalries between and within religions, and contrasting regional identities distinguished by popular culture, history, social structure and politics. The complexity of the German polity is thus moving to the fore, as its dividing lines in part limited, and in part reinforced each other.[39]

Thus, by emphasizing the dynamic nature of that polity too vehemently, we run the risk of underplaying the significance of *both* conflict and complexity as hallmarks of a political system that provided few opportunities without corresponding constraints.

A full consideration of this question would invariably take us too far afield. Nevertheless, if one considers what, for example, the National Liberal government that came to power in the Kingdom of Saxony in October 1918 actually attempted in terms of overturning the political status quo, one discovers more reasons to question liberals' alleged fixation on change. One finds that well into 1918 the National Liberals, left liberals, and Social Democrats in the Saxon *Landtag* continued to postpone domestic quarrels for the sake of the common war effort. These parties "may have asked for the rudder to Saxony's ship of state; but they did not rock the boat when their request was denied."[40] Then, on 26 October 1918, the Saxon king appointed the National Liberal leader in Saxony, Rudolf Heinze, as government leader. For over a fortnight Saxony was ruled according to the principles of parliamentary government.

Because this experiment was effectively freed from the "death throes" of the Hohen-zollern dynasty, we can "look for clues to what the political system of the *Kaiserreich* might have become" if liberals elsewhere had found themselves at the helm.

What did they do with this opportunity? Not very much. The Saxon National Liberal administration proclaimed in its inaugural program of 5 November 1918 that it would "keep the wheels of the state bureaucracy well oiled." Otherwise, it proposed a hybrid system of governance that was "neither democratic nor authoritarian, but a delicate mixture of both, with a corporatist flavor." The liberals, for example, were to enjoy a free rein in the fields of industry and commerce; the Social Democrats would preside over a ministry of labor; and Saxon Conservatives would be allowed to exert decisive influence in the realms of finance, justice, and culture. A state of parliamentary equipoise appears also to have been the liberals' goal when they aimed to introduce proportional representation without, however, abolishing the upper house of the Saxon *Landtag*—the very institution against which they had lobbied for more than two decades. For these reasons, Christoph Nonn has correctly used inverted commas to refer to the "modern" political system that the National Liberals in Saxony intended to introduce with their "new course" in early November 1918. Nonn concedes that the authoritarian political system in Saxony did evolve during the war and would have continued to do so if revolution had not broken out a few days later. However, he concludes that the renowned slipperiness of the term "modern" should make us doubly cautious: cautious about seeing parliamentary democracy as the desired end point of that evolution, in Saxony or elsewhere in Germany, and cautious about imagining that all reformers were in a hurry to implement change. When given the opportunity, National Liberals introduced a political system that was more corporatist than democratic. And to implement it they chose a political process designed quite conspicuously to slow down, not speed up, the pace of future developments.

Drawing together the threads of this argument, my aim has not been to suggest that these decisions were dilatory, or insufficiently modern, or indicative of the unchanging hegemony of established elites in the economic, social, and cultural realms. To argue that many defining features of the Empire's political system remained essentially static between January 1871 and November 1918 is not to resurrect an outdated view of the *Kaiserreich* as "rigidly authoritarian [and] sclerotic."[41] Rather, I have tried to suggest that more Germans avoided firm decisions in favor of reform, and did so at more potentially significant turning points, than historians have generally thought. Putting it more pointedly, if Wilhelminians did not necessarily get the system of governance they envisioned or deserved, in both respects they seem to have gotten what they actually wanted.[42]

Nemesis

There is a certain irony in the fact that historians who consistently stress the new, modern, dynamic nature of Imperial politics beginning in the 1890s have themselves provided key arguments tending to highlight the meanings of stasis after 1871. For example, they have convincingly illuminated the "newness" of political institutions set in place by Bismarck at the founding of the Reich, including the constitutional, administrative, parliamentary, and electoral institutions that remained largely unchanged over the next half-century. They have drawn attention to the relatively early date—certainly not later than the 1870s—at which both bourgeois and (national) liberal Germans can be said to have exerted not only economic, social, and cultural dominance but something approaching political hegemony as well. And they have demonstrated the degree to which party-political conflicts that gave a peculiar openness and dynamism to the decade of the 1870s—the struggles against the Catholic Church and Social Democracy being just the two most obvious examples—had hardened by 1880 into battle lines that remained largely unchanged until just before the war.[43] All new? New and improved? Surely these labels are applied more appropriately to Germany in 1871 and 1919 than in 1900 or 1913.

Elsewhere I have rehearsed questions about what was actually "mass" in the "political mass market" (Hans Rosenberg) and what was "new" about "politics in a new key" (Carl Schorske).[44] Much of the revisionist scholarship of the 1980s and 1990s argued that the decade of the 1890s witnessed the "reconstitution of the political nation." In that literature, any number of recurring phrases were used to give decisive priority to change over stasis. Thus we read that the 1890s constituted "a major moment of flux," a "vital moment of transition," a time of political "fission," a "populist moment," a "major enlargement of the public sphere," a "reordering of the public domain," and "a fundamental change in the scale and intensity of public life."[45] Recently, however, historians have begun to distance themselves from a view that singles out the 1890s so categorically. And certainly when we consider the decades in which truly innovative strategies were not just worked out but implemented by the political parties and leading interest groups,[46] when voter turnout for national elections increased most conspicuously, when the socialist and Catholic milieus were first mobilized, and when party membership in the Social Democratic Party (SPD) rose at its steepest rate (this list of indicators could be extended), then the 1890s recede as a time when the fundamental politicization and democratization of Imperial Germany occurred. When considering larger changes in political ideologies, styles, discourses, and means of mobilization, the discontinuities of 1871 and 1918 seem far more compelling.

Nevertheless—and here we come to the hinge of this chapter's argument—after 1900 Wilhelminians began to feel that political stasis was itself a destabilizing factor in their lives. Stasis began to generate its antithesis. It was *this* dialectic, at least as much as the activities and arguments of flesh-and-blood advocates of change, that now necessitated the accommodation of social, economic, and cultural changes from which politics had been largely insulated up to that point. And it was this dialectic that eventually dissipated a confidence shared by many Wilhelminians that they could continue to build on the achievements of the past. In the final years before the war, Wilhelmine Germans began to recognize that they had no choice—no skirts to hide behind—in confronting challenges and uncertainties that were distinctively twentieth-century in nature.

By and large, such recognition brought with it a clearer, more hard-nosed vision of the future. Thus, for example, Wilhelm's personal rule, precisely because it rested on such pillars of strength, eventually generated its own devastating critiques. The issue of the Prussian three-class suffrage, precisely because it remained unreformed up to 1910 and beyond, fueled suffrage debates in both the Reich and the individual federal states that questioned the political status quo more fundamentally than was possible even in the 1890s. The Bülow Bloc (1907-9), which seemed to epitomize the balancing of right and left, blew apart because of, not despite, the flaw in its founding logic. Subsequent political detonations may have released more heat than light, but their frequency and resonance increased over time. The Black-Blue Bloc (1909-14) satisfied no one, whereupon a continuing left-liberal renaissance in the final prewar years soon brought alternative alignments into focus. In 1914-18, the SPD's integration into the political system—which had long been underway before 1914 but which became apparent to all in the early war years—generated its own internal challenge from an alienated, pacifist rank and file, while Conservative hot-heads opted increasingly for *va banque* solutions to their own marginalization.[47]

What evidence points to a new political dialectic between stasis and reform after 1900?[48] First, the older Bismarckian dichotomy between "friends" and "enemies" of the Reich became increasingly irrelevant as another division arose: that between producers and consumers.[49] Founded upon the "commodification" of politics that was perceived as sharply by contemporaries as by historians, this conflict shifted the initiative toward reformers who, after the turn of the century, began to wrest from the state the power to determine which political discourses resonated most loudly in the public sphere. Second, it was only after 1899 that Wilhelmine debates about civil liberties moved from the realm of discourse (challenges and threats) to one of practical action. When we consider the efforts of Bismarck and his ministers in the 1870s and 1880s to curtail such rights as freedom of association, universal manhood suffrage for Reichstag elections, and freedom of the press, we begin to see that in the 1890s there was nothing new under the sun. At the end of this long period of constitutional incubation, and especially during the Reichstag election campaign of 1898, the Center and the left-liberal parties successfully called attention to the government's and the right-wing parties' plans to amend the Reichstag suffrage. In quick order, other new ideas were subsequently floated about the possibility of plural voting, proportional representation, the abolishment of upper houses of parliament, and the female vote. To be sure, the "pillarization" of political parties conspired against the realization of many of these ideas before 1919. Nonetheless, the broad front on which suffrage reform and other "fairness issues" were pushed after 1900 suggests that the former Bismarckian consensus began to unravel not with the Iron Chancellor's dismissal in March 1890 but only upon his death in July 1898.[50]

Third and lastly, the pluralization of social and regional allegiances after the turn of the century changed the largely static party alignments of the preceding three

decades. Whereas previously electoral coalitions had formed around constitutional
questions of a demonstratively national type (*Kulturkampf*, military budget, anti-
socialist laws), whereby enemies of the Reich could be targeted with relative ease,
conflicts that fell along the urban/rural and consumer/producer axes sundered the
Conservative-Free Conservative-National Liberal *Kartell*. The most conspicuous
aspect of this sundering was to free the National Liberals and a new generation of liberal politicians from their "client" relationship with the two conservative parties. Neither the German Conservative nor the Free Conservative camp threw up leaders after
1900 who could be described as particularly innovative. On that score, both parties
largely abdicated to the leaders of the *völkisch* movement,[51] most of whose factions
offered some combination of *mittelständisch*, hypernationalist, reform-oriented
promises to overcome the stasis on the right. By contrast, both the National Liberal
and the left-liberal parties produced a new generation of spokesmen who were willing
to undertake what has been called both a programmatic and a mental reorientation.

The career of Gustav Stresemann, first in Saxony and then, after 1909, in
national politics, epitomizes three aspects of this new political orientation: its
endorsement of imperialist *Weltpolitik*, its advocacy of urban and industrial interests,
and its fixation on suffrage reform in Germany's federal states. In each respect, and
notwithstanding continuing divisions within their own camp, the National Liberals'
redefinition of their central political goals tended to increase their distance from the
conservative parties and lessen the distance to the left liberals and Social Democrats.
Especially on the regional and local levels, and particularly once changes at the basis
of the moderate and leftist parties' voting constituencies were consolidated in ways
that forced party leaders to move in the same direction, the "learning processes" we
commonly regard as characteristic of the late Wilhelmine years began to overshadow
and displace the political "failures" of the Bismarckian era. Granted, those learning
processes were slow, uneven, and incomplete, as preceding sections of this chapter
have tried to illustrate. However, they would contribute by 1914 to the relative isolation of those Wilhelminians who continued to insist that stasis was the only option.
As Thomas Kühne has written:[52] "The processes of democratization did not overcome the authoritarian condition [*obrigkeitsstaatliche Verfaßtheit*] of Imperial Germany; nor did the beginnings of pluralization and integration neutralize the
sociocultural fragmentation of the party system. But in the half-decade around 1900,
these processes developed a momentum [*Schubkraft*] they did not exhibit either
before or after in the *Kaiserreich*."

Conclusion

The puzzles, paradoxes, and ironies of Wilhelmine Germany cannot be contained
within the framework of "either-or" questions. Although the ambiguous, incongruent
dualisms taken up as topics of debate in recent historical overviews are dissatisfying
to many readers, they contribute to larger reinterpretations in a positive way. In the

case of Wilhelmine Germany, they demonstrate that the growing complexity of the political system (and its individual parts) was balanced by more persistent features already present at the birth of the Reich: the institutionalization of diversity through federalism, the fracturing of political consensus, the persistence of sociocultural milieus, and the gradual accumulation of skirted decisions.

As we cast our gaze back over the Imperial era as a whole, we tend to highlight the dynamic aspect of Wilhelminism because that is the nearer, sharper end of the historical stick we pick up. That dynamism seems all the more compelling when it is associated with a man who was disparaged even in his own time as "His Impulsive Majesty" and "Wilhelm the Sudden." However, Wilhelm has recently been described as a monarch who fulfilled a commitment to an anachronistic Bismarckian legacy rather than one who heralded a new age.[53] Count Harry Kessler recalled: "As life's purpose, he [Wilhelm II] offered us youthful Germans a political retirement, the defense and the enjoyment of what had already been attained. … As was painfully evident to the eye, he represented no beginning but rather an end, a grandiose final chord—*ein Erfüller, kein Verkünder!*"

This essay has tried to demonstrate that a careful attempt to balance elements of reform and stasis, of progressivism and traditionalism, can recover important aspects of *Kaiserreich* history that may have had their historiographical heyday in the 1970s but do not deserve to be disregarded today. Reassessing the degree to which traditionalism continued to influence German life reminds us that many contemporaries foresaw the possibility that the *Kaiserreich* would not only continue to exist, but actually thrive, well into the twentieth century. After all, a typically modern aspect of both state governance and bourgeois taste is to try to monitor, manage, and control change, rather than to embrace it across the board or reject it out of hand. Similarly, the many compromises struck between groups and individuals defending authoritarian and emancipatory political stances have tended to distract attention from those occasions when the sort of compromise that would have permitted further, meaningful political reform of the Reich's central institutions was rejected outright. It is one thing to emphasize how modern, pluralistic, and dynamic life in the Empire was after 1900 and to document the important growth of the Wilhelmine left. It is quite another thing to suggest that the "success"[54] of the opposition parties did not also entail compromises, ambivalences, and outright failures—not ephemeral failures, but arguably ones that reached from the margins of the respective ideologies to their very core.

It is too much to say that historians who study the "meanings of reform" without also studying the "meanings of stasis" steer close to boosterism. Yet to do one without the other presents the sound of only one hand clapping—a non-event that provides neither confirmation of what came before nor transition to something new. Instead, in seeking to recover elements of stasis in the German Empire and in trying to explain why they remained so important until November 1918, we have an opportunity to integrate the more resounding measures of Wilhelmine history with the political silences that also deserve our attention. By listening carefully for both, we may discover some new harmonics—muted and not always benign—lying in between.

Notes

1. Immanuel Kant, *Anthropology from a Pragmatic Point of View*, trans. Mary J. Gregor (The Hague, 1974; orig. 1797), 179-80; emphasis added.
2. See Volker R. Berghahn, "The German Empire, 1871-1914: Reflections on the Direction of Recent Research," and Margaret Lavinia Anderson, "Reply to Volker Berghahn," in *Central European History* 35, no. 1 (2002): 75-82, 83-90. I am grateful to both essayists for sharing their insights with me at proof stage.
3. For example, Dietrich Papenfuß and Wolfgang Schieder, eds., *Deutsche Umbrüche im 20. Jahrhundert* (Cologne, Weimar, and Vienna, 2000).
4. For example, Volker Ullrich, *Die nervöse Großmacht 1871-1918. Aufstieg und Untergang des deutschen Kaiserreichs* (Frankfurt a.M., 1999).
5. For example, Lothar Gall, ed., *Otto von Bismarck und Wilhelm II. Repräsentanten eines Epochen-wechsels?* (Paderborn, 2000).
6. As attempted (unsuccessfully) in Jack R. Dukes and Joachim Remak, eds., *Another Germany: A Reconsideration of the Imperial Era* (Boulder, 1988). See also James Retallack, *Germany in the Age of Kaiser Wilhelm II* (Basingstoke and New York, 1996), esp. 105-7.
7. For example, Simone Lässig, Karl Heinrich Pohl, and James Retallack, eds., *Modernisierung und Region im wilhelminischen Deutschland*, 2nd ed. (Bielefeld, 1998); James Retallack, ed., *Saxony in German History: Culture, Society, and Politics, 1830-1933* (Ann Arbor, 2000).
8. See Ute Frevert, ed., *Das Neue Jahrhundert* (Göttingen, 2000); August Nitschke et al., eds., *Jahrhundertwende*, 2 vols. (Reinbek, 1990); Barbara Beßlich, *Wege in den "Kulturkrieg"* (Darmstadt, 2000); Thomas Rohkrämer, *Eine andere Moderne?* (Paderborn, 1999).
9. See Geoff Eley's contribution to this volume.
10. The following paragraphs draw on David Blackbourn, *The Fontana History of Germany, 1780-1918* (London, 1997), esp. chaps. 7-8, here 313.
11. Klaus Tenfelde, "1890-1914: Durchbruch der Moderne? Über Gesellschaft im späten *Kaiser-reich*," in Gall, *Bismarck und Wilhelm*, 119-41, here 136.
12. Gerhard A. Ritter, "Politische Repräsentation durch Berufsstände. Konzepte und Realität in Deutschland 1871-1933," in *Gestaltungskraft des Politischen*, ed. Wolfram Pyta and Ludwig Richter (Berlin, 1998), 261-80, esp. 269-74; Thomas Kühne, *Dreiklassenwahlrecht und Wahlkul-tur in Preussen 1867-1914* (Düsseldorf, 1994). Cf. idem, "Zur Genese der deutschen Pro-porzkultur im wilhelminischen Preußen," *Politische Vierteljahresschrift* 36, no. 2 (1995): 220-42.
13. Blackbourn, *Fontana History*, 323, and ff. for much of the following.
14. Ibid., 347f.
15. See Joachim Radkau, *Das Zeitalter der Nervosität* (Darmstadt, 1998).
16. Cf. Anson Rabinbach, *The Human Motor: Energy, Fatigue, and the Origins of Modernity* (New York, 1990).
17. Radkau, *Zeitalter*, 26.
18. Ibid., 25.
19. Modris Eksteins, "When Death was Young ...: Germany, Modernism, and the Great War," in *Ideas into Politics*, ed. R. J. Bullen, H. Pogge von Strandmann, and A. B. Polonsky (London, 1984), 25-35, here 29 and f. for following citations. Cf. Wolfgang J. Mommsen, *Bürgerliche Kul-tur und Künstlerische Avantgarde 1870-1918* (Frankfurt a.M. and Berlin, 1994), 98.
20. Peter Jelavich, "Literature and the Arts," in *Imperial Germany*, ed. Roger Chickering (Westport, 1996), 377.
21. Cited in Mommsen, *Bürgerliche Kultur*, 104.
22. Eksteins, "Death," 31.
23. Mommsen, *Bürgerliche Kultur*, 107.
24. Eksteins, "Death," 33.
25. The relevant literature for this section is cited in Retallack, *Germany*, 34-52.
26. Andreas Gawatz, *Wahlkämpfe in Württemberg* (Düsseldorf, 2001); Elvira Döscher and Wolfgang Schröder, *Sächsische Parlamentarier 1869-1918* (Düsseldorf, 2001).

27. Hartmut Pogge von Strandmann, ed., *Walther Rathenau. Industrialist, Banker, Intellectual, and Politician: Notes and Diaries, 1907-1922* (Oxford, 1985), 163-4; emphasis added.

28. Mark Hewitson, *National Identity and Political Thought in Germany* (Oxford, 2000), 253.

29. See Wolfgang J. Mommsen, *Imperial Germany 1867-1918* (London, 1994), 1-40.

30. Mark Hewitson, "The *Kaiserreich* in Question: Constitutional Crisis in Germany before the First World War," *Journal of Modern History* 73 (2001): 725-80, here 725-30.

31. Cited in ibid., 733-34.

32. Ibid., 734 and f. for the following.

33. Alastair P. Thompson, *Left Liberals, the State, and Popular Politics in Wilhelmine Germany* (Oxford, 2000), 7.

34. Ibid., 23 and f. for the following.

35. Emphasis added.

36. Cited in Hewitson, "*Kaiserreich*," 770.

37. Jan Palmowski, "Mediating the Nation: Liberalism and the Polity in Nineteenth-Century Germany," *German History* 18, no. 4 (2001): 573-98, here 584. On the "conserving" ambitions and "modernizing" strategies of German dynastic states, see Jean H. Quataert, *Staging Philanthropy* (Ann Arbor, 2001), and Abigail Green, *Fatherlands* (Cambridge, 2001).

38. Jan Palmowski, *Urban Liberalism in Imperial Germany* (Oxford, 1999). Interestingly, when Friedrich Naumann asked rhetorically, "Can one organize liberals?" his answer conceded that organization was "a liberal idea, but not a liberal habit." Cited in Manfred Hettling, "Partei ohne Parteibeamte. Parteisekretäre im Linksliberalismus von 1900 bis 1913," in *Parteien im Wandel*, ed. Dieter Dowe et al. (Munich, 1999), 109-34, here 109.

39. Palmowski, "Mediating the Nation," 597-98.

40. Christoph Nonn, "Saxon Politics during the First World War: Modernization, National Liberal Style," in Retallack, *Saxony*, 309-21, here 315-16; for the following, 317-21, and Ralph Czychun, "Political Modernisation, Democratisation and Reform during the First World War: The Case of Saxony" (M.A. diss., University of Toronto, 1998).

41. See David Blackbourn, *English Historical Review* 109, no. 432 (June 1994): 667, reviewing vol. 2 of Thomas Nipperdey, *Deutsche Geschichte, 1866-1918* (Munich, 1992).

42. Cf. David Blackbourn and Geoff Eley, *The Peculiarities of German History* (Oxford, 1984).

43. Including three of the most able Anglo-Saxon historians to have focused attention on Bismarckian Germany: David Blackbourn, "New Legislatures: Germany, 1871-1914," *Historical Research* 65 (1992): 201-14; Margaret Lavinia Anderson, "Voter, Junker, *Landrat*, Priest: The Old Authorities and the New Franchise in Imperial Germany," *American Historical Review* 98 (1993): 1448-74; and Geoff Eley, "Society and Politics in Bismarckian Germany," *German History* 15 (1997): 101-32, esp. 111, 121, 128.

44. James Retallack, "Demagogentum, Populismus, Volkstümlichkeit. Überlegungen zur 'Popularitätshascherei' auf dem politischen Massenmarkt des Kaiserreichs," *Zeitschrift für Geschichtswissenschaft* 48, no. 4 (2000): 309-25, where further references can be found.

45. These terms are found in Geoff Eley, "Anti-Semitism, Agrarian Mobilization, and the Conservative Party: Radicalism and Containment in the Founding of the Agrarian League, 1890-93," in *Between Reform, Reaction, and Resistance*, ed. Larry Eugene Jones and James Retallack (Oxford and Providence, 1993), 187-227, here 194; and idem, "Notable Politics, the Crisis of German Liberalism, and the Electoral Transition of the 1890s," in *In Search of a Liberal Germany*, ed. Konrad H. Jarausch and Larry Eugene Jones (New York, Oxford, and Munich, 1990), 187-216, here 192, 210-11. For an appraisal that reflects my own view, see Thompson, *Left Liberals*, 21.

46. See the important study by Axel Grießmer, *Massenverbände und Massenparteien im wilhelminischen Reich. Zum Wandel der Wahlkultur 1903-1912* (Düsseldorf, 2000), esp. 49-50.

47. James Retallack, "The Road to Philippi: The Conservative Party and Bethmann Hollweg's 'Politics of the Diagonal,' 1909-1914," in Jones and Retallack, *Between Reform*, 261-98.

48. Besides works cited in notes 3-9, the following relies heavily on Thomas Kühne, "Die Jahrhundertwende, die 'lange' Bismarckzeit und die Demokratisierung der politischen Kultur," in Gall, *Bismarck und Wilhelm*, 85-118.

49. See Christoph Nonn, *Verbraucherprotest und Parteiensystem im wilhelminischen Deutschland* (Düsseldorf, 1996).

50. See Kühne, "Jahrhundertwende," 118.

51. See Uwe Puschner, *Die völkische Bewegung im wilhelminischen Kaiserreich* (Darmstadt, 2001); also Uwe Puschner et al., eds., *Handbuch zur "Völkischen Bewegung" 1871-1918* (Munich, 1996); Diethart Kerbs and Jürgen Reulecke, eds., *Handbuch der deutschen Reformbewegungen 1880-1933* (Wuppertal, 1998).

52. Kühne, "Jahrhundertwende," 117.

53. Lothar Gall, "Otto von Bismarck und Wilhelm II.: Repräsentanten eines Epochenwechsels?" in Gall, *Bismarck und Wilhelm*, 1-12, including the following passage from Kessler's memoirs (8).

54. Anderson, "Reply," 88.

Notes on Contributors

GEOFF ELEY is the author of *Reshaping the German Right: Radical Nationalism and Political Change since Bismarck* (1980, 2nd ed. 1991), *From Unification to Nazism: Reinterpreting the German Past* (1986), and (with David Blackbourn) *The Peculiarities of German History: Bourgeois Society and Politics in Nineteenth-Century Germany* (1984), as well as editor of *Society, Culture, and the State in Germany 1870-1930* (1996) and *The Goldhagen Effect. History, Memory, Nazism: Facing the German Past* (2000). He is currently finishing another book on liberalism, popular politics, and the creation of the German national state between the 1860s and the 1890s. He has coedited *Becoming National: A Reader* (1996) with Ronald Grigor Suny, and *Culture/Power/History: A Reader in Contemporary Social Theory* (1993) with Nicholas B. Dirks and Sherry B. Ortner. Most recently, he published *Forging Democracy: The History of the Left in Europe, 1850-2000* (2002). His doctoral research was directed by Hartmut Pogge von Strandmann at the University of Sussex in 1970-74, and he taught at Keele and Cambridge before moving to the University of Michigan in 1979.

BRETT FAIRBAIRN attended Oxford University to do a B.A. (Hons.) while holding a Rhodes Scholarship, and stayed on to complete a D.Phil. (1988). He is Professor of History at the University of Saskatchewan and Director of the Centre for the Study of Co-operatives. His interests include the history of democratic politics and movements, and of cooperative organizations in particular. His work on Germany includes *Democracy in the Undemocratic State: The German Reichstag Elections of 1898 and 1903*, as well as numerous papers, articles, and chapters on the history of cooperative movements in Germany between 1850 and the present. He is currently working on a general history and analysis of German co-operatives. In addition, he is author, editor, or coeditor of four other books on cooperative history and theory, particularly as these relate to Canada.

NIALL FERGUSON was a Demy at Magdalen College, Oxford, where he also received his D.Phil. in 1989. He is currently Herzog Professor of Financial History at New York University and Visiting Professor of History at Oxford University. His

first book, *Paper and Iron: Hamburg Business and German Politics in the Era of Inflation 1897-1927* (1995), was short-listed for the *History Today* Book of the Year
award. In 1998 he published *The Pity of War* and *The World's Banker: The History
of the House of Rothschild*, which won the 1998 Wadsworth Prize for Business History and was also short-listed for the Jewish Quarterly/Wingate Literary Award and
the American National Jewish Book Award. His most recent book is *The Cash
Nexus: Money and Power in the Modern World, 1700-2000*. He is currently completing a history of the British Empire to accompany a major television series on
Channel 4 in the U.K.

CONAN FISCHER studied at the Universities of East Anglia and Sussex, receiving
his D.Phil. from the latter in 1980. He is currently Professor of European History
at the University of Strathclyde in Glasgow. He has written *Stormtroopers: A Social,
Economic and Ideological Analysis 1929-35* (1983), *The German Communists and
the Rise of Nazism* (1991), *The Rise of the Nazis* (1995, 2nd ed. 2002), and *The
Ruhr Crisis, 1923-24* (2003), and has edited *The Rise of National Socialism and
the Working Classes in Weimar Germany* (1996). He is currently completing a history of Weimar Germany.

OLIVER WAVELL GRANT studied History and Economics at Oxford University,
graduating in 1977. He then worked for two years as an agricultural economist
before becoming a full-time dairy farmer. In 1992 he installed the first Rotaflow
rotary milking parlor in the United Kingdom, which effectively reintroduced rotary
milking parlors into the United Kingdom after a hiatus of eight years. In 1995 he
returned to Oxford to do an M.Phil. in Economic History, and in 2000 he completed his doctorate on "Internal Migration in Germany 1870-1913," which will
shortly be published by Oxford University Press. He has recently completed an article, "Max Weber and *Die Lage der Landarbeiter im ostelbischen Deutschland*," which
will appear in the *Jahrbuch für Wirtshaftsgeschichte*. He is now working on a project
comparing the impact of science in Britain and Germany, with the provisional title:
*Giant Steps: Science, Education and Economic Progress in Britain and Germany,
1850-1914*. He is currently a Prize Research Fellow at Nuffield College, Oxford.

ERIK GRIMMER-SOLEM studied economics, political science, and history in the
United States and England, receiving a D.Phil. in modern history from Oxford Uni-
versity in 1999. Before joining the History Department of Wesleyan University as
Assistant Professor, he was a lecturer at Balliol College and a Harper Fellow at the
University of Chicago. His first book, *The Rise of Historical Economics and Social
Reform in Germany, 1864-1894*, was published in 2003 by Oxford University Press.
He has published several articles on Gustav Schmoller and other German economists,
focusing on their involvement in social reform during the Imperial era. Among projects
currently in progress is an investigation of the role of the Prussian Statistical Bureau
in the development of German social reform between 1860 and 1890.

MARK HEWITSON studied at University College and St. Antony's College, Oxford. He is currently Lecturer in German Politics and History at University College London. His publications include *National Identity and Political Thought in Germany: Wilhelmine Depictions of the French Third Republic, 1890-1914* (2000), and various articles on German foreign policy, the construction of national identities, and aspects of economic, military, and constitutional history. He is currently writing a book on Germany and the causes of World War I, as well as completing a study of German nationalism between 1848 and 1968.

MATTHEW JEFFERIES studied at the Universities of Sussex and Oxford, where he received his D.Phil. in 1991. He is currently Lecturer in German History at the University of Manchester, England, and Visiting Professor at the Northern Institute of Technology, Hamburg-Harburg, Germany. He is the author of *Politics and Culture in Wilhelmine Germany: The Case of Industrial Architecture* (1995) and *Imperial Culture in Germany, 1871-1918* (2003), as well as many articles on German history and culture. His current research project seeks to uncover the history of naturism and nudism in Germany, from the 1890s to the present day.

NILS OLE OERMANN studied as a Rhodes Scholar at Oxford University, where he completed his D.Phil. in Modern History in 1998. He also received a Ph.D. in Theology from the University of Leipzig in 1999. He is currently a McCloy Scholar at Harvard University. He published *Mission, Church and State Relations in South West Africa under German Rule (1884-1915)* in 1999. In 2001 he published *Einigkeit und Recht und Werte*, together with Johannes Zachhuber, in which the authors examine a High Court case regarding the future relationship of church and state in Germany. He is currently working on his Habilitation in Business Ethics in Berlin and Cambridge, Massachusetts.

KATIANA ORLUC studied History, Comparative Literature, and Law at the Free University of Berlin and took a Master's Degree in Modern History at Oxford University. She is currently a researcher in the Department for History and Civilization at the European University Institute Florence, where she is writing her D.Phil. on European Consciousness after the First World War. She has published several articles on the "European Idea," including "Decline or Renaissance: The Transformation of European Consciousness after the First World War," in Bo Stråth, ed., *Europe and the Other and Europe as the Other* (2000), and "A last Stronghold against Fascism and National Socialism? The Pan-European Debate over the Creation of a European Party in 1932," in Hartmut Kaelble and Luisa Passerini, eds., *European Public Sphere and European Identity* (= *Journal of European Integration History*, vol. 8, no. 2, 2002).

ARNE PERRAS studied colonial and overseas history at the universities of Munich and Oxford , where he received his D.Phil. in 1999. He has focused on colonial politics in Africa and Asia in the nineteenth and twentieth centuries, and has written a political biography of the German colonial agitator Carl Peters, to be published with Oxford University Press. He has worked as a political journalist with various German newspapers, including *Die Zeit* and the *Süddeutsche Zeitung*. He currently works in the Foreign Department of the *Süddeutsche Zeitung* in Munich, focusing on politics and development in sub-Saharan Africa and South and Southeast Asia.

PAUL PROBERT read European History at the University of East Anglia, Norwich, and Modern History at St. Antony's College, Oxford. He was awarded a Hanseatic Scholarship for Britons in 1998, and studied in Hamburg and Bonn before gaining his D.Phil. in 2002, having submitted a thesis on German social democracy and Wilhelmine foreign affairs. He now works for a management consultancy firm in London.

JAMES RETALLACK studied as a Rhodes Scholar at Oxford University, where he received his D.Phil. in 1983. He is currently Professor of History at the University of Toronto. In 2002-3 he held a Visiting Professorship at the University of Göttingen as a *Preisträger* of the Humboldt Foundation. He has published *Notables of the Right: The Conservative Party and Political Mobilization in Germany, 1876-1918* (1988), and *Germany in the Age of Kaiser Wilhelm II* (1996). He has edited two volumes of essays with Larry Eugene Jones (1992, 1993) and (with Simone Lässig and Karl Heinrich Pohl) *Modernisierung und Region im wilhelminischen Deutschland* (1995, 2nd ed. 1998). He recently edited two collections of essays on German regionalism, including *Saxony in German History: Culture, Society, and Politics, 1830-1933* (2000). As well as completing a major study of electoral cultures and the authoritarian state in Saxony and the Reich (1860-1918), he is currently writing a book with the working title *Endgame: The Collapse of the German Empire in 1918*.

WILLEM-ALEXANDER VAN'T PADJE studied at St. John's College, Oxford, as a visiting student in 1994-95 and returned as a graduate student from 1997-2001. He was elected President of the Middle Common Room 2000-1. In July 2002, he received his D.Phil. with a dissertation on diplomatic history entitled "At the Heart of the Growing Anglo-German Imperialist Rivalry: Two British Ambassadors in Berlin, 1884-1908." In 1999, he published an article in the *Bulletin of the Institute for Historical Research*, "Sir Alexander Malet and Prince Otto von Bismarck: An Almost Forgotten Anglo-German Friendship." He is currently working on a scholarly edition tentatively entitled *More Letters from the Berlin Embassy, 1885-1908: Further Selections from the Private Correspondence of British Representatives at Berlin and the Foreign Secretaries at London.*

Publications by Hartmut Pogge von Strandmann

Books

Die Erforderlichkeit des Unmöglichen. Deutschland am Vorabend des Ersten Weltkrieges. Frankfurt a.M., 1965 (with I. Geiss).

Walther Rathenau. Tagebuch 1907-1922. Düsseldorf, 1967 (Book of the Month, January 1968, *Die Zeit*).

Unternehmenspolitik und Unternehmensführung. Der Dialog zwischen Aufsichtsrat und Vorstand bei Mannesmann 1900 bis 1919. Düsseldorf, 1978 (English edition in preparation).

Ideas into Politics: Aspects of European History, 1880-1950 (Festschrift for James Joll). London, 1984 (coeditor with R. J. Bullen and A. B. Polonsky).

Walther Rathenau. Industrialist, Banker, Intellectual, and Politician: Notes and Diaries 1907 – 1922. Oxford, 1985, rpt. 1988.

Britain after 1945: The Beginning of a Modern Age? Bonn, 1988.

The Coming of the First World War. Oxford, 1988, 2nd rpt. 1991 (coeditor with R. J. W. Evans).

Deutschland – Grossbritannien – Europa. Politische Traditionen, Partnerschaft und Rivalität. Essen, 1992 (coeditor with K. Rohe and G. Schmidt).

The Revolutions in Europe 1848-1849: From Reform to Reaction. Oxford, 2000 (coeditor with R. J. W. Evans).

Die Forschungsreisen Paul Pogges in Zentral-Africa, 1874-6 und 1881-4. Berlin, forthcoming 2003.

Articles and Essays

European Imperialism, German Expansionism, Colonial Politics

"The German Empire in Africa and British Perspectives: A Historiographical Essay." In *Britain and Germany in Africa: Imperial Rivalry and Colonial Rule* (Festschrift for H. R. Rudin), ed. P. Gifford and W. R. Louis. New Haven and London, 1967.

"A Place in the Sun." In *History of the Twentieth Century*, ed. J. M. Roberts and A. J. P. Taylor. London, 1968-70.

"Domestic Origins of Germany's Colonial Expansion under Bismarck." *Past & Present* no. 42 (1969).

"Germany and Africa. Politics, Plans and Ambitions." *African Affairs* 69 (1970).

"Nationale Verbände zwischen Weltpolitik und Kontinentalpolitik." In *Marine und Marinepolitik 1871-1914*, ed. H. Schottelius and W. Deist. Düsseldorf, 1972, 2nd ed. 1980.

"Rathenau, die Gebrüder Mannesmann und die Vorgeschichte der Zweiten Marokkokrise." In *Deutschland in der Weltpolitik des 19. und 20. Jahrhunderts. Fritz Fischer zum 65. Geburtstag*, ed. I. Geiss and B.-J. Wendt with P.-C. Witt. Düsseldorf, 1973, 2nd. ed. 1974.

"Deutscher Imperialismus nach 1918." In *Deutscher Konservatismus im 19. und 20. Jahrhundert. Festschrift für Fritz Fischer zum 75. Geburtstag und zum 50. Doktorjubiläum*, ed. D. Stegmann, B.-J. Wendt, and P.-C. Witt. Bonn, 1983.

"Imperialism and Revisionism in Interwar Germany." In *Imperialism and After: Continuities and Discontinuities*, ed. W. J. Mommsen and J. Osterhammel. London, 1986.

"Consequences of the Foundation of the German Empire: Colonial Expansion and the Process of Political-Economic Rationalisation." In *Bismarck, Europe, and Africa: The Berlin Africa Conference 1884/5 and the Onset of Partition*, ed. S. Förster, W. J. Mommsen and R. Robinson. Oxford, 1988.

"In das Innere Afrikas. Forschungsreisen und Initiativen zur Erschließung von Zentralafrika durch Paul Friedrich Pogge." In *Mecklenburger im Ausland. Historische Skizzen zum Leben und Wirken von Mecklenburgern in ihrer Heimat und in der Ferne*, ed. M. Guntau. Bremen, 2001.

"Der Kolonialrat." In *Kolonialmetropole Berlin. Eine Spurensuche*, ed. U. van der Heyden and J. Zeller. Berlin, 2002.

"'Deutsches Land in Fremder Hand' – Der Kolonialrevisionismus." In *Kolonialmetropole Berlin. Eine Spurensuche*, ed. U. van der Heyden and J. Zeller. Berlin, 2002.

World War I and Military History

Three shorter articles in *History of the First World War*, ed. B. Pitt. Bristol, 1968.

"History and War." In *The Institution of War*, ed. R. Hinde. London, 1991.

"Britische Historiker und der Ausbruch des Ersten Weltkrieges." In *Der Erste Weltkrieg. Wirkung, Wahrnehmung, Analyse*, ed. W. Michalka. Munich and Zürich, 1994.

"Nationalisierungsdruck und Königliche Namensänderung in England. Das Ende der Großfamilie Europäischer Dynastien." In *Rivalität und Partnerschaft. Studien zu den deutsch-britischen Beziehungen im 19. und 20. Jahrhundert (Festschrift für Anthony J. Nicholls)*, ed. G. A. Ritter and P. Wende. Paderborn, 1999.

"The Role of British and German Historians in Mobilizing Public Opinion in 1914." In *British and German Historiography 1750-1950: Traditions, Perceptions, and Transfers*, ed. B. Stuchtey and P. Wende. Oxford, 2000.

Russo-German Economic Relations 1917-1941

"Großindustrie und Rapallopolitik. Deutsch-Sowjetische Handelsbeziehungen in der
  Weimarer Republik." *Historische Zeitschrift 222*, no. 2 (1976).

"Industrial Primacy in German Foreign Policy? Myths and Realities in German-Russian
  Relations at the End of the Weimar Republic." In *Social Change and Political
  Development in Weimar Germany*, ed. R. J. Bessel and E. J. Feuchtwanger. London,
  1981.

"Rapallo – Strategy in Preventive Diplomacy? New Sources and New Interpretations." In
  Germany in the Age of Total War (Festschrift for Francis Carsten), ed. V. R. Berghahn
  and M. Kitchen. London, 1981.

"Rapallo or the Immortality of Political Legends." *The Oxford International Review* 1, no.
  1 (1990).

"Rapallo und die Legende von der präventiven Außenpolitik." In *Europa und Rußland –
  das Europäische Haus*, ed. O. Franz. Göttingen, 1993.

"German Industry and the Reconstruction of Russia and Europe in the early 1920s." In *Il
  1922 e la Recostruzione dell' Europa*, ed. W. Abelshauser, P. Hertner, and M.
  Petricioli. Florence, 1996.

"Escalating Paradoxes: German-Soviet Relations 1939-1941." In *The Soviet Union and
  the Outbreak of War, 1939-41*, ed. G. Gorodetsky. Moscow, 1999 (in Russian).

Industrial History and Economic Factors in Foreign Policy

"Widersprüche im Modernisierungsprozeß Deutschlands. Der Kampf der verarbeitenden
  Industrie gegen die Schwerindustrie." In *Industrielle Gesellschaft und Politisches
  System. Beiträge zur politischen Sozialgeschichte. Festschrift für Fritz Fischer zum 70.
  Geburtstag*, ed. D. Stegmann, B.-J. Wendt, and P.-C. Witt. Bonn 1978.

"Entwicklungsstrukturen der Großindustrie im Ruhrgebiet." In *Politik und Gesellschaft im
  Ruhrgebiet*, ed. K. Rohe and H. Kühr. Königstein, 1979.

"Rathenau zwischen Politik und Wirtschaft." In *Am Wendepunkt der europäischen
  Geschichte*, ed. O. Franz. Göttingen, 1981.

"Industry as a Leading Political Factor in Weimar Politics?" In *Ideas into Politics: Aspects
  of European History, 1880-1950* (Festschrift for James Joll), ed. R. J. Bullen, H.
  Pogge von Strandmann, and A. B. Polonsky. London, 1984.

"Wirtschaftliche Entwicklung und industrielle Strategien in Rheinland-Westfalen nach dem
  Ersten Weltkrieg." In *Rheinland und Westfalen im Zeitalter der Industrialisierung*, vol.
  2, ed. W. Köllmann and K. Düwell. Essen, 1984.

"Der Kaiser und die Industriellen. Vom Primat der Rüstung." In *Der Ort Kaiser Wilhelms
  II. in der deutschen Geschichte*, ed. J. C. G. Röhl. Munich, 1991.

"Hochmeister des Kapitalismus. Walther Rathenau als Industrieorganisator, Politiker und
  Schriftsteller." In *Die Extreme berühren sich. Walther Rathenau 1867-1922. Katalog
  zur Rathenau-Ausstellung im Deutschen Museum in Berlin*, ed. H. Wilderotter. Berlin,
  1993.

"Krupp in der Politik." In *Bilder von Krupp. Fotografie und Geschichte im Industriezeitalter*,
  ed. K. Tenfelde. Munich, 1994.

Liberal Parties in Germany and Great Britain, Themes in British History

"Der Nicht-So-Merkwürdige Tod der Liberalen Partei in England." In *Englischer Liberalismus im 19. und frühen 20. Jahrhundert*, ed. K. Rohe. Bochum, 1987.

"Il Monopolio di Potere del Liberalismo nel Governo Locale in Germania Prime del 1914." In *L'Organizzazione della Politica. Cultura, Istituzioni, Partiti nell'Europa Liberale*, ed. N. Matteucci and P. Pombeni. Bologna, 1988.

"Rathenau – ein liberaler Unternehmer?" In *Jüdische Unternehmer in Deutschland im 19. und 20. Jahrhundert* (=Beiheft der *Zeitschrift für Unternehmensgeschichte* 61), ed. W. Mosse und H. Pohl. Bonn, 1992.

"The Liberal Power Monopoly in the Cities of Imperial Germany." In *Elections, Mass Politics, and Social Change in Modern Germany: New Perspectives*, ed. L. E. Jones and J. Retallack. New York and Cambridge, 1992.

"Georg V." In *Englische Könige und Königinnen. Von Heinrich VII. bis Elisabeth II.*, ed. P. Wende. Munich, 1998.

"Von Sponsoren, Stiftern und Heiligen. Namensgebung an britischen Universitäten." In *"... Nicht nur Schall und Rauch." Universitätsreden*, Heft 3, Akademisches Jahr 1998/99. Essen, 2000.

German Revolutionary History

"Deutsche Revolution 1918. Konzepte und Ausführungen." In *Deutschlandstudien II*, ed. R. Picht. Paris and Bonn, 1975.

"The Revolutionary Century in German History 1848-1948." Russell Lecture, Columbia, S.C., 1986.

"Die Revolution von 1848 in Mecklenburg. Die liberale Verfassungsbewegung vom Vormärz bis zum 1850 erfolgten 'Sieg der Reaktion.'" In *Modernisierung und Freiheit. Beiträge zur Demokratiegeschichte in Mecklenburg-Vorpommern*, ed. M. Heinrichs and K. Lüders. Schwerin, 1995.

"Revolutionsfurcht, Sozialreformen und wirtschaftliches Gleichgewicht. Anmerkungen zur Thünenrezeption." In *Politische Deutungskulturen (Festschrift für Karl Rohe)*, ed. O. Haberl and T. Korenke. Baden-Baden, 1999.

Index

A

Africa, 125, 127, 139, 142, 154, 155, 161, 162, 178, 188
    sub-Saharan, 114
Adenauer, Konrad, 209
Agadir, 190, 196
Ahrweiler, 238
Alexander III, 145
Algeciras, 189
Alsace-Lorraine, 56, 125
Altona (near Hamburg), 186
America, 78, 82, 117, 193
    See also United States of America
Amsterdam, 187
Anderson, Benedict, 17
Anderson, Margaret Lavinia, 35
Anglo-German Bank of North-West Africa, 188
Angra Pequena, 155
Applegate, Celia, 3, 20, 22
Arndt, Ernst Moritz, 29
Arnim-Muskau, Count von, 165
Ascona (Switzerland), 99
Ashley, William, 117, 118
Asia, 109, 110, 125, 132, 226
Association for Natural Health Care, 102
Australia, 132
Austria, Austria-Hungary, 114, 126, 132, 134
Auvergne (France), 23

B

Bade, Klaus, 157
Baden, Grand Duchy, 56
Baden, Prince Max of, 193-94
Bairoch, Paul, 52
Balfour, Arthur James, Earl of, 118
Balkans, 127, 130, 132, 191
Ballin, Aby, 192
Ballin, Albert, 189, 190-92

Balliol College, 10
Baltic Sea, 128, 192
Baltzer, Eduard, 93, 94
Barlösius, Eva, 94
Bargash, Said, 161-62
Barrington, Sir Bernard Eric Edward, 146
Barth, Theodor, 78
Bavaria, 21, 27, 42, 56, 110
Bavarian Peasant Association, 42
Bayer Corporation, 209
Bayreuth, 94
Bäumer, Gertrud, 97
Bebel, August, 125-28, 130, 133
Beer, Max, 133-34
Behrens, Peter, 97
Belgium, 193, 195, 208-9
Bennigsen, Rudolf von, 165
Berger, Carl, 173
Berghahn, Volker, ix
Berlant, Lauren, 18
Berlin, 10, 25, 41, 56, 93-95, 97, 98, 101, 103, 112, 123, 126-27, 141-44, 147, 149, 163, 172-74, 176, 179, 180-82, 188, 190-92, 202-3, 206, 208, 211
Berlin Naturalists, 99
Bernstein, Eduard, 126, 129, 133
Bethmann Hollweg, Theobald von, 242
Bielefeld, 3, 75
Biernatzki, Wilhelm, 43
Bircher-Brenner, Max, 94
Birmingham, University of, 117
Bismarck, Herbert von, 149
Bismarck, Otto von, 1, 6, 22, 26, 125, 131, 142, 149, 155-57, 159, 160-66, 210, 240, 243, 246-247
Bloch, Joseph, 130
Blücher von Wahlstatt, Gebhard Leberecht von, 140
Bölsche, Wilhelm, 98, 100
Boers, 114, 145

Bonn, 10
Bonner Borussen, 203
Bormann, Martin, 96, 103
Blackbourn, David, 2, 22
Bracher, Karl Dietrich, 1
Brandenburg, 44, 56, 57
Braun, Carl, 94
Brazil, 114
Brentano, Lujo, 73, 108-9, 110, 115, 119
Brest Litovsk, Treaty of, 193
Britain, 2, 8, 10, 12, 20, 53-55, 63, 65-66,
    78-81, 84, 86, 109-10, 113-15, 117-20,
    123-24, 126-33, 141, 144, 147, 155,
    189-91, 194, 196-97, 222
        See also England
British Bank of West Africa, 188
British Empire
        See Britain
British Expeditionary Force, 123
British Foreign Ministry, 123, 126, 133, 146
British Library, 126
Brockdorff-Rantzau, Count Ulrich von, 194
Brunswick, 56, 68, 94
Bruch, Direktor, 212
Bulgaria, 192
Bülow, Bernhard von, 74, 115, 119, 126,
    134, 178, 189-90
Bund Heimatschutz, 24, 100-1
Bundesrat, 195
Burma, 113

C

Calwer, Richard, 130
Cambon, Paul, 213
Cameroons, 155, 178
Canada, 132, 195
Cape Colony, 148
Caprivi, Leo von, 74, 115-16, 125-26
Carpenter, Edward, 93
Catholics, 4, 22, 85-86
Catholic Church, 246
Central Association of German Banks and
    Bankers, 189
Central Commission for People's Youth Sports,
    25
Centre Party, German, 26, 83, 110, 156, 180-
    81, 203, 247
Chamberlain, Joseph, 117-18
Charles V, Emperor, 159
China, 114, 197
Christian Democratic Union, 103
Christian-Social Association in Elberfeld, 28
Chickering, Roger, 158
Chirol, Sir Valentine, 139-42
Clapham, J. H., 66

Clemenceau, Georges, 86
Cobden, William, 113
Coetzee, Marilyn, 157
Cologne, 124-25
Colonial Institute, 188
Colonial Office
        See German Colonial Office
Combes, Edgar, 83
Combes, Emile, 86
Commerz- und Diskonto Bank, 187
Communists, 210
Conservatives, Conservative Party, 9, 165,
    220, 248
        in Saxony, 245
Conservative Revolutionaries, 224
Confino, Alon, 22
Conwentz, Hugo, 101
Coudenhove-Kalergi, Count Richard, 219-30
Courland, 192
Cowes, 141
Cromwell, Oliver, 159, 160
Cuba, 114, 117
Cuno, Wilhelm, 203
Cyprus, 113

D

Dahl, Robert, 35
Daily Telegraph, 74
Damaschke, Adolf, 93, 100
Darling, M. L., 34, 36-40
Darmstadt, 42
Darwin, Charles, 98
Delagoa Bay, 145
Delbrück, Hans, 82
Denmark, 53-55, 195
Dernburg, Bernhard, 173
Desmond, Olga, 95
Deutschbund (German-Union), 29
Deutsche Kolonialzeitung, 177
Deutsche Bank, 163, 186, 221
Deutsch-Ostafrikanische Gesellschaft. Carl
    Peters und Genossen, 161-64
Diederichs, Eugen, 96
Diefenbach, Karl Wilhelm, 95
Dilke, Charles, 159
Disraeli, Benjamin, 113
Dreibund, 127, 134
Dresden, 93, 96, 100
Dresdner Bank, 221
Dresdner Nachrichten, 82
Dreyfus, Alfred, 82, 83, 85-86
Driesmans, Heinrich, 92
Duez, 83
Duisberg, Carl, 209
Düsseldorf, 125, 208

E

East Africa, 158, 161, 164-65
  See also German East Africa
East Elbia, Elbe River, 51-72 passim
Ebert, Friedrich, 193, 211
Eksteins, Modris, 240
Egypt, 113, 139, 141, 145
"El Dorado," 125
Elberfeld, 28, 161
Eley, Geoff, viii, 2, 36, 102-3, 157, 165-66
Eliasberg, George, 206
Engel, Ernst, 61
Engels, Friedrich, 78
England, vii, viii, 17, 80, 82, 84, 109, 112-
  13, 118, 126, 128-29, 132, 134, 138-45,
  147, 187, 191-93, 244
  See also Britain
English Channel, 127
Entente Cordiale, 118
Erkner (near Berlin), 98
Ernst, Otto, 96
Erzberger, Matthias, 79, 180, 206
Eutin (Holstein, Germany), Johann-Heinrich-
  Voss Gymnasium in, 10
Evangelical Workers' Association, in Elberfeld,
  28
Evans, Richard J., 2

F

Fabri, Friedrich, 154, 157-58
Farnam, Henry W., 117
Faßbender, Martin, 42
Feilitzsch, Max Freiherr von, 42
Feldman, Gerald D., 205
Fenske, Hans, 166
"Fidus," 95-98, 100, 103-4
Fischer, Fritz, vii, 7, 10, 186
Fleischlen, Cäsar, 96
Flürschheim, Michael, 100
Foch, Ferdinand, 213
Foreign Office
  See British Foreign Ministry
  See German Foreign Ministry
France, 2, 8-9, 17, 20-22, 53-55, 76-79, 81-
  88, 94, 114-16, 118, 126, 128, 131, 133-
  34, 143, 145, 155, 189-91, 193, 197,
  202, 204, 208-11, 213-14
Frankfurt a. M., 3, 187, 244
Free Conservatives, 87, 187, 248
Free Union for an Improvement in Women's
  Clothing, 97
Free Union for Naval Lectures (Freie
  Vereinigung für Flottenvorträge), 111-12,
  116, 118-19
Frei, Ernst, 132

Freie Bühne, 98
French Foreign Ministry, 208
French National Assembly, 214
Freyabund, 96
Friedrichshagen (near Berlin), 97-99
Frisch, Geheimrat, 221
Fritsch, Theodor, 99
"Fritz," 175
Frohme, Carl, 125
Fuchs, state attorney, 177-78

G

Gall, Lothar, 3
Garibaldi, Guiseppe, 226
German Democratic Republic (GDR), viii,
  238
Geiss, Imanuel, 11
Gelsenkirchener Mining Company, 212
General German Cultural League, 103
German Colonial Office, 172-73, 177, 179-
  80, 188
German East Africa (Deutsch-Ostafrika),
  154, 174, 178
German Finance Ministry, 192, 212
German Foreign Ministry, 123, 126, 147,
  157, 163-64, 177, 188, 190-92, 203-5,
  221
German Garden City Association (Deutsche
  Gartenstadtgesellschaft), 98-100, 102
German High Command, 123
German Historical Institute (London), 11
German Ministry of the Interior, 192
German Nationalists, 210
German-Portuguese Colonial Syndicate, 188
German Social Democratic Party
  See Social Democracy
Germania, 83
Gibeon (South-West Africa), 178
Gladstone, William, 113
Goethe, Johann Wolfgang von, 159, 239
Goldberger, Ludwig Max, 77
Gosselin, Martin, 145, 146, 148-49
Gneist, Rudolf von, 78
Great Britain
  See Britain
Green, Martin, 101, 103
Grey, Sir Edward, 191
Gropius, Walter, 96
Guttzeit, Johannes, 94, 101
Gwinner, Arthur von, 221

H

Haas, Wilhelm, 41, 42, 44, 48
Haase, Christian, ii
Habermas, Jürgen, 17

Hahn, Kurt, 194
Hahn, Theodor, 94
Halbe, Max, 98-99
Haldane, Viscount Richard Burdon, 191
Halle, Ernst Levy von, 111
Hamburg, 10-11, 23, 68, 75, 124-25, 161-
    63, 177, 186-94
        University of, vii
Hamburg Chamber of Commerce, 189
Hamburg-Morocco Society, 188
Hammer, 99
Hanover, 68, 112
Hannoverscher Courier, 83
Hansabund, 189
Hansing, 161, 163
Hardenberg, Friedrich von, 242
Hart, Heinrich, 96, 98, 100
Hart, Julius, 98, 100
Hartewig, Karin, 206
Hasbach, Wilhelm, 79, 80, 83
Hatzfeldt, Count von, 138, 144, 146, 148
Hauptmann, Gerhart, 98, 102-3
Haussmann, Konrad, 194
Heeringen, August von, 108-11
Heidelberg, 77
Heim, Georg, 42
Heine, Salomon, 187
Heinze, Rudolf, 244
Helfferich, Karl, 192
Helphand, Alexander, 127, 128-29, 133
Hellerau (near Dresden), 100
Hentschel, Volker, 185
Hentschel, Willibald, 99
Herbette, Jules, 140
Herero, 171-73
Herf, Jeffrey, 103
Hertling, Georg von, 87, 193
Hesse, Hermann, 99, 102
Hesse, 56
        Grand Duchy of, 40-42
Hesse-Nassau, 56
Hewitson, Mark, 243
Heydt, Carl von der, 161, 164
Heym, Georg, 96
Heynen, Carl August, 94
Hilfe, Die, 75, 87
Hilferding, Rudolf, 185-86
Hintrager, Oskar, 174
Hintze, Otto, 79-80, 82-85
Hitler, Adolf, 1, 92, 103, 204, 210, 214
Hobohm, Martin, 193
Höllriegelskreuth (Bavaria), 95
Höppener, Hugo, 95
Hoesch, Leopold von, 209
Hoffmann, Walter G., 64-65

Hofmann, Ida, 99
Hohenlohe-Schillingsfürst, Prince Chlodwig
    zu, 74, 143, 145-48
Hohenzollern, dynasty, 25, 74, 160, 245
Hohenzollern, province, 56, 68
Holland
        See Netherlands
Holstein, Friedrich von, 127, 138-42, 148
Holz, Arno, 102
Hong Kong, 110
Howard, 100
Hübbe-Schleiden, Wilhelm, 96, 157
Hué, Otto, 210
Hugenberg, Alfred, 44
Humbert, 83

I

IG-Farben, 230
Imperial Federation (Reichsverband), 42, 44
Imperial Naval Office, 111
Independent Labour Party, 134
India, 34
Information Bureau of the Imperial Naval
        Office, 111
Institute for Tropical Medicine, 188
Italy, 17, 126, 134, 145, 192, 197, 222

J

Jäger, Gustav, 94, 95, 96
Jahrbuch für Gesetzgebung, 118
Japan, 76
Jahn, Friedrich Ludwig, 29
Jaurès, Jean, 86
Jefferies, Richard, 101
Jelavich, Peter, 239
Jellinek, Georg, 77
Jena, 93
Jews, 4
Joll, James, 11
Jühlke, Karl Ludwig, 158
Jugend, Die, 111
Jung, C.G., 99
Just, Adolf, 94

K

Kampffmeyer brothers, 98, 100
Kampffmeyer, Hans, 100
Kant, Immanuel, 235, 238
Kapp, Wolfgang, 206
Kardoff-Wabnitz, Wilhelm von, 165
Karibib (South-West Africa), 179
Kassel, 97
Kautsky, Karl, 126, 129, 133
Kayser, Paul, 145

Kehr, Eckart, 107, 119, 197
Kennedy, Paul, 127, 195
Kerbs, Diethart, 92
Kessler, Count Harry, 249
Kiautschou (China), 114
Kidd, Benjamin, 118
Kiderlen-Wächter, Alfred von, 188
Kiel, 177, 194
Kirdorf, Emil, 212
Klöckner, Peter, 208-9
Kimberley, John Wodehouse, First Earl of, 144, 148
Kneipp, Sebastian, 94
Kocka, Jürgen, 3, 6
Königgrätz, Battle of, 158, 159
Körner, Theodor, 29
Kohn, Gustav, 81
Kolonialrat (Colonial Council), 11
Korthaus, Karl, 46, 47
Koshar, Rudy, 24
Krauel, Friedrich Richard, 163
Krefeld, 97
Kritische Waffengänge, 98
Kropotkin, Peter, 99
Krüger, Ohm, 138-39
Krüger, Peter, 203
Kuhn, Loeb & Co., 187
Kühne, Thomas, 237, 248
Kusserow, Heinrich von, 161-63

L

Lahmann, Heinrich, 96
Lamprecht, Karl, 77
Landauer, Gustav, 98-100
Landesverband (in Bavaria), 42-43
Landmann, Friedrich, 93
Lange, Friedrich, 29
Langewiesche, Dieter, 22
Larsson, Carl, 96
Lascelles, Sir Frank, 139-45
Lasker-Schüler, Elsa, 99
Lassalle, Ferdinand, 129
Latvia, 192
Lawrence, D.H., 99
League of German Land Reformers (Bund Deutscher Bodenreformer), 99, 102
Leavis, F.R., 101
Ledebour, Georg, 98, 126
Legien, Carl, 205
Leipzig, 25, 93
Leipziger Volkszeitung, 124
Lenin, Vladimir, 226
Leroy-Beaulieu, Pierre L., 112
Leuthner, Karl, 80, 130
Leutwein, Theodor von, 173

Liberia, 188
Lichtfreund, Der, 96
Liebknecht, Karl, 206
Liebknecht, Wilhelm, 126, 128-29
Lindequist, Friedrich von, 176-77, 179
Lippe, 23, 68
London, 123, 126-27, 133, 138-39, 143-44, 186-87, 190-91, 203
Lorraine, 208
Lübeck, 68
Ludendorff, Erich von, 193, 204
Lüderitzbucht, 175
Lüneburg Heath, 58
Luxemburg, Rosa, 129, 133, 206

M

Maehl, William H., 127
Magdeburg, 28
Majority Social Democrats
    See Social Democracy, Social Democrats
Malet, Lady Ermyntrude, 146
Malet, Sir Edward Baldwin, 138, 143-49
Maltzan, Ago Count von, 203-4
Manchuria, 76
Mann, Karl, 95
Mann, Klaus, 230
Mann, Thomas, 230
Mannesmann Corporation, 12
Marburg, 40
Marienfeld, Wolfgang, 107
Marshall von Bieberstein, Baron Adolf, 139-49
Marx, Karl, 78, 129, 228
Mayer, Wilhelm, 203
Mecklenburg, 12, 56-58
    -Schwerin and -Strelitz, 68
Mehring, Franz, 129, 133
Meier-Graefe, Julius, 84
Meinecke, Friedrich, 80, 159
Meist, Carl, 125
Meitzen, August, 69
Melanasia, 155
Melchior, Carl, 186
Méline, Jules, 86
Mendelssohn-Bartholdy, 164
Meyenschein, Adam, 41
Michels, Robert, 83
Micronesia, 155
Millerand, Alexandre, 86, 213
Mining Association (Una-Königsborn), 211
Mirbach-Sorquitten, Count Julius von, 165
Mitchell, Brian R., 53, 55
Mittgard colony, 99
Modersohn-Becker, Paula, 98

Moeller-Bruck, Arthur, 98
Molkenbuhr, Hermann, 133
Mommsen, Wolfgang J., 240
"Moritz," 175
Morocco, 188, 197
Morris, William, 99
Mühsam, Erich, 98-99
Müller, F.F., 164
Müller, Hermann, 204
Münchener Neueste Nachrichten, 85
Münsterberg, Hugo, 77
Munich, 42, 103
Mussolini, Benito, 222
Muthesius, Anna, 97
Muthesius, Hermann, 97

N

Nairn, Tom, 18
Nama, 171-73
Namibia, University of, 10
Napoleon, 2
Natal, 113
National Coal Council, 209
National Council, 28
National Festival Society, 25
National Labor Ministry, 207, 209
National Liberalism, National Liberals, 21-22,
    41, 85, 156, 165, 187, 244, 248
    in Saxony, 245
National Socialists, Nazis, 221, 237-38, 241
Naumann, Friedrich, 29, 73-75, 78-81, 86-
    87, 124, 129, 187, 221, 243
Navy League, 111-12
Navy Office, 29
    See also Imperial Naval Office
Netherlands, 81, 114, 193, 195
Neue Gemeinschaft (New Community), 98
Neue Preussische Zeitung, 83
Neuwied (Germany), 41
New Free People's Theater (Berlin), 29
New Guinea, 155
New York, 190
New Zealand, 62
Nicholson, Sir Frederick, 34
Nietzsche, Friedrich, 228, 239
Nipperdey, Thomas, 2, 92-93, 102
Nolde, Emil, 239
Nonn, Christoph, 245
Nord (French departement), 207
Norddeutsche Bank, 187
Nordhausen, 94
North America, 76, 78
North German Confederation, 156
North Sea, 128

O

Oedenkoven, Henri, 99
Offenbach, 42
Oldenburg, 56, 68
Oncken, Hermann, 80
Oranienburg (Berlin), 95
O'Swald, 161-63
Ovambos, 173
Oxford
    University, vii, 10-12, 117
    St. Antony's College, vii, 10
Oxford University Press, 11

P

Pacific Ocean, 155
Palmowski, Jan, 244
Panama, 83
Pan-European Union, 220-21
Pan-German League, 28
Paris, 186-87, 190, 209, 211, 213, 220
Pas-de-Calais, 207
Pasha, Emin, 156, 165
Past & Present, 11
Payer, Friedrich von, 244
Peal, David, 40
Peters, Carl, 12, 154-66
Peukert, Detlev, 8
Pfalz (Bavarian Palatinate), 21-22, 56
Pfalz Historical Association, 21-22
Pfeil, Count von, 158
Philippines, 114
Pogge von Strandmann, Hartmut, ii-iii, vii-viii,
    8-13, 36, 172, 185, 219, 225
Poincaré, Raymond, 204, 211, 213
Pomerania, 39, 45, 56-57
Portugal, 146, 188
Portuguese Angola, 191, 197
Posen, 56, 59
Potsdam, viii, 28
Prague, 203
Preußische Seehandlung, 163-64
Prince Heinrich Gymnasium
    (Schöneberg/Berlin), 25
Progressives (U.S.), 117
Protestants, 4
Provincial Conference of Conservatives
    in the Rhineland, 28
Prussia, 4, 113, 117, 172, 193, 240, 243
    East, 56, 59
    Landtag, 111, 240-41
    West, 56
Prussian Central Cooperative Bank
    (Preußische Central-Genossenschafts-
    Kasse), 43-44
Prussian Ministry of Trade, 210

Prussian Statistical Office (Königlich
    Preußisches Statistisches Bureau), 64-65
Pudor, Heinrich, 95, 97
Puerto Rico, 117

Q

Quai d'Orsay
    See French Foreign Ministry

R

Radicals (in France), 86
Radkau, Joachim, 238-39
Raiffeisen, Friedrich Wilhelm, 34, 38-42, 48
Rapallo, Treaty of, 12, 203
Rassow, Hermann, 28, 29
Rathenau, Walther, viii, 8-9, 11-12, 185-86,
    203-4, 206, 220, 225, 229-30, 242-44
Regendanz, Wilhelm Karl, 188
Reich Loan Consortium, 189
Reichsbank, 190, 192, 196
Reichstag, 7, 9, 22, 110, 116, 124-27, 130,
    134, 141, 156, 161, 180-81, 189, 193,
    195, 241-42, 247
Reichsverband
    See Imperial Federation
Reitmayer, Morten, 186
Repp, Kevin, 99, 103
Retallack, James, 36
Reulecke, Jürgen, 92
Reusch, Paul, 208-9
Reuß, 68
Rhenish Missionary Society (RMS), 173-74
Rhenish Pfalz
    See Pfalz
Rhine River, 21, 202, 209
Rhineland, 38, 56, 203
Richelieu, Cardinal, 159-60
Richter, Klaus, 174
Riehl, Wilhelm Heinrich, 20
Rikli, Arnold, 94
Ritter, Gerhard A., 237
RMS
    See Rhenish Missionary Society
Rochette, 83
Röhl, John C. G. , viii-ix, 6
Rohrkrämer, Thomas, 103
Rollins, William, 101
Romania, 192
Rome, 134
Roosevelt, Theodore, 117
Roscher, Wilhelm, 77
Rosebery, Earl of (Archibald Philip
    Primrose), 149
Rosenberg, Frederic von, 203
Rosenberg, Hans, 246

Rostock, University of, 10
Rother, Eric, 130-33
Rothschilds, 186-87
Royal Navy, 128-29
Royalist Association of Railway Craftsmen, 28
Rudorff, Ernst, 101
Ruhr District, 202, 204, 206-13
Russia, 12, 76, 78, 110, 112-14, 116, 123,
    125-27, 131-32, 134, 143, 187, 189,
    191, 193, 197, 230
    See also Soviet Union

S

Saar District, 208
Salisbury, 3rd Marquess of (Robert Gascoyne-
    Cecil), 138-39, 141-42, 144, 146-49
Samoa, 178
Sarajevo, 191
Saxony, 39, 56, 211, 241, 245, 248
    -Altenburg, 68
    -Coburg-Gotha, 68
    Landtag, 244
    Kingdom of, 59, 244
    -Meiningen, 68
    Province of, and Anhalt, 56, 68
    -Weimar, 68
Schäfer, Dietrich, 80
Scandinavia, 114
Scheulen, Direktor, 212
Schiller, Friedrich, 239
Schippel, Max, 98, 130
Schirmacher, Käthe, 85
Schleswig-Holstein, 43, 56, 68
Schmidt, Karl Eugen
Schmidt, Robert, 208, 211
Schmoller, Gustav, 74-75, 81, 84, 107-20
Schoenlank, Bruno, 124
Schönlanke (Pomerania), 46
Schorske, Carl, 246
Schnee, Heinrich, 158
Schneehagen, Christian, 97
Schneider-Creusot Corp., 230
Schopenhauer, Arthur, 154
Schücking, Walther, 193
Schuckmann, Bruno, 173
Schultze-Naumburg, Paul, 97, 101
Schulze-Delitzsch, Hermann, 41, 43, 48
Schulze-Gävernitz, Gerhard von, 80
Schwarzburg (Thuringia), 68
Schweinburg, Victor, 111
Sedan, 158-59
Seitz (governor in South-West Africa), 179-80
Sera Circle, 96
Serbia, 191
Sethe, Maria, 97

Shouvalov, Count, 145
Siedlungsgemeinschaft Heimland, 99
Siemens, Carl F. von, 163
Siepke, 109
Silesia, 56, 59
Silverberg, Paul, 209
Simmern, Langwerth von, 191
Singer Paul, 131
Smith, Woodruff D., 157
Social Democracy, Social Democrats, 9, 22,
    26, 28, 79, 85-86, 98, 102-3, 123-31,
    133-34, 156, 177, 180-81, 193, 203-8,
    210-13, 220, 244-48
Society for Racial Hygiene, 103
Sombart, Nicolaus, 91
Sombart, Werner, 77, 81
South Africa, 131-32, 138, 143, 145
South America, 109-10
South Carolina, University of, 10
South-West Africa, 171-79, 181-82
Soviet Union, 203, 222
    See also Russia
Sozialist, Der, 98
Sozialistische Monatshefte, 130, 132-33
Spa, 208, 210
Spahn, Martin, 84
Spain, 197
Sparr, Karl, 45
SPD (Social Democratic Party of Germany)
    See Social Democracy
Speyer Volksbank, 46
Stampfer, Friedrich, 203-4
Standard, 141
Stegmann, Dirk, 12
Stegmann, Emmeline, 46
Steiner, Rudolf, 96
Stern, Fritz, 20
Stinnes, Hugo, 205, 208
Stöcker, Adolf, 29
Strasbourg, 112
    University of, 117
Strauss, Emil, 102
Stresemann, Gustav, 203, 210-11, 213, 248
Strindberg, August, 98
Struve, Gustav, 92-94
Stumm, Karl von, 111
Sussex, University of, vii, 10
Swaine, Leopold Victor, 142-43, 146, 149
Sweden, 81, 187, 192, 197
Switzerland, 94, 114, 195
Szoegyenyi, Count, 143

T

Tacke, Charlotte, 22
Tägliche Rundschau, 111

Tag, Der, 84
Tenfelde, Klaus, 7, 237
Times, The, 133, 140
Third Republic (French), 80, 82-83, 85-86
    See also France
Thompson, Alastair, 243-44
Thuringia, 56, 68
Tirpitz, Alfred von, 108-11, 115, 124, 126-
    30, 133, 189
Toeppen, Kurt, 159
Togo, Togoland, 155, 178
Tolstoy, Leo, 93
Toynbee, Arnold, 117
Transvaal, 138-41, 144, 146-48
Treasury Office (German)
        See German Finance Ministry
Treitschke, Heinrich von, 77-80, 86
Trevor-Roper, Hugh, 11
Triple Alliance, 145, 147
"Tuesday Society" in Elberfeld, 28

U

Uelzen (*Kreis* in Prussia), 58
Unna-Königsborn, 212
Ungewitter, Richard, 95
United Kingdom
        See Britain
United States of America, 55, 63, 77-78,
    112-17, 124, 131, 187, 193, 195, 197,
    204, 221
        See also America
Unruh, Fritz von, 227
Upper Bavarian Agricultural Association, 42

V

Vagts, Alfred, 187
Vanselow, Karl, 95
Vatican, 230
Vegetarische Obstbau-Kolonie Eden, 95
Velde, Henry van de, 97
Verein für Sozialpolitik, 60, 74, 81, 108, 111,
    115
Vereinsbank, 187
Versailles, 194, 205, 208
Victoria, Queen, 140
Vienna, 191, 203
Vierbund, 127
Volkswagen Foundation, 11
Vollmar, Georg von, 125
Vorwärts, 103, 124, 132-33, 203
Vossische Zeitung, 82

W

Wagner, Adolph, 73, 79
Wagner, Peter, 55, 223
Wagner, Richard, 93-94, 99
Waldeck, 68
Wallenstein, Albrecht von, 159
Wandres, Carl, 174
Wanne (Ruhr District), 213
Warburg, Felix, 187
Warburg, Max, 185-97, 220
Warburg, Moritz, 187
Warburg, M.M. & Co., 186-88, 191-92
Warburg, Paul, 187
Washington, George, 78
Weber, Ernst von, 157
Weber, Max, 60-62, 74-75, 77-79, 83-84, 87, 99, 222
Wedekind, Frank, 239
Wehler, Hans-Ulrich, vii, 6-7, 11, 108, 155-57
Wellington, Duke of, 140
Werder (on the Havel), 95
West Africa, 161, 188
Westerhold, Johanna, 46
Westphalia, 56, 68, 203
Whitehall
    See British Foreign Ministry

Wilhelm I, 73, 154, 164
Wilhelm II, 6, 13, 73, 87-88, 129, 138, 140-44, 146-49, 186, 189, 191, 196, 205, 240, 247-48
Wilhelmstraße
    See German Foreign Ministry
    See German Colonial Office
Wille, Bruno, 98
Wilson, Woodrow, 193-94, 220
Windhoek, 173-81
Witbooi, Hendrik, 171-72
Wittelsbach, Prince-Regent Luitpold von, 42
Woche, Die, 111
Württemberg, 22, 115, 241
    and Hohenzollern, 56, 68
Wuppertal, 94
Wuttig, Adolf, 40

Y

Yale University, 117

Z

Zanzibar, 161, 163
Zedlitz-Neukirch, Octavio von, 111
Zentral-Arbeitsgemeinschaft, 211
Zimmermann, Arthur, 192
Zollverein, 115